Library of
Davidson College

Leicester's Commonwealth

Woodcut illustration depicting vengeance taken upon the Earl of Leicester, the bear chained to a ragged staff (from *Discours de la vie abominable . . . le my Lorde de Lecestre*, 1585, British Library 10806. a. 10). Used with permission.

LEICESTER'S COMMONWEALTH

*The Copy of a Letter
Written by
a Master of Art of Cambridge
(1584)
and Related Documents*

Edited
by

D. C. PECK

Ohio University Press
Athens, Ohio
London

Introduction and Notes © copyright 1985 by D. C. Peck.
Printed in the United States of America.
All rights reserved.

Library of Congress Cataloging in Publication Data

Leycesters commonwealth.
   Leicester's commonwealth.

   Bibliography: p.
   Includes index.
   1. Leicester, Robert Dudley, Earl of, 1532?-1588.
I. Peck, D. C.   II. Title.
DA358.L5L54   1985   942.05′5′0924   85–4825
ISBN 0–8214–0800–3

To Calvin G. Thayer

CONTENTS

Preface	viii
Acknowledgements	xi
Abbreviations	xii
Introduction to *Leicester's Commonwealth*	1
The Circumstances of Its Publication	5
The Catholic Court Party	13
Authorship	25
Themes, Style, Effects	32
The Black Legend of Leicester	46
Editorial Policies	52
Notes to Introduction	53
Leicester's Commonwealth	63
Notes to *Leicester's Commonwealth*	197
Appendices with Related Notes	
Appendix A. Printed and Manuscript Forms of *Leicester's Commonwealth*	222
Appendix B. The French Translation, 1585, and Its Addition	228
Appendix C. Sidney's *Defense of Leicester*	249
Appendix D. Further Notes	265
Appendix E. Related Documents	279
Appendix F. Genealogical Tables	295
Bibliography of Printed Works Cited	298
Index of Proper Names	310

Preface

The tract known as *Leicester's Commonwealth* is a fascinating book that deserves to be better understood than it is. It has of course been widely read and quoted, but whereas it was once relied upon by serious historians in their remarks upon the Earl of Leicester as if it held the secret "inside" truths about the Elizabethan Court, in this century it has too often been dismissed almost contemptuously as a negligible pack of unsavory lies, that "scurrilous pamphlet." Neither view seems accurate or productive. The purpose of the present edition is to make the book more readily available in a context of supporting references that should help readers better weigh its real value, in general and in any given passage. To this end, I have inclined to fullness in the annotations and other references, risking tedium, I fear, in order to supply as many leads as possible for further investigation. In the Introduction I have ventured some remarks about the political themes in the book, and I have argued that the book was written by Charles Arundell and his circle; I have dwelt at some length on the activities of this group of men, largely because far too little is known about them at present. But the most interesting question—to what extent the book's image of Leicester is an accurate representation of the man himself—I have left largely unanswered. The time has not yet come finally to end controversy on that point, and I have made only a few safe suggestions concerning it.

It will be sufficient to say that the traditional image of Leicester has long been very like the image found in this book. The *Commonwealth* and its progeny have provided the only coherent picture of him in his time; directly and indirectly they have informed every discussion of the Earl into the present century. As one writer has put it, "Seldom can the attempt to transform a living man into a legendary monster have had such a complete and lasting success" (Waldman, p. 171). A more critical interpretation has been slow in coming, but the tide has shifted, and just latterly we have been beneficiaries of a renewed interest in the man, with new studies, including the Earl's first biographies in modern times, attempting more balanced appraisals. Nevertheless, there has been no very clear sense of the man to be found: Was he a responsible statesman and man of principle or a mere opportunist, a worthy adviser to the Queen and commonwealth or a profligate, a grafter, even a murderer? Modern writers have ceased to see him simply as the black sheep of the Golden Age, and indeed a few are becoming quite sympathetic toward him; it is not impossible, however, that we risk moving too far in that direction.

It seems to me that now that we have thrown off the monochrome image originally created by *Leicester's Commonwealth* and have begun to assess his career, his character, and his role at Court afresh, it is necessary also to examine the "black legend" of his life in all its details. In our investigations of individual charges, in this and the other libels against the Earl, we find few to be entirely true, but few to be entirely false—no more than a handful can safely be ignored by anyone seeking to understand the Earl's part in the Elizabethan play, and it must not be thought sufficient to disprove an important allegation by observing that it came from *Leicester's Commonwealth*. Derek Wilson, for example, noting that the *Commonwealth* 'names names' in its circumstantial attack, dismisses the book in part because "they are mostly the names of obscure men (supposing they lived at all) of whom we can now find no trace" (p. 256). But this is not true; we can indeed trace nearly all of those names. Tracing them by no means proves that the allegations are true, only that there is more to be learned about the allegations if we will seek to do so. I hope that this edition, with its annotations and comments, will push forward that examination and provide as much aid to others as is possible at this stage, whilst making more widely available one of the most entertaining pieces of defamatory writing ever seen in English.

This edition of the *Commonwealth* originated in my doctoral dissertation, presented in 1972. Not long thereafter, I began a collaboration with Dr. Peter Roberts of the University of Kent at Canterbury, with a view to using the occasion of the publication of such an edition to study the Earl of Leicester's role in Elizabethan Court affairs in some detail. Dr. Roberts contributed many references for the edition in its present form, but unfortunately other commitments have prevented him from being able to help bring the envisaged project to completion at this time. A confident assessment of the administrative history residing behind the *Commonwealth*'s portrait is a very considerable undertaking, requiring rather more knowledge and space than is available in the present instance, and it must therefore await a future venture. In the meantime, much of Dr. Roberts's work has been incorporated in the following pages, though I must take full responsibility for the opinions expressed and the uses to which his leads have been applied.

I also owe debts of gratitude to Elizabeth Greed Peck, Professor Calvin G. Thayer, the late Professor Frank B. Fieler, Dr. Thomas H. Clancy, S.J., and Jane Wilson, all of whom, in their own ways, contributed much to the completion of this project.

D.C.P.
Leysin, March 1983

Acknowledgements

For permission to quote from materials in their custody, I wish to thank the Folger Shakespeare Library (Washington, D.C.), the Syndics of the Cambridge University Library, the Governors and Guardians of Archbishop Marsh's Library (Dublin), the University Library of the University of Durham, the Bodleian Library in Oxford, the Rectors and Fellows of Exeter College, Oxford, the keepers of the Durning-Lawrence Collection in the University of London Library, the Beinecke Rare Book and Manuscript Library of Yale University, the University of Chicago Press, and of course the British Library. I cannot let pass this opportunity to express my sincere gratitude to the librarians of these and the other collections in which I have studied for their unfailing courtesy and tireless assistance.

Abbreviations

Full reference to printed works may be found in the Bibliography.

A.P.C.	Dasent, *Acts of the Privy Council* (cited by years covered).
C.R.S.	Publications of the Catholic Record Society (cited by volume number).
C.S.P.	*Calendar of State Papers* (cited by series and years covered).
Camden, *Elizabeth*.	Camden, *Historie of the Most Renowned and Virtuous Princess, Elizabeth.* Richard Norton's translation of 1630. (W. T. MacCaffrey's edition of selected chapters, 1970, contains many of the cited passages.)
D.N.B.	*Dictionary of National Biography.*
H.M.C.	Historical Manuscripts Commission reports.
Hardwicke State Papers.	Yorke, *Miscellaneous State Papers.*
Hatton Memoirs.	Nicolas, *Memoirs of the Life and Times of Sir Christopher Hatton.*
Nichols, *Progresses.*	Nichols, *Progresses and Public Processions of Queen Elizabeth.*
O.E.D.	*Oxford English Dictionary.*
S.P.	London, Public Record Office, State Papers (cited by series, volume, and document).
S.T.C.	Pollard and Redgrave, *Short-Title Catalogue . . . 1475–1640.*
Sidney Papers.	Collins, *Letters and Memorials of State.*
Tudor Proclamations.	Hughes and Larkin, *Tudor Royal Proclamations.*

Introduction

Robert Dudley (1532?-1588), Earl of Leicester and Queen Elizabeth's long-time favorite, was the subject of scandal from the very beginnings of the Elizabethan era. His influence with the new Queen was openly resented in 1559, and his "freedom" with her person excited protestations from observers both foreign and domestic throughout the next few years. His rapid rise through virtually all the ranks of power and dignity offended the conservative old nobility, and his ostensibly ornamental status as Court favorite in the 1560s rankled many of the rising class of less glamorous royal servants, among them William Cecil. The Earl, perhaps more than any man at Court during the entire reign, gave his associates ample reason to dislike him.

It is well known today, for example, that at the time of his first wife's death in 1560 he was widely believed to have had her removed in order to clear his matrimonial path to Elizabeth. In 1570 he was rumored to have had two children by the Queen, and by March 1581 the number had grown to five; it was being said that the Queen "never goeth in progress but to be delivered."[1] A certain Charles Ratclif and others were examined in May 1577, and two gentlemen were expelled from the Court in August, all for slandering him; in February 1580 the Earl's dealings in North Wales brought forth "certain Welsh rhymes or libels" against him. Traditions current in the Sheffield and Holles families—of Leicester as poisoner—have been preserved in the family *Memorials*, and grievances peculiar to the Howard clan, often related to the Duke of Norfolk's execution, appear in many documents, as well as in *Leicester's Commonwealth* itself.[2] Examples of anti-Leicestrian gossip could be multiplied indefinitely.

At least by 1580, Leicester was coming in for attacks in print as well, but it is not generally recognized that they came from two more or less distinct directions. One derives from his personal role in the Court, both from his relations with individual courtiers and suitors, especially those of the more conservative families, and from his opponents in factional struggles at Court, most notably in the hectic maneuvering of 1579-1581 surrounding the Queen's proposed marriage to "Monsieur," Francis Duke of Anjou (1554-1584), the heir to the French throne. The other derives more generally from his position among the most influential leaders of the regime, particularly in his growing identification as a leader and protector of the Puritan party at Court. This association had begun by the early 1570s or earlier still, when his advocacy of domestic and foreign left-Protestant causes had begun to assume a public consistency, but it had only become dangerous to the organized Catholic opposition as government harassment of priests and recusants was stepped up around the end of the decade and as his ability to influence the Queen's foreign policy toward more adventurous courses began at last to be taken more seriously in foreign capitals.

As to the first sort, on 30 July 1580 Lord Burghley's ill-fated agent Dr. William Parry reported from Paris that a slanderous book had just appeared "whereunto . . . in requital to that which was written against Monsieur and his ministers in England the lives of the Earl of Leicester and Sir Christopher Hatton are added."[3] And when *Leicester's Commonwealth* first showed up in 1584, Secretary Walsingham asserted that he had heard of "such an intent" three years earlier in a similar context; although he was mistaken in identifying our book with whatever work he had received notice of (perhaps Parry's), it is into this genre that the *Commonwealth* and its immediate relatives must be placed, the tradition of opposition to Leicester at Court resulting largely from personal animosities and from the French-marriage negotiation. The tract reflects a continuing resentment over the thwarted end of the Anjou courtship, and the nature of its grievances very strongly reflects the Court affiliations of those years.

Leicester's leadership of the Puritan cause and his role both in formulation of national policy and in the persecution of Catholics occasioned attacks upon him in *De persecutione Anglicana* (1582) by

Father Robert Parsons (or Persons), S. J. (1546–1610), where the Earl was linked to Walsingham's and Huntingdon's cruelties toward the recusants and priests.[4] Later, Dr. William Allen (1532–1594), *de facto* leader of the English Catholics abroad, fulminated against him in his *Admonition to the Nobility and People of England* (1588), repeating there some of the charges first found in the *Commonwealth*.[5] In the *Flores Calvinistici*, the *Commonwealth*'s accusations are retailed again as part of an attempt to discredit the whole Protestant cause in the religious troubles in the Netherlands, where the Earl had taken command of the anti-Spanish military forces. This strain may be said to have included Leicester in more broadly focused propaganda rather from institutional motives than from personal ones, that is, because he was a prominent member of the regime. The mainstream of Catholic exile propaganda, however, which after about 1580 is represented chiefly by the writings of the Allen-Parsons party, by and large neglected Leicester. To the Catholic cause in general, Lord Burghley was far more often the principal target, as the putative architect of the Settlement that had disenfranchised a Catholic majority at home and looked soon to be interfering in unstable situations on the continent. The *regnum Cecilianum*, not the *Leicestrensem rempublicam*, was the watchword of most resistance literature.[6] After the Babington Plot of 1586, Secretary Walsingham too began to become more frequently associated with Burghley in the obloquy.[7] The *Commonwealth*'s malignant preoccupation with Leicester as a man, its sympathy and respect for both Burghley and Walsingham, suggest more specialized interests than would ordinarily have concerned the Allen-Parsons party, interests that derive from the French match and from factional intrigues at Court.

Leicester's Commonwealth first appeared in 1584. The confusion of these two strains began fairly early, for the book's traditional association with Robert Parsons originated some fifteen years later among his enemies in the Roman Church itself. English government officials seem never to have suspected Parsons during their search for the author, but the legend of "Parsons' Green-Coat" (evidently from the coloring of its leaf edges) was picked up by such Protestant writers as Thomas James in the hysterical years following the "Jesuit" Gunpowder Plot and has been with us, with few demurrers, until this century.[8] There is even an old tradition to the effect that Parsons wrote the book from materials supplied to him by Lord Burghley himself.[9] In 1957 Father Leo Hicks, S. J., undertook to sever the connection in an article that studied in detail the origin of this attribution, and if he had not done so, the religious attitudes that underlie the book should have rendered the idea of Parsons's authorship most implausible long ago.[10] Although Parsons certainly had more to do with the book than either he or Hicks was prepared to admit, as we shall see, the tract can be shown to have emanated, not from Parsons's "Jesuit" party, but from a group of lay Catholic exiles, partisans of the Queen of Scots, who were based principally in Paris, more specifically from a subgroup among them composed of formerly pro-Anjou courtiers recently hounded from the English Court (in their view at least) by Leicester himself.

With only slight oversimplification, the *Commonwealth*'s purposes may be briefly defined as three. The first was to defame the Earl of Leicester in both his private life and his public role, and there seem to be two motives for doing so: a practical motive, to introduce the Earl as a new scapegoat for the rising tensions of the time, thereby diverting malevolent attention from the Queen of Scots; and a personal one, to vilify a hated enemy. The second purpose was to advance again the Scottish claim to the crown of England, chiefly for Queen Mary but newly with her son James in mind as well. The third was to attempt to calm the growing religious anxieties in the realm (in part by writing them off to Leicester's agency) and thereby to procure more favorable treatment for the Catholics at home. The latter two purposes require a reasonable, convincing tone; the first, on the contrary, may well benefit from outrageous charges, salacious details, and a sometimes hysterical tone, not so much to convince as simply to guarantee the book will be read. The *Commonwealth* weaves these three purposes together with admirable logic, and it executes each of these tones masterfully, but if fails signally to solve a basic problem—that however sound the logical connections, these tones do not conjoin easily in the same book. Inevitably, the shrill bitterness seldom far beneath the surface in the discussions of Leicester have almost entirely occluded the nobler purposes. Neither in its own time nor very often since have readers responded to the less defamatory themes; in effect, if not in intent, the book is only a libel. It is to the libellous parts that government and imitators reacted, and it is the libellous parts that have had lasting effect on historiography.

THE CIRCUMSTANCES OF ITS PUBLICATION

The Copy of a Letter Written by a Master of Art of Cambridge first attracted the notice of the English government in August or September 1584.[11] Almost immediately it became known by the more familiar *Leicester's Commonwealth*, though the phrase is actually used only once in the text. Hugh Davies referred to "the Earl of Leicester his Common Wealth" in September 1586, and by 1599 the priest William Watson was giving the new title currency at home and on the continent.[12] At least seven of the contemporary manuscript copies of the tract use this title, and on 2 December 1619 the Lady Anne Clifford recorded having had "a book called *Leicester's Common Wealth*" read to her by a servant.[13] It later appeared on the title pages of the book's 1641 reprints. Although the *Commonwealth*'s authors made use of much material of somewhat earlier date, the final writing seems to have taken place in the late spring of 1584. In the tract both Leicester's son, Robert Lord Denbigh (died 19 July 1584), and the Duke of Anjou himself (d. 31 May/10 June new style 1584) are spoken of as alive, and we may therefore conclude that the book was written no later than the end of June. In the text it is observed that the Lord Deputyship of Ireland will doubtless be filled to Leicester's good liking, but a marginalium, perhaps added while the book was in press, supplies the name of Sir John Perrot, who departed for his new post on 12 May 1584;[14] this may suggest that the printing was in progress no earlier than late May. Thus in all probability the production of the tract can be narrowed to about June, or in any case to summer, 1584.

On 24 August Ambassador Stafford reported from Paris that "the books to answer [Burghley's] *The True Execution of Justice in England* . . . are now come out," one of which books he identified as Dr. Allen's *Defence of English Catholics*, the other of which (if more than one was meant) may have been the *Commonwealth*, as it also makes reply to Lord Burghley's tract.[15] Father Parsons administered from his bases in Paris and Rouen an elaborate system of devices for the transport of books and seminary priests into England, and he had written earlier in August that the lay brother Ralph Emerson had just opened two new routes and brought in eight hundred books, which may have included copies of the *Commonwealth*.[16] On Emerson's next trip in, however, he was certainly bearing a consignment of *Commonwealths*, and both he and his cargo were seized by the authorities.[17] He was committed to the Poultry Street Counter in London, after interrogation, on 26 September 1584.[18] Immediately realizing the potential for scandal that the book presented, the government set about trying to determine its provenance. Lord Mayor Osborne sent a copy to Secretary Walsingham, who in turn read it and deduced from its Marian objectives that it had been set out by her supporters abroad. Writing to Leicester on 29 September, he guessed that "the author thereof is [Thomas] Morgan, the Queen of Scots' agent in France, and as I gather by the course thereof he hath been assisted therein by the Lord Paget, Charles Arundell, and [William] Tresham"; and he reported that he had taken steps to see that the confiscated copies did not get about. He ends, "It behooveth us, considering the malice of this time, to walk very warily in our callings."[19]

Despite the facility of Walsingham's attribution, it soon appeared that no one was yet certain of its author. Leicester himself sent Richard Hakluyt, Stafford's embassy chaplain, back to Paris in October with a demand that the ambassador find out where and by whom it had been published.[20] Stafford, who seems always to have known a good deal more about the *Commonwealth* than he ever told his superiors, replied on 29 October, "I have done what I can to know where they were printed, but far as I can by any means find or hear, they themselves [the English Papists] say in England or in Flanders, which I think to be true, for it hardly can be done either at Rouen or here but I should know of it."[21] Earlier in the same letter, however, he had mentioned that the books had been brought into Paris by a man calling himself Stinter, who had just come out of England and who "was the next day dispatched to Rouen back again"; this must suggest the possibility that "Stinter" had obtained copies of the tract whilst in Rouen *en route* to Paris. One prominent member of the lay exile group, Thomas Fitzherbert, was based in Rouen, and so at this time was Stephen Brinkley, formerly Lord Paget's man, who had managed Father Parsons's secret presswork in England in 1580–1581 and who, a few months after the *Commonwealth*'s appearance, was helping the Jesuit and George Flinton get out the second edition of Parsons's devotional work *The Christian Directory* in that city.[22] Although the writing of the tract was most probably done in Paris, where most of the exiled courtiers principally resided, the printing seems quite likely to have been done in Rouen, therefore, perhaps on George Flinton's press (copies of the *Commonwealth* were being stored with Flinton in the following year) and perhaps on the press of George L'Oyselet, who in 1584 was also printing another Marian tract, Leslie's *Treatise Touching the Right*, from which much material in the *Commonwealth* was directly taken and which has very similar (though not identical) presswork.[23]

Leicester had many enemies, in and out of government, who charged him with many crimes. Many of the charges seem to have been at least partially true. But he was still a Privy Councilor who, for better or worse, enjoyed the favor of the Queen, and so, even though the *Commonwealth* speaks of Elizabeth, Burghley, and Walsingham in the most solicitous and kindly terms, the government treated the book as an attack, not upon Leicester the man, but upon the entire regime and upon the Queen from whom Leicester drew his power. Walsingham had confiscated one consignment, but evidently other copies had got through, for on 12 October in a quite remarkable move a proclamation was issued from Hampton Court that struck out against seditious books in general but was clearly occasioned principally by *Leicester's Commonwealth* and Allen's *Defence* (see Appendix E). In it, the Queen denounced its abominable lies in general terms and required all copies to be surrendered; amnesty was offered to all persons who immediately brought in their copies to the authorities, but those possessing copies who did not come forward were to face indefinite imprisonment. The proclamation did not suffice. On 16 December a bill against "scandalous libelling" received a second reading in the House of Lords and was sent into committee, from which it seems never to have emerged, presumably because the provisions of *13 Elizabeth, cap. 1* (1571), against discussing the succession to the crown, were considered adequate to the *Commonwealth*'s transgressions.[24] On 17 March following, a similar bill was read to the Commons and rejected, probably because the Puritan members feared it could be turned against themselves.[25]

The widespread audience the book was enjoying is attested to by evidence of its circulation: in April 1585, for example, a copy found its way in to William Shelley, a state prisoner in the Tower, and back out again without detection, and it was being read so openly at Court that the Earl of Ormonde teased Sir John Harington by greeting him in the Earl of Leicester's presence with "Good morrow, Mr. Reader." When asked by Leicester what he read, Harington blushed and ("God forgive me for lying") answered, "They were certain cantos of Ariost."[26]

A further indication of its popularity is the fact that these official efforts to suppress it were to continue for some time. Pressure was brought upon King James of Scotland, and on 16 February 1585 there issued from Holyrood House a proclamation against the "Letter of Estate written by a Scholar in Cambridge," that book so "full of ignominious and reproachful calumnies" recently "publicly dispersed in sundry hands within our realm"; James strove to vindicate "the honor and reputation of our right trusty and right well-beloved cousin the Earl of Leicester."[27] Then in June 1585 an even more extraordinary plan was conceived; circular letters were sent out to officials in several (and possibly all) counties from the Privy Council, alluding to the proclamations already made but complaining that despite them the very same "shameful and devilish books and libels have been continually spread abroad." The letter went on to deplore the *Commonwealth*'s charges against the Earl, "of which most malicious and wicked imputations her Majesty in her own clear knowledge doth declare and testify his innocency to all the world" (Appendix E). Evidently, as in the case of the Marprelate attack, the government felt obliged not only to suppress the *Commonwealth*'s slanders but to deny them as best it could as well.

Sometime during the winter of 1584–1585, Sir Philip Sidney also determined to defend his uncle's reputation, and he did so in a hastily written pamphlet now known as the *Defense of Leicester*.[28] Intended evidently for publication but neither published in his own time nor, apparently, very much circulated in manuscript, the *Defense* rather obviously sidesteps the *Commonwealth*'s direct calumnies upon the Earl's morals and concentrates instead upon refuting what had actually been only a secondary line of attack, the charge that Leicester was newly risen from base lineage—Sidney's lineage on his mother's side was, of course, identical with Leicester's own. What seems to have enraged Sir Philip more than anything else about the *Commonwealth*, however, was that he was ignorant of its author's name and did not know to whom he should give the lie; this should indicate that Leicester too and presumably Walsingham had reached no conclusions about its authorship.

In any case Sidney's *Defense* did not find print, probably because the government was understandably wary of opening up a public disputation on the subject of the Earl's morals. One recalls that when in 1573 the publication of the *Treatise of Treasons* so deeply offended Lord Burghley, he drafted notes for a rebuttal but eventually followed Archbishop Parker's advice, that "some things are better put up in silence, than much stirred in."[29] In this and other cases, although there was no settled policy, the officials chose rather to offer categorical denials in the Queen's name than to risk detailed self-exculpations.

Meanwhile the government's search for the persons responsible continued. In May 1585 the French ambassador in London reported that Leicester was still on the hunt for its perpetrators,[30] and Bernardino de Mendoza, the former Spanish ambassador in London, now stationed in Paris, wrote on 1 June that Stafford had been told to bring pressure to bear upon the authorities there; he asserted that the man who had translated the book into French was an Englishman and, without naming him, spoke as if the man's identity were known.[31] Thomas Rogers (alias Nicholas Berden), perhaps Walsingham's best agent, learned in April that one thousand copies of the tract were in the custody of the printer Flinton in Rouen.[32] Later in the year, having infiltrated the exile community in Rouen, he reported that he had won Thomas Fitzherbert's confidence and had been offered the use of his Paris residence, "the lodging of Charles Arundell when he is at Paris"; but "if I be lodged there," he continued, "I must lodge amongst a great number of the libels in French that were written against the Right Honorable the Earl of Leicester."³³

In addition, interrogations were being made of all state prisoners who might have had any knowledge of the book or its authors. Sylvan Scory, the Bishop of Hereford's scapegrace son, was examined on 12 February 1585. He "never saw the book" but "hath heard talk of the said libel . . . commonly at tables." George Errington was examined on 30 August 1585 about a man who had been intercepted at Scarborough bearing copies of the *Commonwealth*. Hugh Davies gave evidence on 6 September 1586 about a Robert Atkins who had extolled the book's virtues to him at offensive length. William Wigges, on 22 June 1587, professed to believe the *Commonwealth* "worthy to be burned." In early 1586 Ambassador Stafford's own man, one Lilly, was detained in London and examined for complicity. And in early 1585 Robert Poley, the "Pooley" whom the *Commonwealth* calls one of Leicester's henchmen, was also interrogated for possessing a copy.³⁴ It seems, however, that at no time did the English government come to any conclusions about the identity of the *Commonwealth*'s authors.

By the spring of 1585 a further complication had developed, the appearance in Paris of a French translation of the *Commonwealth* entitled *Discours de la vie abominable . . . le my Lorde de Lecestre*, the "libels in French" to which Rogers alluded just above. On 30 March Stafford reported to Walsingham that he had heard of it; said to have been printed at Rheims, he related, it had a "villainous addition" tacked onto it. He professed to fear the scandal that would result, and as he had advised when the English version had first appeared, he recommended that he not be ordered to attempt having it suppressed; since his "nearest have a touch in it" (that is, since it mentioned his wife, the former Douglass Sheffield), he might be suspected of personal motives. His greatest fear, however, was that he would be blamed for it, or at least associated with it in Leicester's wrath: "If you command me I will send you [one] of them, for else I will not, for I cannot tell how it will be taken." Neither had he written to Leicester about it, for he "would be loth to do anything subject to bad interpretation." At the end of his dispatch, it appeared that he had known something about it for some time, something that as far as we can tell he had never reported: "I have kept it from the beginning that the other [the *Commonwealth*] came out from translating here, for [Thomas] Throgmorton was even then in hand with it, and by means that I found left it off, and ever since it hath slept, and is but now of a sudden gushed out."[35] To his personal patron Lord Burghley he wrote on the same day the same news, again recommending that the whole matter be left alone. He ended with the same reservation: "If your Lordship will command me, I will send you one as soon as any doth come, but else I will not, for the Earl of Leicester is ever subject to take not well that which cometh from me."[36] Perhaps significantly, Walsingham did not command Stafford to send a copy; little more than a week later, he had his own man bring one to him, and Stafford felt constrained to enclose a copy to Burghley on 10 April for balance.[37]

The French edition is an extremely close and accurate translation of the *Commonwealth*, pretty certainly an attempt by the same men to give Leicester's notoriety a continental coverage, motivated presumably by the same partisan animosity that occasioned its original. Its "villainous addition" (included here as Appendix B) is aimed more pointedly at a French audience and expends considerable energy upon charges against the Earl, such as his subversion of the Duke of Anjou in the Low Countries, which might particularly offend the French reader. Moreover, there are signs that this addition was considered by its author to be the second installment of a continuing campaign against the Earl; he mentions further translations into Latin and Italian shortly to appear (but which, so far as is known, never did) and promises that other men shall "add from day to day such his actions as the time shall discover . . . as soon as they can receive more large advertisement from England, from whence there is already gathered, as I hear, a good quantity that shall be augmented from more to more."[38] Gone from the addition are the *Commonwealth*'s corollary concerns with toleration for English Catholics and the succession to the English crown; here full attention is devoted to Leicester and his Puritan allies.

There is other evidence that a continuing campaign against Leicester had been intended. On 9 March 1586, Sir Francis Englefield, formerly Principal Secretary in Mary I's time and a leading spokesman for the English Catholics at the Spanish Court, wrote a curious letter to an unknown correspondent wherein he linked the *Commonwealth*'s attack upon the Earl to a larger propagandistic undertaking that, in lieu of armed might, must be their only weapon against the English government. In it he wondered at several omissions in the *Commonwealth*'s charges and suggested several new charges to be included in subsequent ventures.

> Instead therefore of the sword, which we cannot obtain, we must fight with paper and pens, which cannot be taken from us. The two books of Justice [Allen's *Defence*] and Leicester's life have raised the building much. Let the same therefore be followed and backed with some pamphlets of like kind fresh and fresh from time to time. The accusation of the Queen of Scots in Throgmorton's confession, her removing from [the Earl of] Shrewsbury to the custody of the Earl of Leicester his allies, their bait at Tutbury being more than half way from Sheffield to Killingworth, and the Oath of Association [of October 1584], excluding whatsoever successor they list to say attempted aught to this Queen of England's annoyance, be all excellent points to be laid forth in proof and confirmation of that which is already set down of the Earl of Leicester's practices. Among which I marvel how the death of the Duke of Lennox was forgotten, and how the King of Scots and his father were pretermitted . . . where mention is made of the Lord Charles [Stuart] and his daughter Arbella, whereat I warrant you some skittish humor will both stumble and kick.[39]

Despite Englefield's suggestions, however, the French translation was the second and last extant production from the exiled courtier group.

Leicester's Commonwealth, however, if it had no more continuations, did leave its mark elsewhere. In February or March 1586 a tiny Latin pamphlet, the *Flores Calvinistici*, was cast abroad in the Netherlands, in two editions, with the intention of discrediting the Protestant cause there.[40] Written by one Julius Briegerus, it includes scandalous anecdotes concerning a number of prominent figures, amongst them Anne Boleyn, Thomas Cranmer, John Knox, and Jean Calvin, but principally concerning Leicester himself. Over one third of its length (some thirty pages) is devoted to the Earl, who was by that time leading the anti-Spanish military effort in the Low Countries, and virtually all of its material concerning him is abstracted from *Leicester's Commonwealth*.[41] In the few years following, the *Commonwealth* was used as a source several times more: loosely, though extensively, in the very amusing twenty-page prose tract in manuscript that comically portrays the Earl's vain attempts to enter Heaven and his subsequent reception in Hell, and in the rather inept manuscript diatribe known as the "Letter of Estate"; and, more exactly, in Thomas Rogers's long poem "Leicester's Ghost."[42] Its presence can be felt in numerous short poetical squibs against the Earl,[43] and it was relied upon or alluded to by such various authors as Camden, Harington, Naunton, Robert Parsons and William Allen, Thomas Wilson, and John Webster, among others. But its original authors were apparently able to add no more to it. Within four years of the book's first appearance, the Paris lay exile group was dispersed—Charles Arundell was dead, Thomas Lord Paget soon to die, Thomas Morgan just released from the Bastille and soon to be imprisoned in the Netherlands–and both Leicester himself, against whom it had been written, and Mary, Queen of Scots, for whom it had been written, were also dead. The next defense of the Earl to appear, the brief prose "The Dead Man's Right" printed anonymously in *The Phoenix Nest* in 1593, arrived, as its title implies, posthumously.[44]

THE CATHOLIC COURT PARTY

It would be impossible now, as it was for the English government in its own time, to identify with certainty the person responsible for *Leicester's Commonwealth*; for one thing, it is evidently the work of several people (which partially explains the diversity of its subject matter and intentions), and for another, we encounter considerable disingenuousness in the statements of those who, like Parsons, Stafford, and Morgan, must have known more about it than they ever told. Nevertheless, by means of what external evidence survives of contemporary attempts to determine its authorship and by means of study of the book's attitudes and interests, we can reach a reasonable certainty about the group of men by whom the tract was produced.[45] The nucleus was composed of Catholic laymen, ex-courtiers who, like Charles Arundell (1540-1587) and Lord Paget (d. 1590), had been members of or attached to the conservative Howard clan and who after two decades of setbacks and renewed hopes had finally been driven from Court by Leicester, Walsingham, and their adherents. Charles Arundell (as will appear) is the man who must be considered central to this group and to the production, and therefore a brief survey of his activities and affiliations both at Court and, after 1583, on the continent will shed light upon the book itself. Arundell was himself a part of the larger Howard family and would have had easy access to those anti-Dudley traditions that passed among the discontented members of that ancient, conservative, and for the most part Catholic house.

The Howard line proper, of importance since the 1200s, had risen sharply in the midfifteenth century and was headed from 1483 to 1572 by the successive Dukes of Norfolk. The clan's principal Elizabethan representative was Thomas, the fourth Duke, son of Surrey the poet and the premier peer of the realm. He was executed in 1572 for his activities in behalf of Mary, Queen of Scots, and her religion, a Roman faith in which, though he denied it on the scaffold, he seems to have believed as much as his temperament allowed him any strong beliefs at all. His eldest son, Philip, later Earl of Arundel, died in the Tower in 1595 after more than a decade's imprisonment for his faith; Norfolk's younger brother, the learned Lord Henry, had been an avowed Papist since the midseventies and received frequent imprisonments of his own for his intrigues in behalf of Queen Mary, until in the next reign he came at last into royal favor.[46] It was to this family, more largely conceived, that Arundell belonged and to which his fortunes were bound. His own father, Sir Thomas Arundell of Wardour, had fallen with Somerset and been executed on Tower Hill on 26 February 1552; it was said that Leicester's father, the Duke of Northumberland, had kept the jury under long restraint until it returned a verdict agains him.[47] Charles had thereafter been taken in by the Howards. Through his mother, sister of Henry VIII's fifth wife, Catherine Howard, he was second cousin to Thomas the fourth Duke and to Lord Harry his brother; he was cousin-german to the Earl of Oxford as well, and second cousin to Queen Elizabeth herself. And he was first cousin once removed to Thomas Radcliffe

(1526?-1583), third Earl of Sussex, the principal patron of both the cause of Anjou's marriage and the Court party that fought to bring it to success.[48] He was also thus related to Ambassador Sir Edward Stafford and to his wife, the Lady Douglass (called Lady Sheffield, from her former marriage), of the Howards of Effingham. These two had long shared the most vehement animosity toward Leicester, the reasons for which will be evident in the text. To them Arundell turned during his exile from England after November 1583, and although his frequenting of Stafford's house in Paris more than once landed him in trouble among the members of the exile community, whilst there he must have found an inexhaustible supply of slanderous anecdotes concerning the Earl.

The origins of the Court group to which Arundell belonged went back some years. During the late 1560s the party lines that were to endure with little alteration for the next two decades and more had already become drawn. As a representative of the old nobility, the Earl of Sussex, once returned from his service in Ireland, had developed something of a history of enmity toward Leicester the opportunist "upstart," as had Sir William Cecil, though more temperately and for different reasons. The young Duke of Norfolk had become a close friend to Sussex, but in 1569 Sussex was residing in the north as Lord President, and without the older man's guidance Norfolk had become involved in a plot to marry the Queen of Scots and to remove Cecil, another "new man," out of his position of influence and into the Tower. The ascertainable details of this intrigue have been recounted elsewhere,[49] but it seems that in some way Leicester had joined its ranks and that when the Queen learned of the affair, he betrayed Norfolk's complicity to her. The contemporaneous Rebellion of the Northern Earls made the matter seem more serious than it probably was, and the Duke came under the gravest royal suspicion. When, not long afterward, he held renewed secret correspondence with Mary and this so-called Ridolfi Plot came to light, he paid the price of his indiscretions, being executed on 2 June 1572. Although Norfolk was much at fault in this matter and by 1571 was certainly verging upon genuine treason, the Howard clan for many years afterward felt that Leicester had been the real culprit, that by luring the Duke into the original plan and then informing upon him, Leicester had initiated the young man's downfall; this interpretation is the one found in the *Commonwealth* and in the other complaints emanating from the Howard interests.

Following Norfolk's execution, the circle of his kinsmen and allies, despite his brother Henry's confinement to Lambeth Palace at the time, seems to have survived with not much loss of favor. The Earl of Arundel was readmitted to the Council. The Duke's cousin and friend the Earl of Oxford married Secretary Cecil's daughter in December 1571, and in May 1573 it was reported that "the Queen's Majesty delighteth more in his personage and his dancing and valiantness than any other."[50] Charles Arundell, referred to as "the Queen's Servant," was one of the courtiers accompanying the Earl of Lincoln's embassy into France for the signing of the Treaty of Blois in April 1572.[51] On 2 June (the same day as Norfolk's execution) he received a grant for life of the reversion of the office of Captain of Portland Castle, and in October 1574 he received, "for his service," the office of Receiver of Crown Lands in the counties of Wilts, Southampton, and Gloucester, with an annuity of one hundred pounds.[52] But then things began to turn sour. In spring 1574 Oxford was implicated belatedly in a 1571 attempt to effect Norfolk's escape abroad; he rashly fled to the continent, but despite (or because of) a hearty welcome from the English exiles there, he sensibly returned at the Queen's command.[53] In early 1575 Lord Harry was reimprisoned after the confessions of Henry Cockyn revealed his renewed correspondence with the Queen of Scots.[54] By the mid-1570s these two men and their friends, amongst them Arundell, had begun to form a dangerous and unstable group with an accumulation of grievances against the state in general and, it seems, against Leicester in particular. As John Bossy has aptly put it, "They had about them a certain sense of 'outness.' "[55]

Most of these men had had deep family roots in the Catholic faith before this, but at some time during these years Arundell, Lord Howard, and another kinsman, Francis Southwell, were formally reconciled to the Roman Church. In mid or late 1576, Oxford too, despite having been raised in Lord Burghley's household, was converted through Arundell's agency.[56] Henceforward, their fates were he informed the Queen of Leicester's more or less secret marriage to the Countess of Essex, which had taken place nearly a year earlier.[64] The effects at first seemed all that he could have hoped for as Leicester and Walsingham were banished from Court, Anjou's passport was signed on 6 July, and talk circulated that Catholics were to be sworn onto the Privy Council, among them the Earl of Northumberland and the Viscount Montagu.[65] In many ways this false dawn of Catholic hopes is the central political event behind *Leicester's Commonwealth*; as Professor Collinson has said, "There was the chance of a real palace revolution."[66]

But it failed. By the end of summer Leicester had returned to the fray and clearly the moment had passed; the Council, in its meeting of 2 October 1579, would no longer advise in favor of the match unless the Queen expressly willed its members to do so. The arguments went back and forth; the Queen turned that way and this; and although Simier was packed off to Paris in November with some inconsequential articles of marriage, the affair dragged on through the next year. During 1580 the hysteria occasioned by Dr. Sander's ill-fated Papal invasion of Ireland, by the Jesuit mission into England, and by the rumored "Holy League" on the continent finally turned Mauvissière away from his Romish allies at Court as he had no use for a relationship that could only work against him. Persecution of Catholics throughout the realm was beginning in earnest at about this time; the Catholic group, though it still supported Sussex and his "peace" platform, was becoming isolated from its chief strength as its adherents found they could no longer trust the French to be working toward common objectives.

During the Christmas season of 1580, Leicester unveiled his answer to Simier's revelation of his marital status. Intent upon rendering Sussex's allies politically useless, he successfully weaned the unstable Oxford away from his friends. The young nobleman confessed to the Queen his intrigues of 1577 with the French ambassador and accused his coreligionists of conspiracy against the state. When his confession and accusations were not immediately believed, he allegedly offered Arundell a thousands pounds to verify his charges and focus the blame upon Howard and Southwell; Arundell, according to his own testimony, refused the offer.[67] Elizabeth told Mauvissière that she had known of the religious persuasions of Howard, Arundell, and Southwell all along but esteemed the men highly anyway, especially in light of their support for her marriage; "she would close her eyes to it" as long as it was not found to go deeper.[68]

When, shortly afterward, Leicester presented to the Queen Oxford's formal statement of his charges against the others,[69] Howard, Arundell, and Southwell received word of their imminent arrest from an unnamed friend on the Privy Council, and the former two took refuge in the Spanish ambassador's house in the middle of the night. Although he had never spoken with them before, Mendoza saw in his hospitality a chance to win valuable contacts; he wrote that Howard was "as intimate with the Earl of Sussex as nail with quick" and that he had "much friendship with the ladies of the privy chamber, who inform him exactly what passes indoors."[70] Indeed, in several of his dispatches of 1582 he indicated that Lord Howard had accepted his offer of a pension and was providing him with "constant information." Soon after their resort to him, however, Howard and Arundell gave themselves up and were committed to the custody of gentlemen.[71] Mendoza reported on 9 January that Leicester had begun to spread rumors, with an eye to discrediting "their close friend" Sussex, that they had been "plotting a massacre of the Protestants, beginning with the Queen."[72] If Leicester was indeed guilty of such hyperbole, the *Commonwealth*'s later attack upon him is no more than repayment in kind.

These tangled affairs shed light upon the elements of *Leicester's Commonwealth*. Arundell's group appears to us as a circle of men of high connection, of considerable if temporary favor with the Queen; they had participated in the short-lived rise of Catholic hopes at Court and had been intimate with the means of knowing everything that "passes indoors" through their contacts with the Sussex group in the Council and the ladies nearest Elizabeth herself. But at the same time they were men who because of their religion were politically vulnerable to the opposition's devices. Their "outness," to recall Mr. Bossy's term, led them into shady dealings with the French ambassador. As their cause came temporarily into favor, they ascended into the center of things, but the reasons for their outness never left them and were soon to drive them into still shadier dealings with Mendoza, whose dispatches home soon began to reflect the Arundell-Howard view of Court life, a view remarkably similar to and often verbally echoing that which we find in the *Commonwealth*. The events of 1579 and 1580, then, explain much in the 1584 book's complex of attitudes, including a veneration of Sussex, as the patron of their cause, a respect for Lord Burghley unusual in Catholic writing, as he too had been their patron, and most of all a virulent hatred for Leicester, the source of all their misfortunes past and present.

Oxford followed their arrest with a flurry of vicious charges against them, most of them frivolous and absurd but some of which must be taken more seriously, especially those involving conspiratorial meetings concerning the Queen of Scots held at Northumberland's Petworth estate in Sussex.[73] Arundell and Howard riposted with several spirited attacks upon Oxford's personal character as well as his activities; these display the same formidable talent for scurrilous invective for which the *Commonwealth* is notorious, and many of them anticipate some of the charges it later levelled at Leicester. For example, Arundell tells of how Oxford hired assassins to murder various men, the Earl's attempt upon Mr. John Cheke supposedly having been revealed to the writer "by the discovery of a gentleman that serves this monster and would not consent to such a villainy,"[74] a strategy employed in the *Commonwealth*. Another document in Arundell's hand was apparently intended to sow division between Oxford and Leicester; it charges Oxford with planning to accuse Leicester of a number of crimes—of storing munitions at Kenilworth under the pretext of supplying fireworks for the Queen's entertainment, of being the only means by which any man could win a suit with the Queen, of knowing of the Earl of Essex's death before it occurred, of "affirming further that he was able to make the proudest subject to sweat that would oppose himself against him, and that he had made the Duke of Norfolk stoop notwithstanding all his bragging"—all of these charges later repeated in the *Commonwealth*.[75] We may, if we wish, consider this period a perverse sort of apprenticeship in defamation.

The Catholic gentlemen remained in restraint from late December until the following autumn; Oxford, when the delivery of his child by Anne Vavasour in March seemed to confirm some of their charges against him, had been remanded to the Tower, later to be released to house arrest in midsummer. The friends of the disputants worked vigorously for resolution of the matter, but the Queen would not entirely free Oxford until he had confronted his antagonists; he in turn would not confront them until after he had been set free. Both Arundell and Howard wrote pleas for intercession to Walsingham and Hatton, whom they appear to have considered sympathetic to their plight;[76] this may partially account for the *Commonwealth*'s strangely softened attitude toward both these men. With Hatton at least they appear to have been fairly successful, for on several occasions Arundell thanked him for various kinds of succor and finally expressed his satisfaction that Hatton, in some capacity, "shall have the hearing of my cause."[77]

Little more is known about the disposition of the matter; the hearing, if there was one, would have been held in October 1581. On the nineteenth of that month, Sussex was sending to Arundell his cautiously worded assurances of what little help he could offer, and on the twenty-seventh Howard, by that time having been released, was attempting a burying of hatchets between himself and Leicester.[78] Nevertheless, as late as May 1583, Walter Raleigh was reporting that the Queen was still concerned about the entire affair and was thinking of reopening it.[79]

By this time the issue of the Anjou marriage had become rather a dead letter, and in February 1582 Anjou was conveyed home from his second visit, with ten thousand pounds in his pocket and a promise of more, but without a wife; for some while the whole idea of a match had been reduced to a pawn in the game of obtaining favorable conditions in an Anglo-French alliance against Spain. To the *Commonwealth*'s authors, however, who had such a stake in the successful conclusion of the marriage, its eventual failure was the result of Leicester's own handiwork, "for his own private lucre."

In these Court intrigues of 1578–1581 reside the formative influences of the *Commonwealth*'s partisan attitudes. These years saw the peak of the Arundell-Howard party's fortunes, and they saw the abrupt reversal of those fortunes in the arrest of its principals and in the dissolution of the marriage cause. Over the next few years Arundell and his friends were in relative retirement, continuing their contacts with Mendoza and working in behalf of the Queen of Scots and the passage of her correspondence (as the spy Henry Fagot reported in April 1583 specifically of Lord Howard and Francis Throgmorton).[80] They were perhaps attempting as well to render financial aid to their exiled friends.[81] Leicester, for his part, continued to hunt down the adherents of the Sussex group; William Tresham, for example, a Catholic Gentleman Pensioner, wrote to Sussex from Paris on 27 January 1582, apologizing for his abrupt flight from the realm without prior consultation but saying that fear of Leicester had left him no alternative.[82] In return, the Papist courtiers were striving to undermine Leicester's positon when they could. To instance one case, in early 1583 two of the Catholic gentlemen, Thomas Lord Paget and the Earl of Northumberland, were urging each other to inform the Queen of Leicester's "practices" against her.[83]

In September 1583 Charles Paget, brother of Arundell's friend Lord Thomas, was sent into England by the Duke of Guise to consult at Petworth with local Catholic magnates about support for a planned invasion of the Sussex coast. While there he talked with his brother, with Northumberland, and with William Shelley of Michelgrove; whether he actually carried out his conspiratorial mission has been doubted by some recent scholarship, but certainly the government was becoming concerned about the increase in exile activities.[84] Accordingly, having missed Paget, Walsingham ordered the arrest of Francis Throgmorton, who had been under careful surveillance since the preceding spring. On 4 or 5 November 1583 Throgmorton and his papers were taken, and on the same day or thereabouts Lord Harry Howard was brought in as well. Lord Paget and Arundell immediately began preparing for flight; and when on 23 November Throgmorton was again put to the rack, they fled to the Sussex coast and crossed over to Dieppe.[85] By early December everyone implicated in their flight or in Charles Paget's mission had been detained and interrogated, and the Earls of Arundel (Philip Howard) and Northumberland were placed under arrest; the former remained in confinement, with one year's intermission, until his death in 1595, while the latter was placed first with Leicester's ally Leighton and then in the Tower, where he is alleged to have committed suicide in June 1585.[86] William Shelley was also arrested and was still a prisoner in the Tower when last heard of in July 1588. Thus were virtually all of the members of the original Catholic courtiers' party rendered politically useless by exile or imprisonment.

Paget and Arundell were probably not themselves guilty of any specific treasonous activity, though the government maintained that Paget had conspired with his brother at Petworth in September.[87] Arundell himself was never charged with anything more than, in Dr. Parry's words, "to have dealt unthankfully with the Queen, unkindly with his friends, and unadvisedly with himself."[88] Paget always claimed that he had long been planning to depart the realm for his conscience' sake (perhaps aided in deciding by his wife's death in April) and that his talk with his brother had been upon that head only.[89] Probably the two men fled in November simply because they panicked, having realized that, given their religion and their known Marian sympathies, they were vulnerable to political arrest; indeed it was widely held that they had fled the implacable cruelty of the Earl of Leicester in particular.[90]

Arundell and Lord Paget arrived in Paris at the beginning of December, and there they joined other exiled laymen, some of them members of their former group: William Tresham, Thomas Throgmorton (brother of Francis), Thomas Fitzherbert of Swinnerton, Thomas Morgan, the Queen of Scots's agent, and others, "all gentlemen of quality and very zealous for religion," as Father Parsons was to describe them. They immediately sought out the new English ambassador to France, their old colleague and kinsman Sir Edward Stafford, and protesting their loyalty *usque ad aras*, they placed themselves at his disposal and waited about in Paris while he tenderly sounded out the possibilities of their reconciliation with the official government. The ambassador's background was in some ways not unlike their own. Like them he had been of the Burghley-Sussex party at Court, he had been a dedicated supporter of the French marriage, and he was closely aligned to the Howard family.[91] He was himself, if not a Catholic (and he may have been), at least sympathetic to their interests and beliefs—both his wife and his mother were indeed Papists—and he had friends as well as intelligence sources amongst the fugitive community. Like Arundell he and his wife both hated Leicester with an inordinate passion, and the fact that he utterly distrusted Leicester's "spirit" Walsingham, who as Principal Secretary was his immediate superior, has led to the argument that he was disloyal to his country.[92] The evidence for this interpretation is by no means conclusive—that Stafford suspected and feared designs against him by Leicester and Walsingham and consequently refused to take them into his confidence provides, as Professor Neale has maintained, sufficient explanation for any mysteries in his intelligence-gathering activities—but certainly the Secretary did what he could to implicate the ambassador in a number of questionable matters and, indeed, occasionally set his spies to watching the embassy.

For a month or two Arundell and Paget merely waited about while Stafford sought their repatriation (or enjoyment of their estates while in exile),[93] but by mid-February Arundell had begun gathering intelligence for the ambassador amongst the fugitive Englishmen. As his hopes for a return to England began to evaporate throughout that spring of 1584, Arundell was a frequent visitor at the embassy, and for the next three and a half years, until his suspicious death in December 1587, he and Stafford worked in close association at the business of monitoring exile activities and the Duke of Guise's ambitions, on the watch for anything that might prove invidious to England's safety.[94] It was during this first spring of Arundell's exile, while he was still based in Paris, that he and the remnants of the old Catholic courtier party found a means of expressing their hopes for the Marian cause and their resentment of Leicester in the composition of *Leicester's Commonwealth*.

AUTHORSHIP

The problem of the *Commonwealth*'s authorship has been much discussed, but we are now in a position to entertain the question more thoroughly. In considering the men most likely to have been involved in the production of the tract, we must begin with Charles Arundell himself. Internal evidence (the book's complex of personal sympathies and enmities and its intimate knowledge of the daily workings of the Court) certainly points to someone very like Arundell, who had shared the varying fortunes and eventual defeat of the

Catholic party but who (unlike Lord Harry Howard and the Earls of Arundel and Northumberland) had escaped to the continent to tell about them. We have seen that Walsingham's first guess about the *Commonwealth*'s authorship, while it specified Thomas Morgan pre-eminently, included Arundell in a supporting role. In January 1585 it was rumored in Paris that, perhaps because of that mention, "an Englishman is here newly arrived, by the practice of Leicester, to kill Charles Arundell and others," and as we have also seen, in August 1585 copies of the French translation were being stored in the lodgings used by Arundell when in Paris.[95] He had been forward in his advocacy of the Queen of Scots's cause for over a decade, and perhaps most importantly, much of the prose of the *Commonwealth* seems very similar indeed to the style of the longer papers surviving in Arundell's handwriting from the 1581 squabbles described earlier.

In 1598 Robert Parsons was accused by Charles Paget of having written the *Commonwealth* himself; in his defense he asserted that the book "is believed to have been due to a combined effort, a number of Catholics having had a part in it, but chiefly Charles Arundell, a nobleman who had recently come to Paris from England and who was extremely hostile to the Earl."[96] In August 1602 the Appellant priest John Cecil also attempted to attribute the book to Parsons, insisting that Arundell had confessed to him that although the materials had been furnished by Arundell himself, the method, style, and form had all come from Parsons.[97] Cecil's concern here had been to smear the Jesuit with unsavory political involvements before his superiors in Rome, and we are by no means obliged to accept his allegation, but his invocation of Arundell's "confession" may indicate that Arundell's name had by that time become sufficiently attached to *Leicester's Commonwealth* to lend credence to his tale. However it was, the association of Parsons's name with the book began to appear more frequently around this time and after; Father Parsons continued to deny it,[98] but by then the matter had passed out of his ability to control it; "Parsons' Green-coat" had become as much a part of the Jesuit's image as the portrait of the furtive and cowardly plotter that Charles Kingsley drew of him in *Westward Ho!*

Nevertheless, Parsons could hardly have been ignorant of the affair. He was in close contact with Arundell in Paris during this spring of 1584, attempting to woo the newcomer away from any allegiance with the anti-Jesuit groups among the exiles. The printing of the *Commonwealth* seems likely (as we have seen) to have been done on a press under Parsons's control, and its conveyance into England was certainly accomplished by his agency. In its content and strategies, the tract is not at all the book Parsons would have written, nor (with his Spanish associations) did he ever show much real interest in the cause of the Queen of Scots. Although it bears little similarity to other works of the Allen-Parsons party, however, it is not so foreign to the Jesuit's positions in the mid-1580s that he would have wished to see it suppressed. One is bound to assume that Parsons must share some responsibility in furthering the book, if not actually in writing it.

Thomas Morgan, the Queen of Scots's chief agent in Paris, may also have taken part in the production, as Leslie Hotson believed, for he was certainly prominent among the lay Catholic Englishmen in France, even after his confinement in the Bastille on 1 March 1585. We have seen that Walsingham at first suspected him of primary responsibility, and it may be that Leicester did as well; on 18 May 1586 Queen Mary wrote to the Archbishop of Glasgow that Morgan's "imprisonment has been procured by the Earl of Leicester, in consequence of an opinion which he has taken, and of which he discoursed fully to Nau [her secretary] at London, that the said Morgan had, with you and my Lord Paget, composed the book which was published against him nearly two years ago; for which he was in the utmost rage against all three."[99] But although Morgan had been (at least ostensibly) in Mary's service since 1568, he had fled to France in 1575 and could have had very little firsthand knowledge of recent English events, certainly none of the Court. What survives of his own correspondence shows a crude style markedly different from that of the *Commonwealth*. In any case, if he had written the book against Leicester and in behalf of his mistress's claim to the throne, he certainly never told her that he had; writing to her on 5 January 1585, for example, he warned her to guard her safety closely because "it was told me that Leicester should say that the book written against him tended all to your honor and his ruin, and therefore he would provide thereafter, meaning by all conjecture to extend his whole force to do your Majesty harm."[100] His colleague Charles Paget had written the same news one day earlier, similarly avoiding taking any credit for its authorship.[101]

Morgan and Paget both may have had a hand in writing or in publishing the book—and, as with Kafka's two assistants in *The Castle*, one can scarcely imagine one of them acting independently of the other—but it must also be pointed out that they were never on good terms with Arundell himself. Father Parsons records that even soon after Arundell's arrival in France he was, at Parsons's instance, avoiding them and their "anti-Jesuit" faction.[102] By January 1585 he and Morgan were openly quarrelling, and in the following September Paget was attempting to land Arundell into trouble with the Papal authorities by exposing him as a spy for England.[103] In December 1585 a fight occurred between the two, in which Arundell "had like to have slain Paget with his dagger."[104] Instances of this hostility between Morgan and Paget on the one side and Arundell on the other continued in overt quarrelling and hidden intrigue until his death,[105] and although they may of course have known something about the *Commonwealth*'s production, it is fair to say that they would not have made ideal collaborators in writing it. Moreover, the hostility between these two and Father Parsons is well known, and it seems unlikely that the Jesuit should have facilitated its publication had he known of their participation in the writing. Professor Hotson, in accepting Walsingham's letter of 29 September as conclusive, seems both to have overrated the Secretary's omniscience (influenced perhaps by the now-discredited idea of the awesome efficiency of Walsingham's "spy service") and to have ignored the unmistakable signs that Leicester and Walsingham continued searching for the author's identity for the next two years, as if that first attribution had never been made.

Thomas Lord Paget, however, was almost certainly involved in some measure. While in England he was sufficiently in touch with Court affairs and indeed was directly involved in some of the incidents charged against Leicester (such as the Drayton Basset affair);

moreover, even though he soon moved to Milan for his health, he remained a close friend of Arundell's on the continent, and they travelled together into Spain in the summer of 1586. He too was cited in Walsingham's letter to Leicester, and he appears in the Queen of Scots's letter to Glasgow. William Tresham, also mentioned by Walsingham, had been a Gentleman Pensioner and an ally of Sussex's until his flight in 1582; he remained close to Arundell (though he was soon spending much of his time with Westmoreland's English Regiment in the Netherlands), and even as the *Commonwealth* was being written, his brother Sir Thomas was suffering in prison for what his family considered Leicester's malice. In fact Sir Thomas's own views on the relative loyalties owed to Queen and Pope, as expressed in several writings, are similar in many respects to those of the *Commonwealth*'s authors.[106]

Thomas Fitzherbert, although never a courtier, had helped Robert Parsons with his clandestine writing in England, had then fled and taken up residence in Paris in 1582, and was a central member of the Paris circle thereafter, as well as a personal friend of Stafford's. Later a priest himself (1602) and finally a Jesuit (1613) until his death in 1640, he also became an estimable writer of controversial literature.[107] As we have seen, copies of the French translation were being stored in his Paris lodgings in 1585. Thomas Throgmorton fled into exile in 1582 and died in 1595. Brother of Francis, whose arrest had precipitated Arundell's flight, he was close to Arundell and Lord Paget, joined in their devotion to the Queen of Scots, shared Arundell's lodgings, and was mentioned by Stafford as having undertaken the translation of the libel into French;[108] an account of Leicester's alleged harassment of his father is included in the *Commonwealth*.

Sir Edward Stafford's own possible involvement must briefly be weighed as well. He, like Arundell, had been associated with the Burghley and Sussex party at Court, and there is no question that he distrusted both Leicester and Walsingham. He was related to Arundell and to the Howards both in his own right and through his wife, and he was in constant contact with Arundell from the spring of 1584 to late 1587. He is known to have suggested coyly a certain loyalty to the Queen of Scots's interests, as long as they did not conflict with his allegiance to Elizabeth during her life. Furthermore, his official reports concerning the *Commonwealth* and the *Discours de la vie* seem always to suggest a greater knowledge than he reveals in them. In late 1585 Lilly, Stafford's secretary, was detained and examined by Walsingham, who wrote to the ambassador chastising him for his insufficient efforts to stop the distribution of the book and advising him of what he considered to be Lilly's implication in the affair. Stafford's answer of 20 January 1586 survives, and in it he stammered out an explanation that he had not thought it fitting for a public official to deal in a private man's cause—he had had orders to the contrary—but protested that he had still burned what copies he could find (thirty-five of them) until he could no longer keep up with them. He attempted to dismiss his man's involvement; "And for Lilly, if he perchance saw or read a book, surely that were in reason no such criminal cause; but sure I had rather cause to think that my Lord of Leicester should be so incensed against him for the love the poor fellow bare to me than for any cause else."[109]

The fact that *Leicester's Commonwealth* is not above breaking a jest or two upon the Lady Sheffield herself and her children by Leicester, however, may suggest that she and Stafford were not in on the production from beginning to end; presumably their participation, if any, extended only as far as after-dinner conversation with Arundell.[110] Yet, as Stafford himself was told by his friends, he had "no cause to be offended" since she is not touched materially in any of the book's references to her. It is quite clear in these passages that Leicester is the villain of the piece and that she had been solidly contracted to him at the time of their liaison, that she was indeed, as the *Commonwealth* says, "the pitifullest abused that ever was poor lady." The ambassador did little enough to have the tract suppressed or to seek out its authors; and if we wish to think his protestations of ignorance about it a bit disingenuous, we shall only be sharing the suspicions of Walsingham and Leicester themselves.[111]

Finally, Lord Harry Howard must be considered. Clearly he was not present at the final composition and publication of the *Commonwealth*, nor is his classically ornate and "asiatic" prose at all reminiscent of the *Commonwealth*'s fluid style, but in at least one sense it seems more his book than anyone else's. As the defunct Catholic Court party's hopes and grievances, from its support of the Anjou marriage to its devotion to the Queen of Scots to its animus against Leicester, inform the book's attitudes and strategies, so Lord Henry, as much as anyone after his brother's execution, shaped that party's attitudes.[112] The *Commonwealth* seems very much a desperate *pis aller* of the conservative old nobility, whose members found themselves being replaced in power and influence by the left-Protestant "new men," and to this extent it is not so much a product of the Catholic laymen merely as a product of Lord Harry's own sensibility, as translated to the Paris circle by his friends Arundell and Lord Paget. And it may even be that some of the anecdotal material is his too, since the *Commonwealth* seems by no means cut of a single fabric. When, in 1584, it was being put into final form, parts of it (in the succession sections) were drawn largely from another book being produced in Rouen at the same time, John Leslie's *Treatise Touching the Right*;[113] some of its defamatory material is of very recent date, but a good deal of it (as in the account of Amy Robsart's death) is much older and must have come to its authors as received tradition. Some of this material may have been written, and it may originally have been written by Lord Henry. But if he personally had no hand in the actual writing, *Leicester's Commonwealth* is nonetheless an expression of the mind of the Howard Court party of which he had been the leader.

To summarize the much-vexed authorship problem, then, our reflections suggest that *Leicester's Commonwealth* was written chiefly by Charles Arundell, probably with the assistance of all or some of the group comprising Lord Paget, Thomas Fitzherbert, William Tresham, Thomas Throgmorton, and possibly still others; so far this conclusion confirms the assertion of Father Parsons and the opinions of the scholars Pollen and Hicks. Parsons probably, and Stafford possibly, to some degree facilitated the production, and both must have known about it. The two other serious candidates for authorship, Parsons himself (advanced by tradition and recently revived by Professor Holmes) and Thomas Morgan (first suggested by Walsingham and latterly accepted by Hotson and Conyers Read) seem quite unlikely to have been involved in the writing. The resulting tract is thus a layman's effort rather than a clerical one, and as we shall see, some notable differences in interpretation can the more clearly be observed once that fact has been recognized.

THEMES, STYLE, EFFECTS

Leicester's Commonwealth is not by any means exclusively a *chronique scandaleuse*. The book is widely known for the rhetorical flights of its railing upon Leicester, and to be sure these are memorable, but elsewhere within it one encounters exploration of serious political ideas, at least one of which, its argument for religious toleration, seems unique in English controversy of its time. Indeed, as noted above, this failure to resolve itself into either primarily a defamatory libel on the one hand or a defense of the Catholics and the Queen of Scots's title on the other is the *Commonwealth*'s chief flaw: While its occasionally hysterical tone may have embarrassed many sober students of the succession, its lengthy legal arguments probably bored the scandalmongers, and even modern scholars find difficulty in agreeing upon exactly what the book was meant to be. Perhaps it was meant to be several things, by several people, but in one's impressions after reading it the assault upon the Earl's reputation and position predominates. Whatever the purpose of the book's political discussions, in the general effect of the book they are secondary; but they are nonetheless worthy of notice.

The political themes entertained in *Leicester's Commonwealth* are basically three: the problem of the loyalty or disloyalty of religious minorities, the problem of religious toleration for those minorities, and the problem of the succession to the crown of England. All three of these were issues of acute seriousness; by the early 1580s, as is well known, the Papists in England were being subjected to systematic government harassment. The execution of Father Edmund Campion and his colleagues on 1 December 1581, convicted on dubious legal grounds, touched off a flurry of criticism of English policy and practice, and the government found itself vulnerable to the polemicists of the opposition and somewhat embarrassed even among its allies. Accordingly, Lord Burghley undertook to explain the government's position; in December 1583 his *Execution of Justice in England* appeared, and in January it was expanded and reissued, bound with Thomas Norton's attempted justification of the use of the rack. These were translated and placed in Courts all over the continent.[114]

The central argument of Cecil's tract was that the Pope had no authority to depose monarchs (as he had done Elizabeth) and that the incoming priests were political agents of the Papacy, sent into England to prepare the Queen's subjects to rise up in support of the invasion that was to enforce that deposition. The Papist's allegiance to his church was a limitation upon his loyalty to the monarch and state, and he could not be trusted, therefore, to remain loyal when the crisis came. There is some justification for Cecil's refusing to distinguish political from spiritual functions in the seminary priests; we know that even as Dr. Allen was publicly disavowing any such intention in his priests, he was himself involved in invasion schemes and was offering their services when the need arose.[115] Nevertheless, Allen made instant rebuttal to Cecil's book in his *True, Sincere, and Modest Defence of English Catholics*, a very well-written reply that is largely concerned only with refuting, point by point and martyr by martyr, Cecil's too-facile identification of priests with fifth columnists.

The authors of *Leicester's Commonwealth* also address themselves directly to Cecil's treatise, but rather than attempt to justify the activities of particular men, they concede that there have been some Catholics justly and accurately called traitors and go straight to the government's premise, that all Catholics are therefore potential traitors. In their "first and second degrees of treason" argument, drawn from the civil law, they affect to appreciate the government's point of view; they admit that there is a certain sense in which men of religions other than the state's will always be traitors to a certain extent, insofar as they (Papists and Puritans alike, and Protestants in Catholic countries) would prefer a ruler of their own faith. They then assert that this is not the same thing as a potential act of genuine treason since there are *other* reasons why a man with such a preference would by no means actually desire a change of rule—that is, reasons of state. As the most likely method of effecting such a change of rule would be by aiding a foreign army, they then adduce a number of examples of minorities expelling coreligionist invaders out of pure "nationalism" and antipathy toward foreigners.

Thus, the *Commonwealth* was able to go right to Cecil's fundamental assumption and show that most Catholics were not even likely to be disloyal in anything more than an irrelevant technical sense. Dr. Allen, a priest and later a cardinal, could not say that if the command to rise up were given from Rome, the Catholic subject would not be bound to do so; the *Commonwealth*, implicitly, says just that. And the *Commmonwealth*'s authors do not feel obliged, as Allen does, to mar their own case by proceeding to a defense of the Papal power of deposition.[116]

Pleas for toleration for the Catholic laymen are not uncommon in Elizabethan Catholic writings, but they are usually of one of two sorts. The clerical writers, when they did beg a lightened load for their coreligionists, nearly always went on to say that the same favor could not reasonably be expected for Protestants in Catholic countries since those people were heretics who had "gone forth" from the true church.[117] The clerical writers sometimes protested against persecution on grounds of inviolability of conscience, a promising idea for wider application, but customarily went on to say that on the other side of it "new religions beginning to bud up" must be "kept down and utterly extinguished by punishment" because of "the truth of [the Catholic] religion and the falsehood of the other, and that it is peculiar to their religion, by promise of Christ, to endure for ever, and triumph over all sects."[118] On the other hand, those Catholic laymen who addressed the question themselves, like the recusant gentlemen in their Toleration Petition of 1585, usually confined themselves more or less to crying out, "O poor worms! what shall become of us!"—seeking only "to present our manifold griefs and miseries to the merciful view of your Majesty."[119]

That is, seldom does one meet with a Catholic writing on the subject that proposes a general theory of toleration. The clerical writers could not follow through the implications of their pleas for toleration, and the laymen normally did not. The *Commonwealth*'s authors, however, affect to be sincere in advocating toleration for all parties. They cite the happy examples of mutual toleration in "Germany, Polonia, Boemland, and Hungary," a toleration that has brought these nations a peace "whereof all Europe besides hath admiration and envy," and suggest that the absence of such toleration will be the real cause of disaster, "for that the prosecution of these differences to extremity cannot but after many wounds and exulcerations being matters finally to rage, fury, and most deadly desperation." Dr. Allen could not admit of any good in the first twelve years of the reign, when religious differences were less cried out upon, because he saw in them only the relaxation of Papist zeal and the decay of his own cause, but from the *Commonwealth*'s point of view, this is the ideal, a nation with all its causes united in quietness and in mutual resistance against foreign oppression. The means to this ideal would be simple: "sweet qualification"—"a little bearing of th' one with th' other." Religion would have its proper place, of course, and provision is made for men of persuasions contrary to one's own, "a certain sweet diligence for their gaining, by good means," but the chief values here are civil peace, security, and prosperity.

Leicester's great crime, therefore, according to the *Commonwealth*'s authors, is that he, "being himself of no religion, feedeth notwithstanding upon our differences in religion, to the fatting of himself and ruin of the realm." Not only is religious dissension an evil in itself, it also permits the destructive opportunism that is manifested in a man like Leicester; he fosters division for his own purposes, and in the end all religions are destroyed. And since men such as he is may use dissension as a convenient blind for their own ambitions, the wise course for England would be to prevent them from riding one party into power by maintaining all factions "at such an equality as destruction may not be feared of the predominant." Thus, from the *Commonwealth*'s perspective, Queen Mary would be an especially desirable successor to Elizabeth because she had already, during her brief reign in Scotland, demonstrated her willingness to permit "all liberty of conscience and free exercise of religion to those of the contrary profession and opinion, without restraint."

Peace, security, and prosperity then, and not true religion, are the ends of the state. These values allow the *Commonwealth*'s authors to extend their proposed toleration to other sects as well: "which only qualification, tolerance, and moderation in our realm," they promise, "would content all divisions, factions, and parties among us for their continuance in peace, be they Papists, Puritans, Familians, or of whatsoever nice difference or section besides, and would be sufficient to retain all parties within a temperate obedience to the magistrate and government for conservation of their country." So often cited for its shrill passions, the *Commonwealth*, some of it at least, speaks with a dignity seldom found in the polarized rhetoric of sixteenth-century English controversy.

We see here something like the *politique* position as it was being developed in France some years earlier; the *Commonwealth* is almost certainly the first English controversial work to show clearly, if only in a general way, the influence of this thought.[120] The French Politiques were moderate Catholics who, amid the violence and fanaticism of the chronic French Religious Wars, were attempting to calm all waters by developing a position in which security of the state was to be everyone's first concern; religious controversy, seen as futile and inherently destructive, was to be resolved within the individual's breast and was not to be allowed to disturb the civil peace. While in Paris, Charles Arundell had many friends among the Politiques, like Jean Bodin, who were associated with the Duke of Anjou, and it may be that he and his friends imbibed these opinions at first hand. They seem just as likely, however, to have arisen from the author's own general attitudes and are not sufficiently specific or developed to permit any ascriptions of source. Whether the *Commonwealth*'s authors were themselves entirely sincere in these beliefs or were merely constructing a plausible argument from them is, of course, open to question, but the important thing is that such beliefs obtained a public hearing at all.

The third important political theme entertained by the *Commonwealth* concerns the succession to the English crown. Its formal arguments in behalf of the Queen of Scots and, to a lesser extent, her son may be as much its *raison d'être* as is its attack upon Leicester himself; even these libellous elements can be seen as an effort to divert some of the growing national anxiety of the 1580s from Mary's door by identifying a new focus for concern, by finding, as it were, a new scapegoat. Its case for Mary consists of two main approaches: an attempt to ensure her life by establishing a connection between her safety and Elizabeth's own welfare and a restatement of the Scottish claim to the throne.

Resentment toward Mary had been in evidence since she first entered England in 1568, but it grew with the years until by the 1580s it had become in some quarters (and especially among Leicester's friends) something of a religious vocation to seek her life. By 1584, certainly, the *Commonwealth*'s fears for her safety were amply justified, as her removal to stricter confinements in that year and the next and her eventual execution in February 1587 are sufficient to prove. Its strategy for defending her is this: After devoting considerable space to a declaration of the dangerous strength of Leicester's party and the heat of his overweening ambition to achieve a crown through his kinsman Huntingdon, the *Commonwealth* attempts to stir the English reader's fear for his sovereign's life by emphasizing her immediate danger at the hands of this her lord and subject. This is a central theme of the book, that the Earl has grown too great for England's good and that Elizabeth's life is the last shield protecting her people from the ultimate triumph of his rapacity. But at one point we find, very neatly worked into this line of attack, the recurring theme of the English Queen's danger enlarged to include the necessity for the safety of Mary right along with that of Elizabeth. The most desirable way to ensure Elizabeth's life, of course, would be to have Leicester brought to book; if that should prove impossible, the second best way would be to preserve the lives of her "next inheritors," Mary and her son James, the "special bulwarks to her Majesty's life and person." As long as these two are alive and sure, it would be no advantage to the Earl to have Elizabeth made away with, for by so doing he would come little closer to realizing his ally's title to the crown.

Most of the *Commonwealth*'s Marian energies, however, are expended upon the prior task of showing that the Scottish pretenders are indeed the "next inheritors," and this involves a fairly complicated legal argument. (The genealogical table supplied in Appendix F may prove helpful here.) During the 1560s the problem of the succession had been a hotly debated one, as Elizabeth herself had terrified all parties by remaining childless and by refusing to name a successor from one of the collateral branches of the royal family. A great many names were to come up, in and out of Parliament, in these early discussions of the soundest claim, but only a few drew sufficient support to come up very often. Mary Stuart, Queen first of France and then of Scotland, was one contender, though the suspicious murder of her husband in 1567 and her subsequent implication in a number of Catholic plots against Elizabeth effectively obviated widespread support. Lady Catherine Grey was another, the favorite of most Protestants, but because her marriage to Lord Hertford had excited Elizabeth's displeasure, her children by him were declared illegitimate; by January 1568 she herself had died, and her backers found difficulty in fixing upon a satisfactory replacement.

Lady Margaret Stuart, the Countess of Lennox, was occasionally mentioned, but she was of doubtfully legal birth, and in any event her claim offered little that was not already found in the Marian; her granddaughter Arabella, however, found some support in the 1590s and was kept under careful scrutiny by both Elizabeth and James I. Another Margaret, the wife of the Earl of Derby, made a fourth, but was never much of a contender since the Catholics found better candidates amongst the Stuarts and the Protestants were understandably chary of the the Stanley family's Catholic connections. Here too, however, the title came up later in the reign, and in the early 1590s her son Lord Strange was the object of some serious conjecture among the Papists abroad; he steadfastly, and wisely, refused to pursue his claim.

The fifth name that occurred with some frequency was that of Leicester's brother-in-law, Henry Hastings (1536–1595), the third Earl of Huntingdon. His title was legally very weak; as the *Commonwealth* points out, naming him successor would only have served to reopen the issues of the Wars of the Roses, since his claim was thoroughly Yorkist and antedated the union of the two houses in its origin. But Huntingdon was a Puritan, and amongst that party he found considerable support (probably chiefly through his kinship with Dudley) in or about the parliamentary year 1563; during the controversies attending the Parliament of 1566 he was very little mentioned.[121] Non-Catholic interests were forced to focus upon one candidate in order to countervail the growing strength of the Stuart claim at that time, and their candidate, as it turned out, was to be the more moderate Protestant Catherine Grey. Robert Dudley's opportunism had led him to interest in other claimants, to Mary Stuart, to Catherine Grey, and back again; and Huntingdon himself, after 1572, spent most of his time in the far north as Lord President of that district, appearing very seldom thereafter at the center of events.

It is accordingly extremely difficult to account for the importance ascribed to him in *Leicester's Commonwealth*, though it expresses a fear commonly found in Catholic circles.[122] He continued to be associated with Leicester, and the answer may lie in that relationship; perhaps he was, as a mainstay of the Puritan movement, just a natural target for Catholic hostility. Because of that connection, because of Mary Stuart's personal fear of him, and because of his relentless prosecution of the Catholics within his jurisdiction, he was very well hated by the Papist writers, but there is little evidence of any renewed attempts to push forward his royal pretensions.[123] The source of most of what evidence there is, however, is significant: Mendoza, in his dispatches of the early 1580s, was reporting such things as Leicester's plan to murder Queen Mary and reopen Huntingdon's claim, and we have already noticed that the Arundell-Howard party had become one of the Spaniard's chief sources of information during those years.[124] But whatever was troubling Queen Mary's friends does not seem to have found much expression elsewhere, and we are left unable fully to explain the vehemence of the *Commonwealth*'s professed fears about him.

After about 1570 and until the 1590s there simply were no clear choices, and consequently the controversies of Elizabeth's first decade simmered down considerably. An act of 1571 (*13 Elizabeth, cap. I, V*) against writing in behalf of any pretender except Elizabeth's own issue further added to the general quiet on the subject. It was only years later, as the Queen was clearly approaching her end, that intrigue and controversy once again resumed on a large scale, this time with different issues and candidates.[125] But it is essentially to the debates of the 1560s that the *Commonwealth* belongs. In restating Mary's claims, the book enters a battle that by 1584 was almost over. In the content of its discussion, it contributes nothing new to the legal debate itself, and its explanatory remarks, as the book's conversants remind us, are intended merely to outline the course of the controversy up to that time; with the only original work being done on the problem during the 1580s, the development of the Spanish claim by the Jesuit party, it has nothing to do. The organization of its discussion, the inclusion of a new if fragmentary case against Huntingdon, and its attempt to link its defense of Mary's title with its hue and cry upon Leicester in an effort to present Mary as the only remaining alternative to the Earl's brutality, these are all its own, but virtually all of its legal points are borrowed *quasi ad verbum* from earlier works, most notably from those of John Leslie, the Bishop of Ross, and seem to derive ultimately from the labors of Edmund Plowden.[126]

But whereas previous writers had been openly argumentative in their advocacy of their chosen candidates, the most striking feature of the *Commonwealth*'s discussion is its sometimes strained but generally consistent air of impartiality. As in the later *Conference about the Next Succession* (1595), which advanced the Spanish Infanta's claim through a very subtle process of elimination, the *Commonwealth* makes effective use of its feigned dialogue to preserve the illusion of a disinterested conversation among friends about the entire problem. As it poses the objections to each of the candidates and the answers that have been offered in defense of each, it is only gradually that we become aware of the preponderance of pro-Marian evidence. In pursuit of this objective atmosphere, the *Commonwealth* goes as far as expressly to avoid considering the principal points of attack against the rival pretenders. Most of these concern questions of legitimacy of birth, and as the *Commonwealth*'s lawyer says, these are best left to qualified legal hearings. In fact, the Marian case is unaffected by the strength of the objections against its rivals, and the authors could easily afford to neglect this line of argument in the interests of a greater plausibility. For Mary had without question the best title to the succession by birthright alone; if the other weaknesses of her claim were to be resolved in her favor, there would be no rival claims to be preferred, how flawless soever they were. And so, very cannily, the *Commonwealth* employs itself in defense rather than offense and avoids the appearance of an obvious bias. The chief objections to her title had traditionally been three—her foreign birth, Henry VIII's last will, and to a lesser extent her religion—and it is these objections that the book endeavors to meet.

How effective as propaganda its succession argument actually was would be impossible to measure. It was used by at least two important later writers, Sir John Harington and Thomas Wilson, both of whom quoted lengthy passages from these pages.[127] Probably, however, the Marian cause had too far degenerated by mid 1584 to admit of many conversions. During the 1580s many people were forsaking Mary herself in favor of a tentative commitment to her son James, and in several places the *Commonwealth* too makes more than a gesture in this direction by expending considerable effort in the repair of his image among Englishmen. Indeed, it almost seems that its authors were attempting simultaneously to connect James's safety and title to their arguments for his mother's and to separate him from her claim as well, to salvage his cause, as it were, if hers should already be lost. In any case, like its remarks concerning toleration, this aspect of the *Commonwealth* had no discernible political effect. Almost every contemporary reaction to its publication centered exclusively upon its defamation of the Earl of Leicester, and certainly its authors, by the extremist shrillness of their *ad hominem* attack, had done little to correct that impression. But whether or not the *Commonwealth* achieved its short-range Marian purposes, it may ultimately have contributed in some small way to a Jacobean one by helping to educate the public into thinking more sympathetically toward the Stuart title, as Harington's use of it may suggest. And, a different kind of success, structurally and stylistically its succession argument is of as high quality as any we are likely to encounter in sixteenth-century propaganda on the subject.

The same observation holds true of the entire book. Artistically (as far as one can use the term of propaganda) it constitutes something of a minor masterpiece. Its language is often vigorous and engaging, in places sharing with Thomas Nashe and Martin Marprelate a delightful quality of outrageous humor. The style is reasonably uniform, and the pace of the discussion is artfully managed so that those drier passages apparently considered necessary are interspersed with livelier writing and the occasional play of wit. If some of its aims and a few of its arguments may seem inconsistent (as Philip Sidney points out), the dialogue technique of presenting them is seldom more faithfully carried through; it is not too much to say that the participants here take on something of the personalities expected of characters from the stage. Despite the heterogeneity of its authors' interests and of the materials they seem to have used, there is no doubt that a single mind has, in tone and verisimilitude, unified them all, largely by this imaginative and credible use of the old, very common, and usually very stiff dialogue form.

The choice of participants in the dialogue is especially skillfully done: As Dr. Clancy points out, the use of two mild Protestants and a moderate Papist relieves the *Commonwealth* "of the task of defending the right-wing Papalist opinions on various disputed questions."[128] By attacking Leicester as Protestants and not as Catholics, and by attacking him primarily as he is a courtier and not as he is a Puritan, the authors seek to avoid dismissal of their book out of hand as a conventional religious polemic. And each of the participants performs a dramatic role as well. The lovable old lawyer brings to the conversation, especially in the succession section, the weight of his authority on legal matters, and in many instances he also, as the only Papist, must allow Protestants to convince him of Leicester's and the Puritans' treachery, rather than the other way about. The worshipful gentleman, in his wise and temperate elder statesman role, lends a note of political experience and inside information to the tract, as well as (because he is not a courtier himself) a kind of country stolidity, while the young scholar displays a pertinent naiveté that demands patient explanation from the others and thus keeps the discussion moving. Some of the latter's own contributions, however, such as his affected "scholar's argument," proved "by a principle of our philosophy," cannot be said to add very much to the force of the points being made.

The gentleman, as might be expected, dominates the conversation arithmetically as well as rhetorically, accounting for 43.4 percent of the book's 113 speeches and, because his remarks are normally longer, 53 percent of the number of lines. The lawyer, by contrast, has 34.5 percent of the speeches and 33.8 percent of the lines, whereas the young scholar, whose role is more often functional than substantial, speaks only 22 percent of the speeches and, with so many brief interjections, only 13 percent of the lines.

Besides the dialogue form, the *Commonwealth* employs other strategies aimed at conferring upon itself a greater plausibility. The epistolary framing device into which the dialogue is placed is no less common a tactic,[129] but here innumerable details are added for further verisimilitude: the cover letter itself, addressed to "G. M." in Gracious Street, London, professing reluctance that the book be printed for fear of Leicester's vengeance; the Christmas occasion of the conference, consistent with the December publication of Burghley's tract, which becomes the springboard for the entire discussion to follow; the promise of continuing reports, especially of the "relation of Gates" being kept safe by one whose name "beginneth with H" (suggesting Hatton?). Circumstantial details are provided throughout the work to testimonies and charges otherwise quite abstract: the Earl of Sussex relaxing by his pond ("where he beheld the taking of a pike or carp"), Leighton and Neville strolling upon the terrace at Windsor, a group of lords and ladies sitting about in leisurely discussion of the state of the commonwealth. Other common controversial devices are also employed both to broaden the focus of the *ad hominem* attack and to mitigate its potential offensiveness. Thus, by use of the venerable "evil counsellors" strategy, the authors fully vent their partisan animosity toward the man himself and, at the same time, make their representations against the policies of the Elizabethan regime without alienating the moderate English reader by direct abuse of his sovereign. By the frequent use of historical parallels (less a "strategy" than a sixteenth-century habit of mind), they intensify the effect of their charges by assimilating even the Earl's known activities into ominous patterns established by the great villains of the past, by rebels like Catiline, by regicides like

Brutus, by corrupt and undeserving favorites like Piers Gaveston and the Duke of Suffolk, and by ambitious seekers after crowns like the initiators of the terrifying Wars of the Roses. And they confirm their warnings about the Earl by linking him to wider phenomena that may have seemed sinister innovations to the average conservative reader, such as the unaccustomed Puritan "prophesyings," the influx of foreign artisans into the realm, the decline of discipline among university students, and (of course) the harassment of law-abiding recusants, perhaps the reader's own neighbors among them, all the while exploiting the traditional country suspicions concerning all courtiers and their activities.

In the libel itself the charges against the Earl are cleverly arranged. Detail after detail is gradually accumulated, but they are sufficiently broken up by intervening digression that the effect is never one of boredom. More importantly, what is on one page introduced somewhat tentatively has some pages later become an assumed fact; the impartial reader is tricked into accepting many details by finding them later used as premises for the next point to be made. Transitions between arguments are prepared for and smoothly executed. All of the worst Elizabethan scare words—the aspirer, the poisoner, the atheist, the Machiavellian, the tyrant who is a law unto himself—all of these are employed and associated with the Earl. Perhaps the most noteworthy of the *Commonwealth*'s techniques, however, is its artful blending of truth and fiction. As the reader will discover from the annotations, very little of what the book says about Leicester and his Puritan supporters is without some foundation in fact, or at least in common rumor, which can now be verified: When he is charged with having caused an obscure riot in Staffordshire, we find that he was indeed involved (and perhaps culpably). When he is charged with having initiated Norfolk's fall, with depredations in North Wales, with having fortified his home, with having harassed Sir Jerome Bowes from Court, we find that there is evidently some truth to all of these; when he is charged with having murdered his first wife and the Earl of Essex, among others, we find that he was believed, at least in many quarters, to have done so. But at the same time, very little does not contain some embroidery upon what we know, and very likely the same is true of what was commonly known in its own day. Probably there is no accusation in the book that was not spun out of facts familiar and recognizable to almost every informed reader. The authors seem to have gone out of their way to have used only those charges against the Earl that were already being widely circulated at least in anti-Dudley circles and probably elsewhere as well as rumors grounded in real events.

It has already been suggested how damaging the *Commonwealth*'s attack upon him has been to Leicester's subsequent reputation, through Camden and Naunton to Strype, Dugdale, Ashmole, Jebb, David Hume, Sir Walter Scott, and the others into our own time. We should also ask whether this attempt to provoke sensational scandal about one of the Queen's foremost ministers may have done harm to the "legitimacy" of the whole regime. In understanding what may have been at stake, we cannot do better than remind ourselves of Darnton's remarks about the similar sorts of libels circulated against the grand persons of the *ancien régime*.

> It is easy to underestimate the importance of personal slander in eighteenth-century French politics, because it is difficult to appreciate that politics took place at court, where personalities counted more than policies. Defamation was a standard weapon of court cabales. And then as now, names made news. . . . The "general public" lived on rumors; and the "general reader" saw politics as a kind of nonparticipant sport, involving villains and heroes but no issues. . . . This was more dangerous propaganda than [Rousseau's] *Contrat social*. It severed the sense of decency that bound the public to its rulers.

Darnton speculates that there may have been an effect of "*désacralisation*, occurring at levels well below the elite," which contributed to the collapse of the existing order in 1789.[130]

These considerations are important ones, and evidently the Elizabethan government, like the Bourbon one, had them uneasily in mind as they acted to suppress such publications and deny their allegations. But Elizabeth's Court was little like Louis's, neither were her people much like his (nor, probably, could as many of them read), and it is difficult to believe that such books as the *Commonwealth*, even if they had appeared far more frequently than they did, could have had a significant depressant effect on the popular support for the Queen's rule, especially since even a Papal bull of excommunication seems not much to have diminished her support, even among Catholics, a decade earlier.[131] Disappointed parties railed against this or that minister, sometimes against the Queen herself, but there were far more important matters in the air than the private morals of a ranking favorite. The claim that if unchecked Leicester should soon be ruler himself seems, frankly, too extraordinary to have been credited by any but the most malevolent. Many readers may have been induced to believe that the Queen harbored near her a very bad man, but that after all was historically more or less to be expected in any Court; it could scarcely, by itself, have depreciated seriously the general loyalty to Gloriana herself. (By contrast, popular distaste for Henri III's minions, cried up by both Huguenot and radical Catholic oppositions, assumed importance only as a reflection of far more substantial divisions within the French state.) It remains doubtful, therefore, that the *Commonwealth* had very much political effect at all. The character of the manuscript extracts made from it in its own time serves further to support that conclusion; the book was evidently enormously popular, but its readers seem generally to have read it for fun.

THE BLACK LEGEND OF LEICESTER

The first question that arises when reading such defamations as *Leicester's Commonwealth*, "News from Heaven and Hell," and the "Letter of Estate" is a simple one: Was Leicester the man the writers portray him to have been? The answer too is simple: He was not. Neither the Queen nor his colleagues would have tolerated his presence if he had been. These are, after all, defamations, unsubtle in their intentions and often hyperbolic in tone. The next questions, however, are more complicated: What sort of man was he in fact? And what was it about the man, about the Court, that gave rise to such attacks? What made them evidently seem so attractive to contemporaries and posterity?

The broad lines of Leicester's life are clear: his devotion to his father and later to the Queen, his rise as essentially a favorite; his left-Protestant domestic religious policies in the early part of the reign, and the shift of his attention in the 1570s to the international Protestant cause, with himself cast in some considerable role as champion of a Reformed alliance on the continent. He was almost indefatigable in his work, and with Burghley, and later Walsingham and Hatton, he remained for thirty years in the innermost policy making circle around the Queen. We've discovered at least something of his activities in the country, his patronage of suitors of all sorts and his efforts toward increasing his own holdings. Rather a good deal is known about his eventual expedition in the Netherlands campaign, as well as about the elements of his character that contributed to its failure.[132] But the man remains elusive. The only really clear images we have are extremes. One is the long-held view of the avaricious, faithless, cunning, and sometimes murderous *luxorioso* emerging from the contemporary libels, given respectability by Camden, and cast into received tradition by the antiquarians of the seventeenth and eighteenth centuries. The other has arrived very recently, in Derek Wilson's self-declared attempt to rehabilitate the Earl's reputation, in a well-written and thoughtful biography that nevertheless has on many disputed questions the false ring of special pleading.[133]

It is impossible yet to characterize the Earl confidently, but a measured picture is emerging gradually in the work of modern historians. The day will soon come when a detailed and coherent assessment can be ventured, but one can suggest that it will be made, indeed is already being made, along the following lines. The sensational murders and "hired cutters" will be cast aside. The gross image of promiscuity and filthy luxury will be somewhat refined into a view of a courtier who did indeed have a few more flings than statesmen like Burghley or Puritan clients like Thomas Wood could approve of, who spent far more on fashion and comfort than he could afford, but who was never monstrous in his inclinations. The personal ambition for power will in general come to be seen as a strong but not uncommon taste for consequence and for preservation of self and family, and to some extent as a not-unworthy attempt to affect the success of policies he believed in, made to appear somewhat more sinister by a political system in which influence with the Queen counted for much. The rapacious avarice common to all early images of Leicester will be resolved into a complex picture that contains more than a few instances of abuse of influence and law but shares much with the practices more or less accepted amongst other magnates, as well as with general pressures already existing in the social and economic situation.

The shameless flattery of the Queen will be seen less as sycophancy than as a necessary, if highly artificial, part of his special relationship with her, one that seemed more natural in the Court language of the time and which provided the Earl with his only hold upon the station to which he had risen. The time serving, the faithless opportunism and fundamental irresponsibility that make the ground rhythm of all early libels and most modern treatments will probably come to be seen, beneath the shifting sands of specific situations and the tentative soundings-out of alternatives, to be unjust; recent studies are revealing more consistency, throughout the reign, in Leicester's underlying beliefs and policies. The hardest work will come in trying finally to draw patterns from the methods used in the Earl's land dealings and in his interventions in behalf of his clients at Court and in the country. Here, I suspect, we shall find much cause for complaint; the Earl seems to have been possessed to an extraordinary degree of arrogance, intolerance, and on occasion vindictiveness in matters touching upon his personal honor or prerogatives. But the common charge that he kept a stranglehold on the granting of all suits at Court now seems not to be particularly true; even though he would, like all courtiers, have involved himself in as much clientage as he could, for the influence and for the fees, the complaints of a monopoly upon favor seem to be only the perceptions of disappointed suitors. An assessment of these allegations will require a thorough understanding of how patronage worked or could work in Elizabethan England, and I believe this will not be long in coming.

Almost a more interesting question to muse upon, if finally a less important one, is what it was about the Earl that gave rise to the black legend in the first place. Other counsellors were slandered but with nothing like the same enthusiasm, imagination, and perseverance. Anti-Dudley propaganda, emerging out of the previous reigns, flowering early in Elizabeth's, and accumulating throughout Leicester's life and beyond it, makes up a whole body of "secret lore" with internal traditions of its own, with sometimes an almost eerie sense of an underground religion shared among initiates. And whereas other politicians were sometimes slandered not only in their policies but also in their personal lives, nowhere else in the reign did there grow up such a cult of the villain, reminiscent of the "Tudor myth" of Richard III. The doctrine that "where there is smoke there is also fire" has probably accounted for much of the influence the black legend has enjoyed over four centuries, and there is something in the idea after all, but it is too simple to explain such a remarkable phenomenon.

I would suggest, somewhat tentatively, that we can point to three reasons that go far to explain the growth and endurance of the anti-Leicestrian lore. The first has to to with the origins of Leicester's influence in English life. All other politicians of the reign (except Hatton) rose to prominence for some political virtue: bureaucratic experience, diplomatic skill, territorial influence, position in the church, and so on, usually after having served apprenticeships in which their skills were developed and observed.[134] The Queen is well known to have been an astute judge of talent and usefulness, and seldom has there been such a congregation of talented individuals as in the Elizabethan government. Dudley's father had been similarly talented, and he too had risen by his service. Robert, however, owed his ascent into prominence to one cause, the Queen's favor. Indeed, it seems reasonably sure that in the early years Elizabeth was, quite simply, in love with him, and as time passed that love evolved into a special relationship that, if it cannot be defined, cannot be missed. It passed through many trials and suffered brief eclipses, but it endured from the first day of her reign to "his last letter" kept at her bedside until her death. Once having gained prominence, Dudley proved himself by no means untalented or unintelligent, but his talents and intelligence were not such as would have recommended him to that elevation in themselves.[135] He was demonstrably the Queen's creation, above his intrinsic merits. His opponents on policy, his rivals for authority, recognized that fact and were jealous. He was in his own way splendid, and the more splendid he made himself, the more offensive he must have seemed, to many men, for that very cause. The base of his power was more personal than institutional, and so the reaction against him took a more personal tone as well.

In practical terms, those men who resented his authority or opposed his policies, understanding that his power depended upon attractive personal qualities, sought to make him unattractive. A favorite who is no longer favored has become virtually nothing. Personal bonds tied him to the Queen and to his own followers, and if these could be loosened, it seemed, he should fall. If the Queen could be got to divert her affection from him, or (if persevering in her affection) could be got to see him as a liability to maintaining the people's love for herself, she must cast him aside. It must have seemed that the key to opposing one so dependent upon favor, so vulnerable to the effects of a blackened reputation, was to blacken that reputation.[136] Scandalous gossip seems indeed all that prevented Dudley from obtaining the Queen in marriage in 1560–1561. Attacks upon him were more comprehensive, *ad hominem*, and scurrilous because curtailing his authority was less a matter of argument or voting than of altering the Queen's affection for him; or failing that, of provoking a popular moral outrage against him that the Queen could not ignore.

The second reason is a bit more speculative, assuming a common source for many libels that can be demonstrated for only some of them. The suggestion is that some of the sense of consistent "lore" and tradition running through the attacks derives from the Earl's having chosen the clan of Howard to offend. We have seen that the *Commonwealth* and its French addition emanated from the remnants of the Howard Court circle, joined with other Catholic interests on the continent. The "Letter of Estate," with its martyrological account of Norfolk's execution, probably came from someone else within the Howard clan in the country,[137] as had many of the spoken slanders being investigated in East Anglia just before and long after the Duke's death in 1572. "News from Heaven and Hell" shows no particular signs of provenance among the Howards, nor does the

Flores Calvinistici, though both have been constructed so as to take part in a tradition already well begun by the others named. Many of the shorter poems and passing shots at the Earl seem at least plausibly to have come out of Howard grievances, and the Holles family complaints, reported in the next century, have Howard connections as well. The attacks individually could have come from any disgruntled libellers, but the sense of consistency, of a somewhat inbred tradition, of something like an anti-Leicestrian cult, may well derive from a common if far-flung source, the clan of Howard and its extensions throughout the old nobility, seeking reasons and laying blame for their own eclipse. The fact that for many years the Howards at Court sheltered under the wings of Cecil and Sussex, who found themselves ranged against Leicester on many issues (in the latter's case with true enmity), may have helped to commend the black legend to William Camden, who worked chiefly out of Cecilian viewpoints; and Camden's adoption of many aspects of the legend in his history virtually assured its longevity.[138]

The third reason for the remarkable growth of this organized animosity toward Leicester may be in the particular nature of some of the better substantiated charges. The murders, the grand plots, the seeking after crowns certainly embellished the legend but need not normally be taken too seriously. The crimes, if that is what they were, which now seem most plausible are not those at the institutional or national levels; they are consequences of the Earl's rough dealings on the personal level. One man is done out of his manor, another is removed from office, another is insulted in the corridors or driven from Court for complaining of Leicester's arrogance or presumption or unmerited favor. The excesses of which Leicester seems most likely to have been guilty seem to be of the sort that would breed, not opposition, but the lust for personal revenge. His political opponents fought against his policies or influence; those individuals who felt they had suffered personally at his hands sought to attack him personally—and with a perverse enthusiasm that argues stronger emotions than those to which most political debates will normally give rise. Evidently Leicester, more than the other Elizabethan leaders, offended more people more deeply in personal ways, and they, like the cast-off Douglass Howard for example, hated him more deeply in return, long after his death had removed his influence from the Court.

But for whatever reasons, the black legend is still very much in evidence, even in this century, and must very carefully be sorted out in the process of reconstructing the Earl's career. Not only must the individual charges be assessed for the light they may or may not shed on what the Earl had actually been up to but the fact that Leicester attracted about him such a consistent body of calumny, some of it absurd, some of it quite plausible, must also be taken into the picture. In any case, it is fair to say that *Leicester's Commonwealth* and its progeny, while they can seldom be relied upon for the facts of the case, can nearly always be taken as reliable guides to the gossip of the period. The evidence indicates that more often they have captured in writing what was already being spoken than they have created the rumors and introduced them into circulation. If that is so, these tracts tell us much about the gossip that was no less a part of Leicester's career than was his Council attendance, his support of poets and actors and preachers, or his periodic tiffs with the Queen.

EDITORIAL POLICIES

The present edition is a collation of nine copies of the 1584 text; Appendix A lists these nine and cites the only three variants found. In order to assist smooth reading and emphasize the book's content rather than its typographical idiosyncracies, I have elected to regularize the spelling in both the text and the other quoted documents, with abbreviations silently expanded. There is an important value to old-spelling texts, but I believe that in this instance a "modernized" version is to be preferred. I should say, however, that where I have deemed different "forms" of a word to have been employed (as in "disgiest" for "digest," "afeard" for "afraid"), rather than merely a variant orthography, I have retained the form found, though again in regularized spelling and with a gloss if required. Similarly, personal names have been regularized in spelling, but where different "forms" appear, they have been retained and followed by their modern equivalents in square brackets or a note (thus Candish becomes Cavendish, and so on). Regnal numbers have been brought to conformity with modern practice (Charles the fifth to Charles V). The marginal speech headings in the original have been inserted into the text, in dialogue fashion, and supplied in brackets where missing. The annotations seek to gloss any words that might give pause, to identify allusions and persons mentioned, and more importantly, to note as much factual material as has so far been unearthed respecting the allegations made. I have tried neither to prove nor to disprove the charges themselves, only first to show that they were plausible enough or were also rumored elsewhere, and second to supply the references to aid further searching; I have also taken pains to indicate several places where the charges show connections with Howard interests, in order further to support my contention that the book emanated from that group of men.

Three other features of the text annotations require mention. The extensive marginalia in the 1584 edition, excepting those that are merely redundant, I have placed in quotation marks in the notes, preceded by the word *Margin.* Second, I have also pointed out a few significant interpolations found in some of the many manuscript copies made directly or indirectly from the 1584 edition. Third, I have referred frequently to the "Marsh annotator"; a hostile reader of the 1584 printed edition now in Archbishop Marsh's Library, Dublin—by his handwriting and other signs a contemporary reader—penned many of his reactions in the margins of his book, and where these seem interesting, I have included them.

NOTES TO INTRODUCTION

1. Lodge, *Illustrations of British History*, 1: 514; Thomas Scot's report to Leicester, S.P. 12/148/34. In 1587 a man of twenty-seven was arrested in Spain; he called himself Arthur Dudley and told a story of having been born to the Queen at Hampton Court, then hidden and brought up in the country (B.C. to _____, Madrid, 28 May 1588 [British Library, Harleian MS. 295, fol. 190^v], and Chamberlin, *Private Character of Queen Elizabeth*, pp. 309–18).

2. Ratclif's examinations, S.P. 12/113/28–30; Edward Cheke to William Davison, Court, 8 Aug. 1577, S.P. 15/25/30; Welsh libels, Hatfield, Cecil Papers 203/81; Holles, *Memorials of the Holles Family*, pp. 70–71; for charges of slander amongst Howard servants, see William Parker to Burghley, 12 July 1580, S.P. 12/140/14.

3. S.P. 15/27/27. The English attack mentioned is John Stubbs's *Discovery of a Gaping Gulf* (1579); the book Parry reports may be the libel seen by Thomas Norton, reported by him on 30 Dec. 1580 to have been written by a group of English Papists (*Hatton Memoirs*, pp. 161–62).

4. In the English translation, *An Epistle of the Persecution of Catholics in England*, the direct references to these men have been removed.

5. Allen, *Admonition*, p. xviii–xix. This attack upon Leicester, however, is included merely as part of a larger attack upon the Queen, who is accused of having raised so profligate a man to favor.

6. The best discussion of the anti-Cecilian tradition is in Clancy's *Papist Pamphleteers*, pp. 14–43 *et passim*, and his "Political Pamphlet."

7. See Southwell, *Humble Supplication to Her Majestie*, pp. 17–23.

8. James repeated the charge in *Jesuits Downfall*, p. 55.

9. Wood, *Athenae Oxonienses*, vol. 2, col. 75. Another tradition credits Sir Walter Raleigh with the authorship! (British Library, Hargrave MS. 311, fol. 2.)

10. Hicks, "Growth of a Myth." J. H. Pollen, in 1919, seems to have been the first to have discarded the attribution to Parsons and to have pointed to Charles Arundell as principally responsible, as "editor" (C.R.S. 21, p. 58).

11. S.T.C. 19399. In Allison and Rogers's *Catalogue of Catholic Books* it is no. 261. The circumstances of the *Commonwealth*'s appearance and government responses to it are studied in the wider context of Catholic printing in Peck, "Government Suppression of Elizabethan Catholic Books."

12. Hugh Davies's charges against Robert Atkins, 6 Sept. 1586, art. 5: "The said Atkins, if Davies would have been resolute, would have showed him a book called the Earl of Leicester his Common Wealth, wherein (he saith) the said Earl is painted out in his colors, and how he hath the disposing of all the bishoprics in England" (S.P. 12/193/18). Watson, letter of Apr. 1599, in Law, *Archpriest Controversy*, 1: 213, and in his *Decacordon of Ten Quodlibetical Questions*, p. 11.

13. Clifford, *Diary*, p. 111.

14. H.M.C. Rutland MSS., 1: 165.

15. Murdin, *State Papers*, p. 418 (see Appendix E). On 1 Apr. 1584 Richard Hakluyt sent word from Paris that a "confutation" of Burghley's book "shall shortly come forth" (S.P. 12/170/1); this is probably Allen's *Defence*.

16. Parsons to Fr. Agazzari, Paris, 10/20 Aug. 1584 (C.R.S. 39, p. 227).

17. Father William Weston's account (C.R.S. 4, pp. 157–59) makes it clear that Emerson was seized at an inn in London. Southern is mistaken, in *Elizabethan Recusant Prose*, p. 35n, in thinking that he might have been the man arrested at Scarborough in early 1585 for possession of copies of the *Commonwealth* (S.P. 12/181/78).

18. Prison lists, C.R.S. 2, p. 149. Emerson was released after Elizabeth's death and died at St. Omer's College in 1604.

19. British Library, Cotton MSS., Titus B. VII, fols. 10–10^v (see Appendix E). Leslie Hotson concluded from this letter that Morgan must have been the book's author; see his essay, and his debate with Hicks over the letter's value for this purpose, in *The Listener*, 43 (1950): 481–83, 567, 659, 745. Hicks had already cited the letter in C.R.S. 39, p. lxviii.

20. Hicks, "Growth of a Myth," p. 95 and note.

21. S.P. 78/12/105 (see Appendix E).
22. C.R.S. 2, p. 35.
23. The S.T.C.'s conjectural "Antwerp" is mistaken since Antwerp was in Protestant hands throughout this time and was in fact soon to be under a year's Catholic siege (Aug. 1584–Aug. 1585).
24. D'Ewes, *Journals of All the Parliaments*, p. 317.
25. D'Ewes, *Journals*, pp. 368, 369; see Neale, *Elizabeth I and Her Parliaments, 1584-1601*, pp. 94–95.
26. Shelley, C.R.S. 21, p. 76; Harington, *Tract on the Succession*, p. 44.
27. Contemporary copy, British Library, Additional MS. 31897, fol. 9. "A Letter of State of a Scholar of Cambridge" is the *Commonwealth*'s running title at the page heads.
28. Included here as Appendix C. In July 1585 the Italian Alberico Gentili defended Leicester in very similar ways in his *De legationibus libri tres*, pp. iv–v.
29. Burghley's rebuttal, *C.S.P. Scots, 1574-81*, pp. 564–61; Parker to Burghley, 11 Sept. 1573, Murdin, *State Papers*, p. 259.
30. C.R.S. 21, p. 112.
31. *C.S.P. Spanish, 1580-86*, p. 538.
32. C.R.S. 21, pp. 72–73.
33. Rogers/Berden to Walsingham, Rouen, 11 Aug. 1585, S.P. 15/29/39.
34. Scory, S.P. 12/176/53, art. 1; Errington, S.P. 12/181/78; Davies, S.P. 12/193/18, art. 5; Wigges, Folger MS. K.b.l., arts. 1, 12, 13; Lilly, S.P. 78/15/15; Poley, S.P. 78/17/26—the date is fixed by Hicks, *Elizabethan Problem*, p. 247.
35. S.P. 78/13/86.
36. S.P. 78/13/87.
37. S.P. 78/13/99.
38. It will be observed that the *Commonwealth* itself, in a marginalium, speaks confidently of an enlarged second edition to follow.
39. S.P. 53/15/552.
40. British Library 1345.a.25 and 1017.a.22. The title page is dated 1585 but also refers to Leicester as "Hollandiae ac Zelandiae pro Elizabetha Angliae Regina Gubernatoris"; as he did not become governor until early Feb. 1585/86, the book probably appeared between that time and the twenty-fifth of March, from which date the year would have been noted as 1586. It seems to have been printed in Holland by John Baptist Zangarum.
41. The *Commonwealth* material has been rearranged, but otherwise Briegerus has rendered it faithfully. He makes only a few additions, the most important of which are the statement that Amy Robsart was "destroyed by a small nail thrust gradually into her head" (p. 14, a gothic detail that persisted into the nineteenth century), the poisoning of Sussex, updated references to the death of Leicester's son and the "slaughter" of Northumberland in the Tower, June 1585 (p. 28), and a page of commentary on the Earl's arrival in the Low Countries.
42. British Library, Sloane MS. 1926, fols. 35-43^v (ca. 1590), printed in Peck, " 'News from Heaven and Hell' "; S.P. 15/28/113, fols. 369-88^v (1585?), printed in Peck, " 'The Letter of Estate' "; Rogers's poem (ca. 1605), printed in F. Williams's edition, Rogers, *Leicester's Ghost*.

43. For examples of poetical progeny, see "Epitaphium" (British Library, Stowe MS. 156, fol. 204^v) and "Notable talk herein taught"(Folger Library MS. G.b.11), both included in Appendix E.

44. "The Dead Man's Right" has been reprinted by D. Wilson, *Sweet Robin*, pp. 339–41. The reply to the *Commonwealth* known as "Father Parsons' Green Coat Well Dusted" (1588) is now considered never to have existed; it was supposedly mentioned in "the first English newspaper," the *English Mercurie* of 1588, which was a hoax perpetrated sometime around 1750. See Hicks, "Growth of a Myth," p. 102n; Tenison, *Elizabethan England*, 5 (1936): 147n; Hazen, "Literary Forgeries and the Library," p. 9.

45. Peter Holmes has performed a service in reminding us that Robert Parsons must have had more knowledge of the book than he ever admitted, and more than Fr. Hicks would admit for him. He goes too far, however, in attempting to reinstate Parsons as principal author and seems to underestimate the differences between the *Commonwealth* and the Jesuit's own opinions or sources of information during this period. See Holmes, "Authorship of 'Leicester's Commonwealth.' "

46. Privy Council and Lord Privy Seal, 1603; created Earl of Northampton, 1604; died, at the age of seventy-four, 14 June 1614.

47. Jordan, *Edward VI: the Threshold of Power*, p. 111. It will be noticed how often the *Commonwealth* returns to these generation-old grievances against Leicester's father.

48. The genealogical table of major Howard connections in Appendix F may be useful here. I am using "party" throughout in a very loose sense, not as an organized political association, but rather as a group of like-minded men who consistently understood their interests on important issues to be similar and the intentions of other groups to be different and possibly opposed.

49. See N. Williams, *Thomas Howard*, chaps. 8–10; on the later Ridolfi Plot see F. Edwards, *This Marvellous Chance*.

50. Gilbert Talbot to Shrewsbury, 11 May 1573, mentioning that Sussex was backing Oxford in his rise (Lodge, *Illustrations of British History*, 2: 16).

51. H.M.C. Salisbury MSS., 1: 146 (misdated 1557).

52. *Calendar of Patent Rolls, 1569–72*, p. 428, no. 2981; *ibid., 1572–75*, p. 227, no. 1210. The latter office he still held in Oct. 1580 (*A.P.C., 1580–81*, pp. 221–22).

53. Read, *Lord Burghley and Queen Elizabeth*, pp. 130–32; *C.S.P. Domestic, Addenda, 1566–79*, p. 469.

54. Howard to Walsingham, 28 May 1575, S.P. 12/103/53.

55. Bossy, "English Catholics and the French Marriage," p. 2; this article is an excellent brief survey of the Howard circle in the late 1570s. Other members of this courtier group seem to have included the Lords Windsor and Compton, the Lords Charles and Thomas Howard, George Gifford, Francis Southwell, Henry Noel, Arthur Gorges, William Tresham, William Cornwallis, and the young Walter Raleigh, as well as others less often at Court, such as the Earls of Northumberland and Southampton, Thomas Lord Paget, and Philip Howard, Norfolk's son and heir. See Peck, "Raleigh, Sidney, Oxford, and the Catholics, 1579," pp. 429–30.

56. Arundell confessed having introduced Oxford to Richard Stephens, a seminary priest (Arundell's Declaration, late Dec. 1580, S.P. 15/27A/46). Oxford

swore the man was a Jesuit and that Arundell had snuck him behind hangings in the Queen's bedchamber to watch the Queen dance.

57. Conyers Read's opinion, in *Burghley*, pp. 200–1, based on Leicester's letter to Walsingham: "You carried a companion over with you who hath played the right Jack since he returned—Charles Arundel. When I first heard of his going I told some of my friends to what end he would go." (Arundell's name is sometimes spelled as above, though he himself preferred the form I have followed.)

58. These tortuous negotiations over the next few years can be followed in detail in Read, *Mr. Secretary Walsingham*, 2: 1–117, and his *Burghley*, pp. 203–71. See also MacCaffrey, "Anjou Match," and his *Queen Elizabeth and the Making of Policy*, chaps. 11 and 12.

59. See Sussex's letter on the subject to the Queen, 28 Aug. 1578, in *Hatton Memoirs*, pp. 81–89, esp. 83–84; Read, *Burghley*, chap. 12.

60. Mendoza reported on 25 Dec. 1581 that Howard was "desirous of bringing about the marriage, as he believed, like many others, that it would result in their being allowed freedom for their faith" (*C.S.P. Spanish, 1580–86*, pp. 245–46); see also Mauvissière to Henri III, 29 Oct. 1579 (S.P. 31/3/27). Compare the sentiments expressed by the *Commonwealth*'s lawyer, below.

61. Stafford's treatise, Mar. 1579, H.M.C. Salisbury MSS., 2: 239–45; Lord Henry's, British Library, Cotton MSS., Titus C. 18, fols. 1–21 (printed in Stubbs, *John Stubbs's Gaping Gulf*, pp. 155–94).

62. Osborn, *Young Philip Sidney*, p. 503; Peck, "Raleigh, Sidney, Oxford, and the Catholics, 1579," pp. 427–28; Howell, *Sir Philip Sidney*, p. 68. The text of Sidney's argument appears in *Miscellaneous Prose of Sir Philip Sidney*.

63. H.M.C. Salisbury MSS., 2: 224.

64. Read, *Burghley*, p. 214; H.M.C. Salisbury MSS., 2: 277–78; Camden, *Elizabeth*, 2: 95. The *Commonwealth* gloats over Leicester's discomfiture at this time but probably exaggerates his will toward violent revenge. The idea that the Queen could have been kept ignorant of his marriage for almost a year's time certainly strains belief but accords with what facts are known; Derek Wilson has argued, however, suggestively if not convincingly, that in fact she learned of it in Apr. 1578 (*Sweet Robin*, pp. 228–30).

65. Bossy, "English Catholics and the French Marriage," p. 7.

66. Collinson, *Elizabethan Puritan Movement*, p. 200.

67. S.P. 15/27A/46.

68. C.R.S. 21, p. 29–30.

69. Arundell's letter to a lady, 1581: The "cause of my stay was a supplication presented to the Queen by Leicester from Oxford" (S.P. 12/151/51).

70. Mendoza's account, 25 Dec. 1581 (*C.S.P. Spanish, 1580–86*, pp. 245–46, and C.R.S. 21, pp. 30–31).

71. Mauvissière to Henri III, 11 Jan. 1581, C.R.S. 21, p. 29–30. Hatton was set over Howard, Walsingham over Southwell, who had surrendered previously; Arundell was confined at Sutton in Surrey, with whom is not known, but probably under Hatton as well. Other Catholic courtiers, while not directly implicated, suffered similar eclipse; Lord Paget, for example, was being pressed at just this time for his failure to attend Protestant services (Paget to Walsingham, 10 Jan. 1581, S.P. 12/147/5).

72. *C.S.P. Spanish, 1580–86*, p. 78.
73. Oxford, "Interrogatories to be demanded of Arundell and Howard," S.P. 12/151/42, art. 1; Arundell denied this charge, S.P. 12/151/43.
74. S.P. 12/151/45, fourth charge.
75. S.P. 12/151/50. Most of these papers, undated but 1581, can be found in S.P. 12/83/41, 12/151/42–57, 15/27A/46.
76. Arundell's supplications, apparently to Walsingham, 1581, S.P. 12/151/51–53; Howard's to Walsingham, 12 Jan. 1581, S.P. 12/147/6, and in later troubles, of 14 Sept. 1582, S.P. 12/155/44, and of 25 Feb. 1583, S.P. 12/158/77. Howard to Hatton, *ca.* July 1581, *Hatton Memoirs*, pp. 376–77 (misdated). Arundell and Lord Paget were said, two years later to "commend[Walsingham] for as real a gentleman as liveth" (Parry to Walsingham, Paris, 8 Dec. 1583, S.P. 15/28/47), and Arundell once wrote that he considered Hatton to be "a man of very good conscience and my honorable friend" (S.P. 12/151/51).
77. Arundell to Hatton, six letters, two from Sutton, 23 May and 20 July 1581, a third *ca.* Aug., *Hatton Memoirs*, pp. 169, 180–81, 216–19.
78. Sussex to Arundell, S.P. 12/150/43; Howard to Leicester, S.P. 12/150/51. See also Howard to Walsingham, 1 Dec. 1581, complaining that Leicester was still trying to "shake and undermine my liberty" (S.P. 12/150/81). On 17 Oct. several of Arundell's servants were summoned before the Privy Council, perhaps for examination in this matter (*A.P.C., 1581–82*, pp. 236, 239).
79. E. Edwards, *Life and Letters of Sir Walter Ralegh*, 2: 21.
80. Read, *Walsingham*, 2: 381–82.
81. S.P. 15/28/2.
82. S.P. 15/27A/57. Tresham later warned Hatton to beware of Leicester in time, for "he affecteth you only to serve his own turn" (*Hatton Memoirs*, pp. 351–53).
83. Paget to Northumberland ?, 4 Mar. 1583 (S.P. 12/159/8): "Your friend in Essex is very desirous that the Queen should have light given her of the practice between Leicester and the Countess [of Shrewsbury] for Arbella" to marry Leicester's son, "for it comes on very lustily, insomuch as the said Earl hath sent down the picture of his baby"—a charge repeated in the *Commonwealth* and, also in Mar. 1583, by Mendoza (*C.S.P. Spanish, 1580–86*, pp. 451–52, also 426).
84. Leo Hicks, echoing the opinion of Parsons (in Knox, *Letters and Memorials of William Cardinal Allen*, pp. 392–94) and others, has tried to demonstrate that both C. Paget and Thomas Morgan were double agents and that Paget may have deliberately failed to broach the matter of invasion in order to sabotage the scheme; see *Elizabethan Problem*, pp. 21–29.
85. Paget to his servant, R. Ensor, 7 Nov. 1583, requiring him to settle his affairs and secretly to forward as much money as could be gathered (S.P. 12/163/52); various examinations, Dec. 1583, S.P. 12/164/23, 26, 45.
86. It was believed by many Catholics that (as C. Paget expressed it in July 1585) Northumberland had been made away with by "the devilish practices of the Earl of Leicester and his confederates" (*C.S.P. Scots, 1584–85*, p. 26).
87. The government case appears in its pamphlets against Throgmorton and against Northumberland, reprinted in Kinney, *Elizabethan Backgrounds*, pp. 138–87.
88. Letter of 12 Feb. 1585, S.P. 15/28/61. Lord Paget's sister Anne Lee mentions

INTRODUCTION TO LEICESTER'S COMMONWEALTH   59

on 29 Jan. 1584 that he, Charles Paget, and Arundell "are called home by proclamation" (S.P. 12/167/51 and mentioned by Parry on 12 Feb.), but what this represents is difficult to tell. In June 1584 the Queen ordered an inventory of all three men's lands, which by Aug. had been completed (*C.S.P. Domestic, 1581–90*, pp. 182, 196, 213); Lord Paget's household goods were confiscated and used to furnish Tutbury Castle for the Queen of Scots's removal there (*C.S.P. Scots, 1584–85*, pp. 437–38). In Feb. 1587 the wardship of William, the son of "the late Lord Paget," was granted to one of Leicester's allies, Sir George Carey (*A.P.C. 1586–87*, p. 352); as Paget did not die until 1590, "late" must refer to his having been attainted, along with Throgmorton and Babington, by the statute *29 Elizabeth, cap. 1*, in the Parliament of 1586–1587 (Bellamy, *Tudor Law of Treason*, p. 212).

89. Lord Paget to his mother, 2 Dec. 1583, S.P. 12/164/5; to Lord Burghley, 2 Dec. 1583, S.P. 12/164/6; to the Council, 12 Oct. 1584, S.P. 15/28/97. In late Oct. 1583 he had been writing to his brother regretting rumors of the latter's activities and threatening to disown him should he forget the loyalty he owed (S.P. 12/163/18).

90. Camden, *Elizabeth*, 3: 33. Also the so-called Somerville Plot was breaking in Oct. and Nov. 1583, and Lord Paget told Stafford upon his arrival in Paris that because of it he feared there was to be "a hard hand over all Papists" (Stafford to Walsingham, 2 Dec. 1583, S.P. 15/28/44).

91. In advising Stafford of the courtiers' flight, Walsingham had warned him against allowing his wife's close alliance with them to affect his duty (2 Dec. 1583, S.P. 78/10/95). Stafford was infuriated at the suggestion and complained to Burghley "that there is an evil meaning in the writer" (19 Dec. 1583, British Library, Cotton MSS., Galba E. vi, fol. 189[v], Hardwicke State Papers, 1: 212).

92. The case against him appears in Conyers Read's two essays "Fame of Sir Edward Stafford," in *American Historical Review*, 1915 and 1930 (less strongly stated in *Walsingham*, 2: 409–15, and *Burghley*, pp. 386–90). Sir John Neale's rebuttal, much the stronger case, appears under the same title in *English Historical Review*, 1929.

93. Efforts were also being made by Dr. Allen and others (Knox, *Allen*, pp. 228, 242) and by the Queen of Scots (Parsons to Englefield, Paris, 24 July 1584, C.R.S. 39, p. 226) to recommend them to the favor of the King of Spain and the Pope.

94. Read interprets these same activities to their disadvantage. Arundell acted as go-between for Stafford, the Duke of Guise, and Mendoza, exchanging news and money for news supposedly out of Stafford's dispatches; Stafford's code name was "Julio," Arundell's "the third party." Stafford had asked permission from home (which, however, was refused) to use such a ruse in order to gain Spanish trust.

Arundell's death invites investigation. When the renegade priest Gifford accused him in Paris of being a spy for Stafford, he countered by delating Gifford to the ecclesiastical authorities for keeping a "quean." Later in the day he learned from Stafford that Gifford had kept an "insurance policy," instructions to him involving the entrapment of Babington and the Queen of Scots signed by Walsingham's man Phelippes. Swearing to retrieve the embarrassing papers or die, Arundell rushed off but was soon after found irremediably ill, and after a week's languishing, he died on Christmas day, 15 Dec. English style. Stafford believed

Arundell to have been poisoned and indicated to Walsingham that he held him in good measure responsible. Gifford's papers were not heard of again.

There is confusion among scholars occasioned by the fact that Arundell was sometimes referred to as Sir Charles, and more often not. In fact, he was knighted by Philip II at the Escorial in summer 1586 and was thus "*miles Hispanicus,*" a knight only to the Catholic writers on the continent.

95. Morgan to the Queen of Scots, Murdin, *State Papers,* pp. 456–57; Rogers/Berden to Walsingham, 11 Aug. 1585, S.P. 15/29/39.

96. Vatican archives, printed in Hicks, "Growth of a Myth," pp. 96–97.

97. "Argumenta quibus probatur Patrem Personium huius libri auctorem fuisse sunt publica fama, stilus optime et familiarissime quamplurimis notus, confession D'ni Caroli Arundelii qui se confessus est huic libro subjectum et materiem subministrasse, P. autem Personium methodum, stilum, et formam" (see Cecil's "Brevis Relatio," in Law, *Archpriest Controversy,* 2: 99).

98. Watson, *Decacordon of Ten Quodlibetical Questions,* p. 266; Parsons, *Warnword to Sir Francis Hastings' Wast-Word,* fol. 2ᵛ.

99. Labanoff, *Letters of Mary Stuart,* p. 362. It is known certainly, however, that his imprisonment was requested by Elizabeth, via the Earl of Derby, because of his implication in the so-called Parry Plot. Observe that Mary evidently has no personal knowledge of the authorship. There is no reason to take the suggestion of Glasgow's participation seriously.

In Nov. 1584 Hieronimo Martelli (*vere* Henri Samerie, S.J.) informed Mary that because Morgan is "vehemently accused" of having written the *Commonwealth,* it is feared that he will soon be in trouble; for this reason "some advise him to disappear," but the writer disagrees, lest Morgan might thus appear guilty (*C.S.P. Scots, 1584–85,* p. 421).

100. Murdin, *State Papers,* p. 456.

101. Leicester "hath said to a friend of his that he will persecute you to the uttermost, for that he supposeth your Majesty to be privy to the setting forth of the book against him" (Murdin, *State Papers,* pp. 436–37).

102. C.R.S. 4, pp. 120–21; C.R.S. 2, p. 33.

103. Rogers/Berden to Walsingham, Paris, 30 Sept. 1585, C.R.S. 21, pp. 80–81. Paget tried again in April of the next year (Murdin, *State Papers,* p. 509).

104. Rogers/Berden to Walsingham, 16 Dec. 1585, S.P. 15/29/55.

105. Their relations can be followed in Hicks, *Elizabethan Problem,* pp. 191–93, 215–18.

106. See Pritchard, *Catholic Loyalism,* pp. 49–56.

107. Fitzherbert, *Defense of the Catholic Cause* and *Treatise Concerning Policy and Religion, inter alia.* See Loomie, *Spanish Elizabethans,* pp. 108–12.

108. *C.S.P. Venetian, 1581–91,* p. 176; S.P. 78/13/86.

109. S.P. 78/15/15 (see Appendix E).

110. Hicks cites instances in which Lady Sheffield is known to have supplied Arundell with vital information on other matters (*Elizabethan Problem,* p. 218 and note).

111. When Richard Verstegan's illustrated book on the English persecution appeared in late 1583 or early 1584, Stafford found no difficulty in having the printing

INTRODUCTION TO LEICESTER'S COMMONWEALTH   61

house raided, the printer arrested, and Verstegan himself imprisoned for a few days' time. See H.M.C. Rutland MSS., 1: 158, and Stafford's dispatches, *C.S.P. Foreign,* for the period 23 Nov. 1583 to 30 Jan. 1584; also A. G. Petti, ed., "Verstegan Papers," C.R.S. 52, p. xxxvii.

112. The *Commonwealth*'s several points of correspondence with Mendoza's dispatches of 1582-1583 serve further to link Lord Harry to the book as at that time Mendoza considered him his primary informant in England.

113. Leslie's *Treatise* is itself a reprint of a part of his 1569 tract, the *Defense of the Honor;* the *Commonwealth*'s authors may have been working from the earlier edition, but as Leslie was living in Rouen, they seem likely to have been in touch with him directly.

114. See Read, "William Cecil and Elizabethan Public Relations," pp. 37-38.

115. See Allen's memorial, "De presenti rerum Anglicarum statu," in Mattingly, "William Allen and Catholic Propaganda in England," pp. 327-28 *et passim.*

116. Allen, *Defence,* pp. 146-72; see also his *Admonition to the Nobility,* pp. 6-7.

117. This oversimplifies a complex controversial problem but is generally a fair characterization; on the Catholic position toward those who have "gone forth," see Clancy, *Papist Pamphleteers,* pp. 146-48.

118. Walpole and Parsons, *News from Spain and Holland,* fols. 26^V-27. Corresponding passages in Parsons, *Brief Discourse Containing Certain Reasons,* unpag. dedication; Parsons, *Epistle of the Persecution,* pp. 5-7; Allen, *Defence,* pp. 93-96. Catholics have "*jus acquisitum,* ancient right over heretics," but Protestants have "*nullum jus acquisitum*" over Catholics; Parsons, *Judgment of a Catholic Englishman,* p. 23, and *Discussion of the Answer of M. William Barlow,* p. 142.

119. This petition was printed with others by Broughton, *English Protestants' Plea and Petition;* passages quoted, pp. 34, 41.

120. Lecler, *Toleration and the Reformation,* 2: 375; Jordan, *Development of Religious Toleration in England,* 1: 404-6.

121. See Levine, *Early Elizabethan Succession Question,* p. 8.

122. This fear of Huntingdon's pursuit of his claim was shared by all of Mary's supporters and by Mary herself (see *C.S.P. Scots, 1584-85,* p. 86).

123. See Cross, *Puritan Earl,* pp. 143-47.

124. See, e.g., *C.S.P. Spanish, 1580-86,* pp. 85, 400. Parsons, too, remarks upon the Earl's claim in a letter of 13 Dec. 1584 (C.R.S. 39, p. 266), and also in Dec. 1584 Englefield identified Huntingdon as the Queen of Scots's "chief competitor" (S.P. 53/15/4). The papers taken about the Scottish Jesuit Creighton (4 Sept. 1584) indicate that for the Lennox Invasion of 1582 proclamations were designed against both Huntingdon and Leicester because "they go about . . . to take away from [James VI] the right to the succession" (Knox, *Allen,* p. 429).

125. See Hurstfield, "The Succession Struggle in Late Elizabethan England," and Hicks, "Sir Robert Cecil."

126. See Axton, "Influence of Edmund Plowden's Succession Treatise."

127. Harington, *Tract on the Succession,* pp. 55-61; T. Wilson, *State of England,* pp. 8-9. Both borrowings are marked in the annotations.

128. Clancy, *Papist Pamphleteers,* p. 56.

129. This is true especially among Catholic writers, e.g., John Leslie's *Copy of a*

Letter Written out of Scotland (1572), Parsons's *Epistle of the Persecution*, the *Copy of a Double Letter* (1582?), Allen's *Copy of a Letter Written by M. Doctor Allen* (1587), Creswell's *Advertisement Written to a Secretary of My Lord Treasurer's* (1592), and Copley's *Answer to a Letter of a Jesuited Gentleman* (1601). On the other side, the government backed Lewis (or Samuel) Lewknor's *A Discourse of the Usage of the English Fugitives* (1595)—in MS., "A Copy of a Letter Sent out of the Low Countries," with Burghley's annotations (British Library, Stowe MS. 159, fols. 276-302)—supposedly a letter from a Catholic Englishman to his nephew, demonstrating why he must not flee the realm in any hope of freedom of conscience and Spanish maintenance.

130. Darnton, *Literary Underground of the Old Regime*, pp. 203-05.
131. Rose, *Cases of Conscience*, p. 42.
132. See C. Wilson, *Queen Elizabeth and the Revolt of the Netherlands*, esp. pp. 101-3.
133. D. Wilson, *Sweet Robin*. A. Kendall's *Robert Dudley* is less interpretive in character; it is largely a chronological tour through the Dudley Papers at Longleat, but the conception of Leicester that lies behind most of its remarks is essentially the older, simpler, and less flattering one.
134. See MacCaffrey, *Queen Elizabeth and the Making of Policy*, p. 437.
135. Pulman, *Elizabethan Privy Council*, pp. 28-29.
136. Opponents of the stature of William Cecil naturally have left no gross diatribes, but as shown by his two memoranda comparing Leicester's qualities with those of the Archduke Charles, Cecil was well aware of the source of Dudley's influence and his vulnerability to unsavory report (printed in D. Wilson, *Sweet Robin*, pp. 188-90).
137. Peck, "Letter of Estate," pp. 25-26. See also the concern of the "Letter" for Norfolk's son Philip (p. 31) and for Sussex (p. 32).
138. Wallace MacCaffrey's introduction to the 1970 edition of Camden, *History of . . . Princess Elizabeth*, p. xxxviii.

Leicester's Commonwealth

The Copy of a Letter

*Written by a Master of Art of Cambridge
to his friend in London, concerning some talk
passed of late between two worshipful and grave
men about the present state and some proceedings
of the Earl of Leicester and his friends in England.
Conceived, spoken and published with most earnest
protestation of all dutiful good will and
affection towards her most excellent Majesty
and the realm, for whose good only it is
made common to many.*
1584.

The Epistle Directory:
To Mr. G. M.
in Gracious Street in London[1]

Dear and loving friend, I received about ten days gone your letter of the ninth of this present, wherein you demand and solicit again the thing that I so flatly denied you at my late being in your chamber; I mean, to put in writing the relation which then I made unto you of the speech had this last Christmas in my presence, between my right worshipful good friend and patron and his guest the old lawyer, of some matters in our state and country. And for that[2] you press me very seriously at this instant, both by request and many reasons, to yield to your desire herein, and not only this, but also to give my consent for the publishing of the same by such secret means as you assure me you can there find out, I have thought good to confer the whole matter with the parties themselves whom principally it concerneth (who at the receipt of your letter were not far off from me). And albeit at the first I found them averse and nothing inclined to grant your demand, yet after, upon consideration of your reasons and assurance of secrecy (especially for that there is nothing in the same contained repugnant to charity or to our bounden duty toward our most gracious Princess or country, but rather for the special good of them both and for the forewarning of some dangers imminent to the same), they have referred over the matter to me, yet with this PROVISO, that they will know nothing nor yet yield consent to the publishing hereof, for fear of some future flourish of the Ragged Staff[3] to come hereafter about their ears if their names should break forth, which (I trust) you will provide shall never happen, both for their security and for your own. And with this I will end, assuring you that within these five or six days you shall receive the whole in writing by another way and secret means; neither shall the bearer suspect what he carrieth, whereof also I thought good to premonish you. And this shall suffice for this time.

The Preface of the Conference

Scholar. Not long before the last Christmas, I was requested by a letter from a very worshipful and grave gentleman, whose son was then my pupil in Cambridge, to repair with my said scholar to a certain house of his near London and there to pass over the holy days in his company; for that it was determined that in Hilary term following his said son should be placed in some Inn of Chancery to follow the study of the common law, and so to leave the University. This request was grateful unto me both in respect of the time as also of the matter, but especially of the company. For that, as I love much the young gentleman my pupil for his towardliness in religion, learning, and virtue, so much more do I reverence his father for the riper possession of the same ornaments, and for his great wisdom, experience, and grave judgment in affairs of the world that do occur; but namely touching our own country, wherein truly I do not remember to have heard any man in my life discourse more substantially, indifferently, and with less passion, more love and fidelity, than I have heard him, which was the cause that I took singular delight to be in his company and refused no occasion to enjoy the same. Which also he perceiving, dealt more openly and confidently with me than with many other of his friends, as by the relation following may well appear.

When I came to the foresaid house by London, I found there among other friends an ancient man that professed the law and was come from London to keep his Christmas in that place, with whom at divers former times I had been well acquainted, for that he haunted much the company of the said gentleman my friend and was much trusted and used by him in matters of his profession, and not a little beloved also for his good conversation, notwithstanding some difference in religion between us. For albeit this lawyer was inclined to be a Papist, yet was it with such moderation and reservation of his duty towards his prince and country, and proceedings of the same, as he seemed always to give full satisfaction in this point to us that were of contrary opinion.

Neither did he let to protest oftentimes with great affection that as he had many friends and kinsfolk of contrary religion to himself, so did he love them never the less for their different conscience, but, leaving that to God, was desirous to do them any friendship or service that he could, with all affection, zeal, and fidelity. Neither was he willful or obstinate in his opinion, and much less reproachful in speech (as many of them be), but was content to hear whatsoever we should say to the contrary (as often we did) and to read any book also that we delivered him for his instruction.

Which temperate behavior induced this gentleman and me to affect the more his company, and to discourse as freely with him in all occurrents as if he had been of our own religion.

The Entrance to the Matter

One day, then, of the Christmas, we three retiring ourselves after dinner into a large gallery for our recreation (as often we were accustomed to do, when other went to cards and other pastimes), this lawyer by chance had in his hand a little book then newly set forth, containing *A Defense of the Public Justice Done of Late in England upon Divers Priests and Other Papists for Treason,*[4] which book the lawyer had read to himself a little before and was now putting it up into his pocket. But the gentleman my friend, who had read over the same once or twice in my company before, would needs take the same into his hand again and asked the lawyer his judgment upon the book.

Lawyer. The lawyer answered that it was not evil penned, in his opinion, to prove the guiltiness of some persons therein named in particular, as also to persuade in general that the Papists both abroad and at home who meddle so earnestly with defense and increase of their religion (for these are not all, said he) do consequently wish and labor some change in the state. But yet whether so far forth and in so deep a degree of proper treason as here in this book both in general and particular is presumed and enforced, that (quoth he) is somewhat hard (I ween) for you or me (in respect of some other difference between us) to judge or discern with indifferency.

Gentleman: Nay truly, said the gentleman, for my part I think not so, for that reason is reason in what religion soever. And for myself I may protest that I bear the honest Papist (if there be any) no malice for his deceived conscience, whereof among others yourself can be a witness; marry, his practices against the state I cannot in any wise disgiest,[5] and much less may the commonwealth bear the same (whereof we all depend), being a sin of all other the most heinous and least pardonable. And therefore, seeing in this you grant the Papist both in general abroad and at home, and in particular such as are condemned, executed, and named in this book to be guilty, how can you insinuate (as you do) that there is more presumed or enforced upon them by this book than there is just cause so to do?

Lawyer. Good Sir, said the other, I stand not here to examine the doings of my superiors, or to defend the guilty, but wish heartily rather their punishment that have deserved the same. Only this I say, for explication of my former speech, that men of a different religion from the state wherein they live may be said to deal against the same state in two sorts: the one, by dealing for the increase of their said different religion, which is always either directly or indirectly against the state. Directly, when the said religion containeth any point or article directly impugning the said state (as perhaps you will say that the Roman religion doth against the present state of England in the point of supremacy), and indirectly, for that every different religion divideth in a sort and draweth from the state, in that there is no man who in his heart would not wish to have the chief governor and state to be of his religion if he could, and consequently misliketh the other in respect of that; and in this kind not only those whom you call busy Papists in England, but also those whom we call hot Puritans among you (whose differences from the state, especially in matters of government, is very well known) may be called all traitors, in mine opinion, for that every one of these indeed do labor indirectly (if not more) against the state, in how much soever each one endeavoreth to increase his part or faction that desireth a governor of his own religion.

And in this case also are the Protestants in France and Flanders under Catholic princes; the Calvinists (as they are called) under the Duke of Saxony, who is a Lutheran; the Lutherans under Casimir, that favoreth Calvinists; the Grecians and other Christians under the Emperor of Constantinople, under the Sophy, under the Great Cham of Tartary, and under other princes that agree not with them in religion. All which subjects do wish (no doubt) in their hearts that they had a prince and state of their own religion, instead of that which now governeth them, and consequently in this first sense they may be called all traitors, and every act they do for advancement of their said different religion (dividing between the state and them) tendeth to treason; which their princes supposing, do sometimes make divers of their acts treasonable or punishable for treason. But yet so long as they break not forth unto the second kind of treason, which containeth some actual attempt or treaty against the life of the prince or state, by rebellion or otherwise, we do not properly condemn them for traitors, though they do some acts of their religion made treason by the prince his laws, who is of a different faith.

And so to apply this to my purpose, I think, Sir, in good sooth, that in the first kind of treason, as well the zealous Papist, as also the Puritans in England, may well be called and proved traitors; but in the second sort (whereof we speak properly at this time) it cannot be so precisely answered, for that there may be both guilty and guiltless in each religion. And as I cannot excuse all Puritans in this point, so you cannot condemn all Papists, as long as you take me and some other to be as we are.[6]

Gentleman: I grant your distinction of treasons to be true (said the gentleman), as also your application thereof to the Papists and Puritans (as you call them) not to want reason, if there be any of them that mislike the present state (as perhaps there be); albeit for my part, I think these two kinds of treasons which you have put down be rather divers degrees than divers kinds; wherein I will refer me to the judgment of our Cambridge friend here present, whose skill is more in logical distinctions. But yet my reason is this, that indeed the one is but a step or degree to the other, not differing in nature, but rather in time, ability, or opportunity. For if (as in your former examples you have showed) the Grecians under the Turk, and other Christians under other princes of a different religion, and as also the Papists and Puritans (as you term them) in England (for now this word shall pass between us for distinction sake), have such alienation of mind from their present regiment and do covet so much a governor and state of their own religion, then no doubt but they are also resolved to employ their forces for accomplishing and bringing to pass their desires, if they had opportunity; and so being now in the first degree or kind of treason do want but occasion or ability to break into the second.

Lawyer. True, Sir, said the lawyer, if there be no other cause or circumstance that may withold them.

Gentleman. And what cause or circumstance may stay them, I pray you (said the gentleman), when they shall have ability and opportunity to do a thing which they so much desire?

Lawyer. Divers causes (quoth the lawyer), but especially and above all other (if it be at home in their own country) the fear of servitude under foreign nations may restrain them from such attempts; as we see in Germany that both Catholics and Protestants would join together against any stranger that should offer danger to their liberty. And so they did, against Charles V.[7] And in France not long ago, albeit the Protestants were up in arms against their king and could have been content, by the help of us in England, to have put him down and placed another of their own religion, yet when they saw us once seized of Newhaven, and so like to proceed to the recovery of some part of our states on that side the sea, they quickly joined with their own Catholics again to expel us.[8]

In Flanders likewise, though Monsieur were called thither by the Protestants especially for defense of their religion against the Spaniard, yet we see how dainty divers chief Protestants of Antwerp, Gaunt, and Bruges were in admitting him, and how quick in expelling, so soon as he put them in the least fear of subjection to the French.[9] And as for Portugal, I have heard some of the chiefest Catholics among them say, in this late contention about their kingdom, that rather than they would suffer the Castilian to come in upon them, they would be content to admit whatsoever aids of a contrary religion to themselves and to adventure whatsoever alteration in religion or other inconvenience might befall them by that means, rather than endanger their subjection to their ambitious neighbor.[10]

The like is reported in divers histories of the Grecians at this day, who do hate so much the name and dominion of the Latins as they had rather to endure all the miseries which daily they suffer under the Turk for their religion and otherwise, than by calling for aid from the west to hazard their subjection to the said Latins. So that by these examples you see that fear and horror of external subjection may stay men in all states, and consequently also both Papists and Puritans in the state of England, from passing to the second kind or degree of treason, albeit they were never so deep in the first and had both ability, time, will, and opportunity for the other.

Scholar. Here I presumed to interrupt their speech, and said that this seemed to me most clear and that now I understood what the lawyer meant before, when he affirmed that albeit the most part of Papists in general might be said to deal against the state of England at this day, in that they deal so earnestly for the maintenance and increase of their religion, and so to incur some kind of treason; yet (perhaps) not so far forth nor in so deep a degree of proper treason as in this book is presumed or enforced; though for my part (said I) I do not see that the book presumeth or enforceth all Papists in general to be properly traitors, but only such as in particular are therein named, or that are by law attainted, condemned, or executed. And what will you say (quoth I) to those in particular?

Lawyer. Surely (quoth he), I must say of these, much after the manner which I spake before, that some here named in this book are openly known to have been in the second degree or kind of treason, as Westmoreland, Norton, Sanders, and the like.[11] But divers others (namely the priests and seminaries[12] that of late have suffered), by so much as I could see delivered and pleaded at their arraignments, or heard protested by them at their deaths, or gathered by reason and discourse of myself (for that no foreign prince or wise counsellor would ever commit so great matters of state to such instruments), I cannot (I say) but think that to the wise of our state that had the doing of this business, the first degree of treason (wherein no doubt they were) was sufficient to dispatch and make them away, especially in such suspicious times as these are; to the end that being hanged for the first, they should never be in danger to fall into the second, nor yet to draw other men to the same, which perhaps was most of all misdoubted.[13]

After the lawyer had spoken this, I held my peace, to hear what the gentleman would answer; who walked up and down two whole turns in the gallery without yielding any word again, and then, staying upon the sudden, cast his eyes sadly upon us both and said:

Gentleman: My masters, howsoever this be, which indeed appertaineth not to us to judge or discuss, but rather to persuade ourselves that the state hath reason to do as it doth and that it must oftentimes as well prevent inconveniences as remedy the same when they are happened, yet for my own part I must confess unto you that upon some considerations which use to come unto my mind, I take no small grief of these differences among us (which you term of divers and different religions), for which we are driven of necessity to use discipline towards divers who possibly otherwise would be no great malefactors. I know the cause of this difference is grounded upon a principle not easy to cure, which is the judgment and conscience of a man, whereunto obeyeth at length his will and affection, whatsoever for a time he may otherwise dissemble outwardly. I remember your speech before of the doubtful and dangerous inclination of such as live discontented in a state of a different religion, especially when either indeed or in their own conceit they are hardly dealt withal, and where every man's particular punishment is taken to reach to the cause of the whole.

I am not ignorant how that misery procureth amity and the opinion of calamity moveth affection of mercy and compassion, even towards the wicked; the better fortune always is subject to envy, and he that suffereth is thought to have the better cause; my experience of the divers reigns and proceedings of King Edward, Queen Mary, and of this our most gracious sovereign hath taught me not a little touching the sequel of these affairs. And finally (my good friends), I must tell you plain (quoth he, and this he spake with great asseveration) that I could wish with all my heart that either these differences were not among us at all, or else that they were so temperately on all parts pursued as the common state of our country, the blessed reign of her Majesty, and the common cause of true religion were not endangered thereby. But now—and there he brake off and turned aside.

Lawyer. The lawyer seeing him hold his peace and depart, he stepped after him and, taking him by the gown, said merrily: Sir, all men are not of your complexion, some are of quicker and more stirring spirits and do love to fish in water that is troubled, for that they do participate [in] the black-moor's humor, that dwell in Guinea (whereof I suppose you have heard and seen also some in this land), whose exercise at home is (as some write) the one to hunt, catch, and sell the other and always the stronger to make money of the weaker for the time. But now if in England we should live in peace and unity of the state, as they do in Germany notwithstanding their differences of religion, and that the one should not prey upon the other, then should the great falcons for the field (I mean the favorites of the time) fail whereon to feed, which were an inconvenience as you know.

Gentleman: Truly, Sir, said the gentleman, I think you rove nearer the mark than you ween, for if I be not deceived the very ground of much of these broils whereof we talk is but a very prey; not in the minds of the prince or state (whose intentions no doubt be most just and holy), but in the greedy imagination and subtile conceit of him who at this present in respect of our sins is permitted by God to tyrannize both prince and state, and, being himself of no religion, feedeth notwithstanding upon our differences in religion, to the fatting of himself and ruin of the realm. For whereas by the common distinction now received in speech there are three notable differences of religion in the land, the two extremes whereof are the Papist and the Puritan, and the religious Protestant obtaining the mean, this fellow being of neither maketh his gain of all, and as he seeketh a kingdom by the one extreme and spoil by the other, so he useth the authority of the third to compass the first two, and the countermine of each one to the overthrow of all three.

Scholar: To this I answered: In good sooth, Sir, I see now where you are, you are fallen into the common place of all our ordinary talk and conference in the University, for I know that you mean my Lord of Leicester, who is the subject of all pleasant discourses at this day throughout the realm.

Gentleman: Not so pleasant as pitiful, answered the gentleman, if all matters and circumstances were well considered, except any man take pleasure to jest at our own miseries, which are like to be greater by his iniquity (if God avert it not) than by all the wickedness of England besides, he being the man that by all probability is like to be the bane and fatal destiny of our state, with the eversion[14] of true religion, whereof by indirect means he is the greatest enemy that the land doth nourish.

Lawyer. Now verily (quoth the lawyer), if you say thus much for the Protestants' opinion of him, what shall I say for his merits towards the Papists? Who for as much as I can perceive do take themselves little beholding unto him, albeit for his gain he was some years their secret friend against you, until by his friends he was persuaded, and chiefly by the Lord North,[15] by way of policy, as the said Lord boasteth, in hope of greater gain to step over to the Puritans against us both, whom notwithstanding it is probable that he loveth as much as he doth the rest.

Gentleman: You know the bear's love, said the gentleman, which is all for his own paunch, and so this Bearwhelp turneth all to his own commodity, and for greediness thereof will overturn all if he be not stopped or muzzled in time.

And surely unto me it is a strange speculation, whereof I cannot pick out the reason (but only that I do attribute it to God's punishment for our sins) that in so wise and vigilant a state as ours is, and in a country so well acquainted and beaten with such dangers, a man of such a spirit as he is known to be, of so extreme ambition, pride, falsehood, and treachery; so born, so bred up, so nuzzled in treason from his infancy; descended of a tribe of traitors, and fleshed in conspiracy against the royal blood of King Henry's children in his tender years, and exercised ever since in drifts against the same by the blood and ruin of divers others; a man so well known to bear secret malice against her Majesty for causes irreconcilable and most deadly rancor against the best and wisest counsellors of her Highness; that such a one (I say), so hateful to God and man and so markable to the simplest subject of this land by the public ensigns of his tyrannous purpose, should be suffered so many years without check to aspire to tyranny by most manifest ways and to possess himself (as now he hath done) of Court, Council, and country without controlment, so that nothing wanteth to him but only his pleasure, and the day already conceived in his mind to dispose as he list both of prince, crown, realm, and religion.

Scholar: It is much, truly (quoth I), that you say, and it ministreth not a little marvel unto many, whereof your worship is not the first nor yet the tenth person of accompt[16] which I have heard discourse and complain. But what shall we say hereunto? There is no man that ascribeth not this unto the singular benignity and most bountiful good nature of her Majesty, who measuring other men by her own heroical and princely sincerity cannot easily suspect a man so much bounden to her grace as he is, nor remove her confidence from the place where she hath heaped so infinite benefits.

Gentleman: No doubt (said the gentleman) but this gracious and sweet disposition of her Majesty is the true original cause thereof, which princely disposition, as in her Highness it deserveth all rare commendation, so lieth the same open to many dangers oftentimes, when so benign a nature meeteth with ingrate and ambitious persons; which observation, perhaps, caused her Majesty's most noble grandfather and father (two renowned wise princes) to withdraw sometime upon the sudden their great favor from certain subjects of high estate. And her Majesty may easily use her own excellent wisdom and memory to recall to mind the manifold examples of perilous haps fallen to divers princes by too much confidence in obliged proditors,[17] with whom the name of a kingdom and one hour's reign weigheth more than all duty, obligation, honesty, or nature in the world. Would God her Majesty could see the continual fears that be in her faithful subjects' hearts whiles that man is about her noble person, so well able and likely (if the Lord avert it not) to be the calamity of her princely blood and name.

The talk will never out of many mouths and minds that divers ancient men of this realm, and once a wise gentleman now a Councillor[18] had with a certain friend of his, concerning the presage and deep impression which her Majesty's father had of the house of Sir John Dudley to be the ruin in time of his Majesty's royal house and blood, which thing was like to have been fulfilled soon after (as all the world knoweth) upon the death of King Edward by the said Dudley this man's father, who at one blow procured to dispatch from all possession of the crown all three children of the said noble king. And yet in the midst of those bloody practices against her Majesty that now is and her sister (wherein also this fellow's hand was so far as for his age he could thrust the same), within sixteen days before King Edward's death he (knowing belike[19] that the king should die) wrote most flattering letters to the Lady Mary (as I have heard by them who then were with her) promising all loyalty and true service to her after the decease of her brother, with no less painted words than this man now doth use to Queen Elizabeth.[20]

So dealt he then with the most dear children of his good king and master, by whom he had been no less exalted and trusted than this man is by her Majesty. And so deeply dissembled he then when he had in hand the plot to destroy them both. And what then (alas) may not we fear and doubt of this his son, who in outrageous ambition and desire of reign is not inferior to his father or to any other aspiring spirit in the world, but far more insolent, cruel, vindicative, expert, potent, subtile, fine, and fox-like than ever he was? I like well the good motion propounded by the foresaid gentleman[21] to his friend at the same time, and do assure myself it would be most pleasant to the realm and profitable to her Majesty, to wit: that this man's actions might be called publicly to trial, and liberty given to good subjects to say what they knew against the same, as it was permitted in the first year of King Henry VIII against his grandfather, and in the first of Queen Mary against his father;[22] and then I would not doubt but if these two his ancestors were found worthy to leese their heads for treason, this man would not be found unworthy to make the third in kindred, whose treacheries do far surpass them both.

Lawyer. After the gentleman had said this, the lawyer stood still, somewhat smiling to himself and looking round about him, as though he had been half afeard, and then said: My masters, do you read over or study the statutes that come forth? Have you not heard of the PROVISO made in the last Parliament for punishment of those who speak so broad of such men as my Lord of Leicester is?[23]

Gentleman: Yes, said the gentleman, I have heard how that my Lord of Leicester was very careful and diligent at that time to have such a law to pass against talkers, hoping (belike) that his Lordship under that general restraint might lie the more quietly in harbrough from the tempest of men's tongues, which tattled busily at that time of divers his Lordship's actions and affairs which perhaps himself would have wished to pass with more secrecy. As of his discontentment and preparation to rebellion upon Monsieur's first coming into the land;[24] of his disgrace and checks received in Court; of the fresh death of the noble Earl of Essex; and of this man's hasty snatching up of the widow, whom he sent up and down the country from house to house by privy ways, thereby to avoid the sight and knowledge of the Queen's Majesty. And albeit he had not only used her at his good liking before, for satisfying of his own lust, but also married and remarried her for contentation of her friends; yet denied he the same by solemn oath to her Majesty and received the holy communion thereupon (so good a conscience he hath) and consequently threatened most sharp revenge towards all subjects which should dare to speak thereof; and so for the concealing both of this and other his doings which he desired not to have public, no marvel though his Lordship were so diligent a procurer of that law for silence.

Scholar. Indeed (said I), it is very probable that his Lordship was in great distress about that time when Monsieur's matters were in hand, and that he did many things and purposed more whereof he desired less speech among the people, especially afterwards when his said designments took not place. I was myself that year not far from Warwick when he came thither from the Court a full *malcontent*, and when it was thought most certainly throughout the realm that he would have taken arms soon after if the marriage of her Majesty with Monsieur had gone forward. The thing in Cambridge and in all the country as I rode was in every man's mouth, and it was a wonder to see not only the countenances, but also the behavior, and to hear the bold speeches of all such as were of his faction.

My Lord himself had given out a little before at Killingworth that the matter would cost many broken heads before Michaelmas day next,[25] and my Lord of Warwick had said openly at his table in Greenwich, Sir Thomas Hennige [Heneage] being by (if I be not deceived), that it was not to be suffered (I mean the marriage), which words of his once coming abroad (albeit misliked by his own lady then also present)[26] every servingman and common companion took then up in defense of his Lordship's part against the Queen's Majesty. Such running there was, such sending and posting about the realm, such amplification of the powers and forces of Casimir and other princes,[27] ready (as was affirmed) to present themselves unto his aid for defense of the realm and religion against strangers (for that was holden to be his cause), such numbering of parties and complices within the realm (whereof himself showed the catalogue to some of his friends for their comfort),[28] such debasing of them that favored the marriage (especially two or three Councillors by name, who were said to be the cause of all and for that were appointed out to be sharply punished to the terror of all others),[29] such letters were written and intercepted of purpose, importing great powers to be ready, and so many other things done and designed, tending all to manifest and open war, as I began heartily to be afeard and wished myself back at Cambridge again, hoping that being there my scholar's gown should excuse me from necessity of fighting, or if not, I was resolved (by my Lord's good leave) to follow Aristotle, who preferreth always the Lion before the Bear; assuring myself withal that his Lordship should have no better success in this (if it came to trial) than his father had in as bad a cause, and so much the more for that I was privy to the minds of some of his friends, who meant to have deceived him if the matter had broken out. And amongst other there was a certain Vicepresident in the world,[30] who being left in the room and absence of another to procure friends, said in a place secretly not far from Ludlow that if the matter came to blows he would follow his Mistress and leave his master in the briars.

Gentleman: Marry, Sir (quoth the gentleman), and I trow many more would have followed that example. For albeit I know that the Papists were most named and misdoubted of his part in that cause, for their open inclination towards Monsieur, and consequently for greater discredit of the thing itself it was given out everywhere by this champion of religion that her Majesty's cause was the Papists' cause (even as his father had done in the like enterprise before him, though all upon dissimulation as appeared at his death, where he professed himself an earnest Papist);[31] yet was there no man so simple in the realm which descried not this vizard at the first, neither yet any good subject (as I suppose) who, seeing her Majesty on the one part, would not have taken against the other part, whatsoever he had been. And much more the thing itself in controversy (I mean the marriage of her royal Majesty with the brother and heir apparent of France), being taken and judged by the best, wisest, and faithfullest

Protestants of the realm to be both honorable, convenient, profitable, and needful. Whereby only, as by a most sovereign and present remedy, all our maladies both abroad and at home had at once been cured: all foreign enemies and domestical conspirators, all differences, all dangers, all fears had ceased together, France had been ours most assured, Spain would not a little have trembled, Scotland had been quiet, our competitors in England would have quaked, and for the Pope, he might have put up his pipes. Our differences in religion at home had been either less or no greater than now they are, for that Monsieur, being but a moderate Papist and nothing vehement in his opinions, was content with very reasonable conditions for himself and his strangers only in use of their conscience, not unlikely (truly) but that in time he might by God's grace and by the great wisdom and virtue of her Majesty have been brought also to embrace the gospel, as King Ethelbert, an heathen, was by noble Queen Bertha his wife, the first Christian of our English princes.[32]

Unto all which felicity, if the Lord in mercy should have added also some issue of their royal bodies (as was not impossible when first this noble match was moved), we then (doubtless) had been the most fortunate people under heaven and might have been (perhaps) the mean to have restored the gospel throughout all Europe besides, as our brethren of France well considered and hoped.

Of all which singular benefits both present and to come, both in RE and in SPE,[33] this tyrant for his own private lucre (fearing lest hereby his ambition might be restrained and his treachery revealed) hath bereaved the realm and done what in him lieth besides to alienate forever and make our mortal enemy this great prince, who sought the love of her Majesty with so much honor and confidence as never prince the like, putting twice his own person to jeopardy of the sea and to the peril of his malicious enviers here in England for her Majesty's sake.

Lawyer. When you speak of Monsieur (said the laywer), I cannot but greatly be moved, both for these considerations well touched by you, as also for some other; especially one wherein (perhaps) you will think me partial, but truly I am not, for that I speak it only in respect of the quiet and good of my country, and that is, that by

Monsieur's match with our noble Princess, besides the hope of issue (which was the principal), there wanted not also probability that some union or little toleration in religion between you and us might have been procured in this state, as we see that in some other countries is admitted to their great good. Which thing (no doubt) would have cut off quite all dangers and dealings from foreign princes and would have stopped many devices and plots within the realm; whereas now by this breach with France we stand alone, as me seemeth, without any great unition[34] or friendship abroad, and our differences at home grow more vehement and sharp than ever before. Upon which two heads, as also upon infinite other causes, purposes, drifts, and pretenses, there do ensue daily more deep, dangerous, and desperate practices, every man using either the commodity or necessity of the time and state for his own purpose. Especially now when all men presume that her Majesty (by the continual thwartings which have been used against all her marriages) is not like to leave unto the realm that precious jewel so much and long desired of all English hearts, I mean the royal heirs of her own body.

Gentleman: Thwartings call you the defeating of all her Majesty's most honorable offers of marriage? (said the other); truly in my opinion you should have used another word to express the nature of so wicked a fact, whereby alone, if there were no other, this unfortunate man hath done more hurt to his commonwealth than if he had murdered many thousands of her subjects or betrayed whole armies to the professed enemy. I can remember well myself four treatises to this purpose undermined by his means: the first with the Swethen king, the second with the Archduke of Austria, the third with Henry King of France that now reigneth, and the fourth with the brother and heir of the said kingdom.[35] For I let pass many other secret motions made by great potentates to her Majesty for the same purpose, but these four are openly known and therefore I name them. Which four are as well known to have been all disturbed by this DAVUS[36] as they were earnestly pursued by the other.

And for the first three suitors, he drove them away by protesting and swearing that himself was contracted unto her Majesty, whereof her Highness was sufficiently advertised by Cardinal Châtillon in the first treaty for France, and the Cardinal soon after punished (as is thought) by this man wit~~h~~ ~~...~~ yet this speech he gave out then everywhere among h~~is~~ ~~...~~ h strangers and other, that he (foresooth) was assured ~~...~~ and consequently that all other princes must give over their suits for him. Whereunto notwithstanding, when the Swethen would hardly give ear, this man conferred with his privado[37] to make a most unseemly and disloyal proof thereof for the other's satisfaction, which thing I am enforced by duty to pass over with silence for honor to the parties who are touched therein, as also I am to conceal his said filthy privado, though worthy otherwise for his dishonesty to be displayed to the world; but my Lord himself, I am sure, doth well remember both the man and the matter. And albeit there was no wise man at that time who, knowing my Lord, suspected not the falsehood and his arrogant affirmation touching this contract with her Majesty, yet some both abroad and at home might doubt thereof perhaps; but now of late, by his known marriage with his minion Dame Lettice of Essex, he hath declared manifestly his own most impudent and disloyal dealing with his sovereign in this report.

Lawyer. For that report (quoth the lawyer), I know that it was common and maintained by many for divers years; yet did the wiser sort make no accompt thereof, seeing it came only from himself and in his own behalf. Neither was it credible that her Majesty, who refused so noble knights and princes as Europe hath not the like, would make choice of so mean a peer as Robin Dudley is, noble only in two descents and both of them stained with the block, from which also himself was pardoned but the other day, being condemned thereunto by law for his deserts, as appeareth yet in public records.[38] And for the widow of Essex, I marvel, Sir (quoth he), how you call her his wife, seeing the canon law standeth yet in force touching matters of marriage within the realm.

Gentleman: Oh (said the gentleman, laughing), you mean for that he procured the poisoning of her husband in his journey from Ireland. You must think that Doctor Dale will dispense in that matter, as he did (at his Lordship's appointment) with his Italian physician Doctor Julio to have two wives at once; at the leastwise the matter was permitted and borne out by them both publicly (as all the world knoweth) and that against no less persons than the Archbishop of Canterbury himself, whose overthrow was principally wrought by this tyrant for contrarying his will in so beastly a demand.[39] But for this controversy whether the marriage be good or no, I leave it to be tried hereafter between my young Lord of Denbigh and Mr. Philip Sidney, whom the same most concerneth.[40] For that it is like to deprive him of a goodly inheritance if it take place, as some will say that in no reason it can, not only in respect of the precedent adultery and murder between the parties, but also for that my Lord was contracted at least to another lady before that yet liveth, whereof Mr. Edward Dyer and Mr. Edmund Tilney, both courtiers, can be witnesses, and consummated the same contract by generation of children.[41] But this (as I said) must be left to be tried hereafter by them which shall have most interest in the case. Only for the present I must advertise you that you may not take hold so exactly of all my Lord's doings in women's affairs, neither touching their marriages, neither yet their husbands.

For first his Lordship hath a special fortune, that when he desireth any woman's favor, then what person soever standeth in his way hath the luck to die quickly for the finishing of his desire. As for example, when his Lordship was in full hope to marry her Majesty and his own wife stood in his light, as he supposed, he did but send her aside to the house of his servant Forster of Cumnor by Oxford, where shortly after she had the chance to fall from a pair of stairs and so to break her neck, but yet without hurting of her hood that stood upon her head.[42] But Sir Richard Varney, who by commandment remained with her that day alone, with one man only, and had sent away perforce all her servants from her to a market two miles off, he (I say) with his man can tell how she died, which man, being taken afterward for a felony in the marches of Wales and offering to publish the manner of the said murder, was made away privily in the prison. And Sir Richard himself, dying about the same time in London, cried piteously and blasphemed God, and said to a gentleman of worship of mine acquaintance not long before his death that all the devils in hell did tear him in pieces. The wife also of Bald Buttler, kinsman to my Lord,⁴³ gave out the whole fact a little before her death. But to return unto my purpose, this was my Lord's good fortune to have his wife die at that time when it was like to turn most to his profit.⁴⁴

Long after this, he fell in love with the Lady Sheffield, whom I signified before, and then also had he the same fortune to have her husband die quickly with an extreme rheum in his head (as it was given out), but as other say of an artificial catarrh that stopped his breath.⁴⁵ The like good chance had he in the death of my Lord of Essex (as I have said before) and that at a time most fortunate for his purpose; for when he was coming home from Ireland with intent to revenge himself upon my Lord of Leicester for begetting his wife with child in his absence (the child was a daughter and brought up by the Lady Shandoies, W. Knooles his wife),⁴⁶ my Lord of Leicester hearing thereof, wanted not a friend or two to accompany the deputy, as among other, a couple of the Earl's own servants, Crompton (if I miss not his name), yeoman of his bottles, and Lloyd, his secretary, entertained afterward by my Lord of Leicester.⁴⁷ And so he died in the way, of an extreme flux, caused by an Italian *recipe*, as all his friends are well assured, the maker whereof was a surgeon (as is believed) that then was newly come to my Lord from Italy. A cunning man and sure in operation, with whom if the good lady had been sooner acquainted and used his help, she should not have needed to have sitten so pensive at home and fearful of her husband's former return out of the same country, but might have spared the young child in her belly, which she was enforced to make away (cruelly and unnaturally) for clearing the house against the goodman's arrival.

Neither must you marvel though all these died in divers manners of outward diseases, for this is the excellency of the Italian art, for which this surgeon and Dr. Julio were entertained so carefully, ⁴⁸ who can make a man die in what manner or show of sickness you will; by whose instructions no doubt but his Lordship is now cunning, especially adding also to these the counsel of his Doctor Bayley,⁴⁹ a man also not a little studied (as he seemeth) in this art. For I heard him once myself in a public act in Oxford (and that in presence of my Lord of Leicester, if I be not deceived) maintain that poison might be so tempered and given as it should not appear presently, and yet should kill the party afterward at what time should be appointed. Which argument belike pleased well his Lordship, and therefore was chosen to be discussed in his audience, if I be not deceived of his being that day present. So though one die of a flux and another of a catarrh, yet this importeth little to the matter, but showeth rather the great cunning and skill of the artificer.

So Cardinal Châtillon (as I have said before), having accused my Lord of Leicester to the Queen's Majesty and after that passing from London towards France about the marriage, died by the way at Canterbury of a burning fever and so proved Dr. Bayley's assertion true, that poison may be given to kill at a day.[50]

Scholar. At this the lawyer cast up his eyes to heaven, and I stood somewhat musing and thinking of that which had been spoken of the Earl of Essex, whose case indeed moved me more than all the rest, for that he was a very noble gentleman, a great advancer of true religion, a patron to many preachers and students, and towards me and some of my friends in particular he had been in some things very beneficial; and therefore I said that it grieved me extremely to hear or think of so unworthy a death contrived by such means to so worthy a peer. And so much the more, for that it was my chance to come to the understanding of divers particulars concerning that thing, both from one Lea, an Irishman,[51] Robin Hunnis, and other, that were present at Penteneis the merchant's house in Develing upon the quay,[52] where the murder was committed. The matter was wrought especially by Crompton, yeoman of the bottles, by the procurement of Lloyd, as you have noted before, and there was poisoned at the same time and with the same cup (as given of courtesy by the Earl) one Mistress Alice Draycot, a goodly gentlewoman whom the Earl affectioned much, who departing thence towards her own house (which was eighteen miles off), the foresaid Lea accompanying her and waiting upon her, she began to fall sick very grievously upon the way, and continued with increase of pains and excessive torments by vomiting until she died, which was the Sunday before the Earl's death ensuing the Friday after; and when she was dead, her body was swollen unto a monstrous bigness and deformity, whereof the good Earl hearing the day following, lamented the case greatly and said in the presence of his servants: Ah, poor Alice, the cup was not prepared for thee, albeit it were thy hard destiny to taste thereof.

Young Hunnis also, whose father is Master of the Children of her Majesty's Chapel,[53] being at that time page to the said Earl and accustomed to take the taste of his drink (though since entertained also among other by my Lord of Leicester for better covering of [the] matter), by his taste that he then took of the compound cup (though in very small quantity, as you know the fashion is), yet was he like to have lost his life, but escaped in the end (being young) with the loss only of his hair; which the Earl perceiving and taking compassion of the youth, called for a cup of drink a little before his death and drank to Hunnis, saying: I drink to thee, my Robin, and be not afeard, for this is a better cup of drink than that whereof thou tookest the taste when we were both poisoned, and whereby thou hast lost thy hair and I must leese my life. This hath young Hunnis reported openly in divers places and before divers gentlemen of worship sithence his coming into England, and the foresaid Lea, Irishman, at his passage this way towards France, after he had been present at the forenamed Mistress Draycot's death, with some other of the Earl's servants have and do most constantly report the same where they may do it without the terror of my Lord of Leicester's revenge. Wherefore in this matter there is no doubt at all, though most extreme vile and intolerable indignity, that such a man should be so openly murdered without punishment.[54] What nobleman within the realm may be safe if this be suffered? Or what worthy personage will adventure his life in her Majesty's service if this shalbe his reward? But (Sir) I pray you pardon me, for I am somewhat perhaps too vehement in the case of this my patron and noble peer of our realm. And therefore I beseech you to go forward in your talk whereas you left.

Gentleman: I was recounting unto you others (said the gentleman) made away by my Lord of Leicester with like art, and the next in order I think was Sir Nicholas Throgmorton, who was a man whom my Lord of Leicester used a great while (as all the world knoweth) to overthwart and cross the doings of my Lord Treasurer then Sir William Cecil, a man especially misliked always of Leicester, both in respect of his old master the Duke of Somerset, as also for that his great wisdom, zeal, and singular fidelity to the realm was like to hinder much this man's designments; wherefore understanding after a certain time that these two knights were secretly made friends, and that Sir Nicholas was like to detect his doings (as he imagined), which might turn to some prejudice of his purposes (having conceived also a secret grudge and grief against him, for that he had written to her Majesty at his being ambassador in France that he heard reported at Duke Memorance's [Montmorency's] table that the Queen of England had a meaning to marry her horsekeeper);[55] he invited the said Sir Nicholas to a supper at his house in London and at supper time departed to the Court, being called for (as he said) upon the sudden by her Majesty, and so perforce would needs have Sir Nicholas to sit and occupy his Lordship's place, and therein to be served as he was; and soon after by a surfeit there taken he died of a strange and incurable vomit. But the day before his death, he declared to a dear friend of his all the circumstance and cause of his disease, which he affirmed plainly to be of poison given him in a salad at supper, inveighing most earnestly against the Earl's cruelty and bloody disposition, affirming him to be the wickedest, most perilous and perfidious man under heaven. But what availed this, when he had now received the bait?[56]

This then is to show the man's good fortune, in seeing them dead whom for causes he would not have to live. And for his art of poisoning, it is such now and reacheth so far as he holdeth all his foes in England and elsewhere, as also a good many of his friends, in fear thereof, and if it were known how many he hath dispatched or assaulted that way, it would be marvelous to the posterity. The late Earl of Sussex wanted not a scruple for many years before his death of some dram received that made him incurable. And unto that noble gentleman Monsieur Simiers, it was discovered by great providence of God that his life was to be attempted by that art, and that not taking place (as it did not through his own good circumspection), it was concluded that the same should be assaulted by violence, whereof I shall have occasion to say more hereafter.

It hath been told me also by some of the servants of the late Lady

Lennox, who was also of the blood royal by Scotland, as all men know, and consequently little liked by Leicester, that a little before her death or sickness, my Lord took the pains to come and visit her with extraordinary kindness at her house at Hackney, bestowing long discourses with her in private; but as soon as he was departed, the good lady fell into such a flux as by no means could be stayed so long as she had life in her body, whereupon both she herself and all such as were near about her and saw her disease and ending day were fully of opinion that my Lord had procured her dispatch at his being there. Whereof let the women that served her be examined, as also Fowler, that then had the chief doings in her affairs and since hath been entertained by my Lord of Leicester. Mallet also, a stranger born, that then was about her, a sober and zealous man in religion and otherwise well qualified, can say somewhat in this point (as I think) if he were demanded.[57] So that this art and exercise of poisoning is much more perfect with my Lord than praying, and he seemeth to take more pleasure therein.

Now for the second point which I named, touching marriages and contracts with women; you must not marvel though his Lordship be somewhat divers, variable, and inconstant with himself, for that according to his profit or his pleasure, and as his lust and liking shall vary (wherein by the judgment of all men he surpasseth not only Sardanapalus and Nero, but even Heliogabalus himself),[58] so his Lordship also changeth wives and minions by killing the one, denying the other, using the third for a time, and the[n] fawning upon the fourth. And for this cause he hath his terms and pretenses (I warrant you) of contracts, precontracts, postcontracts, protracts, and retracts; as for example, after he had killed his first wife and so broken that contract, then forsooth would he needs make himself husband to the Queen's Majesty and so defeat all other princes by virtue of his precontract. But after this, his lust compelling him to another place, he would needs make a postcontract with the Lady Sheffield, and so he did, begetting two children upon her, the one a boy called Robin Sheffield now living, some time brought up at Newington, and the other a daughter, born (as is known) at Dudley Castle.[59] But yet after, his concupiscence changing again (as it never stayeth), he resolved to make a retract of this postcontract (though it were as surely done, as I have said, as bed and bible could make the same), and to make a certain new protract (which is a continuation of using her for a time) with the widow of Essex. But yet to stop the mouths of outcriers and to bury the Synagogue with some honor (for these two wives of Leicester were merrily and wittily called his Old and New Testaments by a person of great excellency within the realm), he was content to assign to the former a thousand pounds in money with other petty considerations (the pitifullest abused that ever was poor lady) and so betake his limbs to the latter, which latter notwithstanding he so useth (as we see), now confessing, now forswearing, now dissembling the marriage, as he will always yet keep a void place for a new surcontract with any other, when occasion shall require.

Scholar. Now, by my truth, Sir (quoth I), I never heard nor read the like to this in my life, yet have I read much in my time of the carnality and licentiousness of divers outrageous persons in this kind of sin, as namely these whom you have mentioned before: especially the Emperor Heliogabalus, who passed all other and was called Varius, of the variety of filth which he used in this kind of carnality or carnal beastliness. Whose death was, that being at length odious to all men, and so slain by his own soldiers, [he] was drawn through the city upon the ground like a dog and cast into the common privy, with this epitaph: *Hic projectus est indomitae et rabide libidinus catulus*—Here is thrown in the whelp of unruly and raging lust, which epitaph may also one day chance to serve my Lord of Leicester (whom you call the Bearwhelp) if he go forward as he hath begun and die as he deserveth.

But (good Sir) what a compassion is this, that among us Christians, and namely in so well governed and religious a commonwealth as ours is, such a riot should be permitted upon men's wives, in a subject; whereas we read that among the very heathens less offenses than these, in the same kind, were extremely punished in princes themselves, and that not only in the person delinquent alone, but also by extirpation of the whole family for his sake, as appeareth in the example of the Tarquinians among the Romans. And here also in our own realm, we have registered in chronicle how that one King Edwin above six hundred years past was deprived of his kingdom for much less scandalous facts than these.[60]

Gentleman: I remember well the story (quoth the gentleman) and thereby do easily make conjecture what difference there is betwixt those times of old and our days now; seeing then, a crowned prince could not pass unpunished with one or two outrageous acts, whereas now a subject raised up but yesterday from the meaner sort rangeth at his pleasure in all licentiousness, and that with security, void of fear both of God and man. No man's wife can be free from him, whom his fiery lust liketh to abuse, nor their husbands able to resist nor save from his violence if they show dislike or will not yield their consent to his doings. And if I should discover in particular how many good husbands he had plagued in this nature, and for such delights, it were intolerable; for his concupiscence and violence do run jointly together, as in furious beasts we see they are accustomed. Neither holdeth he any rule in his lust besides only the motion and suggestion of his own sensuality. Kindred, affinity, or any other band of consanguinity, religion, honor, or honesty taketh no place in his outrageous appetite. What he best liketh, that he taketh as lawful for the time. So that kinswoman, ally, friend's wife or daughter, or whatsoever female sort besides doth please his eye (I leave out of purpose and for honor sake terms of kindred more near), that must yield to his desire.

The keeping of the mother with two or three of her daughters at once or successively is no more with him than the eating of an hen and her chicken[s] together. There are not (by report) two noblewomen about her Majesty (I speak upon some accompt of them that know much) whom he hath not solicited by potent ways; neither contented with this place of honor, he hath descended to seek pasture among the waiting gentlewomen of her Majesty's Great Chamber, offering more for their allurement than I think Lais did commonly take in Corinth, if three hundred pounds for a night will make up the sum;[61] or if not, yet will he make it up otherwise, having reported himself (so little shame he hath) that he offered to another of higher place an hundred pound lands by the year with as many jewels as most women under her Majesty used in England, which was no mean bait to one that used traffic in such merchandise, she being but the leavings of another man before him,[62] whereof my Lord is nothing squeamish for satisfying of his lust but can be content (as they say) to gather up crumbs when he is hungry, even in the very laundry itself or other place of baser quality.

And albeit the Lord of his great mercy, to do him good, no doubt, if he were revocable, hath laid his hand upon him in some chastisement in this world by giving him a broken belly on both sides of his bowels, whereby misery and putrifaction is threatened to him daily, and to his young son by the widow of Essex (being *filius peccati*) such a strange calamity of the falling sickness in his infancy as well may be a witness of the parents' sin and wickedness and of both their wasted natures in iniquity;[63] yet is this man nothing amended thereby, but according to the custom of all old adulterers is more libidinous at this day than ever before, more given to procure love in others by conjuring, sorcery, and other such means. And albeit for himself, both age and nature spent do somewhat tame him from the act, yet wanteth he not will, as appeareth by the Italian ointment procured not many years past by his surgeon or mountebank of that country, whereby (as they say) he is able to move his flesh at all times, for keeping of his credit, howsoever his inability be otherwise for performance; as also one of his physicians reported to an earl of this land, that his Lordship had a bottle for his bedhead of ten pounds the pint to the same effect. But, my masters, whither are we fallen unadvised? I am ashamed to have made mention of so base filthiness.

Scholar. Not without good cause (quoth I) but that we are here alone and no man heareth us. Wherefore I pray you let us return whereas we left; and when you named my Lord of Leicester's daughter born of the Lady Sheffield in Dudley Castle, there came into my head a pretty story concerning that affair, which now I will recompt (though somewhat out of order), thereby to draw you from the further stirring of this unsavory puddle and foul dunghill whereunto we are slipped by following my Lord somewhat too far in his paths and actions.

Wherefore to tell you the tale as it fell out: I grew acquainted these months past with a certain minister that now is dead and was the same man that was used at Dudley Castle for complement of some sacred ceremonies at the birth of my Lord of Leicester's daughter in that place, and the matter was so ordained by the wily wit of him that had sowed the seed that for the better covering of the harvest and secret delivery of the Lady Sheffield, the good wife of the castle[64] also (whereby Leicester's appointed gossips might without other suspicion have access to the place) should feign herself to be with child, and after long and sore travail (God wot) to be delivered of a cushion (as she was indeed), and a little after a fair coffin was buried with a bundle of clouts in show of a child; and the minister caused to use all accustomed prayers and ceremonies for the solemn interring thereof, for which thing afterward, before his death, he had great grief and remorse of conscience, with no small detestation of the most irreligious device of my Lord of Leicester in such a case.[65]

Lawyer. Here the lawyer began to laugh apace both at the device and at the minister, and said: Now truly, if my Lord's contracts hold no better, but hath so many infirmities, with subtilties and by-places besides, I would be loth that he were married to my daughter, as mean as she is.

Gentleman. But yet (quoth the gentleman), I had rather of the two be his wife for the time than his guest, especially if the Italian surgeon or physician be at hand.

Lawyer. True it is (said the lawyer), for he doth not poison his wives, whereof I somewhat marvel; especially his first wife, I muse why he chose rather to make her away by open violence than by some Italian confortive.[66]

Gentleman. Hereof (said the gentleman) may be divers reasons alleged. First that he was not at that time so skillful in those Italian wares, nor had about him so fit physicians and surgeons for the purpose; nor yet in truth do I think that his mind was so settled then in mischief as it hath been sithence. For you know that men are not desperate the first day, but do enter into wickedness by degrees and with some doubt or staggering of conscience at the beginning. And so he at that time might be desirous to have his wife made away, for that she letted him in his designments, but yet not so stony-hearted as to appoint out the particular manner of her death, but rather to leave that to the discretion of the murderer.

Secondly, it is not also unlikely that he prescribed unto Sir Richard Varney at his going thither that he should first attempt to kill her by poison, and if that took not place, then by any other way to dispatch her howsoever. This I prove by the report of old Doctor Bayley [67] who then lived in Oxford (another manner of man than he who now liveth about my Lord of the same name) and was Professor of the Physic Lecture in the same University. This learned grave man reported for most certain that there was a practice in Cumnor among the conspirators to have poisoned the poor lady a little before she was killed, which was attempted in this order:

They seeing the good lady sad and heavy (as one that well knew by her other handling that her death was not far off) began to persuade her that her disease was abundance of melancholy and other humors, and therefore would needs counsel her to take some potion, which she absolutely refusing to do, as suspecting still the worst, they sent one day (unawares to her) for Doctor Bayley and desired him to persuade her to take some little potion at his hands, and they would send to fetch the same at Oxford upon his prescription, meaning to have added also somewhat of their own for her comfort, as the Doctor upon just causes suspected, seeing their great importunity and the small need which the good lady had of physic; and therefore he flatly denied their request, misdoubting (as he after reported) lest if they had poisoned her under the name of his potion he might after have been hanged for a cover of their sin. Marry, the said Doctor remained well assured that this way taking no place she should not long escape violence, as after ensued. And the thing was so beaten into the heads of the principal men of the University of Oxford, by these and other means—as for that she was found murdered (as all men said) by the crowner's [68] inquest, and for that she being hastily and obscurely buried at Cumnor (which was condemned above as not advisedly done), my good Lord, to make plain to the world the great love he bare to her in her life and what a grief the loss of so virtuous a lady was to his tender heart, would needs have her taken up again and reburied in the University church at Oxford, with great pomp and solemnity—that Doctor Babington, my Lord's chaplain, making the public funeral sermon at her second burial, tript once or twice in his speech by recommending to their memories that virtuous lady so pitifully murdered, instead of so pitifully slain.[69]

A third cause of this manner of the lady's death may be the disposition of my Lord's nature, which is bold and violent where it feareth no resistance (as all cowardly natures are by kind), and where any difficulty or danger appeareth, there more ready to attempt all by art, subtilty, treason, and treachery. And so for that he doubted no great resistance in the poor lady to withstand the hands of them which should offer to break her neck, he durst the bolder attempt the same openly.

But in the men whom he poisoned, for that they were such valiant knights, the most part of them, as he durst as soon have eaten his scabbard as draw his sword in public against them, he was enforced (as all wretched, ireful, and dastardly creatures are) to supplant them by fraud and by other men's hands. As also at other times he hath sought to do unto divers other noble and valiant personages, when he was afeard to meet them in the field as a knight should have done.

His treacheries towards the noble late Earl of Sussex in their many breaches is notorious to all England. As also the bloody practices against divers others.

But as among many, none were more odious and misliked of all men than those against Monsieur Simiers, a stranger and ambassador; whom first he practised to have poisoned (as hath been touched before) and when that device took not place, then he appointed that Robin Tider his man (as after upon his ale bench he confessed) should have slain him at the Blackfriars at Greenwich as he went forth at the garden gate;[70] but missing also of that purpose, for that he found the gentleman better provided and guarded than he expected, he dealt with certain Flushingers and other pirates[71] to sink him at sea with the English gentlemen his favorers that accompanied him at his return into France. And though they missed of this practice also (as not daring to set upon him for fear of some of her Majesty's ships, who to break off this designment attended by special commandment to waft him over in safety), yet the foresaid English gentlemen were holden four hours in chase at their coming back, as Mr. Rawley [Raleigh] well knoweth, being then present, and two of the chasers named Clark and Harris confessed afterward the whole designment.[72]

The Earl of Ormonde in like wise hath often declared, and will avouch it to my Lord of Leicester's face whensoever he shalbe called to the same, that at such time as this man had a quarrel with him and thereby was likely to be enforced to the field (which he trembled to think of), he first sought by all means to get him made away by secret murder, offering five hundred pounds for the doing thereof, and secondly, when that device took no place, he appointed with him the field, but secretly suborning his servant William Killigrew to lie in the way where Ormonde should pass and so to massacre him with a caliver before he came to the place appointed. Which murder though it took no effect, for that the matter was taken up before the day of meeting, yet was Killigrew placed afterward in her Majesty's Privy Chamber by Leicester, for showing his ready mind to do for his master so faithful a service.[73]

Scholar. So faithful a service? (quoth I). Truly, in my opinion, it was but an unfit preferment for so facinorous[74] a fact. And as I would be loth that many of his Italians or other of that art should come nigh about her Majesty's kitchen, so much less would I that many such his bloody champions should be placed by him in her Highness' chamber. Albeit for this gentleman in particular, it may be that with change of his place in service he hath changed also his mind and affection, and received better instruction in the fear of the Lord.

But yet in general I must needs say that it cannot be but prejudicial and exceeding dangerous unto our noble prince and realm that any one man whatsoever (especially such a one as the world taketh this man to be) should grow to so absolute authority and commandry in the Court, as to place about the Princess' person (the head, the heart, the life of the land) whatsoever people liketh him best, and that not upon their deserts towards the prince but towards himself, whose fidelity being more obliged to their advancer than to their sovereign, do serve for watchmen about the same, for the profit of him by whose appointment they were placed. Who by their means casting indeed but nets and chains and invisible bands about that person whom most of all he pretendeth to serve, he shutteth up his prince in a prison most sure, though sweet and senseless.

Neither is this art of aspiring new or strange unto any man that is experienced in affairs of former time, for that it hath been from the beginning of all government a trodden path of all aspirers. In the stories both sacred and profane, foreign and domestical, of all nations, kingdoms, countries, and states, you shall read that such as meant to mount above other and to govern all at their own discretion did lay this for the first ground and principle of their purpose, to possess themselves of all such as were in place about the principal; even as he who intending to hold a great city at his own disposition nor dareth make open war against the same, getteth secretly into his hands or at his devotion all the towns, villages, castles, fortresses, bulwarks, rampires,[75] waters, ways, ports, and passages about the same, and so without drawing any sword against the said city he bringeth the same into bondage to abide his will and pleasure.

This did all these in the Roman Empire who rose from subjects to be great princes and to put down emperors. This did all those in France and other kingdoms who at sundry times have tyrannized their princes. And in our own country the examples are manifest of Vortiger[n], Harold, Henry of Lancaster, Richard of Warwick, Richard of Gloucester, John of Northumberland, and divers others who by this mean specially have pulled down their lawful sovereigns.[76]

And to speak only a word or two of the last, for that he was this man's father, doth not all England know that he first overthrew the good Duke of Somerset by drawing to his devotion the very servants and friends of the said Duke? And afterward, did not he possess himself of the king's own person, and brought him to the end which is known, and before that, to the most shameful disheriting of his own royal sisters; and all this, by possessing first the principal men that were in authority about him?

Wherefore, Sir, if my Lord of Leicester have the same plot in his head (as most men think) and that he meaneth one day to give the same push at the crown by the house of Huntingdon, against all the race and line of King Henry VII in general, which his father gave before him by pretense of the house of Suffolk against the children of King Henry VIII in particular, he wanteth not reason to follow the same means and platform of planting special persons for his purpose about the prince; for surely his father's plot lacked no witty device or preparation, but only that God overthrew it at the instant, as happily he may do this man's also, notwithstanding any diligence that human wisdom can use to the contrary.

Gentleman: To this said the gentleman: That my Lord of Leicester hath a purpose to shoot one day at the diadem by the title of Huntingdon is not a thing obscure in itself, and it shalbe more plainly proved hereafter. But now will I show unto you, for your instruction, how well this man hath followed his father's platform (or rather passed the same) in possessing himself of all her Majesty's servants, friends, and forces to serve his turn at that time for execution, and in the mean space for preparation.

First, in the Privy Chamber, next unto her Majesty's person, the most part are his own creatures (as he calleth them), that is, such as acknowledge their being in that place from him; and the rest he so overruleth either by flattery or fear as none may dare but to serve his turn. And his reign is so absolute in this place (as also in all other parts of the Court) as nothing can pass but by his admission; nothing can be said, done, or signified whereof he is not particularly advertised; no bill, no supplication, no complaint, no suit, no speech can pass from any man to the Princess (except it be from one of the Council) but by his good liking; or if there do, he being admonished thereof (as presently he shall), the party delinquent is sure after to abide the smart thereof. Whereby he holdeth as it were a lock upon the ears of his prince, and the tongues of all her Majesty's servants so surely chained to his girdle as no man dareth to speak any one thing that may offend him, though it be never so true or behoveful for her Majesty to know.

As well appeared in his late marriage with Dame Essex, which albeit it was celebrated twice—first at Killingworth and secondly at Wanstead (in presence of the Earl of Warwick, Lord North, Sir Francis Knollys, and others) and this exactly known to the whole Court, with the very day, the place, the witnesses, and the minister that married them together[77]—yet no man durst open his mouth to make her Majesty privy thereunto until Monsieur Simiers disclosed the same (and thereby incurred his high displeasure), nor yet in many days after for fear of Leicester. Which is a subjection most dishonorable and dangerous to any prince living, to stand at the devotion of his subject what to hear or not to hear of things that pass within his own realm.

And hereof it followeth that no suit can prevail in Court, be it never so mean, except he first be made acquainted therewith and receive not only the thanks, but also be admitted unto a great part of the gain and commodity thereof. Which, as it is a great injury to the suitor, so is it a far more greater to the bounty, honor, and security of the prince, by whose liberality this man feedeth only and fortifieth himself, depriving his sovereign of all grace, thanks, and good will for the same.[78] For which cause also he giveth out ordinarily to every suitor that her Majesty is nigh and parsimonious of herself and very difficile to grant any suit, were it not only upon his incessant solicitation. Whereby he filleth his own purse the more and emptieth the hearts of such as receive benefit from due thanks to their Princess for the suit obtained.[79]

Hereof also ensueth that no man may be preferred in Court (be he otherwise never so well a deserving servant to her Majesty), except he be one of Leicester's faction or followers; none can be advanced, except he be liked and preferred by him; none receive grace, except he stand in his good favor, no one may live in countenance or quiet of life, except he take it, use it, and acknowledge it from him, so as all the favors, graces, dignities, preferments, riches, and rewards which her Majesty bestoweth or the realm can yield must serve to purchase this man private friends and favorers, only to advance his party and to fortify his faction. Which faction if by these means it be great (as indeed it is) you may not marvel, seeing the riches and wealth of so worthy a commonweal do serve him but for a price to buy the same.

Which thing himself well knowing, frameth his spirit of proceeding accordingly. And first, upon confidence thereof is become so insolent and impotent of his ire[80] that no man may bear the same, how justly or injustly soever it be conceived; for albeit he begin to hate a man upon bare surmises only (as commonly it falleth out, ambition being always the mother of suspicion), yet he prosecuteth the same with such implacable cruelty as there is no long abiding for the party in that place. As might be showed by the examples of many whom he hath chased from the Court upon his only displeasure, without other cause, being known to be otherwise zealous Protestants, as Sir Jerome Bowes, Mr. George Scott, and others that we could name.[81]

To this insolency is also joined (as by nature it followeth) most absolute and peremptory dealing in all things whereof it pleaseth him to dispose, without respect either of reason, order, due, right, subordination, custom, conveniency, or the like, whereof notwithstanding princes themselves are wont to have regard in disposition of their matters; as for example, among the servants of the Queen's Majesty's household it is an ancient and most commendable order and custom that when a place of higher room falleth void, he that by succession is next and hath made proof of his worthiness in an inferior place should rise and possess the same (except it be for some extraordinary cause), to the end that no man unexperienced or untried should be placed in the higher rooms the first day to the prejudice of others and disservice of the prince.

Which most reasonable custom this man contemning and breaking at his pleasure, thrusteth into higher rooms any person whatsoever, so he like his inclination or feel his reward, albeit he neither be fit for the purpose nor have been so much as clerk in any inferior office before.

The like he useth out of the Court, in all other places where matters should pass by order, election, or degree; as in the Universities, in election of scholars and heads of houses, in ecclesiastical persons for dignities of church, in officers, magistrates, stewards of lands, sheriffs and knights of the shires, in burgesses of the Parliament, in commissioners, judges, justices of the peace (whereof many in every shire must wear his livery), and all other the like, where this man's will must stand for reason and his letters for absolute laws; neither is there any man, magistrate or commoner, in the realm who dareth not sooner deny their petition of her Majesty's letters upon just causes (for that her Highness is content after to be satisfied with reason) than to resist the commandment of this man's letters, who will admit no excuse or satisfaction but only the execution of his said commandment, be it right or wrong.

Lawyer. To this answered the lawyer: Now verily (Sir), you paint unto me a strange pattern of a perfect potentate in the Court; belike that stranger who calleth our state in his printed book *Leicestrensem rempublicam*, a Leicestrian commonwealth, or the commonwealth of my Lord of Leicester, knoweth much of these matters.[82] But to hold (Sir) still within the Court, I assure you that by considerations which you have laid down I do begin now to perceive that his party must needs be very great and strong within the said Court, seeing that he hath so many ways and means to increase, enrich, and encourage the same, and so strong abilities to tread down his enemies. The common speech of many wanteth not reason, I perceive, which calleth him the heart and life of the Court.

Gentleman: They which call him the heart (said the gentleman) upon a little occasion more would call him also the head, and then I marvel what should be left for her Majesty when they take from her both life, heart, and headship in her own realm? But the truth is that he hath the Court at this day in almost the same case as his father had it in King Edward's days, by the same device (the Lord forbid that ever it come fully to the same state, for then we know what ensued to the principal), and if you will have an evident demonstration of this man's power and favor in that place, call you but to mind the times when her Majesty upon most just and urgent occasions did withdraw but a little her wonted favor and countenance towards him; did not all the Court, as it were, mutiny presently? Did not every man hang the lip, except a few, who afterward paid sweetly for their mirth? Were there not every day new devices sought out, that some should be on their knees to her Majesty; some should weep and put finger in their eyes; other should find out certain covert manner of threatening; other, reasons and persuasions of love; other, of profit; other, of honor; other, of necessity; and all to get him recalled back to favor again? And had her Majesty any rest permitted unto her until she had yielded and granted to the same?

Consider then (I pray you) that if at that time, in his disgrace, he had his faction so fast assured to himself, what hath he now in his prosperity, after so many years of fortification? Wherein by all reason he hath not been negligent, seeing that in policy the first point of good fortification is to make that fort impregnable which once hath been in danger to be lost. Whereof you have an example in Richard Duke of York, in the time of King Henry VI, who being once in the king's hands by his own submission and dismissed again (when for his deserts he should have suffered), provided after that the king should never be able to overreach him the second time, or have him in his power to do him hurt, but made himself strong enough to pull down the other with extirpation of his family.[83]

And this of the Court, household, and chamber of her Majesty. But now if we shall pass from Court to Council we shall find him no less fortified, but rather more, for albeit the providence of God hath been such that in this most honorable assembly there hath not wanted some two or three of the wisest, gravest, and most experienced in our state that have seen and marked this man's perilous proceedings from the beginning (whereof notwithstanding two are now deceased, and their places supplied to Leicester's good liking),[84] yet (alas) the wisdom of these worthy men hath discovered always more than their authorities were able to redress (the other's great power and violence considered); and for the residue of that bench and table, though I doubt not but there be divers who do in heart detest his doings (as there were also no doubt among the Councillors of King Edward who misliked this man's father's attempts, though not so hardy as to contrary the same), yet for most part of the Council present, they are known to be so affected in particular, the one for that he is to him a brother, the other a father, the other a kinsman, the other an ally, the other a fast obliged friend, the other a fellow or follower in faction, as none will stand in the breach against him; none dare resist or encounter his designments; but every man yielding rather to the force of his flow permitteth him to pierce and pass at his pleasure in whatsoever his will is once settled to obtain.

And hereof (were I not stayed for respect of some whom I may not name) I could allege strange examples, not so much in affairs belonging to subjects and to private men (as were the cases of Snowden Forest, [of] Denbigh, of Killingworth, of his fair pastures foully procured by Southam, of the Archbishop of Canterbury, of the Lord Berkeley, of Sir John Throgmorton, of Mr. Robinson, and the like)[85] wherein those of the Council that disliked his doings least dared to oppose themselves to the same, but also in things that appertain directly to the crown and dignity, to the state and commonweal, and to the safety and continuance thereof. It is not secure for any one Councillor or other of authority to take notice of my Lord's errors or misdeeds but with extreme peril of their own ruin.

As for example, in the beginning of the rebellion in Ireland, when my Lord of Leicester was in some disgrace and consequently, as he imagined, but in frail state at home, he thought it not unexpedient for his better assurance to hold some intelligence also that way for all events, and so he did, whereof there was so good evidence and testimony found upon one of the first of accompt that was there slain (as honorable personages of their knowledge have assured me) as would have been sufficient to touch the life of any subject in the land, or in any state Christian, but only my Lord of Leicester, who is a subject without subjection.[86]

For what think you? Durst any man take notice hereof or avouch that he had seen thus much? Durst he that took it in Ireland deliver the same where especially he should have done? Or they who received it in England (for it came to great hands) use it to the benefit of their Princess and country? No, surely; for if it had been but only suspected that they had seen such a thing, it would have been as dangerous unto them as it was to Acteon to have seen Diana and her maidens naked;[87] whose case is so common now in England as nothing more, and so do the examples of divers well declare, whose unfortunate knowledge of too many secrets brought them quickly to unfortunate ends.

For we hear of one Salvatore, a stranger, long used in great mysteries of base affairs and dishonest actions, who afterward (upon what demerit I know not) sustained a hard fortune, for being late with my Lord in his study (well near until midnight, if I be rightly informed), went home to his chamber and the next morning was found slain in his bed.[88] We hear also of one Doughty, hanged in haste by Captain Drake upon the sea, and that by order (as is thought) before his departure out of England, for that he was over-privy to the secrets of this good Earl.[89]

There was also this last summer past one Gates hanged at Tyburn, among others, for robbing of carriers,[90] which Gates had been lately clerk of my Lord's kitchen and had laid out much money of his own (as he said) for my Lord's provision, being also otherwise in so great favor and grace with his Lordship as no man living was thought to be more privy of his secrets than this man, whereupon also it is to be thought that he presumed the rather to commit this robbery (for to such things doth my Lord's good favor most extend), and being apprehended and in danger for the same, he made his recourse to his honor for protection (as the fashion is) and that he might be borne out, as divers of less merit had been by his Lordship in more heinous causes before him.

The good Earl answered his servant and dear privado courteously and assured him for his life, howsoever for utter show or complement the form of law might pass against him. But Gates, seeing himself condemned and nothing now between his head and the halter but the word of the magistrate, which might come in an instant, when it would be too late to send to his Lord, remembering also the small assurance of his said Lord's word by his former dealings towards other men, whereof this man was too much privy, he thought good to solicit his case also by some other of his friends, though not so puissant as his Lord and master; who dealing indeed both diligently and effectually in his affair found the matter more difficult a great deal than either he or they had imagined, for that my Lord of Leicester was not only not his favorer but a great hastener of his death under hand and that with such care, diligence, vehemency, and irresistable means (having the law also on his side) that there was no hope at all of escaping; which thing when Gates heard of he easily believed, for the experience he had of his master's good nature, and said that he always mistrusted the same, considering how much his Lordship was in debt to him and he made privy to his Lordship['s] foul secrets, which secrets he would there presently have uttered in the face of all the world but that he feared torments or speedy death with some extraordinary cruelty if he should so have done, and therefore he disclosed the same only to a gentleman of worship whom he trusted specially, whose name I may not utter for some causes (but it beginneth with H.). And I am in hope ere it be long, by means of a friend of mine, to have a sight of that discourse and report of Gates, which hitherto I have not seen nor ever spake I with the gentleman that keepeth it, though I be well assured that the whole matter passed in substance as I have here recounted it.[91]

Scholar. Whereunto I answered that in good faith it were pity that this relation should be lost, for that it is very like that many rare things be declared therein, seeing it is done by a man so privy to the affairs themselves, wherein also he had been used an instrument.[92]

[*Gentleman:*] I will have it (quoth the gentleman), or else my friends shall fail me, howbeit not so soon as I would, for that he is in the west country that should procure it for me and will not return for certain months, but after I shall see him again I will not leave him until he procure it for me as he hath promised.

[*Scholar.*] Well (quoth I), but what is become of that evidence found in Ireland under my Lord's hand, which no man dare pursue, avouch, or behold?

Gentleman: Truly (said the gentleman), I am informed that it lieth safely reserved in good custody, to be brought forth and avouched whensoever it shall please God so to dispose of her Majesty's heart as to lend an indifferent ear as well to his accusers as to himself in judgment.

Neither must you think that this is strange, nor that the things are few which are in such sort reserved in deck for the time to come, even among great personages and of high calling, for seeing the present state of his power to be such and the tempest of his tyranny to be so strong and boisterous as no man may stand in the rage thereof without peril—for that even from her Majesty herself in the lenity of her princely nature he extorteth what he designeth either by fraud, flattery, false information, request, pretense, or violent importunity to the over-bearing of all whom he meanth to oppress—no marvel then though many even of the best and faithfullest subjects of the land do yield to the present time and do keep silence in some matters that otherwise they would take it for duty to utter.

And in this kind, it is not long sithence a worshipful and wise friend of mine told me a testimony in secret from the mouth of as noble and grave a Councillor as England hath enjoyed these many hundred years, I mean the late Lord Chamberlain,[93] with whom my said friend being alone at his house in London not twenty days before his death, conferred somewhat familiarly about these and like matters, as with a true father of his country and commonwealth; and after many complaints in the behalf of divers who had opened their griefs unto Councillors and saw that no notice would be taken thereof, the said nobleman, turning himself somewhat about from the water (for he sat near his pondside, where he beheld the taking of a pike or carp), said to my friend: It is no marvel (Sir), for who dareth intermeddle himself in my Lord's affairs? I will tell you (quoth he), in confidence between you and me, there is as wise a man and as grave and as faithful a Councillor as England breedeth (meaning thereby the Lord Treasurer) who hath as much in his keeping of Leicester's own handwriting as is sufficient to hang him, if either he durst present the same to her Majesty or her Majesty do justice when it should be presented. But indeed (quoth he), the time permitteth neither of them both, and therefore it is in vain for any man to struggle with him.

These were that noble man's words, whereby you may consider whether my Lord of Leicester be strong this day in Council or no, and whether his fortification be sufficient in that place.

But now if out of the Council we will turn but our eye in the country abroad, we shall find as good fortification also there as we have perused already in Court and Council, and shall well perceive that this man's plot is no fond or indiscreet plot, but excellent well grounded and such as in all proportions hath his due correspondence.[94]

Consider then the chief and principal parts of this land for martial affairs, for use and commodity of armor, for strength, for opportunity, for liberty of the people, as dwelling farthest off from the presence and aspect of their prince, such parts (I say) as are fittest for sudden enterprises without danger of interception, as are the north, the west, the countries of Wales, the islands round about the land, and sundry other places within the same; are they not all at this day at his disposition? Are they not all (by his procurement) in the only hands of his friends and allies, or of such as by other matches have the same complot and purpose with him?

In York is President the man that of all other is fittest for that place, that is, his nearest in affinity, his dearest in friendship, the head of his faction and open competitor of the scepter.[95] In Berwick is Captain his wife's uncle, most assured to himself and Huntingdon as one who at convenient time may as much advance their designments as any one man in England.[96]

In Wales the chief authority from the prince is in his own brother-in-law, [97] but among the people, of natural affection, [it] is in the Earl of Pembroke, who both by marriage of his sister's daughter is made his ally and by dependence is known to be wholly at his disposition.[98] The west part of England is under Bedford, a man wholly devoted to his and the Puritans' faction.[99] In Ireland was governor of late the principal instrument[100] appointed for their purposes, both in respect of his heat and affection toward their designments, as also of some secret discontentment which he hath towards her Majesty and the state present for certain hard speeches and ingrate recompences, as he pretendeth;[101] but indeed for that he is known to be of nature fiery and impatient of stay from seeing that commonwealth on foot which the next competitors for their gain have painted out to him and such others, more pleasant than the Terrestrial Paradise itself.

This then is the Hector, this is the Ajax, appointed for the enterprise when the time shall come. This must be (forsooth) another Richard of Warwick, to gain the crown for Henry IX of the house of York, as the other Richard did put down Henry VI of the house of Lancaster and placed Edward IV, from whom Huntingdon deriveth his title; therefore this man is necessarily to be entertained from time to time (as we see now he is) in some charge and martial action, to the end his experience, power, and credit may grow the more and he be able at the time to have soldiers at his commandment. And for the former charge which [he] held of late in Ireland, as this man had not been called away but for execution of some other secret purpose[102] for advancement of their designments, so be well assured that for the time to come it is to be furnished again with a sure and fast friend to Leicester and to that faction.[103]

In the Isle of Wight I grant that Leicester hath lost a great friend and a trusty servant by the death of Captain Horsey,[104] but yet the matter is supplied by the succession of another no less assured unto him than the former, or rather more, through the band of affinity by his wife.[105] The two islands of Jersey and Guernsey are in the possession of two friends and most obliged dependents. The one, by reason he is exceedingly addicted to the Puritan proceedings;[106] the other, as now being joined unto him by the marriage of Mistress Bess his wife's sister, both daughters to Sir Francis or (at least) to my Lady Knollys, and so become a rival, companion, and brother, who was before (though trusty) yet but his servant.[107]

And these are the chief keys, fortresses, and bulwarks within, without, and about the realm, which my Lord of Leicester possessing (as he doth), he may be assured of the body within; where notwithstanding (as hath been showed) he wanteth no due preparation for strength, having at his disposition (besides all aids and other helps specified before) her Majesty's horse and stable, by interest of his own office; her armor, artillery, and munition, by the office of his brother the Earl of Warwick;[108] The Tower of London and treasure therein, by the dependence of Sir Owen Hopton, his sworn servant, as ready to receive and furnish him with the whole (if occasion served) as one of his predecessors was to receive his father in King Edward's days, for the like effect, against her Majesty and her sister.[109]

And in the city of London itself, what this man at a pinch could do by the help of some of the principal men and chief leaders and (as it were) commanders of the commons there,[110] and by the bestirring of Fleetwood, his mad Recorder,[111] and other such his instruments; as also in all other towns, ports, and cities of importance, by such of his own setting up as he hath placed there to serve his designments, and justices of [the] peace with other, that in most shires do wear his livery and are at his appointment, the simplest man within the realm doth consider.

Whereunto if you add now his own forces and furniture which he hath in Killingworth Castle and other places, as also the forces of Huntingdon in particular, with their friends, followers, allies, and compartners, you shall find that they are not behind in their preparations.

Scholar. For my Lord of Huntingdon's forwardness in the cause (said I), there is no man, I think, which maketh doubt; marry, for his private forces, albeit they may be very good for anything I do know to the contrary (especially at his house within twenty-five miles of Killingworth,[112] where one told me some years past that he had furniture ready for five thousand men), yet do I not think but that they are far inferior to my Lord of Leicester's, who is taken to have excessive store, and that in divers places. And as for the castle last mentioned by you, there are men of good intelligence and of no small judgment who report that in the same he hath well to furnish ten thousand good soldiers of all things necessary both for horse and man, besides all other munition, armor, and artillery (whereof great store was brought thither under pretense of triumph when her Majesty was there and never as yet carried back again),[113] and besides the great abundance of ready coin there laid up (as is said), sufficient for any great exploit to be done within the realm.

And I know that the estimation of this place was such among divers many years ago, as when at a time her Majesty lay dangerously sick and like to die at Hampton Court, a certain gentleman of the Court[114] came unto my Lord of Huntingdon and told him that for so much as he took his Lordship to be next in succession after her Majesty he would offer him a mean of great help for compassing of his purpose after the decease of her Majesty, which was the possession of Killingworth Castle (for at that time these two Earls were not yet very friends, nor confederate together), and that being had, he showed to the Earl the great furniture and wealth which thereby he should possess for pursuit of his purpose.

The proposition was well liked, and the matter esteemed of great importance, and consequently received with many thanks. But yet afterward her Majesty by the good providence of God recovering again letted the execution of the bargain, and my Lord of Huntingdon, having occasion to join amity with Leicester, had more respect of his own commodity than to his friend's security (as commonly in such persons and cases it falleth out) and so discovered the whole device unto him, who forgot not after, from time to time, to plague the deviser by secret means, until he hath brought him to that poor estate as all the world seeth, though many men be not acquainted with the true cause of this his disgrace and bare fortune.

Lawyer. To this answered the lawyer: In good faith (gentlemen), you open great mysteries unto me, which either I knew not or considered not so particularly before, and no marvel, for that my profession and exercise of law restraineth me from much company keeping, and when I happen to be among some that could tell me much herein, I dare not either ask or hear if any of himself begin to talk, lest afterward the speech coming to light I be fetched over the coals (as the proverb is) for the same, under pretense of another thing. But you (who are not suspected for religion) have much greater privilege in such matters both to hear and speak again, which men of mine estate dare not do. Only this I knew before, that throughout all England my Lord of Leicester is taken for *Dominus factotum,* whose excellency above others is infinite, whose authority is absolute, whose commandment is dreadful, whose dislike is dangerous, and whose favor is omnipotent.

And for his will, though it be seldom law, yet always is his power above law, and therefore we lawyers in all cases brought unto us have as great regard to his inclination as astronomers[115] have to the planet dominant, or as seamen have to the North Pole.

For as they that sail do direct their course according to the situation and direction of that star which guideth them at the Pole, and as astronomers who make prognostications do foretell things to come according to the aspect of the planet dominant or bearing rule for the time, so we do guide our client's bark and do prognosticate what is like to ensue of his cause by the aspect and inclination of my Lord of Leicester. And for that reason, as soon as ever we hear a case proposed, our custom is to ask what part my Lord of Leicester is like to favor in the matter (for in all matters lightly[116] of any importance he hath a part) or what may be gathered of his inclination therein, and according to that we give a guess, more or less, what end will ensue.

But this (my masters) is from the purpose, and therefore returning to your former speech again, I do say that albeit I was not privy before to the particular provisions of my Lord and his friends in such and such places, yet seeing him accompted Lord General over all the realm, and to have at his commandment all these several commodities and forces pertaining to her Majesty which you have mentioned before, and so many more as be in the realm and not mentioned by you (for in fine he hath all), I could not but accompt him (as he is) a potent prince of our state, for all furniture needful to defense or offense, or rather the only monarch of our nobility, who hath sufficient of himself to plunge his prince if he should be discontented, especial for his abundance of money (which by the wise is termed the sinours[117] of martial actions), wherein by all men's judgments he is better furnished at this day than ever any subject of our land either hath been heretofore or lightly may be hereafter, both for banks without the realm and stuffed coffers within. Insomuch that being myself in the last Parliament when the matter was moved for the grant of a subsidy, after that one for her Majesty[118] had given very good reasons why her Highness was in want of money and consequently needed the assistance of her faithful subjects therein, another that sat next me of good accompt said in mine ear secretly: These reasons I do well allow and am contented to give my part in money, but yet, for her Majesty's need, I could make answer as one answered once the Emperor Tiberius in the like case and cause: *Abunde ei pecuniam fore, si a liberto suo in societatem reciperetur*—that her Majesty should have money enough if one of her servants would vouchsafe to make her Highness partaker with him, meaning thereby my Lord of Leicester, whose treasure must needs in one respect be greater than that of her Majesty, for that he layeth up whatsoever he getteth and his expenses he casteth upon the purse of his Princess.

Gentleman: For that (said the gentleman), whether he do or no it importeth little to the matter, seeing both that which he spendeth and that he hoardeth is truly and properly his Princess' treasure, and seeing he hath so many and divers ways of gaining, what should he make accompt of his own private expenses? If he lay out one for a thousand, what can that make him the poorer—he that hath so goodly lands, possessions, seignories, and rich offices of his own as he is known to have; he that hath so special favor and authority with the prince as he can obtain whatsoever he listeth to demand; he that hath his part and portion in all suits besides that pass by grace or else (for the most part) are ended by law; he that may chop and change what lands he listeth with her Majesty, despoil them of all their woods and other commodities, and rack them afterward to the uttermost penny, and then return the same so tenter-stretched and bare shorn into her Majesty's hands again by fresh exchange, rent for rent, for other lands never enhanced before;[119] he that possesseth so many gainful licenses to himself alone, of wine, oils, currants, cloth, velvets, with his new office for license of alienation,[120] most pernicious unto the commonwealth as he useth the same, with many other the like, which were sufficient to enrich whole towns, corporations, countries, and commonwealths; he that hath the art to make gainful to himself every offense, displeasure, and falling out of her Majesty with him, and every angry countenance cast upon him; he that hath his share in all offices of great profit and holdeth an absolute monopoly of the same; he that disposeth at his will the ecclesiastical livings of the realm, maketh bishops none but such as will do reason or of his chaplains whom he listeth and retaineth to himself so much of the living as liketh him best; he that sweepeth away the glebe from so many benefices throughout the land and compoundeth with the parson for the rest; he that so scoureth the University and colleges where he is Chancellor and selleth both headships and scholars' places and all other offices, rooms, and dignities that by art or violence may yield money; he that maketh title to what land or other thing he please and driveth the parties to compound for the same; he that taketh in whole forests, commons, woods, and pastures to himself, compelling the tenants to pay him new rent and what he cesseth; he that vexeth and oppresseth whomsoever he list, taketh from any what he list, and maketh his own claim, suit, and end as he list; he that selleth his favor with the prince, both abroad in foreign countries and at home, and setteth the price thereof what himself will demand; he that hath and doth all this, and besides this hath infinite presents daily brought unto him of great value, both in jewels, plate, all kind of furniture, and ready coin, this man (I say) may easily bear his own expenses and yet lay up sufficiently also to weary his prince when needs shall require.

Lawyer. You have said much, Sir (quoth the lawyer), and such matter as toucheth nearly both her Majesty and the commonwealth, and yet, in my conscience, if I were to plead at the bar for my Lord, I could not tell which of all these members to deny. But for that which you mention in the last part, of his gaining by her Majesty's favor both at home and abroad: touching his home gain it is evident, seeing all that he hath is gotten only by the opinion of her Majesty's favor towards him, and many men do repair unto him with fat presents rather for that they suppose he may by his favor do them hurt if he feel not their reward than for that they hope he will labor anything in their affairs.

You remember (I doubt not) the story of him that offered his prince a great yearly rent to have but this favor only, that he might come every day in open audience and say in his ear God save your Majesty, assuring himself that by the opinion of confidence and secret favor which hereby the people would conceive to be in the prince towards him, he should easily get up his rent again doubletold. Wherefore my Lord of Leicester, receiving daily from her Majesty greater tokens of grace and favor than this, and himself being no evil merchant to make his own bargain for the best of his commodities, cannot but gain exceedingly at home by his favor.

And for his lucre abroad upon the same cause I leave to other men to conceive what it may be sithence the beginning of her Majesty's reign; the times whereof and condition of all Christendom hath been such as all the princes and potentates round about us have been constrained at one time or other to sue to her Highness for aid, grace, or favor, in all which suits men use not to forget (as you know) the parties most able by their credit to further or let the same.

In particular only this I can say, that I have heard of sundry Frenchmen that at such time as the treaty was between France and England for the redelivery of Calais unto us again in the first year of her Majesty's reign that now is, when the Frenchmen were in great distress and misery and King Philip refused absolutely to make peace with them except Calais were restored to England (whither for that purpose he had now delivered the French hostages), the Frenchmen do report (I say) that my Lord of Leicester stood them in great stead at that necessity, for his reward (which you may well imagine was not small for a thing of such importance), and became a suitor that peace might be concluded with the release of Calais to the French, which was one of the most impious facts (to say the truth) that ever could be devised against his commonwealth.[121]

Gentleman: A small matter in him (said the gentleman), for in this he did no more but as Christ said of the Jews, that they filled up the measure of their fathers' sins. And so if you read the story of King Edward's time you shall find it most evident that this man's father before him sold Boulogne to the French by like treachery. For it was delivered up upon composition, without necessity or reason, the 25 of April in the fourth year of King Edward VI, when he (I mean Duke Dudley) had now put in the Tower the Lord Protector and thrust out of the Council whom he listed, as namely the Earls of Arundel and Southampton, and so invaded the whole government himself, to sell, spoil, and dispose at his pleasure.[122] Wherefore this is but natural to my Lord of Leicester by descent to make merchandise of the state, for his grandfather Edmund also was such a kind of copesman.[123]

Lawyer. An evil race of merchants for the commonwealth (quoth the lawyer), but yet, Sir, I pray you (said he), expound unto me somewhat more at large the nature of these licenses which you named, as also the changing of lands with her Majesty, if you can set it down any plainer, for they seem to be things of excessive gain, especially his way of gaining by offending her Majesty or by her Highness' offense towards him, for it seemeth to be a device above all skill or reason.

[*Gentleman:*] Not so (quoth the gentleman), for you know that every falling out must have an atonement again, whereof he being sure by the many and puissant means of his friends in Court, as I have showed before, who shall not give her Majesty rest until it be done, then for this atonement, and in perfect reconciliation on her Majesty's part, she must grant my Lord some suit or other which he will have always ready provided for that purpose, and this suit shall be well able to reward his friends that labored for his reconcilement and leave also a good remainder for himself. And this is now so ordinary a practice with him as all the realm observeth the same and disdaineth that her Majesty should be so unworthily abused. For if her Highness fall not out with him as often as he desireth to gain this way, then he picketh some quarrel or other to show himself discontented with her, so that one way or other this gainful reconciliation must be made, and that often, for his commodity. The like art he exerciseth in inviting her

Majesty to his banquets and to his houses, where if she come she must grant him in suits ten times so much as the charges of all amount unto; so that Robin playeth the broker in all his affairs and maketh the uttermost penny of her Majesty every way.

Now for his change of lands, I think I have been reasonable plain before, yet for your fuller satisfaction, you shall understand his further dealing therein to be in this sort. Besides the good lands and of ancient possession to the crown procured at her Majesty's hand and used as before was declared, he useth the same trick for his worst lands that he possesseth any way, whether they come to him by extort means and plain oppression, or through maintenance and broken titles, or by cozenage of simple gentlemen to make him their heir,[124] or by what hard title or unhonest means soever (for he practiceth store of such and thinketh little of the reckoning), after he hath tried them likewise to the uttermost touch and letten them out to such as shall gain but little by the bargain, then goeth he and changeth the same with her Majesty for the best lands he can pick out of the crown, to the end that hereby he may both enforce her Majesty to the defense of his bad titles and himself fill his coffers with the fines and uttermost commodity of both the lands.

His licenses do stand thus: first he got license for certain great numbers of cloths to be transported out of this land, which might have been an undoing to the merchant subject if they had not redeemed the same with great sums of money, so that it redounded to great damage of all occupied about that kind of commodity.[125] After that he had the grant for carrying over of barrel staves and of some other such like wares. Then procured he a monopoly for bringing in of sweet wines, oils, currants, and the like, the gain whereof is inestimable.[126] He had also the forfeit of all wine that was to be drawn above the old ordinary price, with license to give authority to sell above that price, wherein Captain Horsey was his instrument;[127] by which means it is incredible what treasure and yearly rent was gathered of the vintners throughout the land.

To this add now his license of silks and velvets, which only were enough to enrich the Mayor and aldermen of London if they were all decayed (as often I have heard divers merchants affirm). And his license of alienation of lands, which (as in part I have opened before) serveth him not only to excessive gain, but also for an extreme scourge wherewith to plague whom he please in the realm. For seeing that without this license, no man can buy, sell, pass, or alienate any land that any ways may be drawn to that tenure as holden in chief of the prince (as commonly now most land may), he calleth into question whatsoever liketh him best, be it never so clear, and under this color not only enricheth himself without all measure, but revengeth himself also where he will, without all order.

Lawyer. Here the lawyer stood still a pretty while, biting his lip as he were astonished, and then said: Verily, I have not heard so many and so apparent things or so odious of any man that ever lived in our commonwealth. And I marvel much of my Lord of Leicester, that his grandfather's fortune doth not move him much, who lost his head in the beginning of King Henry VIII's days for much less and fewer offenses in the same kind committed in the time of King Henry VII; for he was thought to be the inventor of these poolings[128] and molestations wherewith the people were burdened in the later days of the said king. And yet had he great pretense of reason to allege for himself, in that these exactions were made to the king's use and not to his (albeit no doubt but his own gain was also there).[129] Mr. Stow writeth in his *Chronicle* that in the time of his imprisonment in the Tower he wrote a notable book entitled *The Tree of Commonwealth*, which book the said Stow saith that he hath delivered to my Lord of Leicester many years gone.[130] And if the said book be so notable as Mr. Stow affirmeth, I marvel that his Lordship in so many years doth not publish the same for the glory of his ancestors.

Gentleman: It may be (said the gentleman) that the secrets therein contained be such as it seemeth good to my Lord to use them only himself and to gather the fruit of that tree into his own house alone. For if the tree of the commonwealth in Edmund Dudley's book be the prince and his race, and the fruits to be gathered from that tree be riches, honors, dignities, and preferments, then no doubt but as the writer Edmund was cunning therein, so have his two followers John and Robert well studied and practiced the same, or rather have exceeded and far passed the author himself.[131] The one of them gathering so eagerly and with such vehemency as he was like to have broken down the main boughs for greediness; the other yet plucking and heaping so fast to himself and his friends as it is and may be most justly doubted that when they have cropped all they can from the tree left them by their father Edmund (I mean the race of King Henry VII), then will they pluck up the stem itself by the roots as unprofitable and pitch in his place another trunk (that is, the line of Huntingdon) that may begin to feed anew with fresh fruits again and so for a time content their appetites, until of gatherers they may become trees (which is their final purpose) to feed themselves at their own discretion.

And howsoever this be, it cannot be denied but that Edmund Dudley's brood have learned by this book and by other means to be more cunning gatherers than ever their first progenitor was, that made the book. First, for that he made profession to gather to his prince (though wickedly), and these men make demonstration that they have gathered for themselves, and that with much more iniquity. Secondly, for that Edmund Dudley, though he got himself near about the tree, yet was he content to stand on the ground and to serve himself from the tree as commodity was offered, but his children, not esteeming that safe gathering, will needs mount aloft upon the tree to pull, crop, and rifle at their pleasure. And as in this second point the son John Dudley was more subtile than Edmund the father, so in a third point the nephew[132] Robert Dudley is more crafty than they both [were]. For that, he seeing the evil success of those two that went before him, he hath provided to gather so much in convenient time and to make himself therewith so fat and strong (wherein the other two failed), as he will never be in danger more to be called to any accompt for the same.

Lawyer. In good faith, Sir (quoth the lawyer), I thank you heartily for this pleasant discourse upon Edmund Dudley's tree of commonwealth. And by your opinion, my Lord of Leicester is the most learned of all his kindred and a very cunning logicianer indeed, that can draw for himself so commodious conclusions out of the perilous premises of his progenitors.

Gentleman. No marvel (quoth the gentleman), for that his Lordship is Master of Art in Oxford and Chancellor besides of the same University, where he hath store (as you know) of many fine wits and good logicianers at his commandment and where he learneth not only the rules and art of cunning gathering, but also the very practice (as I have touched before), seeing there is no one college or other thing of commodity within that place wherehence he hath not pulled whatsoever was possibly to be gathered either by art or violence.

Scholar. Touching Oxford (said I), for that I am an University man myself and have both experience of Cambridge and good acquaintance with divers students of the other University, I can tell you enough, but in fine all tendeth to this conclusion, that by his Chancellorship is cancelled almost all hope of good in that University,[133] and by his protection it is like soon to come to destruction. And surely if there were no other thing to declare the odds and difference betwixt him and our Chancellor[134] (whom he cannot bear, for that every way he seeth him to pass him in all honor and virtue), it were sufficient to behold the present state of the two Universities whereof they are heads and governors.

For our own, I will not say much, lest I might perhaps seem partial, but let the thing speak for itself. Consider the fruit of the garden, and thereby you may judge of the gardener's diligence. Look upon the bishoprics, pastorships, and pulpits of England and see whence principally they have received their furniture for advancement of the gospel. And on the contrary side, look upon the seminaries of Papistry at Rome and Rheims, upon the colleges of Jesuits and other companies of Papists beyond the seas, and see wherehence they are especially fraught.[135]

The priests and Jesuits here executed within the land and other that remain either in prison or abroad in corners, are they not all (in a manner) of that University? I speak not to the disgrace of any good that remain there or that have issued out thence into the Lord's vineyard, but for the most part there, of this our time, have they not either gone beyond the seas, or left their places for discontentment in religion, or else become servingmen, or followed the bare name of law or physic, without profiting greatly therein or furthering the service of God's Church or their commonwealth?

And wherehence (I pray you) ensueth all this but by reason that the chief governor thereof is an atheist himself and useth the place only for gain and spoil? For herehence it cometh that all good order and discipline is dissolved in that place, the fervor of study extinguished, the public lectures abandoned (I mean of the more part), the taverns and ordinary tables frequented, the apparel of students grown monstrous, and the statutes and good ordinance both of the University and of every college and hall in private broken and infringed at my Lord's good pleasure, without respect either of oath, custom, or reason to the contrary. The heads and officers are put in and out at his only discretion, and the scholars' places either sold or disposed by his letters or by these of his servants and followers; nothing can be had there now without present money; it is as common buying and selling of places in that University as of horses in Smithfield, whereby the good and virtuous are kept out and companions thrust in, fit to serve his Lordship afterward in all affairs that shall occur.[136]

And as for leases of farms, woods, pastures, parsonages, benefices, or the like, which belong any way to any part of the University to let or bestow, these his Lordship and his servants have so fleeced, shorn, and scraped already that there remaineth little to feed upon hereafter, albeit he want not still his spies and intelligencers in the place to advertise him from time to time when any little new morsel is offered. And the principal instruments which for this purpose he hath had there before this have been two physicians, Bayley and Culpepper, both known Papists a little while ago but now just of Galen's religion and so much the fitter for my Lord's humor;[137] for his Lordship doth always covet to be furnished with certain chosen men about him, for divers affairs, as these two Galenists for agents in the University, Dee and Allen (two atheists) for figuring and conjuring,[138] Julio the Italian and Lopez the Jew for poisoning and for the art of destroying children in women's bellies,[139] Verneys for murdering, Digbys for bawds,[140] and the like in other occupations which his Lordship exerciseth.

Wherefore to return to the speech where we began, most clear it is that my Lord of Leicester hath means to gain and gather also by the

University as well as by the country abroad. Wherein (as I am told) he beareth himself so absolute a lord as if he were their king and not their Chancellor; nay, far more than if he were the general and particular founder of all the colleges and other houses of the University, no man daring to contrary or interrupt the least word or signification of his will but with his extreme danger, which is a proceeding more fit for Phalaris the Tyrant[141] or some governor in Tartary than for a Chancellor of a learned University.

Lawyer. To this answered the lawyer: For my Lord's wrath towards such as will not stand to his judgment and opinion I can myself be a sufficient witness, who, having had often occasion to deal for composition of matters betwixt his Lordship and others, have seen by experience that always they have sped best who stood least in contention with him, whatsoever their cause were. For as a great and violent river, the more it is stopped or contraried, the more it riseth and swelleth big and in the end dejecteth with more force the thing that made resistance, so his Lordship, being the great and mighty potentate of this realm and accustomed now to have his will in all things, cannot bear to be crossed or resisted by any man, though it were in his own necessary defense.

Hereof I have seen examples, in the causes of Snowden Forest in Wales, of Denbigh, of Killingworth, of Drayton, and others, where the parties that had interest or thought themselves wronged had been happy if they had yielded at the first to his Lordship's pleasure without further question, for then had they escaped much trouble, charges, displeasure, and vexation which by resistance they incurred to their great ruin (and loss of life to some,)[142] and in the end were fain also to submit themselves unto his will with far worse conditions than in the beginning were offered unto them, which thing was pitiful indeed to behold, but yet such is my Lord's disposition.

Gentleman: A noble disposition (quoth the gentleman), that I must give him my coat if he demand the same, and that quickly also, for fear lest if I stagger or make doubt thereof he compel me to yield both coat and doublet in penance of my stay. I have read of some such tyrants abroad in the world; marry, their end was always according to their life, as it is very like that it wilbe also in this man, for that there is small hope of his amendment and God passeth not over commonly such matters unpunished in this life as well as in the life to come.

But I pray you, Sir, seeing mention is now made of the former oppressions so much talked of throughout the realm, that you will take the pains to explain the substance thereof unto me, for albeit in general every man doth know the same and in heart do detest the tyranny thereof, yet we abroad in the country do not understand it so well and distinctly as you that be lawyers, who have seen and understood the whole process of the same.

Lawyer. The case of Killingworth and Denbigh (said the Lawyer) are much alike in matter and manner of proceeding, though different in time, place, and importance. For that the lordship of Denbigh in North Wales being given unto him by her Majesty a great while ago[143] at the beginning of his rising (which is a lordship of singular great importance in that country, having, as I have heard, well near two hundred worshipful gentlemen freeholders to the same), the tenants of the place, considering the present state of things and having learned the hungry disposition of their new lord, made a common purse of a thousand pounds to present him withal at his first entrance. Which though he received (as he refuseth nothing), yet accompted he the sum of small effect for satisfaction of his appetite, and therefore applied himself not only to make the uttermost that he could by leases and such like ways of commodity, but also would needs enforce the freeholders to raise their old rent of the lordship from two hundred and fifty pounds a year or thereabouts (at which rate he had received the same in gift from her Majesty) unto eight or nine hundred pounds by the year. For that he had found out (forsooth) an old record (as he said) whereby he could prove that in ancient time long past that lordship had yielded so much old rent, and therefore he would now enforce the present tenants to make up so much again upon their lands, which they thought was against all reason for them to do; but my Lord perforce would have it so and in the end compelled them to yield to his will, to the impoverishing of all the whole country about.[144]

The like proceeding he used with the tenants about Killingworth, where he, receiving the said lordship and castle from the prince in gift of twenty-four pounds yearly rent or thereabout,[145] hath made it now better than five hundred by [the] year, by an old record also, found by great fortune in the hole of a wall as is given out (for he hath singular good luck always in finding out records for his purpose); by virtue whereof he hath taken from the tenants round about their lands, woods, pastures, and commons to make himself parks, chases, and other commodities therewith, to the subversion of many a good family which was maintained there before this devourer set foot in that country.

But the matter of Snowden Forest doth pass all the rest both for cunning and cruelty, the tragedy whereof was this: he had learned by his intelligencers abroad (whereof he hath great store in every part of the realm) that there was a goodly ancient forest in North Wales which hath almost infinite borderers about the same, for it lieth in the midst of the country, beginning at the hills of Snowden (whereof it hath his name) in Carnarvonshire and reacheth every way towards divers other shires. When my Lord heard of this, he entered presently into the conceit of a singular great prey and, going to her Majesty, signified that her Highness was oftentimes abused by the encroaching of such as dwelt upon her forests, which was necessary to be restrained, and therefore beseeched her Majesty to bestow upon him the encroachments only which he should be able to find out upon the forest of Snowden, which was granted.[146]

And thereupon he chose out commissioners fit for the purpose and sent them into Wales with the like commission as a certain Emperor was wont to give his magistrates when they departed from him to govern, as Suetonius writeth: *Scitis quid velim, et quibus opus habeo*[147]— you know what I would have and what I have need of. Which recommendation these commissioners taking to heart, omitted no diligence in execution of the same, and so going into Wales, by such means as they used of setting one man to accuse another, brought quickly all the country round about in three or four shires within the compass of forest ground and so entered upon the same for my Lord of Leicester. Whereupon, when the people were amazed and expected what order my Lord himself would take therein, his Lordship was so far off from refusing any part of that which his commissioners had presented and offered him as he would yet further stretch the forest beyond the sea into the Isle of Anglesey, and make that also within his compass and bounder.

Which when the commonalty saw, and that they profited nothing by their complaining and crying out of this tyranny, they appointed to send some certain number of themselves to London to make supplication to the prince, and so they did, choosing out for that purpose a dozen gentlemen and many more of the commons of the country of Lleyn to deal for the whole. Who coming to London and exhibiting a most humble supplication to her Majesty for redress of their oppression, received an answer by the procurement of my Lord of Leicester that they should have justice if the commonalty would return home to their houses and the gentlemen remain there to solicit the cause. Which as soon as they had yielded unto, the gentlemen were all taken and cast into prison, and there kept for a great space, and afterward were sent down to Ludlow (as the place most eminent of all these countries), there to wear papires of perjury[148] and receive other punishments of infamy for their complaining; which punishments notwithstanding, afterward upon great suit of the parties and their friends, were turned into great fines of money, which they were constrained to pay and yet besides to agree also with my Lord of Leicester for their own lands, acknowledging the same to be his and so to buy it of him again.

Whereby not only these private gentlemen but all the whole country thereabout was and is (in a manner) utterly undone. And the participation of this injury reacheth so far and wide and is so general in these parts as you shall scarce find a man that cometh from that coast who feeleth not the smart thereof, being either impoverished, beggared, or ruinated thereby.

Whereby I assure you that the hatred of all that country is so universal and vehement against my Lord as I think never thing created by God was so odious to that nation as the very name of my Lord of Leicester is. Which his Lordship well knowing, I doubt not but that he will take heed how he go thither to dwell or send thither his posterity.[149]

Gentleman: For his posterity (quoth the gentleman), I suppose he hath little cause to be solicitous, for that God himself taketh care commonly that goods and honors so gotten and maintained as his be shall never trouble the third heir. Marry, for himself, I confess (the matter standing as you say) that he hath reason to forbear that country and to leave off his building begun at Denbigh, as I hear say he hath done.[150] For that the universal hatred of a people is a perilous matter. And if I were in his Lordship's case, I should often think of the end of Nero, who, after all his glory, upon fury of the people was adjudged to have his head thrust into a pillory and so to be beaten to death with rods and thwongs.[151]

Or rather I should fear the success of Vitellius, the third Emperor after Nero, who for his wickedness and oppression of the people was taken by them at length, when fortune began to fail him, and led out of his palace naked, with hooks of iron fastened in his flesh, and so drawn through the city with infamy, where, loaden in the streets with filth and ordure cast upon him and a prick put under his chin to the end he should not look down or hide his face, [he] was brought to the bank of Tiber and there, after many hundred wounds received, was cast into the river.[152] So implacable a thing is the furor of a multitude when it is once stirred and hath place of revenge. And so heavy is the hand of God upon tyrants in this world, when it pleaseth his divine Majesty to take revenge of the same.

I have read in Leander, in his description of Italy,[153] how that in Spoleto (if I be not deceived), the chief city of the country of Umbria, there was a strange tyrant who in the time of his prosperity contemned all men and forbare to injury no man that came within his claws, esteeming himself sure enough for ever being called to render accompt in this life, and for the next he cared little. But God upon the sudden turned upsidedown the wheel of his felicity and cast him into the people's hands, who took him and bound his naked body upon a plank in the market place, with a fire and iron tongs by him, and then made proclamation that, seeing this man was not otherwise able to make satisfaction for the public injuries that he had done, every private person annoyed by him should come in order and with the hot burning tongs there ready should take of his flesh so much as was correspondent to the injury received, as indeed they did until the miserable man gave up the ghost, and after too, as this author writeth.

But to the purpose: seeing my Lord careth little for such examples and is become so hardy now as he maketh no accompt to injury and oppress whole countries and commonalties together, it shalbe bootless to speak of his proceedings towards particular men, who have not so great strength to resist as a multitude hath. And yet I can assure you that there are so many and so pitiful things published daily of his tyranny in this kind as do move great compassion towards the party that do suffer and horror against him who shameth not daily to offer such injury.

As for example, whose heart would not bleed to hear the case before mentioned of Mr. Robinson of Staffordshire, a proper young gentleman and well given both in religion and other virtues. Whose father died at Newhaven in her Majesty's service under this man's brother the Earl of Warwick and recommended at his death this his eldest son to the special protection of Leicester and his brother, whose servant also this Robinson hath been from his youth upward and spent the most of his living in his service. Yet notwithstanding all this, when Robinson's lands were entangled with a certain Londoner upon interest for his former maintenance in their service, whose title my Lord of Leicester (though craftily, yet not covertly) under Ferris his cloak[154] had gotten to himself, he ceased not to pursue the poor gentleman even to imprisonment, arraignment, and sentence of death, for greediness of the said living; together with the vexation of his brother-in-law Mr. Harcourt and all other his friends, upon pretense, forsooth, that there was a man slain by Robinson's party in defense of his own possession against Leicester's intruders that would by violence break into the same.[155]

What shall I speak of others, whereof there would be no end? As of his dealing with Mr. Richard Lee for his manor of Hook Norton (if I fail not in the name);[156] with Mr. Lodovick Greville, by seeking to bereave him of all his living at once if the drift had taken place;[157] with George Whitney, in the behalf of Sir Henry Lee, for enforcing him to forgo the Controllership of Woodstock which he holdeth by patent from King Henry VII?[158] With my Lord Berkeley, whom he enforced to yield up his lands to his brother Warwick which his ancestors had held quietly for almost two hundred years together?[159]

What shall I say of his intolerable tyranny upon the last Archbishop of Canterbury for Doctor Julio his sake, and that in so foul a matter?[160] Upon Sir John Throgmorton, whom he brought pitifully to his grave before his time by continual vexations for a piece of faithful service done by him to his country and to all the line of King Henry against this man's father in King Edward and Queen Mary's days?[161] Upon divers of the Lanes, for one man's sake of that name before mentioned, that offered to take Killingworth Castle? Upon some of the Giffords and other for Throgmorton's sake[162] (for that is also his Lordship's disposition, for one man's cause whom he brooketh not to plague a whole generation that any way pertaineth or is allied to the same)? His endless persecuting of Sir Drew Drury and many other courtiers both men and women?[163] All these (I say) and many others who daily suffer injuries, rapines, and oppressions at his hands throughout the realm, what should it avail to name them in this place, seeing neither his Lordship careth anything for the same, neither the parties aggrieved are like to attain any least release of affliction thereby, but rather double oppression for their complaining.

Wherefore, to return again whereas we began, you see by this little who and how great and what manner of man my Lord of Leicester is this day in the state of England. You see and may gather in some part by that which hath been spoken his wealth, his strength, his cunning, his disposition. His wealth is excessive in all kind of riches for a private man and must needs be much more than anybody lightly can imagine, for the infinite ways he hath had of gain so many years together. His strength and power is absolute and irresistable, as hath been showed, both in Chamber, Court, Council, and country. His cunning in plotting and fortifying the same, both by force and fraud, by mines and countermines, by trenches, bulwarks, flankers, and rampires, by friends, enemies, allies, servants, creatures, and dependents, or any other that may serve his turn, is very rare and singular. His disposition to cruelty, murder, treason, and tyranny, and by all these to supreme sovereignty over other, is most evident and clear. And then judge you whether her Majesty that now reigneth (whose life and prosperity the Lord in mercy long preserve) have not just cause to fear in respect of these things only, if there were no other particulars to prove his aspiring intent besides?

Lawyer. No doubt (quoth the lawyer) but these are great matters in the question of such a cause as is a crown. And we have seen by example that the least of these four which you have here named, or rather some little branch contained in any of them, hath been sufficient to found just suspicion, distrust, or jealousy in the heads of most wise princes towards the proceedings of more assured subjects than my Lord of Leicester in reason may be presumed to be. For that the safety of a state and prince standeth not only in the readiness and ability of resisting open attempts when they shall fall out, but also (and that much more, as statists[164] write) in a certain provident watchfulness, of preventing all possibilities and likelihoods of danger or suppression, for that no prince commonly will put himself to the courtesy of another man (be he never so obliged) whether he shall retain his crown or no, seeing the cause of a kingdom acknowledgeth neither kindred, duty, faith, friendship, nor society.

I know not whether I do expound and declare myself well or no, but my meaning is that whereas every prince hath two points of assurance from his subject, the one in that he is faithful and lacketh will to annoy his sovereign, the other for that he is weak and wanteth ability to do the same, the first is always of more importance than the second and consequently more to be eyed and observed in policy, for that our will may be changed at our pleasure but not our ability.

Considering then upon that which hath been said and specified before, how that my Lord of Leicester hath possessed himself of all the strength, powers, and sinews of the realm, hath drawn all to his own direction, and hath made his party so strong as it seemeth not resistable, you have great reason to say that her Majesty may justly conceive some doubt, for that if his will were according to his power most assured it is that her Majesty were not in safety.

Scholar. Say not so, good Sir (quoth I), for in such a case truly I would repose little upon his will, which is so many ways apparent to be most insatiable of ambition. Rather would I think that as yet his ability serveth not, either for time, place, force, or some other circumstance, than that any part of good will should want in him, seeing that not only his desire of sovereignty but also his intent and attempt to aspire to the same is sufficiently declared (in my conceit) by the very particulars of his power and plots already set down. Which if you please to have the patience to hear a scholar's argument, I will prove by a principle of our philosophy.

For if it be true which Aristotle saith, there is no agent so simple in the world which worketh not for some final end (as the bird buildeth not her nest but to dwell and hatch her young ones therein), and not only this, but also that the same agent doth always frame his work according to the proportion of his intended end (as when the fox or badger maketh a wide earth or den it is a sign that he meaneth to draw thither great store of prey); then must we also in reason think that so wise and politic an agent as is my Lord of Leicester for himself wanteth not his end in these plottings and preparations of his, I mean an end proportionable in greatness to his preparations. Which end can be no less nor meaner than supreme sovereignty, seeing his provision and furniture do tend that way and are in every point fully correspondent to the same.

What meaneth his so diligent besieging of the Princess' person? His taking up the ways and passages about her? His insolency in Court? His singularity in the Council? His violent preparation of strength abroad? His enriching of his complices? The banding of his faction, with the abundance of friends everywhere? What do these things signify (I say) and so many other, as you have well noted and mentioned before, but only his intent and purpose of supremacy? What did the same things protend[165] in times past in his father but even that which now they protend in the son? Or how should we think that the son hath another meaning in the very same actions than had his father before him, whose steps he followeth?

I remember I have heard oftentimes of divers ancient and grave men in Cambridge how that in King Edward's days the Duke of Northumberland this man's father was generally suspected of all men to mean indeed as afterward he showed, especially when he had once joined with the house of Suffolk and made himself a principal of that faction by marriage. But yet for that he was potent, and protested everywhere and by all occasions his great love, duty, and special care, above all others, that he bare towards his prince and country, no man durst accuse him openly until it was too late to withstand his power (as commonly it falleth out in such affairs), and the like is evident in my Lord of Leicester's actions now (albeit to her Majesty I doubt not but that he will pretend and protest, as his father did to her brother), especially now after his open association with the faction of Huntingdon, which no less impugneth under this man's protection the whole line of Henry VII for right of the crown than the house of Suffolk did under his father the particular progeny of King Henry VIII.

Gentleman: Nay, rather much more (quoth the gentleman), for that I do not read in King Edward's reign (when the matter was in plotting notwithstanding) that the house of Suffolk durst ever make open claim to the next succession. But now the house of Hastings is become so confident upon the strength and favor of their fautors[166] as they dare both plot, practice, and pretend all at once, and fear not to set out their title in every place whereas they come.

Lawyer: And do they not fear the statute (said the lawyer), so rigorous in this point as it maketh the matter treason to determine of titles?[167]

Gentleman: No, they need not (quoth the gentleman), seeing their party is so strong and terrible as no man dare accuse them; seeing also they well know that the procurement of that statute was only to endanger or stop the mouths of the true successors whiles themselves in the mean space went about underhand to establish their own ambushment.

Lawyer: Well (quoth the lawyer), for the pretense of my Lord of Huntingdon to the crown I will not stand with you, for that it is a matter sufficiently known and seen throughout the realm. As also that my Lord of Leicester is at this day a principal favorer and patron of that cause, albeit some years past he were an earnest adversary and enemy to the same. But yet I have heard some friends of his in reasoning of these matters deny stoutly a point or two which you have touched here, and do seem to believe the same.

And that is, first, that howsoever my Lord of Leicester do mean to help his friend when time shall serve, yet pretendeth he nothing to the crown himself. The second is that whatsoever may be meant for the title, or compassing the crown after her Majesty's death, yet nothing is intended during her reign. And of both these points they allege reasons.

As for the first, that my Lord of Leicester is very well known to have no title to the crown himself, either by descent in blood, alliance, or otherways. For the second, that his Lordship hath no cause to be a malcontent in the present government nor hope for more preferment if my Lord of Huntingdon were king tomorrow next than he receiveth now at her Majesty's hands, having all the realm (as hath been showed) at his own disposition.

Gentleman: For the first (quoth the gentleman), whether he mean the crown for himself or for his friend it importeth not much, seeing both ways it is evident that he meaneth to have all at his own disposition. And albeit now for the avoiding of envy he give it out, as a crafty fox, that he meaneth not but to run with other men and to hunt with Huntingdon and other hounds in the same chase, yet is it not unlike but that he will play the Bear when he cometh to dividing of the prey and will snatch the best part to himself. Yea, and these selfsame persons of his train and faction whom you call his friends, though in public, to excuse his doings and to cover the whole plot, they will and must deny the matters to be so meant, yet otherwise they both think, hope, and know the contrary and will not stick in secret to speak it, and among themselves it is their talk of consolation.

The words of his special counsellor the Lord North are known, which he uttered to his trusty Pooley upon the receipt of a letter from Court of her Majesty's displeasure towards him for his being a witness at Leicester's second marriage with Dame Lettice (although I know he was not ignorant of the first) at Wanstead, of which displeasure this Lord making far less accompt than in reason he should of the just offense of his sovereign, said that for his own part he was resolved to sink or swim with my Lord of Leicester, who (saith he) if once the cards may come to shuffling (I will use but his very own words), I make no doubt but he alone shall bear away the bucklers.[168]

The words also of Sir Thomas Leighton to Sir Henry Neville, walking upon the terrace at Windsor, are known, who told him, after long discourse of their happy conceived kingdom, that he doubted not but to see him one day hold the same office in Windsor of my Lord of Leicester which now my Lord did hold of the Queen. Meaning thereby the goodly office of Constableship, with all royalties and honors belonging to the same, which now the said Sir Henry exerciseth only as deputy to the Earl.[169] Which was plainly to signify that he doubted not but to see my Lord of Leicester one day king, or else his other hope could never possibly take effect or come to pass.

To the same point tended the words of Mistress Anne West, Dame Lettice's sister, unto the Lady Anne Askew in the Great Chamber, upon a day when her brother Robert Knowles had danced disgraciously and scornfully before the Queen in presence of the French.[170] Which thing for that her Majesty took to proceed of will in him, as for dislike of the strangers in presence and for the quarrel of his sister Essex, it pleased her Highness to check him for the same, with addition of a reproachful word or two (full well deserved), as though done for despite of the forced absence from that place of honor of the good old gentlewoman (I mitigate the words) his sister. Which words the other younger twig receiving in deep dudgeon, brake forth in great choler to her forenamed companion and said that she nothing doubted but that one day she should see her sister, upon whom the Queen railed now so much (for so it pleased her to term her Majesty's sharp speech), to sit in her place and throne, being much worthier of the same for her qualities and rare virtues than was the other. Which undutiful speech, albeit it were overheard and condemned of divers that sat about them, yet none durst ever report the same to her Majesty, as I have heard sundry courtiers affirm, in respect of the revenge which the reporters should abide at my Lord of Leicester's hands whensoever the matter should come to light.

And this is now concerning the opinion and secret speech of my Lord's own friends, who cannot but utter their conceit and judgment in time and place convenient, whatsoever they are willed to give out publicly to the contrary for deceiving of such as will believe fair painted words against evident and manifest demonstration of reason.

I say reason, for that if none of these signs and tokens were, none of these preparations nor any of these speeches and detections by his friends that know his heart, yet in force of plain reason I could allege unto you three arguments only which to any man of intelligence would easily persuade and give satisfaction that my Lord of Leicester meaneth best and first for himself in this suit. Which three arguments, for that you seem to be attent, I will not stick to run over in all brevity.

And the first is the very nature and quality of ambition itself, which is such (as you know) that it never stayeth, but passeth from degree to degree, and the more it obtaineth the more it coveteth and the more esteemeth itself both worthy and able to obtain. And in our matter that now we handle, even as in wooing, he that sueth to a lady for another and obtaineth her good will entereth easily into conceit of his own worthiness thereby, and so commonly into hope of speeding himself while he speaketh for his friend; so much more in kingdoms, he that seeth himself of power to put the crown off another man's head will quickly step to the next degree, which is to set it of [on] his own, seeing that always the charity of such good men is wont to be so orderly as (according to the precept) it beginneth with itself first.

Add to this that ambition is jealous, suspicious, and fearful of itself, especially when it is joined with a conscience loaden with the guilt of many crimes, whereof he would be loth to be called to accompt or be subject to any man that might by authority take review of his life and actions when it should please him. In which kind, seeing my Lord of Leicester hath so much to increase his fear, as before hath been showed, by his wicked dealings, it is not like that ever he will put himself to another man's courtesy for passing his audit in particular reckonings which he can no way answer or satisfy, but rather will stand upon the gross sum and general *quietus est* by making himself chief auditor and master of all accompts for his own part in this life, howsoever he do in the next, whereof such humors have little regard. And this is for the nature of ambition in itself.

The second argument may be taken from my Lord's particular

disposition, which is such as may give much light also to the matter in question, being a disposition so well liking and inclined to a kingdom as it hath been tampering about the same from the first day that he came in favor. First by seeking openly to marry with the Queen's Majesty herself, and so to draw the crown upon his own head and to his posterity. Secondly, when that attempt took not place, then he gave it out, as hath been showed before, how that he was privily contracted to her Majesty (wherein as I told you his dealing before for satisfaction of a stranger, so let him with shame and dishonor remember now also the spectacle he secretly made for the persuading of a subject and Councillor of great honor in the same cause)[171] to the end that if her Highness should by any way have miscarried, then he might have entitled any one of his own brood (whereof he hath store in many places, as is known) to the lawful succession of the crown under color of that privy and secret marriage, pretending the same to be by her Majesty, wherein he will want no witnesses to depose what he will. Thirdly, when he saw also that this device was subject to danger, for that his privy contract might be denied more easily than he able justly to prove the same after her Majesty's decease, he had a new fetch to strengthen the matter, and that was to cause these words of NATURAL ISSUE to be put into the statute of succession for the crown, against all order and custom of our realm and against the known common style of law accustomed to be used in statutes of such matter, whereby he might be able after the death of her Majesty to make legitimate to the crown any one bastard of his own by any of so many hackneys as he keepeth, affirming it to be the natural issue of her Majesty by himself. For no other reason can be imagined why the ancient usual words of LAWFUL ISSUE should so cunningly be changed into NATURAL ISSUE. Thereby not only to endanger our whole realm with new quarrels of succession, but also to touch (as far as in him lieth) the royal honor of his sovereign, who hath been to him but too bountiful a Princess.[172]

Fourthly, when after a time these fetches and devices began to be discovered, he changed straight his course and turned to the Papists' and Scottish faction, pretending the marriage of the Queen in prison.[173] But yet after this again, finding therein not such success as contented him thoroughly and having in the mean space a new occasion offered to bait, he betook himself fifthly to the party of Huntingdon, having therein (no doubt) as good meaning to himself as his father had by joining with Suffolk. Marry, yet of late he hath cast anew about once again for himself in secret by treating the marriage of young Arbella with his son entitled the Lord Denbigh.[174]

So that by this we see the disposition of this man bent wholly to a scepter. And albeit in right, title, and descent of blood (as you say), he can justly claim neither kingdom nor cottage (considering either the baseness or disloyalty of his ancestors), if in respect of his present state and power, and of his natural pride, ambition, and crafty conveyance received from his father, he hath learned how to put himself first in possession of chief rule, under other pretenses, and after to devise upon the title at his leisure.

But now to come to the third argument: I say more and above all this that the nature and state of the matter itself permitteth not that my Lord of Leicester should mean sincerely the crown for Huntingdon, especially seeing there hath passed between them so many years of dislike and enmity, which albeit for the time and present commodity be covered and pressed down, yet by reason and experience we know that afterward when they shall deal together again in matters of importance, and when jealousy shalbe joined to other circumstances of their actions, it is impossible that the former mislike should not break out in far higher degree than ever before.

As we saw in the examples of the reconciliation made betwixt this man's father and Edward Duke of Somerset, bearing rule under King Edward VI, and between Richard of York and Edmund Duke of Somerset, bearing rule in the time of King Henry VI. Both which Dukes of Somerset, after reconciliation with their old, crafty, and ambitious enemies, were brought by the same to their destruction soon after.[175] Whereof I doubt not but my Lord of Leicester will take good heed in joining by reconciliation with Huntingdon after so long a breach, and will not be so improvident as to make him his sovereign who now is but his dependent. He remembereth too well the success of the Lord Stanley, who helped King Henry VII to the crown, of the Duke of Buckingham, who did the same for Richard III, of the Earl of Warwick, who set up King Edward IV, and of the three Percies, who advanced to the scepter King Henry IV. All which noblemen upon occasions that after fell out were rewarded with death by the selfsame princes whom they had preferred.[176]

And that not without reason, as Seignior Machavel my Lord's counsellor affirmeth.[177] For that such princes afterward can never give sufficient satisfaction to such friends for so great a benefit received. And consequently, lest upon discontentment they may chance do as much for others against them as they have done for them against others, the surest way is to recompense them with such a reward as they shall never after be able to complain of.

Wherefore I can never think that my Lord of Leicester will put himself in danger of the like success at Huntingdon's hands, but rather will follow the plot of his own father with the Duke of Suffolk, whom no doubt but he meant only to use for a pretext and help whereby to place himself in supreme dignity, and afterwards, whatsoever had befallen of the state, the other's head could never have come to other end than it enjoyed. For if Queen Mary had not cut it off, King John of Northumberland would have done the same in time, and so all men do well know that were privy to any of his cunning dealings.[178]

And what Huntingdon's secret opinion of Leicester is (notwithstanding this outward show of dependence) it was my chance to learn from the mouth of a special man of that Hasty king who was his ledger or agent in London,[179] and at a time falling in talk of his master's title declared that he had heard him divers times in secret complain to his lady (Leicester's sister) as greatly fearing that in the end he would offer him wrong and pretend some title for himself.

Lawyer. Well (quoth the lawyer), it seemeth by this last point that these two lords are cunning practitioners in the art of dissimulation, but for the former whereof you spake, in truth, I have heard men of good discourse affirm that the Duke of Northumberland had strange devices in his head for deceiving of Suffolk (who was nothing so fine as himself) and for bringing the crown to his own family. And among other devices it is thought that he had most certain intention to marry the Lady Mary himself (after once he had brought her into his own hands) and to have bestowed her Majesty that now is upon some one of his children (if it should have been thought best to give her life) and so consequently to have shaken off Suffolk and his pedigree, with condign punishment for his bold behavior in that behalf.

Scholar. Verily (quoth I), this had been an excellent stratagem if it had taken place. But I pray you (Sir), how could himself have taken the Lady Mary to wife, seeing he was at that time married to another?[180]

Gentleman: Oh (quoth the gentleman), you question like a scholar. As though my Lord of Leicester had not a wife alive when he first began to pretend marriage to the Queen's Majesty. Do not you remember the story of King Richard III, who at such time as he thought best for the establishing of his title to marry his own niece, that afterward was married to King Henry VII, how he caused secretly to be given abroad that his own wife was dead, whom all the world knew to be then alive and in good health, but yet soon afterward she was seen dead indeed?[181] These great personages, in matters of such weight as is a kingdom, have privileges to dispose of women's bodies, marriages, lives and deaths, as shalbe thought for the time most convenient.

And what do you think (I pray you) of this new TRIUMVIRATE so lately concluded about Arbella (for so I must call the same, though one of the three persons be no *vir*, but virago)?[182] I mean of the marriage between young Denbigh and the little daughter of Lennox, whereby the father-in-law, the grandmother, and the uncle of the new designed queen have conceived to themselves a singular triumphant reign. But what do you think may ensue hereof? Is there nothing of the old plot of Duke John of Northumberland in this?

Lawyer. Marry, Sir (quoth the lawyer), if this be so, I dare assure you there is sequel enough pretended hereby. And first no doubt but there goeth a deep drift by the wife and son against old Abraham (the husband and father) with the well-lined large pouch. And secondly a far deeper by trusty Robert against his best mistress; but deepest of all by the whole crew against the designments of the Hasty Earl, who thirsteth a kingdom with great intemperance and seemeth (if there were plain dealing) to hope by these good people to quench shortly his drought. But either part, in truth, seeketh to deceive other, and therefore it is hard to say where the game in fine will rest.

Gentleman: Well, howsoever that be (quoth the gentleman), I am of opinion that my Lord of Leicester will use both this practice and many mo for bringing the scepter finally to his own head, and that he will not only employ Huntingdon to defeat Scotland and Arbella to defeat Huntingdon, but also would use the marriage of the Queen imprisoned to defeat them both if she were in his hand; and any one of all three to dispossess her Majesty that now is, as also the authority of all four to bring it to himself; with many other fetches, flings, and friscoes besides which simple men as yet do not conceive.

And howsoever these two conjoined Earls do seem for the time to draw together and to play booty, yet am I of opinion that th'one will beguile th'other at the upshot. And Hastings, for aught I see, when he cometh to the scambling is like to have no better luck by the Bear than his ancestor had once by the Boar.[183] Who using his help first in murdering the son and heir of King Henry VI and after in destroying the faithful friends and kinsmen of King Edward V, for his easier way to usurpation, made an end of him also in the Tower at the very same day and hour that the other were by his counsel destroyed in Pontefract Castle.[184] So that where the goal and prize of the game is a kingdom, there is neither faith, neither good fellowship, nor fair play among the gamesters. And this shalbe enough for the first point, *viz.*, what good my Lord of Leicester meaneth to himself in respect of Huntingdon.

Touching the second, whether the attempt be purposed in her Majesty's days or no, the matter is much less doubtful to him that knoweth or can imagine what a torment the delay of a kingdom is to such a one as suffereth hunger thereof and feareth that every hour may breed some alteration to the prejudice of his conceived hope. We see oftentimes that the child is impatient in this matter, to expect the natural end of his parent's life. Whom notwithstanding by nature he is enforced to love and who also by nature is like long to leave this world before him, and after whose decease he is assured to obtain his desire, but most certain of dangerous event if he attempt to get it while yet his parent liveth. Which four considerations are (no doubt) of great force to contain a child in duty and bridle his desire, albeit some times not sufficient to withstand the greedy appetite of reigning.

But what shall we think where none of these four considerations do restrain? Where the present possessor is no parent? Where she is like by nature to outlive the expecter? Whose death must needs bring infinite difficulties to the enterprise? And in whose lifetime the matter is most easy to be achieved, under color and authority of the present possessor? Shall we think that in such a case the ambitious man will overrule his own passion and leese his commodity?

As for that which is alleged before for my Lord in the reason of his defenders, that his present state is so prosperous as he cannot expect better in the next change whatsoever [it] should be, is of small moment in the conceit of an ambitious head, whose eye and heart is always upon that which he hopeth for and enjoyeth not, and not upon that which already he possesseth, be it never so good. Especially in matters of honor and authority, it is an infallible rule that one degree desired and not obtained afflicteth more than five degrees already possessed can give consolation; the story of Duke Aman confirmeth this evidently,[185] who being the greatest subject in the world under King Assuerus, after he had reckoned up all his pomp, riches, glory, and felicity to his friends, yet he said that all this was nothing unto him until he could obtain the revenge which he desired upon Mardocheus his enemy,[186] and hereby it cometh ordinarily to pass that among highest in authority are found the greatest store of malcontents that most do endanger their prince and country.

When the Percies took part with Henry of Bolingbroke against King Richard II, their lawful sovereign, it was not for lack of preferment, for they were exceedingly advanced by the said king and possessed the three earldoms of Northumberland, Worcester, and Stafford together, besides many other offices and dignities of honor.

In like sort, when the two Nevilles took upon them to join with Richard of York to put down their most benign prince King Henry VI, and after again in the other side to put down King Edward IV, it was not upon want of advancement, they being Earls both of Salisbury and Warwick and lords of many notable places besides.[187] But it was upon a vain imagination of future fortune, whereby such men are commonly led, and yet had not they any smell in their nostrils of getting the kingdom for themselves as this man hath to prick him forward.

If you say that these men hated their sovereign and that thereby they were led to procure his destruction, the same I may answer of my Lord living, though of all men he hath least cause so to do. But yet such is the nature of wicked ingratitude that where it oweth most and disdaineth to be bound, there upon every little discontentment it turneth double obligation into triple hatred.

This he showed evidently in the time of his little disgrace, wherein he not only did diminish, vilipend,[188] and debase among his friends the inestimable benefits he hath received from her Majesty, but also used to exprobate his own good services and merits and to touch her Highness with ingrate consideration and recompense of the same. Which behavior, together with his hasty preparation to rebellion and assault of her Majesty's royal person and dignity upon so small a cause given, did well show what mind inwardly he beareth to his sovereign, and what her Majesty may expect if by offending him she should once fall within the compass of his furious paws, seeing such a smoke of disdain could not proceed but from a fiery furnace of hatred within.

And surely it is a wonderful matter to consider what a little check, or rather the bare imagination of a small overthwart, may work in a proud and disdainful stomach. The remembrance of his marriage missed that he so much pretended and desired with her Majesty doth stick deeply in his breast and stirreth him daily to revenge. As also doth the disdain of certain checks and disgraces received at some times, especially that of his last marriage, which irketh him so much the more by how much greater fear and danger it brought him into at that time and did put his widow in such open frenzy as she raged many months after against her Majesty and is not cold yet, but remaineth as it were a sworn enemy for that injury, and standeth like a fiend or fury at the elbow of her Amadis to stir him forward when occasion shall serve.[189] And what effect such female suggestions may work when they find an humor proud and pliable to their purpose, you may remember by the example of the Duchess of Somerset, who enforced her husband to cut off the head of his only dear brother, to his own evident destruction, for her contentation.[190]

Wherefore, to conclude this matter without further dispute or reason, seeing there is so much discovered in the case as there is, so great desire of reign, so great impatience of delay, so great hope and ability of success if it be attempted under the good fortune and present authority of the competitors, seeing the plots be so well laid, the preparation so forward, the favorers so furnished, the time so propitious, and so many other causes conviting together; seeing that by deferring all may be hazarded and by hastening little can be endangered, the state and condition of things well weighed; finding also the bands of duty so broken already in the conspirators, the causes of mislike and hatred so manifest, and the solicitors to execution so potent and diligent as women, malice, and ambition are wont to be; it is more than probable that they will not leese their present commodity, especially seeing they have learned by their archetype or protoplot which they follow (I mean the conspiracy of Northumberland and Suffolk in King Edward's days) that herein there was some error committed at that time which overthrew the whole, and that was the deferring of some things until after the king's death which should have been put in execution before.

For if in the time of their plotting, when as yet their designments were not published to the world, they had under the countenance of the king (as well they might have done) gotten into their hands the two sisters and dispatched some other few affairs before they had caused the young prince to die, no doubt but in man's reason the whole designment had taken place, and consequently it is to be presupposed that these men (being no fools in their own affairs) will take heed of falling into the like error by delay, but rather will make all sure by striking while the iron is hot, as our proverb warneth them.

Lawyer. It cannot be denied in reason (quoth the lawyer) but that they have many helps of doing what they list now, under the present favor, countenance, and authority of her Majesty, which they should not have after her Highness' decease, when each man shall remain more at liberty for his supreme obedience by reason of the statute provided for uncertainty of the next succession,[191] and therefore I for my part would rather counsel them to make much of her Majesty's life, for after that they little know what may ensue or befall their designments.

Gentleman: They will make the most thereof (quoth the gentleman) for their own advantage, but after that what is like to follow the examples of Edward and Richard II, as also of Henry and Edward VI, do sufficiently forewarn us, whose lives were prolonged until their deaths were thought more profitable to the conspirators and not longer. And for the statute you speak of, procured by themselves for establishing the incertainty of the next true successor (whereas all our former statutes were wont to be made for the declaration and certainty of the same), it is with PROVISO (as you know) that it shall not endure longer than the life of her Majesty that now reigneth; that is, indeed, no longer than until themselves be ready to place another.[192] For then, no doubt but we shall see a fair proclamation that my Lord of Huntingdon is the only next heir, with a bundle of halters to hang all such as shall dare once open their mouth for denial of the same.

Lawyer: At these words the old lawyer stepped back, as somewhat astonied, and began to make crosses in the air after their fashion,[193] whereat we laughed, and then he said: Truly, my masters, I had thought that no man had conceived so evil imagination of this statute as myself, but now I perceive that I alone am not malicious. For my own part, I must confess unto you that as often as I read over this statute, or think of the same (as by divers occasions many times I do), I feel myself much grieved and afflicted in mind, upon fears which I conceive what may be the end of this statute to our country and what privy meaning the chief procurers thereof might have for their own drifts against the realm and life of her Majesty that now reigneth.

And so much more it maketh me to doubt for that in all our records of law you shall not find (to my remembrance) any one example of such a device for concealing of the true inheritor, but rather in all ages, states, and times (especially from Richard I downward),[194] you shall find statutes, ordinances, and provisions for declaration and manifestation of the same, as you have well observed and touched before. And therefore this strange and new device must needs have some strange and unaccustomed meaning, and God of his mercy grant that it have not some strange and unexpected event.

In sight of all men this is already evident, that never country in the world was brought into more apparent danger of utter ruin than ours is at this day by pretense of this statute. For whereas there is no gentleman so mean in the realm that cannot give a guess more or less who shall be his next heir, and his tenants soon conjecture what manner of person shalbe their next lord, in the title of our noble crown, whereof all the rest dependeth, neither is her Majesty permitted to know or say who shalbe her next successor, nor her subjects allowed to understand or imagine who in right may be their future sovereign, an intolerable injury in a matter of so singular importance.[195]

For (alas) what should become of this our native country if God should take from us her most excellent Majesty (as once he will) and so leave us destitute upon the sudden? What should become of our lives, of our states, and of our whole realm or government? Can any man promise himself one day longer of rest, peace, possession, life, or liberty within the land than God shall lend us her Majesty to reign over us? Which albeit we do and are bound to wish that it may be long, yet reason telleth us that by course of nature it cannot be of any great continuance, and by a thousand accidents it may be much shorter. And shall then our most noble commonwealth and kingdom, which is of perpetuity and must continue to ourselves and our posterity, hang only upon the life of her Highness alone, well strocken in years and of no great good health or robustious and strong complexion.

I was within hearing some six or seven years ago when Sir Christopher Hatton, in a very great assembly, made an eloquent oration (which after I ween was put in print) at the pardoning and delivery of him from the gallows that by error (as was thought) had discharged his piece upon her Majesty's barge and hurt certain persons in her Highness' presence.[196] And in that oration he declared and described very effectually what inestimable damage had ensued to the realm if her Majesty by that or any other means should have been taken from us. He set forth most lively before the eyes of all men what division, what dissension, what bloodshed had ensued, and what fatal dangers were most certain to fall upon us whensoever that doleful day should happen, wherein no man should be sure of his life, of his goods, of his wife, of his children; no man certain whither to fly, whom to follow, or where to seek repose and protection.

And as all the hearers there present did easily grant that he therein said truth and far less than might have been said in that behalf, things standing as they do, so many [a] one (I trow) that heard these words proceed from a Councillor that had good cause to know the state of his own country, entered into this cogitation, what punishment they might deserve then at the whole state and commonwealth's hands who first by letting her Majesty from marriage and then by procuring this statute of dissembling the next inheritor had brought their realm into so evident and inevitable dangers? For every one well considered and weighed with himself that the thing which yet only letted these dangers and miseries set down by Sir Christopher must necessarily one day fail us all, that is, the life of her Majesty now present; and then (say we) how falleth it out that so general a calamity as must needs overtake us ere it be long (and may, for anything we know, tomorrow next) is not provided for, as well as foreseen.

Is there no remedy but that we must willingly and wittingly run into our own ruin? And for the favor or fear of some few aspirers betray our country and the blood of so many thousand innocents as live within the land?

For tell me (good Sirs), I pray you, if her Majesty should die tomorrow next (whose life God long preserve and bless)—but if she should be taken from us (as by condition of nature and human frailty she may), what would you do? Which way would you look? Or what head or part knew any good subject in the realm to follow? I speak not of the conspirators, for I know they wilbe ready and resolved whom to follow, but I speak of the plain, simple, and well meaning subject, who following now the utter letter of this fraudulent statute (fraudulent, I mean, in the secret conceit of the cunning aspirers) shalbe taken at that day upon the sudden and, being put in a maze by the unexpected contention about the crown, shalbe brought into a thousand dangers both of body and goods, which now are not thought upon by them who are most in danger of the same. And this is for the commonwealth and country.

But unto her Majesty, for whose good and safety the statute is only pretended to be made, no doubt but that it bringeth far greater dangers than any device that they have used besides. For hereby under color of restraining the claims and titles of true successors (whose endeavors notwithstanding are commonly more calm and moderate than [those] of usurpers), they make unto themselves a mean to foster and set forward their own conspiracy without controlment, seeing no man of might may oppose himself against them but with suspicion that he meaneth to claim for himself. And so they being armed on the one side with their authority and force of present fortune and defended on the other side by the pretense of the statute, they may securely work and plot at their pleasure, as you have well proved before that they do. And whensoever their grounds and foundations shalbe ready, it cannot be denied but that her Majesty's life lieth much at their discretion, to take it or use it to their best commodity (and there is no doubt but they will), as such men are wont to do in such affairs. Marry, one thing standeth not in their powers so absolutely, and that is to prolong her Majesty's days or favor towards themselves at their pleasures, whereof it is not unlike but they will have due consideration, lest perhaps upon any sudden accident they might be found unready.

Gentleman: They have good care thereof, I can assure you (quoth the gentleman), and mean not to be prevented by any accident or other mishap whatsoever; they wilbe ready for all events, and for that cause they hasten so much their preparations at this day more than ever before by sending out their spies and solicitors everywhere to prove and confirm their friends, by delivering their common watchword, by complaining on all hands of our Protestant bishops and clergy and of all the present state of our irreformed religion (as they call it), by amplifying only the danger of Papists and Scottish faction, by giving out openly that now her Majesty is past hope of childbirth and consequently seeing God hath given no better success that way in two women one after the other, it were not convenient (say they) that another of that sex should ensue, with high commendation of the Law Salic in France whereby women are forbidden to succeed. Which speech, though in show it be delivered against the Queen of Scots and other of King Henry VII his line that descend of sisters, yet all men see that it toucheth as well the disabling of her Majesty that is present as others to come, and so tendeth directly to maturation of the principal purpose, which I have declared before.

Scholar. Here said I: For the rest which you speak of, besides the watchword, it is common and everywhere treated in talk among them, but yet for the watchword itself (for that you name it), I think (Sir) many know it not, if I were the first that told you the story, as perchance I was. For in truth I came to it by a rare hap (as then I told you), the thing being uttered and expounded by a baron of their own faction to another nobleman of the same degree and religion, though not of the same opinion in these affairs. And for that I am requested not to utter the second, who told it me in secret, I must also spare the name of the first, which otherwise I would not, nor the time and place where he uttered the same.

Lawyer. To this said the lawyer: You do well in that, but yet I beseech you, let me know this watchword (if there be any such) for mine instruction and help, when need shall require. For I assure you that this gentleman's former speech of halters hath so terrified me as if any should come and ask or feel my inclination in these matters, I would answer them fully to their good contentment, if I knew the watchword whereby to know them. For of all things I love not to be hanged for quarrels of kingdoms.

[*Scholar*]: The watchword is (said I) WHETHER YOU BE SETTLED OR NO? and if you answer yea and seem to understand the meaning thereof, then are you known to be of their faction, and so to be accompted and dealt withal for things to come.[197] But if you stagger or doubt in answering, as if you knew not perfectly the mystery (as the noble man my good Lord did, imagining that it had been meant of his religion, which was very well known to be good and settled in the gospel), then are you descried thereby, either not to be of their side or else to be but a puny[198] not well instructed, and consequently he that moveth you the question will presently break off that speech and turn to some other talk until afterward occasion be given to persuade you or else instruct you better in that affair.

Marry, the nobleman whereof I spake before, perceiving by the demanding that there was some mystery in covert under the question, took hold of the words and would not suffer the propounder to slip away (as he endeavored), but with much entreaty brought him at length to expound the full meaning and purpose of the riddle. And this was the first occasion (as I think) whereby this secret came abroad. Albeit afterwards at the public communions which were made throughout so many shires the matter became more common, especially among the strangers that inhabit (as you know) in great numbers with us at this day. All which (as they say) are made most assured to this faction and ready to assist the same with great forces at all occasions.[199]

Lawyer. Good Lord (quoth the lawyer), how many mysteries and secrets be there abroad in the world whereof we simple men know nothing and suspect less. This watchword should I never have imagined, and for the great and often assemblies under pretense of communions, though of themselves and of their own nature they were unaccustomed and consequently subject to suspicion, yet did I never conceive so far forth as now I do, as neither of the lodging and entertaining of so many strangers in the realm, whereof our artisans do complain everywhere. But now I see the reason thereof, which (no doubt) is founded upon great policy for the purpose. And by this also I see that the house of Huntingdon presseth far forward for the game and shouldereth near the goal to lay hands upon the same. Which to tell you plainly liketh me but a little, both in respect of the good will I bear to the whole line of King Henry, which hereby is like to be dispossessed, as also for the misery which I do foresee must necessarily ensue upon our country if once the challenge of Huntingdon take place in our realm. Which challenge being derived from the title of Clarence only, in the house of York, before the union of the two great houses, raiseth up again the old contention between the families of York and Lancaster wherein so much English blood was spilt in times past, and much more like to be poured out now if the same contention should be set on foot again. Seeing that to the controversy of titles would be added also the controversy of religion, which of all other differences is most dangerous.

Gentleman: Sir (quoth the gentleman), now you touch a matter of consequence indeed and such as the very naming thereof maketh my heart to shake and tremble. I remember well what Philippe Comines setteth down in his history of our country's calamity by that contention of those two houses distinguished by the red rose and the white, but yet both in their arms might justly have borne the color of red with a fiery sword in a black field to signify the abundance of blood and mortality which ensued in our country by that most woeful and cruel contention.[200]

I will not stand here to set down the particulars observed and gathered by the foresaid author, though a stranger, which for the most part he saw himself while he lived about the Duke of Burgundy and King Louis of France of that time, namely the pitiful description of divers right noblemen of our realm, who besides all other miseries were driven to beg openly in foreign countries and the like.[201] Mine own observation in reading over our country['s] affairs is sufficient to make me abhor the memory of that time and to dread all occasion that may lead us to the like in time to come, seeing that in my judgment neither the civil wars of Marius and Sulla or of Pompey and Caesar among the Romans, nor yet the Guelphians and Ghibellines among the Italians did ever work so much woe as this did to our poor country. Wherein by reason of the contention of York and Lancaster were foughten sixteen or seventeen pitched fields in less than an hundred years. That is, from the eleventh or twelfth year of King Richard II his reign (when this controversy first began to bud up) unto the thirteenth year of King Henry VII. At what time by cutting off the chief titler of Huntingdon's house, to wit, young Edward Plantagenet, Earl of Warwick,[202] son and heir to George Duke of Clarence, the contention most happily was quenched and ended, wherein so many fields (as I have said) were foughten between brethren and inhabitants of our own nation. And therein and otherwise only about the same quarrel were slain, murdered, and made away about nine or ten kings and kings' sons, besides above forty earls, marquesses, and dukes of name, but many mo lords, knights, and great gentlemen and captains, and of the common people without number, and by particular conjecture very near two hundred thousand. For that in one battle foughten by King Edward IV[203] there are recorded to be slain on both parts five and thirty thousand seven hundred and eleven persons, besides other wounded and taken prisoners to be put to death afterward at the pleasure of the conqueror; at divers battles after, ten thousand slain at a battle, as in those of Barnet and Tewkesbury foughten both in one year.[204]

This suffered our afflicted country in those days by this infortunate and deadly contention, which could never be ended but by the happy conjunction of those two houses together in Henry VII; neither yet so (as appeareth by chronicle) until (as I have said) the state had cut off the issue male of the Duke of Clarence, who was cause of divers perils to King Henry VII though he were in prison. By whose sister the faction of Huntingdon at this day doth seek to raise up the same contention again, with far greater danger both to the realm and to her Majesty that now reigneth than ever before.

And for the realm it is evident, by that it giveth room to strangers' competitors of the house of Lancaster, better able to maintain their own title by sword than ever was any of that lineage before them. And for her Majesty's peril present, it is nothing hard to conjecture, seeing the same title in the foresaid Earl of Warwick was so dangerous and troublesome to her grandfather (by whom she holdeth) as he was fain twice to take arms in defense of his right against the said title, which was in those days preferred and advanced by the friends of Clarence before that of Henry, as also this of Huntingdon is at this day by his faction before that of her Majesty, though never so unjustly.

Lawyer. Touching Huntingdon's title before her Majesty (quoth the lawyer) I will say nothing, because in reason I see not by what pretense in the world he may thrust himself so far forth, seeing her Majesty is descended not only of the house of Lancaster but also before him most apparently from the house of York itself, as from the eldest daughter of King Edward IV, being the eldest brother of that house. Whereas Huntingdon claimeth only by the daughter of

George Duke of Clarence, the younger brother. Marry, yet I must confess that if the Earl of Warwick's title were better than that of King Henry VII (which is most false, though many attempted to defend the same by sword), then hath Huntingdon some wrong at this day by her Majesty. Albeit in very truth, the attaints of so many of his ancestors by whom he claimeth would answer him also sufficiently in that behalf if his title were otherwise allowable.[205]

But I know besides this they have another fetch of King Richard III, whereby he would needs prove his elder brother King Edward to be a bastard and consequently his whole line as well male as female to be void. Which device, though it be ridiculous and was at the time when it was first invented, yet as Richard found at that time a Doctor Shaw that shamed not to publish and defend the same at Paul's Cross in a sermon,[206] and John of Northumberland, my Lord of Leicester's father, found out divers preachers in his time to set up the title of Suffolk and to debase the right of King Henry's daughter both in London, Cambridge, Oxford, and other places, most apparently against all law and reason, so I doubt not but these men would find out also both Shaws, Sands, and others to set out the title of Clarence before the whole interest of King Henry VII and his posterity if occasion served.[207] Which is a point of importance to be considered by her Majesty, albeit for my part I mean not now to stand thereupon but only upon that other of the house of Lancaster, as I have said.

For as that most honorable, lawful, and happy conjunction of the two adversary houses in King Henry VII and his wife made an end of the shedding of English blood within itself and brought us that most desired peace which ever sithence we have enjoyed by the reign of their two most noble issue, so the plot that now is in hand for the cutting off the residue of that issue and for recalling back of the whole title to the only house of York again is like to plunge us deeper than ever in civil discord and to make us the bait of all foreign princes; seeing there be among them at this day some of no small power (as I have said) who pretend to be the next heirs by the house of Lancaster[208] and consequently are not like to give over or abandon their own right if once the door be opened to contention for the same by disannulling the line of King Henry VII, wherein only the keys of all concord remain knit together.

And albeit I know well that such as be of my Lord of Huntingdon's party will make small accompt of the title of Lancaster, as less rightful a great deal than that of York (and I for my part mean not greatly to avow the same as now it is placed, being myself no favorer of foreign titles), yet indifferent men have to consider how it was taken in times past and how it may again in time to come if contention should arise; how many noble personages of our realm did offer themselves to die in defense thereof; how many oaths and laws were given and received throughout the realm for maintenance of the same against the other house of York forever; how many worthy kings were crowned and reigned of that house and race, to wit, the four most noble Henrys, one after another, the fourth, the fifth, the sixth, and the seventh, who both in number, government, sanctity, courage, and feats of arms were nothing inferior (if not superior) to those of the other house and line of York after the division between the families.

It is to be considered also as a special sign of the favor and affection of our whole nation unto that family that Henry Earl of Richmond, though descending but of the last son and third wife of John of Gaunt, Duke of Lancaster,[209] was so respected for that only by the universal realm as they inclined wholly to call him from banishment and to make him king, with the deposition of Richard which then ruled of the house of York, upon condition only that the said Henry should take to wife a daughter of the contrary family; so great was in those days the affection of English hearts towards the line of Lancaster for the great worthiness of such kings as had reigned of that race, how good or bad soever their title were; which I stand not here at this time to discuss, but only to insinuate what party the same found in our realm in times past and consequently how extreme dangerous the contention for the same may be hereafter, especially seeing that at this day the remainder of that title is pretended to rest wholly in a stranger whose power is very great. Which we lawyers are wont to esteem as a point of no small importance for justifying of any man's title to a kingdom.

Scholar. You lawyers want not reason in that, Sir (quoth I), howsoever you want right, for if you will examine the succession of governments from the beginning of the world unto this day, either among Gentile, Jew, or Christian people, you shall find that the sword hath been always better than half the title, to get, establish, or maintain a kingdom, which maketh me the more appalled to hear you discourse in such sort of new contentions and foreign titles accompanied with such power and strength of the titlers. Which cannot be but infinitely dangerous and fatal to our realm, if once it come to action, both for the division that is like to be at home and the variety of parties from abroad. For as the prince whom you signify will not fail (by all likelihood) to pursue his title with all forces that he can make, if occasion were offered, so reason of state and policy will enforce other princes adjoining to let and hinder him therein what they can, and so by this means shall we become Judah and Israel among ourselves, one killing and vexing the other with the sword; and to foreign princes we shalbe as the island of Salamina [Salamis] was in old time to the Athenians and Megarians, and as the island of Sicilia was afterward to the Grecians, Carthaginians, and Romans, and as in our days the kingdom of Naples hath been to the Spaniards, Frenchmen, Germans, and Venetians; that is, a bait to feed upon and a game to fight for.

Wherefore I beseech the Lord to avert from us all occasions of such miseries. And I pray you, Sir, for that we are fallen into the mention of these matters, to take so much pains as to open unto me the ground of these controversies so long now quiet between York and Lancaster, seeing they are now like to be raised again. For albeit in general I have heard much thereof, yet in particular I either conceive not or remember not the foundation of the same, and much less the state of their several titles at this day, for that it is a study not properly pertaining unto my profession.

Lawyer. The controversy between the houses of York and Lancaster (quoth the lawyer) took his actual beginning in the issue of King Edward III, who died somewhat more than two hundred years gone, but the occasion, pretense, or cause of that quarrel began in the children of King Henry III, who died an hundred years before that and left two sons: Edward, who was king after him by the name of Edward I and was grandfather to Edward III, and Edmund (for his deformity called Crookback), Earl of Lancaster and beginner of that house, whose inheritance afterward in the fourth descent fell upon a daughter named Blanche, who was married to the fourth son of King Edward III, named John of Gaunt for that he was born in the city of Gaunt in Flanders, and so by this his first wife he became Duke of Lancaster and heir of that house. And for that his son Henry of Bolingbroke (afterward called King Henry IV) pretended among other things that Edmund Crookback, great-grandfather to Blanche his mother, was the elder son of King Henry III and injustly put by the inheritance of the crown for that he was crookbacked and deformed, he took by force the kingdom from Richard II, nephew to King Edward III by his first son,[210] and placed the same in the house of Lancaster where it remained for three whole descents, until afterward Edward Duke of York, descended of John of Gaunt's younger brother, making claim to the crown by title of his grandmother that was heir to Lionel Duke of Clarence, John of Gaunt's elder brother, took the same by force from Henry VI of the house of Lancaster and brought it back again to the house of York, where it continued with much trouble in two kings only, until both houses were joined together in King Henry VII and his noble issue.

Hereby we see how the issue of John of Gaunt, Duke of Lancaster, fourth son to King Edward III, pretended right to the crown by Edmund Crookback before the issue of all the other three sons of Edward III, albeit they were the elder brothers, whereof we will speak more hereafter. Now John of Gaunt, though he had many children, yet had he four only of whom issue remain, two sons and two daughters. The first son was Henry of Bolingbroke, Duke of Lancaster, who took the crown from King Richard II, his uncle's son, as hath been said, and first of all planted the same in the house of Lancaster where it remained in two descents after him, that is, in his son Henry V and in his nephew Henry VI, who was afterward destroyed together with Henry Prince of Wales, his only son and heir,[211] and consequently all that line of Henry Bolingbroke extinguished by Edward IV of the house of York.

The other son of John of Gaunt was John Duke of Somerset, by Katherine Swynford, his third wife;[212] which John had issue another John, and he, Margaret his daughter and heir, who being married to

Edmund Tudor, Earl of Richmond, had issue Henry Earl of Richmond, who after was named King Henry VII, whose line yet endureth.

The two daughters of John of Gaunt were married to Portugal and Castile; that is, Philippe born of Blanche, heir to Edmund Crookback as hath been said, was married to John King of Portugal, of whom is descended the king that now possesseth Portugal and the other princes which have or may make title to the same; and Katherine, born of Constance, heir of Castile, was married back again to Henry King of Castile in Spain, of whom King Philip is also descended.[213] So that by this we see where the remainder of the house of Lancaster resteth if the line of King Henry VII were extinguished, and what pretext foreign princes may have to subdue us if my Lord of Huntingdon either now or after her Majesty's days will open to them the door by shutting out the rest of King Henry's line and by drawing back the title to the only house of York again, which he pretendeth to do upon this that I will now declare.

King Edward III, albeit he had many children, yet five only will we speak of at this time, whereof three were elder than John of Gaunt and one younger. The first of the elder was named Edward the Black Prince, who died before his father leaving one only son named Richard, who afterward being king and named Richard II was deposed without issue and put to death by his cousin german named Henry Bolingbroke, Duke of Lancaster, son to John of Gaunt as hath been said, and so there ended the line of King Edward's first son.

King Edward's second son was William of Hatfield, that died without issue.

His third son was Lionel Duke of Clarence, whose only daughter and heir, called Philippe, was married to Edmund Mortimer, Earl of March, and after that, Anne, the daughter and heir of Mortimer,[214] was married to Richard Plantagenet, Duke of York, son and heir to Edmund of Langley, the first Duke of York,[215] which Edmund was the fifth son of King Edward III and younger brother to John of Gaunt. And this Edmund of Langley may be called the first beginner of the house of York, even as Edmund Crookback the beginner of the house [of] Lancaster.

This Edmund Langley then, having a son named Richard that married Anne Mortimer, sole heir to Lionel Duke of Clarence, joined two lines and two titles in one; I mean the line of Lionel and of Edmund Langley, who were (as hath been said) the third and the fifth sons to King Edward III. And for this cause, the child that was born of this marriage, named after his father Richard Plantagenet, Duke of York, seeing himself strong and the first line of King Edward III's eldest son to be extinguished in the death of King Richard II, and seeing William of Hatfield, the second son, dead likewise without issue, made demand of the crown for the house of York by the title of Lionel the third son of King Edward. And albeit he could not obtain the same in his days, for that he was slain in a battle against King Henry VI at Wakefield, yet his son Edward got the same and was called by the name of King Edward IV.

This king at his death left divers children, as namely two sons, Edward V and his brother, who after were both murdered in the Tower, as shalbe showed; and also five daughters, to wit: Elizabeth, Cecily, Anne, Katherine, and Bridget. Whereof the first was married to Henry VII, the last became a nun, and the other three were bestowed upon divers other husbands.[216]

He had also two brothers: the first was called George Duke of Clarence, who afterward upon his deserts (as is to be supposed) was put to death in Calais by commandment of the king and his attainder allowed by Parliament. And this man left behind him a son named Edward Earl of Warwick, put to death afterward without issue by King Henry VII, and a daughter named Margaret Countess of Salisbury who was married to a mean gentleman named Richard Poole,[217] by whom she had issue Cardinal Poole that died without marriage and Henry Poole that was attainted and executed in King Henry VIII his time (as also herself was), and this Henry Poole left a daughter married afterward to the Earl of Huntingdon, by whom this Earl that now is maketh title to the crown.[218] And this is the effect of my Lord of Huntingdon's title.

The second brother of King Edward IV was Richard Duke of Gloucester, who after the king's death caused his two sons to be murdered in the Tower and took the kingdom to himself.[219] And afterward he being slain by King Henry VII at Bosworth field, left no issue behind him. Wherefore King Henry VII, descending as hath been showed of the house of Lancaster, by John of Gaunt's last son and third wife, and taking to wife Lady Elizabeth, eldest daughter of King Edward IV of the house of York, joined most happily the two families together and made an end of all controversies about the title.

Now King Henry VII had issue three children of whom remaineth posterity. First, Henry VIII, of whom is descended our sovereign her Majesty that now happily reigneth and is the last that remaineth alive of that first line. Secondly, he had two daughters, whereof the first, named Margaret, was married twice, first to James King of Scotland, from whom are directly descended the Queen of Scotland that now liveth and her son, and, King James being dead, Margaret was married again to Archibald Douglas, Earl of Anguish,[220] by whom she had a daughter named Margaret which was married afterward to Matthew Steward, Earl of Lennox, whose son Charles Steward was married to Elizabeth Candish [Cavendish], daughter to the present Countess of Shrewsbury,[221] and by her hath left his only heir, a little daughter named Arbella, of whom you have heard some speech before. And this is touching the line of Scotland, descending from the first and eldest daughter of King Henry VII.

The second daughter of King Henry VII, called Mary, was twice married also, first to the king of France, by whom she had no issue,[222] and after his death to Charles Brandon, Duke of Suffolk, by whom she had two daughters, that is, Frances, of which the children of my Lord of Hertford do make their claim, and Eleanor, by whom the issue of the Earl of Derby pretendeth right, as shalbe declared. For that Frances, the first daughter of Charles Brandon by the Queen of France, was married to the Marquess of Dorset, who after Charles Brandon's death was made Duke of Suffolk in right of his wife and was beheaded in Queen Mary's time for his conspiracy with my Lord of Leicester's father. And she had by this man three daughters: that is, Jane, that was married to my Lord of Leicester's brother and proclaimed queen after King Edward's death, for which both she and her husband were executed; Catherine, the second daughter, who had two sons yet living by the Earl of Hertford; and Mary, the third daughter, which left no children.

The other daughter of Charles Brandon by the Queen of France, called Eleanor, was married to George Clifford, Earl of Cumberland,[223] who left a daughter by her named Margaret, married to the Earl of Derby, which yet liveth and hath issue. And this is the title of all the house of Suffolk, descended from the second daughter of King Henry VII, married (as hath been showed) to Charles Brandon, Duke of Suffolk. And by this you see also how many there be who do think their titles to be far before that of my Lord of Huntingdon's, if either right, law, reason, or consideration of home affairs may take place in our realm; or if not, yet you cannot but imagine how many great princes and potentates abroad are like to join and buckle with Huntingdon's line for the pre-eminence if once the matter fall again to contention by excluding the line of King Henry VII, which God forbid.

Scholar. Truly, Sir (quoth I), I well perceive that my Lord's turn is not so nigh as I had thought, whether he exclude the line of King Henry or no. For if he exclude that, then must he enter the combat with foreign titlers of the house of Lancaster, and if he exclude it not, then in all appearance of reason and in law too (as you have said) the succession of the two daughters of King Henry VII (which you distinguish by the two names of Scotland and Suffolk) must needs be as clearly before him and his line, that descendeth only from Edward IV his brother, as the Queen's title that now reigneth is before him. For that both Scotland, Suffolk, and her Majesty do hold all by one foundation, which is the union of both houses and titles together in King Henry VII, her Majesty's grandfather.

Gentleman. That is true (quoth the gentleman) and evident enough in every man's eye, and therefore no doubt but that as much is meant against her Majesty, if occasion serve, as against the rest that hold by the same title. Albeit her Majesty's state (the Lord be praised) be such at this time as it is not safety to pretend so much against her as against the rest, whatsoever be meant. And that in truth more should be meant 'gainst her Highness than against all the rest there is this reason, for that her Majesty by her present possession letteth more their desires than all the rest together with their future pretenses. But as I have said, it is not safety for them, nor yet good policy, to declare openly what they mean against her Majesty; it is the best way for the present to hew down the rest and to leave her Majesty for the last blow and upshot to their game. For which cause, they will seem to make great difference at this day between her Majesty's title and the rest that descend in like wise from King Henry VII, avowing the one and disallowing the other. Albeit my Lord of Leicester's father preferred that of Suffolk, when time was, before this of her Majesty and compelled the whole realm to swear thereunto. Such is the variable policy of men that serve the time, or rather that serve themselves of all times, for their purposes.

Scholar. I remember (quoth I) that time of the Duke and was present myself at some of his proclamations for that purpose. Wherein my Lord his son that now liveth being then a doer (as I can tell he was), I marvel how he can deal so contrary now, preferring not only her Majesty's title before that of Suffolk (whereof I wonder less because it is more gainful to him), but also another much further off. But you have signified the cause, in that the times are changed, and other bargains are in hand of more importance for him. Wherefore leaving this to be considered by others whom it concerneth, I beseech you, Sir (for that I know your worship hath been much conversant among their friends and favorers), to tell me what are the bars and lets which they do allege why the house of Scotland and Suffolk descending of King Henry VII his daughters should not succeed in the crown of England after her Majesty, who endeth the line of the same king by his son, for in my sight the matter appeareth very plain.

Gentleman: They want not pretenses of bars and lets against them all (quoth the gentleman), which I will lay down in order as I have heard them alleged. First, in the line of Scotland there are three persons, as you know, that may pretend right; that is, the Queen and her son by the first marriage of Margaret, and Arbella by the second. And against the first marriage I hear nothing affirmed, but against the two persons proceeding thereof I hear them allege three stops: one, for that they are strangers born out of the land and consequently incapable of inheritance within the same; another, for that by a special testament of King Henry VIII, authorized by two several Parliaments, they are excluded; the third, for that they are enemies to the religion now received among us and therefore to be debarred.

Against the second marriage of Margaret, with Archibald Douglas, whereof Arbella is descended, they allege that the said Archibald had a former wife at the time of that marriage which lived long after, and so neither that marriage lawful nor the issue thereof legitimate.[224]

The same bar they have against all the house and line of Suffolk, for first they say that Charles Brandon, Duke of Suffolk, had a known wife alive when he married Mary Queen of France, and consequently that neither the Lady Frances nor Eleanor born of that marriage can be lawfully born.[225] And this is all I can hear them say against the succession of the Countess of Derby, descended of Eleanor. But against my Lord of Hertford's children that come from Frances the eldest daughter I hear them allege two or three bastardies more besides this of the first marriage. For first, they affirm that Henry Marquess Dorset, when he married the Lady Frances, had to wife the old Earl of Arundel's sister, who lived both then and many years after and had a provision out of his living to her dying day, whereby that marriage could no way be good.[226] Secondly, that the Lady Catherine, daughter to the said Lady Frances by the Marquess (by whom the Earl of Hertford had his children) was lawfully married to the Earl of Pembroke that now liveth, and consequently could have no lawful issue by any other during his life.[227] Thirdly, that the said Catherine was never lawfully married to the said Earl of Hertford, but bare him those children as his concubine. Which (as they say) is defined and registered in the Archbishop of Canterbury's court, upon due examination taken by order of her Majesty that now reigneth, and this is in effect so much as I have heard them allege about these affairs.[228]

Scholar. It is much (quoth I) that you have said, if it may be all proved. Marry, yet by the way, I cannot but smile to hear my Lord of Leicester allow of so many bastardies now upon the issue of Lady Frances, whom in time past, when Jane her eldest daughter was married to his brother, he advanced in legitimation before both the daughters of King Henry VIII. But to the purpose: I would gladly know what grounds of verity these allegations have and how far in truth they may stop from inheritance, for indeed I never heard them so distinctly alleged before.

Gentleman: Whereto answered the gentleman that our friend the lawyer could best resolve that, if it pleased him to speak without his fee, though in some points alleged every other man (quoth he) that knoweth the state and common government of England may easily give his judgment also. As in the case of bastardy, if the matter may be proved there is no difficulty, but that no right to inheritance can justly be pretended; as also (perhaps) in the case of foreign birth, though in this I am not so cunning; but yet I see by experience that foreigners born in other lands can hardly come and claim inheritance in England, albeit to the contrary I have heard great and long disputes but such as indeed passed my capacity. And if it might please our friend here present to expound the thing unto us more clearly, I for my part would gladly bestow the hearing, and that with attention.

Lawyer. To this answered the lawyer: I will gladly, Sir, tell you my mind in any thing that it shall please you demand, and much more in this matter wherein by occasion of often conference I am somewhat perfect.

The impediments which these men allege against the succession of King Henry VIII his sisters are of two kinds, as you see, the one known and allowed in our law, as you have well said, if it may be proved, and that is bastardy, whereby they seek to disable all the whole line and race of Suffolk, as also Arbella of the second and later house of Scotland. Whereof it is to small purpose to speak anything here, seeing the whole controversy standeth upon a matter of fact only, to be proved or improved by records and witnesses. Only this I will say, that some of these bastardies before named are rife in many men's mouths and avowed by divers that yet live; but let other men look to this, who have most interest therein and may be most damnified by them if they fall out true.

The other impediments which are alleged only against the Queen of Scots and her son are in number three, as you recite them: that is, foreign birth, King Henry's testament, and religion, whereof I am content to say somewhat seeing you desire it, albeit there be so much published already in books of divers languages beyond the sea, as I am informed, concerning this matter as more cannot be said. But yet so much as I have heard pass among lawyers my betters in conference of these affairs I will not let to recite unto you, with this proviso and protestation always, that what I speak I speak by way of recital of other men's opinions, not meaning myself to incur the statute of affirming or avowing any person's title to the crown whatsoever.

First then,[229] touching foreign birth, there be some men in the world that will say that it is a common and general rule of our law that no stranger at all may inherit anything by any means within the land, which in truth I take to be spoken without ground, in that general sense. For I could never yet come to the sight of any such common or universal rule, and I know that divers examples may be alleged in sundry cases to the contrary; and by that which is expressly set down in the seventh and ninth years of King Edward IV, and in the eleventh and fourteenth of Henry IV, it appeareth plainly that a stranger may purchase lands in England, as also inherit by his wife if he marry an inheritrix. Wherefore this common rule is to be restrained from that generality into proper inheritance only; in which sense I do easily grant that our common law hath been of ancient, and is at this day, that no person born out of the allegiance of the king of England whose father and mother were not of the same allegiance at the time of his birth shalbe able to have or demand any heritage within the same allegiance as heir to any person. And this rule of our common law is gathered in these selfsame words of a statute made in the twenty-fifth year of King Edward III, which indeed is the only place of effect that can be alleged out of our law against the inheritance of strangers in such sense and cases as we now treat of.

And albeit now the common law of our country do run thus in general, yet will the friends of the Scottish claim affirm that hereby that title is nothing let or hindered at all towards the crown, and that for divers manifest and weighty reasons, whereof the principal are these which ensue.

First, it is common and a general rule of our English laws that no rule, axiom, or maxima of law (be it never so general) can touch or bind the crown except express mention be made thereof in the same, for that the king and crown have great privilege and prerogative above the state and affairs of subjects and great differences allowed in points of law.

As for example, it is a general and common rule of law that the wife, after the decease of her husband, shall enjoy the third of his lands, but yet the queen shall not enjoy the third part of the crown after the king's death, as well appeareth by experience and is to be seen by law, Anno 5. and 21. of Edward III and Anno 9. and 28. of Henry VI.[230] Also it is a common rule that the husband shall hold his wife's lands after her death as tenant by courtesy during his life, but yet it holdeth not in a kingdom.

In like manner, it is a general and common rule that if a man die seized of land in fee simple, having daughters and no son, his lands shalbe divided by equal portions among his daughters, which holdeth not in the crown, but rather the eldest daughter inheriteth the whole as if she were the issue male. So also it is a common rule of our law that the executor shall have all the goods and chattels of the testator, but yet not in the crown. And so in many other cases which might be recited it is evident that the crown hath privilege above others and can be subject to no rule, be it never so general, except express mention be made thereof in the same law, as it is not in the former place and a statute alleged; but rather to the contrary (as after shalbe showed), there is express exception for the prerogative of such as descend of royal blood.

Their second reason is for that the demand or title of a crown cannot in true sense be comprehended under the words of the former statute forbidding aliens to demand heritage within the allegiance of England, and that for two respects. The one, for that the crown itself cannot be called an heritage of allegiance or within allegiance, for that it is holden of no superior upon earth but immediately from God himself; the second, for that this statute treateth only and meaneth of inheritance by descent, as heir to the same (for I have showed before that aliens may hold lands by purchase within our dominion), and then say they, the crown is a thing incorporate and descendeth not according to the common course of other private inheritances, but goeth by succession as other incorporations do. In sign whereof, it is evident that albeit the king be more favored in all his doings than any common person shalbe, yet cannot he avoid by law his grants and letters patent by reason of his nonage (as other infants and common heirs under age may do), but always be said to be of full age in respect of his crown, even as a prior, parson, vicar, dean, or other person incorporate shalbe, which cannot by any means in law be said to be within age, in respect of their incorporations.

Which thing maketh an evident difference in our case from the meaning of the former statute, for that a prior, dean, or parson, being aliens and no denizens, might always in time of peace demand lands in England in respect of their corporations, notwithstanding the said statute or common law against aliens, as appeareth by many book-cases yet extant, as also by the statute made in the time of King Richard II, which was after the foresaid statute of King Edward III.[231]

The third reason is for that in the former statute itself of King Edward there are excepted expressly from this general rule INFANTES DU ROY, that is, the king's offspring or issue, as the word INFANT doth signify both in France, Portugal, Spain, and other countries, and as the Latin word *liberi* (which answereth the same) is taken commonly in the civil law. Neither may we restrain the French words of that statute, INFANTES DU ROY, to the king's children only of the first degree (as some do, for that the barrenness of our language doth yield us no other word for the same), but rather that thereby are understood as well the nephews and other descendants of the king or blood royal as his immediate children. For it were both unreasonable and ridiculous to imagine that King Edward by this statute would go about to disinherit his own nephews if he should have any born out of his own allegiance (as easily he might at that time, his sons being much abroad from England, and the Black Prince, his eldest son, having two children born beyond the seas), and consequently it is apparent that this rule or maxima set down against aliens is no way to be stretched against the descendants of the king or of the blood royal.

Their fourth reason is that the meaning of King Edward and his children (living at such time as this statute was made) could not be that any of their lineage or issue might be excluded in law from inheritance of their right to the crown by their foreign birth wheresoever. For otherwise it is not credible that they would so much have dispersed their own blood in other countries as they did by giving their daughters to strangers and other means. As Lionel the king's third son was married in Milan, and John of Gaunt the fourth son gave his two daughters Philippe and Katherine to Portugal and Castile and his niece Joan to the king of Scots; as Thomas of Woodstock also, the youngest brother, married his two daughters, the one to the king of Spain, and the other to the Duke of Brittany. Which no doubt they (being wise princes and so near of the blood royal) would never have done if they had imagined that hereby their issue should have lost all claim and title to the crown of England, and therefore it is most evident that no such bar was then extant or imagined.

Their fifth reason is that divers persons born out of all English dominion and allegiance, both before the Conquest and sithence, have been admitted to the succession of our crown as lawful inheritors without any exception against them for their foreign birth. As before the Conquest is evident in young Edgar Etheling, born in Hungary and thence called home to inherit the crown by his great uncle King Edward the Confessor with full consent of the whole realm, the Bishop of Worcester being sent as ambassador to fetch him home with his father, named Edward the Outlaw.[232]

And since the Conquest, it appeareth plainly in King Stephen and King Henry II, both of them born out of English dominions and of parents that at their birth were not of the English allegiance, and yet were they both admitted to the crown. Young Arthur also, Duke of Bretaigne[233] by his mother Constance that matched with Geoffrey, King Henry II's son, was declared by King Richard his uncle at his departure towards Jerusalem, and by the whole realm, for lawful heir apparent to the crown of England, though he were born in Bretaigne out of English allegiance, and so he was taken and adjudged by all the world at that day; albeit after King Richard's death his other uncle John most tyrannously took both his kingdom and his life from him.[234] For which notable injustice he was detested of all men both abroad and at home, and most apparently scourged by God with grievous and manifold plagues both upon himself and upon the realm which yielded to his usurpation. So that by this also it appeareth what the practice of our country hath been from time to time in this case of foreign birth, which practice is the best interpreter of our common English law, which dependeth especially and most of all upon custom; nor can the adversary allege any one example to the contrary.

Their sixth is of the judgment and sentence of King Henry VII and of his Council, who being together in consultation at a certain time about the marriage of Margaret his eldest daughter into Scotland, some of his Council moved this doubt, what should ensue if by chance the king's issue male should fail and so the succession devolve to the heirs of the said Margaret as now it doth? Whereunto that wise and most prudent prince made answer that if any such event should be, it could not be prejudicial to England, being the bigger part, but rather beneficial, for that it should draw Scotland to England, that is, the lesser to the more, even as in times past it happened in Normandy, Aquitaine, and some other provinces. Which answer appeased all doubts and gave singular content[at]ion to these of his Council, as Polydore writeth that lived at that time and wrote the special matters of that reign by the king's own instruction.[235] So that hereby we see no question made of King Henry or his Councillors touching foreign birth to let the succession of Lady Margaret's issue, which no doubt would never have been omitted in that learned assembly if any law at that time had been esteemed or imagined to bar the same.

And these are six of their principalest reasons to prove that neither by the words nor meaning of our common laws, nor yet by custom or practice of our realm an alien may be debarred from claim of his interest to the crown when it falleth to him by rightful descent in blood and succession. But in the particular case of the Queen of Scots and her son they do add another reason or two, thereby to prove them in very deed to be no aliens. Not only in respect of their often and continual mixture with English blood from the beginning (and especially of late, the Queen's grandmother and husband being English, and so her son begotten of an English father), but also for two other causes and reasons, which seem in truth of very good importance.

The first is for that Scotland by all Englishmen (howsoever the Scots deny the same) is taken and holden as subject to England by way of homage, which many of their kings at divers times have acknowledged; and consequently the Queen and her son being born in Scotland are not born out of the allegiance of England, and so no foreigners.[236]

The second cause or reason is for that the forenamed statute of foreigners in the five and twenty year of King Edward III is entitled *of those that are born beyond the seas*. And in the body of the same statute the doubt is moved of children born out of English allegiance beyond the seas, whereby cannot be understood Scotland for that it is a piece of the continent land within the seas. And all our old records in England that talk of service to be done within these two countries have usually these Latin words, *infra quatuor maria*, or in French, *deins lez quatre mers*; that is, within the four seas, whereby must needs be understood as well Scotland as England, and that perhaps for the reason before mentioned, of the subjection of Scotland by way of homage to the crown of England. In respect whereof it may be that it was accompted of old but one dominion or allegiance, and consequently no man born therein can be accompted an alien to England.[237] And this shall suffice for the first point, touching foreign nativity.[238]

For the second impediment objected, which is the testament of King Henry VIII,[239] authorized by Parliament, whereby they affirm the succession of Scotland to be excluded, it is not precisely true that they are excluded, but only that they are put back behind the succession of the house of Suffolk. For in that pretended testament (which after shalbe proved to be none indeed), King Henry so disposeth that after his own children (if they should chance to die without issue) the crown shall pass to the heirs of Frances and of Eleanor, his nieces by his younger sister Mary Queen of France; and after them (deceasing also without issue) the succession to return to the next heirs again. Whereby it is evident that the succession of Margaret Queen of Scotland, his eldest sister, is not excluded, but thrust back only from their due place and order to expect the remainder which may in time be left by the younger. Whereof in mine opinion do ensue some considerations against the present pretenders themselves.

First, that in King Henry's judgment the former pretended rule of foreign birth was no sufficient impediment against Scotland, for if it had been, no doubt but that he would have named the same in his alleged testament and thereby have utterly excluded that succession. But there is no such thing in the testament.

Secondly, if they admit this testament, which alloteth the crown to Scotland next after Suffolk, then, seeing that all the house of Suffolk (by these men's assertion) is excluded by bastardy, it must needs follow that Scotland by their own judgment is next, and so this testament will make against them, as indeed it doth in all points most apparently but only that it preferreth the house of Suffolk before that of Scotland. And therefore I think (Sir) that you mistake somewhat about their opinion in alleging this testament. For I suppose that no man of my Lord of Huntingdon's faction will allege or urge the testimony of this testament, but rather some friend of the house of Suffolk, in whose favor I take it that it was first of all forged.

Gentleman: It may be (quoth the gentleman), nor will I stand obstinately in the contrary, for that it is hard sometime to judge of what faction each one is who discourseth of these affairs. But yet I marvel (if it were as you say) why Leicester's father after King Edward's death made no mention thereof in the favor of Suffolk in the other testament which then he proclaimed, as made by King Edward deceased, for preferment of Suffolk before his own sisters?

Lawyer: The cause of this is evident (quoth the lawyer), for that it made not sufficiently for his purpose, which was to disinherit the two daughters of King Henry himself and advance the house of Suffolk before them both.[240]

Gentleman: A notable change (quoth the gentleman), that a title so much exalted of late by the father, above all order, right, rank, and degree, should now be so much debased by the son, as though it were not worthy to hold any degree, but rather to be trodden under foot for plain bastardy. And you see by this how true it is which I told you before, that the race of Dudleys are most cunning merchants to make their gain of all things, men, and times. And as we have seen now two testaments alleged, the one of the king father and the other of the king son, and both of them in prejudice of the testators' true successors, so many good subjects begin greatly to fear that we may chance to see shortly a third testament of her Majesty for the entitling of Huntingdon and extirpation of King Henry's blood, and that before her Majesty can think of sickness, wherein I beseech the Lord I be no prophet. But now (Sir), to the foresaid will and testament of King Henry, I have often heard in truth that the thing was counterfeit, or at the least not able to be proved, and that it was discovered, rejected, and defaced in Queen Mary's time; but I would gladly understand what you lawyers esteem or judge thereof.

Lawyer. Touching this matter (quoth the lawyer), it cannot be denied but that in the twenty and eighth and thirty and sixth years of King Henry's reign,[241] upon consideration of some doubt and irresolution which the king himself had showed to have about the order of succession in his own children, as also for taking away all occasions of controversies in those of the next blood, the whole Parliament gave authority unto the said king to debate and determine those matters himself, together with his learned Council, who best knew the laws of the realm and titles that any man might have thereby; and that whatsoever succession his Majesty should declare as most right and lawful under his letters patent sealed, or by his last will and testament rightfully made and signed with his own hand, that the same should be received for good and lawful.

Upon pretense whereof, soon after King Henry's death there was showed a will with the king's stamp at the same and the names of divers witnesses, wherein (as hath been said) the succession of the crown, after the king's own children, is assigned to the heirs of Frances and of Eleanor, nieces to the king by his younger sister. Which assignation of the crown, being as it were a mere gift in prejudice of the elder sister's right (as also of the right of Frances and Eleanor themselves, who were omitted in the same assignation and their heirs entitled only), was esteemed to be against all reason, law, and nature, and consequently not thought to proceed from so wise and sage a prince as King Henry was known to be, but rather either the whole forged or at leastwise that clause inserted by other and the king's stamp set unto it after his death, or when his Majesty lay now past understanding. And hereof there wanteth not divers most evident reasons and proofs.

For first, it is not probable or credible that King Henry would ever go about, against law and reason, to disinherit the line of his eldest sister without any profit or interest to himself, and thereby give most evident occasion of civil war and discord within the realm, seeing that in such a case of manifest and apparent wrong in so great a matter the authority of Parliament taketh little effect against the true and lawful inheritor, as well appeared in the former times and contentions of Henry VI, Edward IV, and Richard III, in whose reigns the divers and contrary Parliaments made and holden against the next inheritor held no longer with any man than until the other was able to make his own party good.

So likewise in the case of King Edward III his succession to France in the right of his mother, though he were excluded by the general assembly and consent of their parliaments, yet he esteemed not his right extinguished thereby, as neither did other kings of our country that ensued after him. And for our present case, if nothing else should have restrained King Henry from such open injustice towards his eldest sister, yet this cogitation at least would have stayed him, that by giving example of supplanting his elder sister's line by virtue of a testament or pretense of Parliament, some other might take occasion to displace his children by like pretense, as we see that Duke Dudley did soon after by a forged testament of King Edward VI. So ready scholars there are to be found which easily will learn such lessons of iniquity.

Secondly, there be too many incongruities and indignities in the said pretended will to proceed from such a prince and learned Council as King Henry's was. For first, what can be more ridiculous than to give the crown unto the heirs of Frances and Eleanor and not to any of themselves? Or what had they offended that their heirs should enjoy the crown in their right and not they themselves? What if King Henry's children should have died whiles Lady Frances had been yet alive? Who should have possessed the kingdom before her, seeing her line was next? And yet by this testament she could not pretend herself to obtain it. But rather, having married Adrian Stokes her horsekeeper, she must have suffered her son by him (if she had any) to enjoy the crown, and so Adrian of a servingman and master of horses should have become the Great Master and Protector of England.[242] Of like absurdity is that other clause also, wherein the king bindeth his own daughters to marry by consent and direction of his Council or otherwise to leese the benefit of their succession, but yet bindeth not his nieces' daughters, to wit, the daughters of Frances and Eleanor (if that they had any) to any such condition.

Thirdly, there may be divers causes and arguments alleged in law why this pretended will is not authentical, if otherwise it were certain that King Henry had meant it. First, for that it is not agreeable to the mind and meaning of the Parliament, which intended only to give authority for declaration and explication of the true title and not for donation or intricating of the same to the ruin of the realm. Secondly, for that there is no lawful and authentical copy extant thereof, but only a bare enrollment in the Chancery, which is not sufficient in so weighty an affair;[243] no witness of the Privy Council or of nobility to the same, which had been convenient in so great a case (for the best of the witnesses therein named is Sir John Gates, whose miserable death is well known);[244] no public notary; no probation of the will before any bishop or any lawful court for that purpose; no examination of the witnesses or other thing orderly done for lawful authorizing of the matter.

But of all other things this is most of importance, that the king never set his own hand to the foresaid will, but his stamp was put thereunto by others, either after his death or when he was past remembrance, as the late Lord Paget in the beginning of Queen Mary's days, being of the Privy Council, first of all other discovered the same of his own accord and upon mere motion of conscience, confessing before the whole Council and afterward also before the whole Parliament how that himself was privy thereunto and partly also culpable (being drawn thereunto by the instigation and forcible authority of others), but yet afterward upon other more godly motions detested the device and so of his own free will very honorably went and offered the discovery thereof to the Council.[245] As also did Sir Edward Montague, Lord Chief Justice, that had been privy and present at the said doings,[246] and one William Clark, that was the man who put the stamp unto the paper and is ascribed among the other pretensed witnesses, confessed the whole premises to be true and purchased his pardon for his offense therein.[247] Whereupon

Queen Mary and her Council caused presently the said enrollment lying in the Chancery to be cancelled, defaced, and abolished.

And sithence that time, in her Majesty's days that now liveth about the eleventh or twelfth year of her reign (if I compt not amiss), by occasion of a certain little book spread abroad at that time very secretly for advancing of the house of Suffolk by pretense of this testament,[248] I remember well the place where the late Duke of Norfolk, the Marquess of Winchester (which then was Treasurer), the old Earls of Arundel and Pembroke that now are dead, with my Lord of Pembroke that yet liveth (as also my Lord of Leicester himself, if I be not deceived), with divers others, met together upon this matter; and after long conference about the foresaid pretensed will and many proofs and reasons laid down why it could not be true or authentical, the old Earl of Pembroke protesting that he was with the king in his chamber from the first day of his sickness unto his last hour and thereby could well assure the falsification thereof, at length it was moved that from that place they should go, with the rest of the nobility, and proclaim the Queen of Scotland heir apparent in Cheapside. Wherein my Lord of Leicester (as I take it) was then as forward as any man else, howbeit now for his profit he be turned aside, and would turn back again tomorrow next for a greater commodity.

And albeit, for some causes to themselves best known, they proceeded not in the open publishing of their determination at that time, yet my Lord of Pembroke now living can bear witness that thus much is true, and that his father the old Earl at that time told him openly before the other noblemen that he had brought him to that assembly and place to instruct him in that truth, and to charge him to witness the same and to defend it also with his sword (if need required) after his death.[249] And I know that his Lordship is of that honor and nobility as he cannot leave off easily the remembrance or due regard of so worthy an admonition. And this shall suffice for the second impediment, imagined to proceed of this supposed testament of King Henry VIII.

As for the third impediment,[250] of religion, it is not general to all, for that only one person (if I be not deceived) of all the competitors in King Henry's line can be touched with suspicion of different religion from the present state of England. Which person notwithstanding (as is well known) while she was in government in her own realm of Scotland permitted all liberty of conscience and free exercise of religion to those of the contrary profession and opinion, without restraint. And if she had not, yet do I not see either by prescript of law or practice of these our times that diversity of religion may stay just inheritors from enjoying their due possessions in any state or degree of private men, and much less in the claim of a kingdom, which always in this behalf (as hath been said before) is preferred in privilege.

This we see by experience in divers countries and parts of the world at this day, as in Germany, where among so many princes and so divided in religion as they be, yet everyone succeedeth to the state whereto he hath right without resistance for his religion. The examples also of her Majesty that now is and of her sister before is evident, who being known to be of two different inclinations in religion and the whole realm divided in opinion for the same cause, yet both of them at their several times with general consent of all were admitted to their lawful inheritance, excepting only a few traitors against the former,[251] who withstood her right as also in her the right of her Majesty that is present, and that not for religion (as appeared by their own confession after), but for ambition and desire of reign. Monsieur, the king's brother and heir of France, as all the world knoweth, is well accepted, favored, and admitted for successor of that crown by all the Protestants at this day of that country, notwithstanding his opinion in religion known to be different. And I doubt not but the King of Navarre or Prince of Condé, in the contrary part, would think themselves greatly injured by the state of France, which is different from them in religion at this day, if after the death of the king that now is and his brother without issue (if God so dispose) they should be barred from inheriting the crown under pretense only of their religion.[252] My Lord of Huntingdon himself also, is he not known to be of a different religion from the present state of England? And that if he were king tomorrow next, he would alter the whole government, order, condition, and state of religion now used and established within the realm?

But as I said in the beginning, if one of a whole family or of divers families be culpable or to be touched herein, what have the rest offended thereby? Will you exclude all, for the mislike of one? And to descend in order, if the first of King Henry's line after her Majesty may be touched in this point, yet why should the rest be damnified thereby? The King of Scotland her son, that next ensueth (to speak in equity), why should he be shut out for his religion? And are not all the other in like manner Protestants whose descent is consequent by nature, order, and degree?

Scholar. For the young King of Scotland (quoth I), the truth is that always for mine own part I have had great hope and expectation of him, not only for the conceit which commonly men have of such orient youths born to kingdoms, but especially for that I understood from time to time that his education was in all learning, princely exercises, and instruction of true religion, under rare and virtuous men for that purpose. Whereby I conceived hope that he might not only become in time an honorable and profitable neighbor unto us for assurance of the gospel in these parts of the world, but also (if God should deprive us of her Majesty without issue) might be a mean by his succession to unite in concord and government the two realms together, which heretofore hath been sought by the price of many a thousand men's blood and not obtained.

Marry, yet now of late (I know not by what means) there is begun in men's hearts a certain mislike or grudge against him, for that it is given out everywhere that he is inclined to be a Papist and an enemy to her Majesty's proceedings. Which argueth him verily of singular ingratitude if it be true, considering the great helps and protection which he hath received from her Highness ever sithence he was born.[253]

Gentleman: And are you so simple (quoth the gentleman) as to believe every report that you hear of this matter? Know you not that it is expedient for my Lord of Leicester and his faction that this youth above all other be held in perpetual disgrace with her Majesty and with this realm? You know that Richard of Gloucester had never been able to have usurped as he did if he had not first persuaded King Edward IV to hate his own brother the Duke of Clarence, which Duke stood in the way between Richard and the thing which he most of all things coveted, that is, the possibility to the crown. And so in this case is there the like device to be observed.

For truly, for the young King of Scotland's religion, it is evident to as many as have reason that it can be no other of itself but inclined to the best, both in respect of his education, instruction, and conversation with those of true religion, as also by his former actions, edicts, government, and private behavior he hath declared. Marry, these men, whose profit is nothing less than that he or any other of that race should do well, do not cease daily by all secret ways, drifts, and molestations possible to drive him either to mislike of our religion or else to incur the suspicion thereof with such of our realm as otherwise would be his best friends; or if not this, yet for very need and fear of his own life to make recourse to such other princes abroad as may most offend or mislike this state.

And for this cause, they suborn certain busy fellows of their own crew and faction pertaining to the ministry of Scotland (but unworthy of so worthy a calling) to use such insolency towards their king and prince as is not only undecent but intolerable. For he may do nothing but they will examine and discuss the same in pulpit. If he go but on hunting when it pleaseth them to call him to their preaching; if he make but a dinner or supper when, or where, or with whom they like not; if he receive but a couple of horses or other present from his friends or kinsmen beyond the seas; if he salute or use courteously any man or messenger which cometh from them (as you know princes of their nobility and courtesy are accustomed, though they come from their enemies, as often hath been seen and highly commended in her Majesty of England); if he deal familiarly with any ambassador which liketh not them; or finally if he do, say, or signify any one thing whatsoever that pleaseth not their humor, they will presently, as seditious tribunes of the people, exclaim in public and, stepping to the pulpit where the word of the Lord only ought to be preached, will excite the commonalty to discontentation, inveighing against their sovereign with such bitterness of speech, unreverend terms, and insolent controlments as is not to be spoken.[254] Now imagine what her Majesty and her grave Council would do in England if such proceedings should be used by the clergy against them.

Scholar. No doubt (quoth I) but that such unquiet spirits should be punished in our realm. And so I said of late to their most reverend and worthy prelate and primate the Archbishop of St. Andrews, with whom it was my luck to come acquainted in London, whither he was come by his king's appointment (as he said) to treat certain affairs with our Queen and Council.[255] And talking with him of this disorder of his ministry, he confessed the same with much grief of mind and told me that he had preached thereof before the king himself, detesting and accusing divers heads thereof, for which cause he was become very odious to them and other of their faction both in Scotland and England. But he said that as he had given the reasons of his doings unto our Queen, so meaneth he shortly to do the same unto Monsieur Beza and to the whole church of Geneva,[256] by sending thither the articles of his and their doings; protesting unto me that the proceedings and attempts of those factious and corrupt men was most scandalous, seditious, and perilous both to the king's person and to the realm, being sufficient indeed to alienate wholly the young prince from all affection to our religion when he shall see the chief professors thereof to behave themselves so undutifully towards him.

Gentleman: That is the thing which these men his competitors most desire (quoth the gentleman), hoping thereby to procure him most evil will and danger both at home and from England. For which cause also they have practiced so many plots and treacheries with his own subjects against him, hoping by that means to bring the one in distrust and hatred of the other and consequently the king in danger of destruction by his own. And in this machination they have behaved themselves so dexterously, so covertly used the manage and contriving hereof, and so cunningly conveyed the execution of many things, as it might indeed seem apparent unto the young king that the whole plot of treasons against his realm and person doth come from England, thereby to drive him into jealousy of our state and our state of him; and all this for their own profit.

Neither is this any new device of my Lord of Leicester, to draw men for his own gain into danger and hatred with the state under other pretenses. For I could tell you divers stories and stratagems of his cunning in this kind, and the one far different from the other in device but yet all to one end. I have a friend yet living that was towards the old Earl of Arundel[257] in good credit and by that means had occasion to deal with the late Duke of Norfolk in his chiefest affairs before his troubles. This man is wont to report strange things from the Duke's own mouth of my Lord of Leicester's most treacherous dealing towards him for gaining of his blood, as after appeared, albeit the Duke, when he reported the same, mistrusted not so much my Lord's malice therein. But the sum of all is this, in effect, that Leicester, having a secret desire to pull down the said Duke, to the end that he might have no man above himself to hinder him in that which he most desireth, by a thousand cunning devices drew in the Duke to the cogitation of that marriage with the Queen of Scotland which afterward was the cause or occasion of his ruin. And he behaved himself so dexterously in this drift, by setting on the Duke on the one side and entrapping him on the other, as Judas himself never played his part more cunningly when he supped with his master and set himself so near as he dipped his spoon in the same dish, and durst before others ask who should betray him, meaning that night to do it himself, as he showed soon after supper when he came as a captain with a band of conspirators and with a courteous kiss delivered his person into the hands of them whom he well knew to thirst after his blood.

The very like did the Earl of Leicester with the Duke of Norfolk for the art of treason, though in the parties betrayed there were great difference of innocency. Namely at one time, when her Majesty was at Basing in Hampshire[258] and the Duke attended there to have audience, with great indifferency in himself to follow or leave off his suit for marriage (for that now he began to suspect her Majesty liked not greatly thereof), my Lord of Leicester came to him and counselled him in any case to persevere and not to relent, assuring him with many oaths and protestations that her Majesty must and should be brought to allow thereof whether she would or no, and that himself would seal that purpose with his blood. Neither was it to be suffered that her Majesty should have her will herein; with many other like speeches to this purpose, which the Duke repeated again then presently to my said friend, with often laying his hand upon his bosom and saying: I have here [that] which assureth me sufficiently of the fidelity of my Lord of Leicester, meaning not only the foresaid speeches, but also divers letters which he had written to the Duke to that effect, as likewise he had done to some other person of more importance in the realm; which matter coming afterward to light, he cozened most notably her Majesty by showing her a reformed copy of the said letter for the letter itself.²⁵⁹

But now how well he performed his promise in dealing with her Majesty for the Duke, or against the Duke, in this matter, her Highness can best tell and the event itself showed. For the Duke, being admitted soon after to her Majesty's speech at another place and receiving a far other answer than he had in hope conceived upon Leicester's promises, retired himself to London, where the same night following he received letters both from Leicester and Sir Nicholas Throgmorton upon Leicester's instigation (for they were at that time both friends and of a faction) that he should presently flee into Norfolk, as he did, which was the last and final complement of all Leicester's former devices whereby to plunge his friend over the ears in suspicion and disgrace, in such sort as he should never be able to draw himself out of the ditch again, as indeed he was not, but died in the same.²⁶⁰

And herein you see also the same subtile and Machavellian sleight which I mentioned before, of driving men to attempt somewhat whereby they may incur danger or remain in perpetual suspicion or disgrace. And this practice he hath long used and doth daily against such as he hath will to destroy. As for example, what say you to the device he had of late to entrap his well deserving friend Sir Christopher Hatton in the matter of Hall, his priest, whom he would have had Sir Christopher to send away and hide, being touched and detected in the case of Arden, thereby to have drawn in Sir Christopher himself, as Sir Charles Candishe can well declare if it please him, being accessory to this plot for the otherthrow of Sir Christopher.²⁶¹ To which intent and most devilish drift pertained (I doubt not), if the matter were duly examined, the late interception of letters in Paris from one Aldred of Lyons then in Rome, to Henry Umpton, servant to Sir Christopher, in which letters Sir Christopher is reported to be of such credit and special favor in Rome as if he were the greatest Papist in England.²⁶²

What meaneth also these pernicious late dealings against the Earl of Shrewsbury, a man of the most ancient and worthiest nobility of our realm? What mean the practices with his nearest both in bed and blood against him? What mean these most false and slanderous rumors cast abroad of late of his disloyal demeanor towards her Majesty and his country with the great prisoner committed to his charge?[263] Is all this to any other end but only to drive him to some impatience, and thereby to commit or say something which may open the gate unto his ruin? Divers other things could I recite of his behavior towards other noblemen of the realm, who live abroad in their countries much injured and malcontented by his insolency, albeit in respect of his present power they dare not complain. And surely it is strange to see how little accompt he maketh of all the ancient nobility of our realm, how he contemneth, derideth, and debaseth them, which is the fashion of all such as mean to usurp, to the end they may have none who shall not acknowledge their first beginning and advancement from themselves.

Lawyer. Not only usurpers (quoth the lawyer), but all others who rise and mount aloft from base lineage be ordinarily most contemptuous, contumelious, and insolent against others of more antiquity. And this was evident in this man's father, who being a buck of the first head[264] (as you know) was intolerable in contempt of others, as appeareth by those whom he trod down of the nobility in his time, as also by his ordinary jests against the Duke of Somerset and others. But among other times, sitting one day at his own table (as a Councillor told me that was present), he took occasion to talk of the Earl of Arundel, whom he then had not only removed from the Council but also put into the Tower of London, being (as is well known) the first and chiefest earl of the realm.[265] And for that the said Earl showed himself somewhat sad and afflicted with his present state (as I marvel not, seeing himself in prison and within the compass of so fierce a Bear's paws), it pleased this goodly Duke to vaunt upon this Earl's misery at his own table (as I have said) and asked the noblemen and gentlemen there present what crest or cognizance my Lord of Arundel did give? And when everyone answered that he gave the white horse—I thought so (quoth the Duke) and not without great cause, for as the white palfrey when he standeth in the stable and is well provendered is proud and fierce and ready to leap upon every other horse's back, still neighing and prancing and troubling all that stand about him, but when he is once out of his hot stable and deprived a little of his ease and fat feeding every boy may ride and master him at his pleasure, so is it (quoth he) with my Lord of Arundel. Whereat many marveled that were present to hear so insolent speech pass from a man of judgment against a peer of the realm cast into calamity.[266]

Gentleman: But you would more have marveled (quoth the gentleman) if you had seen that which I did afterward, which was the most base and abject behavior of the same Duke to the same Earl of Arundel at Cambridge and upon the way towards London, when this Earl was sent to apprehend and bring him up as prisoner. If I should tell you how he fell down on his knees, how he wept, how he besought the said Earl to be good lord unto him, whom a little before he had so much contemned and reproached, you would have said that himself might as well be compared to this his white palfrey as the other.[267] Albeit in this I will excuse neither of them both, neither almost any other of these great men who are so proud and insolent in their prosperous fortune as they are easily led to contemn any man, albeit themselves be most contemptible of all others whensoever their fortune beginneth to change; and so will my Lord of Leicester be also, no doubt, at that day, though now in his wealth he triumph over all and careth not whom or how many he offend or injury.

Scholar: Sir, therein I believe you (quoth I), for we have had sufficient trial already of my Lord's fortitude in adversity. His base and abject behavior in his last disgrace about his marriage well declared what he would do in a matter of more importance. His fawning and flattering of them whom he hated most; his servile speeches, his feigned and dissembled tears are all very well known; then Sir Christopher Hatton must needs be enforced to receive at his hands the honorable and great office of Chamberlainship of Chester,[268] for that he would by any means resign the same unto him whether he would or no, and made him provide (not without his charge) to receive the same, though his Lordship never meant it, as after well appeared. For that the present pang being past, it liked my Lord to fulfill the Italian proverb of such as in dangers make vows to saints: *Scampato il pericolo, gabbato il Santo*—the danger escaped, the saint is deceived.[269]

Then, and in that necessity, no men of the realm were so much honored, commended, and served by him as the noble Chamberlain deceased and the good Lord Treasurer yet living, to whom at a certain time he wrote a letter, in all fraud and base dissimulation, and caused the same to be delivered with great cunning in the sight of her Majesty, and yet so as to show a purpose that it should not be seen, to the end her Highness might the rather take occasion to call for the same and read it, as she did. For Mistress Frances Howard[270] (to whom the stratagem was committed) playing her part dexterously, offered to deliver the same to the Lord Treasurer near the door of the withdrawing chamber, he then coming from her Majesty. And to draw the eye and attention of her Highness the more unto it, she let fall the paper before it touched the Treasurer's hand and by that occasion brought her Majesty to call for the same. Which after she had read and considered the style together with the mettle and constitution of him that wrote it, and to whom it was sent, her Highness could not but break forth in laughter with detestation of such absurd and abject dissimulation, saying unto my Lord Treasurer there present: My Lord, believe him not, for if he had you in like case he would play the Bear with you, though at this present he fawn upon you never so fast.

But now, Sir, I pray you go forward in your speech of Scotland, for there I remember you left off when by occasion we fell into these digressions.

[*Gentleman*:] Well then (quoth the gentleman), to return again to Scotland (as you move) from whence we have digressed; most certain and evident it is to all the world that all the broils, troubles, and dangers procured to the prince in that country, as also the vexations of them who any way are thought to favor that title in our own realm, do proceed from the drift and complot of these conspirators. Which besides the great dangers mentioned before both domestical and foreign, temporal and of religion, must needs infer great jeopardy also to her Majesty's person and present reign that now governeth, through the hope and heat of the aspirers' ambition, enflamed and increased so much the more by the nearness of their desired prey.

For as soldiers entered into hope of a rich and well furnished city are more fierce and furious when they have gotten and beaten down the bulwarks round about, and as the greedy burglarer that hath pierced and broken down many walls to come to a treasure is less patient of stay, stop, and delay when he cometh in sight of that which he desireth, or perceiveth only some partition of wainscot or the like betwixt his fingers and the coffers or moneybags, so these men, when they shall see the succession of Scotland extinguished, together with all friends and favorers thereof (which now are to her Majesty as bulwarks and walls and great obstacles to the aspirers), and when they shall see only her Majesty's life and person to stand betwixt them and their fiery desires (for they make little accompt of all other competitors by King Henry's line), no doubt but it wilbe to them a great prick and spur to dispatch her Majesty also, the nature of both Earls being well considered, whereof the one killed his own wife (as hath been showed before) only upon a little vain hope of marriage with a queen, and the other being so far blinded and borne away with the same furious fume and most impotent itching humor of ambition as his own mother, when she was alive, seemed greatly to fear his fingers if once the matter should come so near as her life had only stood in his way. For which cause the good old Countess was wont to pray God (as I have heard divers say) that she might die before her Majesty (which happily was granted unto her),[271] to the end that by standing in her son's way (whom she saw to her grief furiously bent to wear a crown) there might not some dangerous extremity grow to her by that nearness. And if his own mother feared this mischance, what may her Majesty doubt at his and his companions' hands, when she only shalbe the obstacle of all their unbridled and impatient desires?

Lawyer. Clear it is (quoth the lawyer) that the nearness of aspirers to the crown endangereth greatly the present possessors, as you have well proved by reason and I could show by divers examples if it were need. For when Henry Bolingbroke, Duke of Lancaster, saw not only Richard II to be without issue, but also Roger Mortimer, Earl of March, that should have succeeded in the crown to be slain in Ireland, though before (as is thought) he meant not to usurp, yet seeing the possibility and near cut that he had, was invited therewith to lay hands of his sovereign's blood and dignity, as he did. The like is thought of Richard Duke of Gloucester, that he never meant the murder of his nephews until he saw their father dead and themselves in his own hands, his brother also, Duke of Clarence, dispatched and his only son and heir Earl of Warwick within his own power.

Wherefore seeing it hath not pleased Almighty God, for causes to himself best known, to leave unto this noble realm any issue by her most excellent Majesty, it hath been a point of great wisdom in mine opinion and of great safety to her Highness' person, state, and dignity to preserve hitherto the line of the next inheritors by the house of Scotland (I mean both the mother and the son), whose deaths hath been so diligently sought by the other competitors and had been long ere this achieved if her Majesty's own wisdom and royal clemency (as is thought) had not placed special eye upon the conservation thereof from time to time. Which princely providence, so long as it shall endure, must needs be a great safety and fortress to her Majesty not only against the claims, aids, or annoyance of foreign princes, who will not be so forward to advance strange titles while so manifest heirs remain at home nor yet so willing (in respect of policy) to help that line to possession of the whole island, but also against practices of domestical aspirers (as you have showed) in whose affairs no doubt but these two branches of Scotland are great blocks, as also special bulwarks to her Majesty's life and person, seeing (as you say) these compartners make so little accompt of all the other of that line who should ensue by order of succession.

Marry, yet of the two, I think the youth of Scotland be of much more importance for their purpose to be made away, both for that he may have issue and is like in time to be of more ability for defense of his own inheritance, as also for that he being once dispatched his mother should soon ensue by one sleight or other, which they would devise unwitting to her Majesty, albeit I must needs confess that her Highness hath used most singular prudence for prevention thereof in placing her restraint with so noble, strong, and worthy a peer of our realm as the Earl of Shrewsbury is, whose fidelity and constancy being nothing pliable to the others' faction giveth them little contentation. And for that cause, the world seeth how many sundry and divers devices they have used and do use daily to slander and disgrace him and thereby to pull from him his charge committed.[272]

Gentleman: To this the gentleman answered nothing at all, but stood still musing with himself, as though he had conceived some deep matter in his head, and after a little pause he began to say as followeth:

I cannot truly but much marvel when I do compare some things of this time and government with the doings of former princes, progenitors to her Majesty. Namely of Henry VII and Henry VIII, who had so vigilant an eye to the lateral line of King Edward IV by his brother of Clarence as they thought it necessary not only to prevent all evident dangers that might ensue that way but even the possibilities of all peril; as may well appear by the execution of Edward Earl of Warwick before named, son and heir to the said Duke of Clarence, and of Margaret his sister, Countess of Salisbury, with the Lord Henry Montagu her son, by whose daughter the Earl of Huntingdon now claimeth. All which were executed for avoiding of inconveniences, and that at such times when no imminent danger could be much doubted by that line, especially by the latter. And yet now when one of the same house and line, of more ability and ambition than ever any of his ancestors were, maketh open title and claim to the crown, with plots, packs,[273] and preparations to most manifest usurpation, against all order, all law, and all rightful succession, and against a special statute provided in that behalf, yet is he permitted, borne out, favored, and friended therein, and no man so hardy as in defense of her Majesty and realm to control him for the same.

It may be that her Majesty is brought into the same opinion of my Lord of Huntingdon's fidelity as Julius Caesar was of Marcus Brutus, his dearest obliged friend, of whose ambitious practices and aspiring when Caesar was advertised by his careful friends, he answered that he well knew Brutus to be ambitious; but I am sure (quoth he) that my Brutus will never attempt anything for the Empire while Caesar liveth, and after my death let him shift for the same among others as he can. But what ensued? Surely I am loth to tell the event, for omination's sake, but yet all the world knoweth that ere many months passed this most noble and clement emperor was pitifully murdered by the same Brutus and his partners in the public Senate when least of all he expected such treason. So dangerous a thing it is to be secure in a matter of so great sequel, or to trust them with a man's life who may pretend preferment or interest by his death.

Wherefore, would God her Majesty in this case might be induced to have such due care and regard of her own estate and royal person as the weighty moment of the matter requireth, which containeth the bliss and calamity of so noble and worthy a kingdom as this is.

I know right well that most excellent natures are always furthest off from diffidence in such people as profess love and are most bounden by duty, and so it is evident in her Majesty. But yet surely this confidence so commendable in other men is scarce allowable oftentimes in the person of a prince, for that it goeth accompanied with so great peril as is inevitable to him that will not suspect, principally when dangers are foretold or presaged (as commonly by God's appointment they are, for the special hand he holdeth over princes' affairs), or when there is probable conjecture or just surmise of the same.

We know that the forenamed Emperor Caesar had not only the warning given him of the inclination and intent of Brutus to usurpation, but even the very day when he was going towards the place of his appointed destiny, there was given up into his hands a detection of the whole treason with request to read the same presently, which he upon confidence omitted to do. We read also of Alexander the Great, how he was not only forbidden by a learned man to enter into Babylon (whither he was then going), for that there was treason meant against him in the place, but also that he was foretold of Antipater's mischievous meaning against him in particular. But the young prince, having so well deserved of Antipater, could not be brought to mistrust the man that was so dear unto him, and by that means was poisoned in a banquet by three sons of Antipater which were of most credit and confidence in the king's chamber.

Scholar. Here, truly, my heart did somewhat tremble with fear, horror, and detestation of such events. And I said unto the gentleman: I beseech you, Sir, to talk no more of these matters, for I cannot well abide to hear them named, hoping in the Lord that there is no cause nor ever shalbe to doubt the like in England, specially from these men who are so much bounden to her Majesty and so forward in seeking out and pursuing all such as may be thought to be dangerous to her Majesty's person, as by the sundry late executions we have seen, and by the punishments every way of Papists we may perceive.

Gentleman: Truth it is (quoth the gentleman) that justice hath been done upon divers of late, which contenteth me greatly, for the terror and restraint of others of what sect or religion soever they be. And it is most necessary (doubtless) for the compressing of parties that great vigilance be used in that behalf. But when I consider that only one kind of men are touched herein, and that all speech, regard, doubt, distrust, and watch is of them alone without reflexion of eye upon any other men's doings or designments; when I see the double diligence and vehemency of certain instruments which I like not, bent wholly to raise wonder and admiration [274] of the people, fear, terror, and attention to the doings, sayings, and meanings of one part or faction alone, and of that namely and only which these conspirators esteem for most dangerous and opposite to themselves, I am (believe me) often tempted to suspect fraud and false measure, and that these men deal as wolves by nature in other countries are wont to do, which going together in great numbers to assail a flock of sheep by night do set some one or two of their company upon the wind side of the fold afar off, who partly by their scent and other bruitling [275] which of purpose they make may draw the dogs and shepherds to pursue them alone, whiles the other do enter and slay the whole flock. Or as rebels that meaning to surprise a town, to turn away the inhabitants from consideration of the danger and from defense of that place where they intend to enter, do set on fire some other parts of the town further off and do sound a false alarm at some gate where is meant least danger.

Which art was used cunningly by Richard Duke of York in the time of King Henry VI when he, to cover his own intent, brought all the realm in doubt of the doings of Edmund Duke of Somerset, his enemy. But John of Northumberland, father to my Lord of Leicester, used the same art much more skillfully when he put all England in a maze and musing of the Protector and of his friends, as though nothing could be safe about the young king until they were suppressed, and consequently all brought into his own authority without obstacle. I speak not this to excuse Papists or to wish them any way spared wherein they offend, but only to signify that in a country where so potent factions be it is not safe to suffer the one to make itself so puissant by pursuit of the other as afterwards the prince must remain at the devotion of the stronger; but rather as in a body molested and troubled with contrary humors, if all cannot be purged, the best physic is without all doubt to reduce and hold them at such an equality as destruction may not be feared of the predominant.

Lawyer. To this said the lawyer, laughing: Yea, marry, Sir, I would to God your opinion might prevail in this matter, for then should we be in other terms than now we are. I was not long since in company of a certain honorable lady of the Court, who, after some speech passed by gentlemen that were present of some apprehended and some executed and such like affairs, brake into a great complaint of the present time and therewith (I assure you) moved all the hearers to grief (as women you know are potent in stirring of affections) and caused them all to wish that her Majesty had been nigh to have heard her words.

I do well remember (quoth she) the first dozen years of her Highness' reign, how happy, pleasant, and quiet they were, with all manner of comfort and consolation. There was no mention then of factions in religion, neither was any man much noted or rejected for that cause, so otherwise his conversation were civil and courteous. No suspicion of treason, no talk of bloodshed, no complaint of troubles, miseries, or vexations. All was peace, all was love, all was joy, all was delight. Her Majesty (I am sure) took more recreation at that time in one day than she doth now in a whole week, and we that served her Highness enjoyed more contentation in a week than we can now in divers years. For now there are so many suspicions everywhere, for this thing and for that, as we cannot tell whom to trust. So many melancholic in the Court, that seem malcontented; so many complaining or suing for their friends that are in trouble; other slip over the sea or retire themselves upon the sudden; so many tales brought us of this or that danger, of this man suspected, of that man sent for up, and such like unpleasant and unsavory stuff as we can never almost be merry one whole day together.

Wherefore (quoth this lady) we that are of her Majesty's train and special service and do not only feel these things in ourselves but much more in the grief of her most excellent Majesty, whom we see daily molested herewith (being one of the best natures, I am sure, that ever noble princess was endued withal), we cannot but moan to behold contentions advanced so far forth as they are, and we could wish most heartily that for the time to come these matters might pass with such peace, friendship, and tranquility as they do in other countries, where difference in religion breaketh not the band of good fellowship or fidelity. And with this in a smiling manner she brake off, asking pardon of the company if she had spoken her opinion overboldly like a woman.

To whom answered a courtier that sat next her: Madam, your Ladyship hath said nothing in this behalf that is not daily debated among us in our common speech in Court, as you know. Your desire also herein is a public desire, if it might be brought to pass, for there is no man so simple that seeth not how perilous these contentions and divisions among us may be in the end. And I have heard divers gentlemen that be learned discourse at large upon this argument, alleging old examples of the Athenians, Lacedaemonians, Carthaginians, and Romans who received notable damages and destruction also in the end by their divisions and factions among themselves, and specially from them of their own cities and countries who upon factions lived abroad with foreigners and thereby were always as firebrands to carry home the flame of war upon their country.

The like they also showed by the long experience of all the great cities and states of Italy which by their factions and foruscites [276] were in continual garboil, bloodshed, and misery. Whereof our own country hath tasted also her part by the odious contention between the houses of Lancaster and York, wherein it is marvelous to consider what trouble a few men oftentimes, departing out of the realm, were able to work by the part of their faction remaining at home (which commonly increaseth towards them that are absent) and by the readiness of foreign princes to receive always and comfort such as are discontented in another state, to the end that by their means they might hold an oar in their neighbor's boat, which princes that are nigh borderers do always above all other things most covet and desire.

This was that courtier's speech and reason, whereby I perceived that as well among them in Court as among us in the realm and country abroad the present inconvenience and dangerous sequel of this our home dissension is espied, and consequently most English hearts inclined to wish the remedy or prevention thereof by some reasonable moderation or reunion among ourselves. For that the prosecution of these differences to extremity cannot but after many wounds and exulcerations bring matters finally to rage, fury, and most deadly desperation.

Whereas on the other side, if any sweet qualification or small toleration among us were admitted, there is no doubt but that affairs would pass in our realm with more quietness, safety, and public weal of the same than it is like it will do long, and men would easily be brought, that have English bowels, to join in the preservation of their country from ruin, bloodshed, and foreign oppression which desperation of factions is wont to procure.

Gentleman: I am of your opinion (quoth the gentleman) in that, for I have seen the experience thereof, and all the world beholdeth the same at this day in all the countries of Germany, Polonia, Boemland,[277] and Hungary, where a little bearing of th'one with th'other hath wrought them much ease and continued them a peace whereof all Europe besides hath admiration and envy. The first dozen years also of her Majesty's reign, whereof your lady of the Court discoursed before, can well be a witness of the same, wherein the commiseration and lenity that was used towards those of the weaker sort, with a certain sweet diligence for their gaining, by good means, was the cause of much peace, contentation, and other benefit to the whole body.

We see in France that by overmuch pressing of one part only a fire was enkindled not many years since, like to have consumed and destroyed the whole had not a necessary mollification been thought upon by the wisest of that king's Council, full contrary to the will and inclination of some great personages who meant perhaps to have gained more by the other.[278] And since that time we see what peace, wealth, and reunion hath ensued in that country, that was so broken, dissevered, and wasted before. And all this, by yielding a little in that thing which no force can master, but exulcerate rather and make worse; I mean the conscience and judgment of men in matters of religion.

The like also I could name you in Flanders, where after all these broils and miseries of so many years' wars (caused principally by too much straining in such affairs at the beginning), albeit the king be never so strict-laced in yielding to public liberty and free exercise on both parts, yet is he descended to this at length (and that upon force of reason), to abstain from the pursuit and search of men's consciences, not only in the towns which upon composition he receiveth, but also where he hath recovered by force, as in Tournay and other places, where I am informed that no man is searched, demanded, or molested for his opinion or conscience, nor any act of Papistry or contrary religion required at their hands, but are permitted to live quietly to God and themselves at home in their own houses, so they perform otherwise their outward obedience and duties to their prince and country.[279] Which only qualification, tolerance, and moderation in our realm (if I be not deceived, with many more that be of my opinion) would content all divisions, factions, and parties among us for their continuance in peace, be they Papists, Puritans, Familians,[280] or of whatsoever nice difference or section besides, and would be sufficient to retain all parties within a temperate obedience to the magistrate and government for conservation of their country, which were of no small importance to the contentation of her Majesty and weal public of the whole kingdom.

But what should I talk of this thing, which is so contrary to the desires and designments of our puissant conspirators? What should Cicero the Senator use persuasions to Captain Catiline and his crew that quietness and order were better than hurley-burlies?[281] Is it possible that our aspirers will ever permit any such thing, cause, or matter to be treated in our state as may tend to the stability of her Majesty's present government? No, surely, it standeth nothing with their wisdom or policy, especially at this instant, when they have such opportunity of following their own actions in her Majesty's name under the vizard and pretext of her defense and safety; having sowed in every man's head so many imaginations of the dangers present both abroad and at home, from Scotland, Flanders, Spain, and Ireland, so many conspiracies, so many intended murders, and others so many contrived or conceived mischiefs as my Lord of Leicester assureth himself that the troubled water can not be cleared again in short space, nor his baits and lines laid therein easily espied, but rather that hereby ere long he will catch the fish he gapeth so greedily after, and in the meantime, for the pursuit of these crimes and other that daily he will find out, himself must remain perpetual dictator.

But what meaneth this so much inculcating of troubles, treasons, murders, and invasions? I like not surely these ominous speeches. And as I am out of doubt that Leicester, the caster of these shadows, doth look to play his part first in these troublesome affairs, so do I heartily fear that, unless the tyranny of this Leicestrian fury be speedily stopped, that such misery to prince and people (which the Lord for his mercy's sake turn from us) as never greater fell before to our miserable country is far nearer hand than is expected or suspected.

And therefore for prevention of these calamities, to tell you plainly mine opinion (good Sirs) and therewith to draw to an end of this our conference (for it waxeth late), I would think it the most necessary point of all for her Majesty to call his Lordship to accompt among other and to see what other men could say against him at length, after so many years of his sole accusing and pursuing of others. I know and am very well assured that no one act which her Majesty hath done since her coming to the crown (as she hath done right many most highly to be commended), nor any that lightly her Majesty may do hereafter, can be of more utility to herself and to the realm or more grateful unto her faithful and zealous subjects than this noble act of justice would be, for trial of this man's deserts towards his country.

I say it would be profitable to her Majesty and to the realm, not only in respect of the many dangers before mentioned hereby to be avoided, which are like to ensue most certainly if his courses be still permitted, but also for that her Majesty shall by this deliver herself from that general grudge and grief of mind, with great mislike, which many subjects otherwise most faithful have conceived against the excessive favor showed to this man so many years without desert or reason. Which favor he having used to the hurt, annoyance, and oppression both of infinite several persons and the whole commonwealth (as hath been said), the grief and resentment thereof doth redound commonly in such cases not only upon the person delinquent alone, but also upon the sovereign by whose favor and authority he offereth such injuries, though never so much against the other's intent, will, desire, or meaning.

And hereof we have examples of sundry princes in all ages and countries whose exorbitant favor to some wicked subject that abused the same hath been the cause of great danger and ruin, the sins of the favorite being returned and revenged upon the favorer. As in the history of the Grecians is declared by occasion of the pitiful murder of that wise and victorious prince Philip of Macedony, who albeit that he were well assured to have given no offense of himself to any of his subjects and consequently feared nothing, but conversed openly and confidently among them, yet for that he had favored too much one Duke Attalus, a proud and insolent courtier, and had borne him out in certain of his wickedness, or at least not punished the same after it was detected and complained upon, the parties grieved, accompting the crime more proper and heinous on the part of him who by office should do justice and protect other than of the perpetrator, who followeth but his own passion and sensuality, let pass Attalus and made their revenge upon the blood and life of the king himself, by one Pausanias, suborned for that purpose, in the marriage day of the king's own daughter.[282]

Great store of like examples might be repeated out of the stories of other countries, nothing being more usual or frequent among all nations than the afflictions of realms and kingdoms and the overthrow of princes and great potentates themselves by their too much affection towards some unworthy particular persons, a thing indeed so common and ordinary as it may well seem to be the specialest rock of all other whereat kings and princes do make their shipwracks.

For if we look into the states and monarchies of all Christendom and consider the ruins that have been of any prince or ruler within the same, we shall find this point to have been a great and principal part of the cause thereof, and in our own state and country the matter is too too evident. For whereas since the Conquest we number principally three just and lawful kings to have come to confusion by alienation of their subjects, that is, Edward II, Richard II, and Henry VI, this only point of too much favor towards wicked persons was the chiefest cause of destruction in all three. As in the first, the excessive favor towards Peter Gaveston and two of the Spencers. In the second, the like extraordinary and indiscreet affection towards Robert Vere, Earl of Oxford and Marquess of Dublin, and Thomas Mowbray, two most turbulent and wicked men, that set the king against his own uncles and the nobility.[283]

In the third (being a simple and holy man), albeit no great exorbitant affection was seen towards any, yet his wife Queen Margaret's too much favor and credit (by him not controlled) towards the Marquess of Suffolk that after was made Duke, by whose instinct[284] and wicked counsel she made away first the noble Duke of Gloucester and afterward committed other things in great prejudice of the realm and suffered the said most impious and sinful Duke to range and make havoc of all sort of subjects at his pleasure (much after the fashion of the Earl of Leicester now, though yet not in so high and extreme a degree)—this I say was the principal and original cause, both before God and man (as Polydore well noteth),[285] of all the calamity and extreme desolation which after ensued both to the king, queen, and their only child, with the utter extirpation of their family.

And so likewise now to speak in our particular case, if there be any grudge or grief at this day, any mislike, repining, complaint, or murmur against her Majesty's government in the hearts of her true and faithful subjects, who wish amendment of that which is amiss and not the overthrow of that which is well (as I trow it were no wisdom to imagine there were none at all), I dare avouch upon conscience that either all or the greatest part thereof proceedeth from this man, who by the favor of her Majesty so afflicteth her people as never did before him either Gaveston, or Spencer, or Vere, or Mowbray, or any other mischievous tyrant that abused most his prince's favor within our realm of England. Whereby it is evident how profitable a thing it should be to the whole realm, how honorable to her Majesty, and how grateful to all her subjects, if this man at length might be called to his accompt.

Lawyer. Sir (quoth the lawyer), you allege great reason, and verily I am of opinion that if her Majesty knew but the tenth part of this which you have here spoken, as also her good subjects' desires and complaint in this behalf, she would well show that her Highness feareth not to permit justice to pass upon Leicester or any other within her realm for satisfaction of her people, whatsoever some men may think and report to the contrary or howsoever otherwise of her own mild disposition or good affection towards the person she have borne with him hitherto. For so we see that wise princes can do at times convenient for peace, tranquility, and public weal, though contrary to their own particular and peculiar inclination.

As to go no further than to the last example named and alleged by yourself before: though Queen Margaret, the wife of King Henry VI, had favored most unfortunately many years together William Duke of Suffolk (as hath been said), whereby he committed manifold outrages and afflicted the realm by sundry means, yet she being a woman of great prudence, when she saw the whole commonalty demand justice upon him for his demerits, albeit she liked and loved the man still, yet for satisfaction of the people upon so general a complaint she was content first to commit him to prison and afterward to banish him the realm. But the providence of God would not permit him so to escape, for that he being encountered and taken upon the sea in his passage, he was beheaded in the ship and so received some part of condign punishment for his most wicked, loose, and licentious life.[286]

And to seek no more examples in this case, we know into what favor and special grace Sir Edmund Dudley, my Lord of Leicester's good grandfather, was crept with King Henry VII in the later end of his reign, and what intolerable wickedness and mischief he wrought against the whole realm and against infinite particular persons of the same by the poolings and oppressions which he practiced, whereby though the king received great temporal commodity at that time (as her Majesty doth nothing at all by the present extortions of his nephew), yet for justice sake and for mere compassion towards his afflicted subjects that complained grievously of this iniquity, that most virtuous and wise prince King Henry was content to put from him this lewd instrument and devilish suggester of new exactions; whom his son Henry, that ensued in the crown, caused presently before all other business to be called publicly to accompt and for his deserts to leese his head. So as where the interest of a whole realm or common cause of many taketh place, the private favor of anyone cannot stay a wise and godly prince (such as all the world knoweth her Majesty to be) from permitting justice to have her free passage.

Gentleman: Truly, it should not (quoth the gentleman), for to that end were princes first elected, and upon that consideration do subjects pay them both tribute and obedience: to be defended by them from injuries and oppressions, and to see laws executed and justice exercised upon and towards all men with indifferency.[287] And as for our particular case of my Lord of Leicester, I do not see in right and equity how her Majesty may deny this lawful desire and petition of her people. For if her Highness do permit and command the laws daily to pass upon thieves and murderers without exception, and that for one fact only, as by experience we see, how then can it be denied in this man who in both kinds hath committed more enormous acts than may be well recompted.

As in the first, of theft, not only by spoiling and oppressing almost infinite private men, but also whole towns, villages, corporations, and countries, by robbing the realm with inordinate licenses, by deceiving the crown with racking, changing, and embezzling the lands, by abusing his prince and sovereign in selling his favor both at home and abroad, with taking bribes for matter of justice, grace, request, supplication, or whatsoever suit else may depend upon the court or of the prince's authority; with setting at sale and making open market of whatsoever her Majesty can give, do, or procure, be it spiritual or temporal. In which sort of traffic he committeth more theft oftentimes in one day than all the waykeepers, cutpurses, cozeners, pirates, burglars, or other of that art in a whole year within the realm.

And as for the second, which is murder, you have heard before somewhat said and proved, but yet nothing to that which is thought to have been in secret committed upon divers occasions at divers times, in sundry persons of different calling in both sexes, by most variable means of killing, poisoning, charming, enchanting, conjuring, and the like, according to the diversity of men, places, opportunities, and instruments for the same. By all which means, I think, he hath more blood lying upon his head at this day, crying vengeance against him at God's hands and her Majesty's, than ever had private man in our country before, were he never so wicked.

Whereto now if we add his other good behavior, as his intolerable licentiousness in all filthy kind and manner of carnality, with all sort of wives, friends, and kinswomen; if we add his injuries and dishonors done hereby to infinite; if we add his treasons, treacheries, and conspiracies about the crown; his disloyal behavior and hatred against her Majesty; his ordinary lying and common perjuring himself in all matters for his gain both great and small; his rapes and most violent extortions upon the poor; his abusing of the Parliament and other places of justice, with the nobility and whole commonalty besides; if we add also his open injuries which he offereth daily to religion and the ministers thereof, by tithing them and turning all to his own gain; together with his manifest and known tyranny practiced towards all estates abroad, throughout all shires of the kingdom; his despoiling of both the Universities and discouraging of infinite notable wits there from seeking perfection of knowledge and learning (which otherwise were like to become notable), especially in God's word (which giveth life unto the soul), by defrauding them of the price and reward proposed for their travail in that kind through his insatiable simoniacal contracts; if, I say, we should lay together all these enormities before her Majesty, and thousands more in particular which might and would be gathered if his day of trial were but in hope to be granted, I do not see in equity and reason how her Highness, sitting in throne and at the Royal Stern as she doth, could deny her subjects this most lawful request, considering that every one of these crimes apart requireth justice of his own nature, and much more all together ought to obtain the same at the hands of any good and godly magistrate in the world.

Scholar. No doubt (quoth I) but that these considerations must needs weigh much with any zealous prince, and much more with her most excellent Majesty, whose tender heart towards her realm and subjects is very well known of all men. It is not to be thought also but that her Highness hath intelligence of divers of these matters alleged, though not perhaps of all. But what would you have her Majesty to do? Perhaps the consultation of this affair is not what were convenient but what is expedient; not what ought to be done in justice, but what may be done in safety. You have described my Lord before to be a great man, strongly furnished and fortified for all events. What if it be not secure to bark at the Bear that is so well britched? I speak unto you but that which I hear in Cambridge and other places where I have passed, where every man's opinion is that her Majesty standeth not in free choice to do what herself best liketh in that case at this day.

Gentleman: I know (said the gentleman) that Leicester's friends give it out everywhere that her Majesty now is their good Lord's prisoner, and that she either will or must be directed by him for the time to come, except she will do worse; which thing his Lordship is well contented should be spread abroad and believed, for two causes: the one, to hold the people thereby more in awe of himself than of their sovereign, and secondly, to draw her Majesty indeed by degrees to fear him. For considering with himself what he hath done and that it is impossible in truth that ever her Majesty should love him again or trust him after so many treacheries as he well knoweth are come to her Highness' understanding, he thinketh that he hath no way of sure standing but by terror and opinion of his puissant greatness, whereby he would hold her Majesty and the realm in thraldom as his father did in his time before him. And then for that he well remembereth the true saying, *malus custos diuturnitatis metus*,[288] he must provide shortly that those which fear him be not able to hurt him; and consequently you know what must follow by the example of King Edward, who feared Duke Dudley extremely for that he had cut off his two uncles' heads, and the Duke took order that he should never live to revenge the same. For it is a settled rule of Machivel which the Dudleys do observe, *that where you have once done a great injury, there must you never forgive.*

But I will tell you (my friends), and I will tell you no untruth, for that I know what I speak herein and am privy to the state of my Lord in this behalf, and of men's opinions and affections towards him within the realm. Most certain it is that he is strong by the present favor of the prince (as hath been showed before), in respect whereof he is admitted also as chief patron of the Huntingdon faction, though neither loved nor greatly trusted of the same; but let her Majesty once turn her countenance aside from him in good earnest and speak but the word only that justice shall take place against him, and I will undertake with gaging of both my life and little lands that God hath given me that without stir or trouble or any danger in the world the Bear shalbe taken to her Majesty's hand and fast chained to a stake, with muzzle-cord, collar, and ring, and all other things necessary, so that her Majesty shall bait him at her pleasure without all danger of biting, breaking loose, or any other inconvenience whatsoever.

For (Sirs) you must not think that this man holdeth anything abroad in the realm but by violence, and that only upon her Majesty's favor and countenance towards him. He hath not anything of his own, either from his ancestors or of himself, to stay upon in men's hearts or conceits; he hath not ancient nobility as other of our realm have, whereby men's affections are greatly moved. His father John Dudley was the first noble of his line, who raised and made himself big by supplanting of other and by setting debate among the nobility, as also his grandfather Edmund, a most wicked promoter and wretched pettifogger, enriched himself by other men's ruins—both of them condemned traitors, though different in quality, the one being a cozener and the other a tyrant, and both of their vices conjoined, collected, and comprised (with many more additions) in this man (or beast rather) which is Robert, the third of their kin and kind. So that from his ancestors this Lord receiveth neither honor nor honesty, but only succession of treason and infamy.

And yet in himself hath he much less of good wherewith to procure himself love or credit among men than these ancestors of his had, he being a man wholly abandoned of human virtue and devoted to wickedness, which maketh men odible both to God and man. In his father (no doubt) there were to be seen many excellent good parts if they had been joined with faith, honesty, moderation, and loyalty. For all the world knoweth that he was very wise, valiant, magnanimous, liberal, and assured friendly where he once promised; of all which virtues my Lord his son hath neither show nor shadow, but only a certain false representation of the first, being crafty and subtile to deceive and ingenious to wickedness. For as for valor, he hath as much as hath a mouse; his magnanimity is base sordidity; his liberality, rapine; his friendship, plain fraud, holding only for his gain and no otherwise though it were bound with a thousand oaths, of which he maketh as great accompt as hens do of cackling, but only for his commodity, using them specially and in greatest number when most he meaneth to deceive. Namely, if he swear solemnly by his George[289] or by the eternal God, then be sure it is a false lie; for these are observations in the Court and sometimes in his own lodging, in like case his manner is to take up and swear by the Bible, whereby a gentleman of good accompt and one that seemeth to follow him (as many do that like him but a little) protested to me of his knowledge that in a very short space he observed him wittingly and willingly to be forsworn sixteen times.

    This man, therefore, so contemptible by his ancestors, so odible of himself, so plunged, overwhelmed, and defamed in all vice, so envied in the Court, so detested in the country, and not trusted of his own and dearest friends; nay (which I am privy to), so misliked and hated of his own servants about him for his beastly life, niggardy, and atheism (being never seen yet to say one private prayer within his chamber in his life) as they desire nothing in this world so much as his ruin and that they may be the first to lay hands upon him for revenge. This man (I say) so broken both within and without, is it possible that her Majesty and her wise Council should fear? I can never believe it; or if it be so, it is God's permission without all cause for punishment of our sins, for that this man, if he once perceive indeed that they fear him, will handle them accordingly and play the Bear indeed, which inconvenience I hope they will have care to prevent, and so I leave it to God and them, craving pardon of my Lord of Leicester for my boldness if I have been too plain with him. And so I pray you let us go to supper, for I see my servant expecting yonder at the gallery door to call us down.

Lawyer. To that said the lawyer: I am content with all my heart, and I would it had been sooner, for that I am afeard lest any by chance have overheard us here since night. For my own part, I must say that I have not been at such a conference this seven years, nor mean to be hereafter if I may escape well with this; whereof I am sure I shall dream this fortnight and think oftener of my Lord of Leicester than ever I had intended—God amend him and me both. But if ever I hear at other hands of these matters hereafter, I shall surely be quakebritch and think every bush a thief. And with that came up the mistress of the house to fetch us down to supper, and so all was whusht, saving that at supper a gentleman or two began again to speak of my Lord, and that so conformable to some of our former speech (as indeed it is the common talk at tables everywhere) that the old

lawyer began
to shrink and be ap-
palled, and
to
cast dry
looks upon the
gentleman our friend,
doubting lest something
had been discovered
of our confer-
ence. But
in-
deed, it was not so.
F I N I S.

A Godly and Profitable Meditation taken out of the 20th chapter of the Book of Job.[290]

This I know from the first that man was placed upon earth, that the praise (or applause) given to wicked men endureth but a little, and the joy of an hypocrite is but for a moment. Though his pride were so great as to mount to heaven, and his head should touch the skies, yet in the end shall he come to perdition as a dung hill, and they who beheld him (in glory before) shall say, where is he? He shalbe found as a flying dream, and as a fantasy by night shall fade away. The eye that beheld him before shall no more see him, nor yet shall his place (of honor) ever more behold him. His children shall be worn out with beggary, and his own hands shall return upon him his sorrow. His (old) bones shall be replenished with the vices of his youth, and they shall sleep with him in his grave. His bread in his belly shalbe turned inwardly into the gall of serpents. The riches which he hath devoured he shall vomit forth again, and God shall pull them forth of his belly. He shall suck the head of cockatrices, and the (venomous) tongues of adders shall slay him. He shall sustain due punishment for all the wickedness that he hath committed, nor yet shall he have end or consummation thereof. He shall suffer according to the multitude of all his wicked inventions. For that by violence he hath spoiled the poor, made havoc of his house, and not builded the same. His womb is never satisfied, and yet when he hath that which he desired, he shall not be able to possess the same. There remaineth no part of his meat (for the poor), and therefore there shall remain nothing of his goods. When his belly is full, then shall he begin to be straitened, then shall he swear, and all kind of sorrow shall rush upon him. I would his belly were once full, that God might send forth upon him the rage of his fury, and rain upon him his war. He shall fly away from iron weapons and run upon a bow of brass. A drawn sword coming out of his scabbard shall flash as lightning in his bitterness. All darkness lie hidden for him in secret; the fire that needeth no kindling shall devour him, and he shalbe tormented alone in his tabernacle. The offspring of his house shalbe made open and pulled down in the day of God's fury. This is the portion of a wicked man from God, and this is the inheritance of his substance from the Lord.

Notes to *Leicester's Commonwealth*

1. Gracious Street, now Gracechurch Street, near London Bridge; Walpole and Parsons's *News from Spain and Holland* (1593) is similarly addressed, as is the "Letter of Estate."
2. "For that": because (commonly used in this sense).
3. Frequent allusion is made throughout to both elements of Leicester's crest, the "bear" chained to a ragged post or "staff" (as in bearbaiting).
4. Lord Burghley's *Execution of Justice in England* (1583), stating the government's position toward Catholic priests. Consistent with this "Christmas conference," Cecil's book bears the date 17 Dec. 1583 on its first edition.
5. "Disgiest": digest (*O.E.D.*, a common form).
6. Sir Edward Stafford quotes C. Paget making a similar distinction between "Papists of state" and those of religion only, in a letter to Walsingham, 27 Oct. 1583 (S.P. 78/10/66).
7. The so-called War of Liberation (1552), in which Charles's Lutheran and Catholic allies joined with his enemies, the regional princes, to resist his Spanish-enforced Augsburg Interim.
8. In 1562 the English under the Earl of Warwick occupied Newhaven (Le Havre) as security for aid to the Huguenot rebels; shortly after, the rebel leader Condé signed the Peace of Amboise, and the French combatants joined to dislodge the garrison. Decimated by plague, besieged by a combined French army, Warwick surrendered on 28 July 1563.
9. The Duke of Anjou ("Monsieur": heir to the French throne), whom the Dutch Protestants named their sovereign in 1581, was expelled from the Low Countries in Feb. 1583 after his attempt to arrogate several towns to himself. "Gaunt" is Ghent.
10. On the death of the childless Portuguese king (Jan. 1580), Philip II of Spain ("the Castilian") enforced his claim to the throne; having overcome the opposition by August, he was proclaimed king by the Cortes in Apr. 1581.
11. Charles Neville (1543?–1601), sixth Earl of Westmoreland, and the "Old Rebel" Richard Norton lived in exile after the Northern Rebellion of 1569; Norton is not mentioned by name in Cecil's book. Dr. Nicholas Sander (or Sanders), a leading Jesuit controversialist, joined the ill-fated Papal invasion of Ireland (1579) and died of exposure in that country two years later.
12. That is, priests trained at the seminaries at Douai, Rheims, Rome, etc.
13. This may reflect growing lay Catholic distrust of the foreign-trained priests who were, in this view, inciting the government to severity against all Papists. The best short discussions of this and other distinctions among Catholic groups are in Bossy's "Character of Elizabethan Catholicism" and his *English Catholic Community*, pp. 11–74.
14. "Eversion": overthrowing (*O.E.D.*).
15. Roger, second Lord North (Privy Council, 1596; d. 1600), one of Leicester's chief allies.
16. That is, man of social standing.

17. "Obliged proditors": sworn traitors, betrayers (*O.E.D.*).
18. Margin: "Sir Francis Walsingham" (1532-1590). The syntax of this sentence is a little odd.
19. "Belike": probably (*O.E.D.*).
20. On 21 May 1553 John Dudley, Duke of Northumberland, married his son Guildford to the chief Suffolk claimant, Jane Grey, and procured Edward VI's signature to a "device" deflecting the succession from the Catholic Mary to his daughter-in-law. The king died on 6 July (the *Commonwealth* authors believe the Duke had contrived his death). Jane was proclaimed on 10 July, and Robert Dudley was dispatched to arrest Mary, only to find her already fled to her Howard supporters. Northumberland surrendered at Cambridge on 20 July. On the "letters to Mary," see Harbison, *Rival Ambassadors at the Court of Queen Mary*, p. 34.
21. Margin: "Sir Francis Walsingham."
22. Margin: "Edmund Dudley," who paid for his financial malfeasances by standing trial for "constructive treason" on 16-18 July 1509 and by his execution on 17 Aug. 1510, and "John Dudley," who was tried on 18 and executed on 22 Aug. 1553.
23. The "last Parliament" (1581) saw enactment of *23 Elizabeth, cap. 2*, which only provided against speaking or writing slander of the Queen herself. According to Neale, the Lords did pass and send down a bill against slandering noblemen and lords of the clergy, but it was killed after its second reading by the Puritans in the Commons. Apparently, then, the "proviso" never became law. See Neale, *Elizabeth I and Her Parliaments, 1559-1581*, p. 398.
24. This and the following matters are dealt with in more detail below.
25. "Killingworth": Kenilworth Castle, Warwickshire; Leicester's principal seat. The events described, though exaggerated, refer to the situation in summer 1579, when the Earl was in disgrace over his revealed marriage and Anjou had just arrived for his first visit. Michaelmas: 29 September.
26. Heneage (d. 1595), Vice Chamberlain of the Household. Warwick's lady was his third wife, Anne Russell, daughter of the Earl of Bedford, whom he married in Nov. 1565.
27. John Casimir (d. 1592), younger son of Frederick III of the Palatinate, a Calvinist condottiere often hired to fight Catholic enemies; in Jan. 1579 he was in England and was entertained by Leicester. "Amplification": exaggeration (*O.E.D.*).
28. Margin: "To Sir Thomas Leighton"; see note 107 below.
29. Margin: "Lord Treasurer, Lord Chamberlain, Master Comptroller," i.e., Burghley, Sussex, and Sir James Croft (d. 1590), Comptroller of the Household from 1570 until his death, all active in behalf of the Anjou marriage. Croft was a Catholic with a Spanish pension; Mendoza regularly referred to him as his "first confidant" and to Lord Harry Howard as his "second."
30. Margin: "Sir John Hibbott," alias Huband (d. 1583), a member of the Council of Wales (based at Ludlow) and steward of several of Leicester's lordships, including Kenilworth; never "Vicepresident" of the Council, though nominated as such in 1576.
31. This appears to have been the received Catholic view, e.g., in Parsons, *A*

Temperate Ward-word to . . . *Sir Francis Hastings*, p. 44, and Broughton, *English Protestants Plea*, p. 16, and accepted by most modern writers; it has been questioned by Beer, *Northumberland*, p. 162.

32. Margin: "Ethelbert, King of Kent, converted A.D. 603"; according to Bede, softened by Bertha and converted by St. Augustine in about 597. The date 603 is found in Polydore Vergil's *Anglica historia*, 1846, p. 129, which seems to have been the *Commonwealth*'s chief source for English history.

33. That is, both in fact and in hope.

34. "Unition": union (*O.E.D.*, citing this passage).

35. Prince Eric of Sweden (later Eric XIV), suitor in 1559–1560; Charles, younger son of the Emperor Ferdinand I, whose suit reached a high point in 1565–1566; Henri Duke of Anjou (later Henri III), a suitor in 1571; and Anjou, whose suit extended from 1572 to 1582. Leicester at one time or another fought against each of these matches.

36. Printed DAVVS, thus either "Daws," a fool or lazy person (O.E.D.) or probably "Davus," a cunning slave, as in the proverb *Davus sum, non Oedipus*, a quotation from Terence's *Andria*. "News from Heaven and Hell" similarly describes Leicester as "being *Davus non Edipus*" (p. 145).

37. "Privado": confidant, favorite (*O.E.D.*). Prince Eric never visited England but was represented there by his brother Duke John of Finland.

38. Margin: "Anno 1. R. Mary." Lord Robert was attainted of treason and condemned to death on 22 Jan. 1554; he was pardoned on 18 Oct. 1554, and the removal of attainder was ratified in Parliament on 7 March 1558. (D. Wilson argues that Dudley's release from prison did not occur until Jan. 1555; *Sweet Robin*, p. 316).

39. Dr. Valentine Dale (d. 1589), sometime ambassador to France (1573–1576), Master of Requests at the beginning of the Julio affair, on which see Appendix D (6).

40. Robert, Lord Denbigh (born 1578 or 1579, d. 19 July 1584), Leicester's son by Lady Essex. All of Dudley's brothers died childless, as did his sister the Countess of Huntingdon, and the only heirs to the family estates were Denbigh and the children of his other sister, the wife of Sir Henry Sidney, of which Philip was the eldest; both Denbigh and Sir Philip having predeceased Leicester, Robert Sidney became general heir to the Dudleys.

41. Margin: "The Lady Sheffield, now Ambassadess in France," discussed again below; Dyer (knighted 1596, d. 1607), courtier and poet, a protégé of Leicester's; Tilney (d. 1610), Lady Sheffield's kinsman, Master of the Revels from July 1579 until his death.

42. Cf. *The Yorkshire Tragedy* (ca. 1606), scene 5, lines 13–14: "The surest way to charm a woman's tongue/ Is break her neck; a politician did it" (Brooke, *Shakespeare Apocrypha*, p. 257b). Also: "You that were held the famous politician;/ Whose art was poison. . . . That would have broke your wife's neck down the stairs/ Ere she was poisoned" (John Webster's *White Devil*, ca. 1612; act 5, scene 3, lines 155–58); Webster alludes in the next line to Leicester's alleged salad poisoning of Throgmorton.

43. Bald Buttler is unidentified. Leicester had distant kinship to the Butlers of Ashton in the Walls, and two Butlers are mentioned in his will, but as it was rather

among his wife's kinsmen that suspicions ran high, the text's "my L." may be an error for "my La."; in which case the correction has been made in the French translation ("*parent de la dame,*" *Discours de la vie,* fol. 16).

44. On Amy Robsart's death, see Appendix D (1).

45. John, second Lord Sheffield of Butterwick, who died in 1568. There seems to have been no public suspicion concerning his death, but among his own family it was attributed to Leicester's poison; see Holles, *Memorials of the Holles Family,* pp. 70–71.

46. Dorothy Braye (d. 1605), widow of Edmund Brydges, Lord Chandos, and wife of William Knollys (d. 1632), an ally of Leicester's who was Lady Essex's eldest brother and, much later, the first Earl of Banbury. Concerning the putative child, see Appendix D (2).

47. Essex's man Richard Lloyd was later employed as Leicester's secretary (Bruce, *Correspondence of Robert Dudley,* p. 26; John Dee's diary, p. 21). On Rowland Crompton, yeoman of Essex's cellar, see discussion of Essex's death in Appendix D (2).

48. On Dr. Julio, see Appendix D (6).

49. Margin: "Doctor Bayley the younger," i.e., Walter Bayley (d. 1593), M.D., Regius Professor of Physic in 1561, later physician to the Queen.

50. Odet, Cardinal de Châtillon, brother of the Huguenot leader Coligny, lived in refuge in England, 1568–1571, attempting to further the marriage to Henri of Anjou. Returning to France, he was taken ill at Canterbury and died on 24 Mar. 1571; tradition ascribes his death both to Catherine de Medici and to the Guisan Cardinal de Lorraine. Elizabeth's investigating team reported directly to Leicester and was headed by his ally Leighton. See Atkinson, "Cardinal of Châtillon," which charges Lorraine with the crime (pp. 254–55).

51. Possibly Sir Henry Lee's kinsman Thomas (executed 1601), younger son of Benedict Lee of Bigging and the Earl of Essex's second cousin, who although not an Irishman was serving with Essex in Ireland at this time. See Chambers, *Sir Henry Lee,* pp. 185–201.

52. "Develing": Dublin. "Penteneis" is unidentified.

53. William Hunnis, Master of the Children from 1566 until his death in 1597.

54. On the death of the Earl of Essex, see Appendix D (2).

55. This joke originated with the Queen of Scots, then still in France, on the occasion of Amy's death; Leicester was Elizabeth's Master of the Horse. Throgmorton sent word of it from Paris to Cecil via his secretary, Robert Jones (26 Nov. 1560); Cecil told the Queen, who in turn twitted Dudley with it, and he learned its provenance by interrogation of Jones. See Jones to Throgmorton, 30 Nov. 1560, Hardwicke State Papers, 1: 164. Anne de Montmorency (d. 1567), Constable of France, was then close to Mary's kinsmen the Guises.

56. Sir Nicholas, uncle of Francis and Thomas Throgmorton, died on 25 Feb. 1571. Camden's account follows the *Commonwealth*'s: "In [Leicester's] house as he fed hard at supper on salads, he was taken (as some report) with an impostume of the lungs, as others say with a vehement catarrh, not without suspicion of poison, and died in a good time for himself and his, being in great danger of life and estate by reason of his restless spirit" (*Elizabeth,* 2: 14).

57. Margaret, daughter of Henry VIII's sister and wife of Matthew Stuart, Earl of Lennox, died at sixty-two at Hackney in London on 9 May 1578, apparently with no suspicions attending. Thomas Fowler, who administered her affairs (H.M.C. Salisbury MSS., 3: 105), became Leicester's steward before 1580 (A. Kendall, *Robert Dudley*, p. 186); his son William was one of Walsingham's agents but in Aug. 1584 was used by Leicester in some dealing in Scotland that the Earl kept secret even from Walsingham (*C.S.P. Scots, 1584-85*, pp. 258, 300).

58. Sardanapalus, legendary king of Assyria; Nero, Roman Emperor A.D. 54-68; Varius Avitus Bassanius (called Heliogabalus), Emperor at fourteen, murdered at eighteen by his Praetorian Guard in A.D. 222.

59. On the Earl's relationship with Lady Sheffield, see Appendix D (3).

60. Margin: "A.D. 959." Edwy, or Eadwig, was deprived of the northern half of his kingdom in 957; when he died in 959 it was reunited in his brother Edgar. The date 959 follows Polydore Vergil (1846), p. 241.

61. William Painter twice recounts the adventures of this fourth-century B.C. courtesan who was accustomed to demand a sum "amounting very near to three hundred pound of our money" (*Palace of Pleasure* [1566], bk. 1, chap. 15; bk. 2, chap. 13).

62. Margin: "Anne Vavasour," on whom see Appendix D (4). "Another man" is the Earl of Oxford.

63. Margin: "The children of adulterers shall be consumed, and the seed of a wicked bed shall be rooted out, saith God. *Sap.* 3"; in the Douai-Rheims, Wisdom 3:16. The Marsh annotator points out the unwisdom of this reference: The "author of this discourse will needs forsooth have [his] gentleman to be a protestant: But here you see he is bewrayed. . . . No protestant acc[epte]th the book of Wisdom to be the book of God."

64. "Wife of the castle": Mary (d. 1600), Lady Sheffield's sister, wife of Edward Sutton (d. 1586), Lord Dudley of Dudley Castle, Staffordshire. "Gossips": female attendants at a birth (*O.E.D.*).

65. For comment on this daughter's existence, see Appendix D (3).

66. "Confortive": something of comfort (*O.E.D.*), with the ironic sense of a medical prescription.

67. Margin: "Doctor Bayley the elder," i.e., Henry Bayley, Proctor of New College (1547), M.D. (1563).

68. "Crowner": coroner (*O.E.D.*). The jury seems to have suspected murder at first (Blount's report, Adlard, *Amye Robsart*, p. 40), but its verdict was accidental death.

69. As far as is known, Amy was buried only once, at Our Lady of Oxford on 22 Sept.; Dudley did not attend. Dr. Francis Babington was Leicester's chaplain and later Vice Chancellor of Oxford; in 1565 he was reconciled to Rome and fled into exile, where he died in 1569. Tradition had it that Edmund Campion delivered this sermon, but a contemporary account of the funeral confirms the identification here (Adlard, *Amye Robsart*, p. 55).

70. Of an attempt to poison Jean de Simier, Anjou's agent in the marriage talks, nothing is known, though he was ill in summer 1579. After his revelation of Leicester's marriage early in July, he was shot at in the grounds of Greenwich Palace by

one Tider or Teuder of the Queen's Guard (Camden, *Elizabeth*, 2: 95), and he himself believed Leicester to have been behind the attack. At about this time (on 17 July) a man fired upon the Queen's barge, in which Simier was sitting (see below), and this too he considered an attempt on his life. Sometime in 1579 Simier was informed that he was soon to be stabbed, and he sent to Charles Arundell to borrow a "privy doublet," a coat of mail to be worn beneath his outer clothing; Arundell did not know by whom Simier had been threatened (Arundell's answers, S.P. 12/151/48, arts. 6 and 7).

71. The seamen of Flushing and all the Dutch coast thereabouts were known chiefly for their privateering activities.

72. Simier returned into France in late Nov. 1579, but there is no evidence of any untoward incident. Walter Raleigh was amongst Arundell's circle until at least 1580 (see Peck, "Raleigh, Sidney, Oxford, and the Catholics, 1579"); Edward Stafford was also one of the gentlemen accompanying Simier. Clark and Harris have common names, but the former is probably Capt. Augustine Clerk who in spring 1580 brought his "well-armed" ship over to the Spanish service. Checking on him, Mendoza learned that he had earlier arrived in England from Gravelines (cf. "certain Flushingers"), and he concluded that the man was a spy from Walsingham; accordingly, on 15 Aug. King Philip reported Clerk's arrest (*C.S.P. Spanish, 1580–86*, pp. 29, 36, 49).

73. William Killigrew (d. 1622), a courtier attached to Leicester's party; it was to Burghley, however, that his brother Sir Henry applied to win him a place among the Grooms of the Privy Chamber in Mar. 1573 (*C.S.P. Scots, 1571–74*, p. 519). "Caliver": a light musket. The Queen's kinsman Thomas Butler (1532–1614), tenth Earl of Ormonde, was a major force in Irish affairs, and he was generally aligned with Cecil and Sussex, while Leicester and Lord Deputy Sidney backed his rival the Earl of Desmond. The enmity between Leicester and Ormonde was notorious, whereas the latter "always had good liking to the house of Howard" (H.M.C. Rutland MSS., 1: 144) and was a friend of Charles Arundell's in particular (Ormonde to Hertford, 26 Mar. 1574, H.M.C. Bath MSS., 4: 140), with whom he corresponded regularly in "causes of friendship" (S.P. 12/151/48, art. 4). In 1565 both Ormonde and Desmond were in England, their differences to be heard by the Council, and several instances of violence are recorded from that summer (e.g., *A.P.C., 1558–70*, pp. 215, 219, 235).

74. "Facinorous": vile, extremely wicked (*O.E.D.*).

75. "Rampires": ramparts (*O.E.D.*).

76. Vortigern (fifth century) controlled, then murdered Constans, and crowned himself; Harold ruled Edward the Confessor, then succeeded him in 1066 (well disputed by William the Conqueror); Henry IV deposed Richard II in 1399; Warwick deposed Edward IV in 1470; Richard III became king in 1483.

77. Margin: "Leicester married at Wanstead when her Majesty was at Mr. Stonor's house, Doctor Culpepper, physician, minister." The Kenilworth ceremony is unconfirmed, but a letter from Philip Sidney of Dec. 1577, if indeed addressed to Leicester, seems to indicate that he knew of such a marriage (*Prose Works of Sidney*, 3: 119). The other, at Leicester's Wanstead House in Essex, a few miles from London, occurred on 20 Sept. 1578, while the Queen was stopped on progress

LEICESTER'S COMMONWEALTH   203

at Loughton, the home of Francis Stonor, whence she proceeded to Wanstead. In addition to these named, the Earl of Pembroke was present; the minister cited here would be Dr. Martin Colepeper, but it was actually Humfrey Tindall, Master of Queen's College, Oxford (later Dean of Ely, d. 1614). See the depositions of all those present, dated 13 Mar. 1581 (S.P. 12/148/24; printed in Hawarde, *Reportes del cases in Camera Stellata*, appendix 13).

78. Margin: "Read Polydore in the 7. year of King Richard II and you shall find this proceeding of certain about that king to be put as a great cause of his overthrow."

79. The Elizabethan "system" of patronage is only coming to be understood in detail, but good discussions can be found in MacCaffrey, "Place and Patronage in Elizabethan Politics" and *Queen Elizabeth*, chap. 16; P. Williams, *Tudor Regime*, chap. 3 and pp. 371–74; Neale, "Elizabethan Political Scene"; A. Smith, *Government of Elizabethan England*, pp. 57–69. In general, Leicester seems to have "had a lesser say in the distribution of patronage than Burghley" did (A. Smith, *Servant of the Cecils*, p. 53), and in the tentative opinion of Peter Roberts, now studying royal household reforms, Leicester's "power was not as all-pervasive or as malignant as alleged. What evidence there is reveals a positive, constructive interest in clearing things up as Lord Steward in the last years" (letter, 1 July 1977). Dudley's assistance to literary men has been well studied by Rosenberg, *Leicester*.

80. "Impotent of his ire": incapable of restraining his anger (following O.E.D.).

81. Edward Cheke to William Davison, Court, 8 Aug. 1577: "Sir Jerome Bowes and my cousin George Scott are banished the Court for a slanderous speech they should speak of my Lord of Leicester" (S.P. 15/25/30).

82. This book is unidentified; "stranger" means foreigner. "*Leicestrensem rempublicam*" may have been its title, as normally assumed, but the syntax may as easily indicate that it is rather what the stranger "calleth our state" in a book here untitled. Either way, the conclusion is unwarranted that the book is an earlier original of which our text is an English translation (as in Chamberlin, *Elizabeth and Leycester*, p. 417).

83. Margin: "Anno Regni 31" (1453); perhaps an error for "A. R. 34," as in Sept. 1456 York was trapped into submitting himself at Coventry but was then released.

84. Margin: "Lord Keeper, Lord Chamberlain," i.e., Sir Nicholas Bacon (d. 1579) and the Earl of Sussex (d. 1583). According to Conyers Read, Lord Hunsdon was the only man added to the Council between 1573 and 1586 who was not more or less of Leicester's camp ("Walsingham and Burghley in Queen Elizabeth's Privy Council," p. 41).

85. All of these cases but one are discussed in greater detail below. Southam is in Warwickshire, some ten miles from Kenilworth; despite the fact that Leicester acquired a great deal of land in the area, this reference is unidentified.

86. On 16 June 1566, Sussex was called by the Queen to explain his remark that Lord Deputy Sidney was in league with Shan O'Neill, the rebel chief; he demanded to know who accused him of having made it, and Leicester stepped forward to repeat the allegation. Sussex seems then to have accused Leicester of

having written encouragements to O'Neill (S.P. 63/18/19; Read, *Mr. Secretary Cecil,* pp. 332–33; D. Wilson, *Sweet Robin,* p. 184; on Dudley's earlier support of O'Neill against Sussex, see Canny, *Elizabethan Conquest of Ireland,* pp. 42–43). Cyril Falls prints a letter, 4 May 1570, from the Irish rebels to their agent in Spain, which includes mention of communications received from "certain Engishmen of the Council in England who have favored us, albeit clandestinely" (*Elizabeth's Irish Wars,* p. 140).

87. Acteon was transformed into a stag and torn apart by his own hounds; see Ovid, *Metamorphoses,* bk. 3 (lines 205–304 in Golding's translation, 1567).

88. The reference may be to Bartolome Salvariccia, a Genoese in London who in June 1583 sought Mendoza's protection from harassment by the Leicester-Walsingham group (*C.S.P. Spanish, 1580–86,* p. 478).

89. One MS. copy of the *Commonwealth* adds to Doughty's name "of the Inner Temple," and has a marginal comment: "Doughty, this man I knew and was acquainted with; he was with the Earl of Essex at his death and afterwards entertained by my Lord of Leicester" (British Library, Harleian MS. 4020, fol. 43). Thomas Doughty, said to have been dismissed from Essex's service (1574) for creating dissension between his commander and Leicester, sailed with his friend Francis Drake on the circumnavigation (Nov. 1577), probably as a spy for Burghley. After stirring up trouble among the crew, he was tried and executed on shipboard off the Patagonian coast in Aug. 1578 (see Corbett, *Drake and the Tudor Navy,* 1: 201–13, 221–47). When news reached home, it was rumored that he had been killed on Leicester's orders, "for that he had reported abroad that the Earl of Essex was made away by the cunning practices of Leicester" (Camden, *Elizabeth,* 2: 112).

90. "Carriers": bearers of letters, transporters of goods.

91. Gates is unidentified; various MSS. of the *Commonwealth* specify him as John or Henry Gates but on doubtful authority. Perhaps he was a kinsman of Sir John Gates, who was executed with Leicester's father in 1553. That this man was hanged at Tyburn "this last summer past" accords with a lost ballad concerning a robbing of "curriers" near London which was entered for publication in Aug. 1583 (Arber, *Transcript of the Registers,* 2: 427), and which may refer to the same man. This passage served Thomas Kyd as a source for his *Spanish Tragedy;* see Bowers's "Kyd's Pedringano," Baldwin's *On the Literary Genetics of Shakspere's Plays,* pp. 185–98, and Freeman's *Thomas Kyd,* p. 58. Cf. the analogous tale of the Yorkshire gentleman in Peck, "Letter of Estate," pp. 33–34.

92. Margin: "This relation of Gates' may serve hereafter for an addition in the second edition of this book."

93. Margin: "The Earl of Sussex his speech of the Earl of Leicester." Sussex died at Bermondsey in London on 9 June 1583.

94. Mendoza reported in Jan. 1582 that the Queen had told Simier that she could do nothing to diminish Leicester's power, "as he had taken advantage of the authority she had given him to place kinsmen and friends of his in almost every post and principal place in the kingdom" (*C.S.P. Spanish, 1580–86,* pp. 266–67); Arundell and Howard constituted the only known link between Simier and the Spaniard.

95. Margin: "York, the Earl of Huntingdon" (Henry Hastings), Leicester's

brother-in-law, based in York as President of the Council of the North from 1572 until his death in 1595.

96. Margin: "Berwick, the Lord Hunsdon" (Henry Carey), Warden of the East March (based at Berwick) from 1568 until his death in 1596. His sister was the mother of Leicester's wife Lettice. He was more often counted among Burghley's adherents than among Leicester's.

97. Margin: "Wales, Sir Henry Sidney" (d. 1586), President of the Council in the Marches of Wales from 1560 until his death, who had married Leicester's sister Mary in 1551.

98. Henry Herbert (d. 1601), second Earl of Pembroke, one of Leicester's closest friends, had married Sidney's daughter Mary in Apr. 1577; she it was to whom her brother dedicated his *Arcadia*.

99. Francis Russell (d. 1585), second Earl of Bedford, an active Puritan, was Warwick's father-in-law as well.

100. Margin: "The Lord Grey," i.e., Arthur (d. 1593), Lord Grey of Wilton, whose ferocity as Lord Deputy of Ireland, especially in the massacre of the Spanish garrison at Smerwick (Nov. 1580), was notorious. He returned to England in Nov. 1582, where his severities earned him a "great displeasure with the Queen," which "was kindled against him by Sussex, his heavy adversary" (Camden, *Elizabeth*, 2: 119).

101. Margin: "Her Majesty (as he saith), for striking of Mr. Fortescue, called him lame wretch; that grieved him so (for that he was hurt in her service at Lieth) as he said he would live to be revenged." Grey was wounded while serving under his father at the siege of Lieth in Scotland in May 1560. The incident with Mr. (later Sir) John Fortescue of Salden occurred in Oct. 1573, when Grey used "uncivil language" to him in the Presence Chamber; in Dec. Fortescue complained that Grey had had him beaten up in Chancery Lane, all apparently resulting from a dispute over hunting rights (*C.S.P. Domestic, 1547–80*, pp. 467, 468, 470).

102. Margin: "In Scotland or elsewhere against the next inheritors or present possessors."

103. Margin: "Sir John Perrot" (d. 1592), who departed for Ireland as the new Lord Deputy on 12 May 1584 (H.M.C. Rutland MSS., 1: 165); possibly this marginalium was added upon arrival of that news. As early as Nov. 1582 it was thought that he would be Grey's successor (*ibid.*, p. 144), but the post remained vacant for a year and a half.

104. Margin: "Sir Edward Horsey" (kt. 1577, d. 1583); after entering exile upon the failure of the "Dudley Plot" of 1556, he progressed from agent for Ambassador Throgmorton to Leicester's service, thence to Captain of the Isle of Wight (*ca.* 1566–1583). Like another former rebel, Leighton, he was a follower of Leicester and was often used on diplomatic assignments (e.g., to France, 1573), but he was never, as in *D.N.B.*, a member of the Privy Council.

105. Margin: "Sir George Carew" (Carey), who succeeded his father Henry in the barony of Hunsdon in 1596. He was Captain of the Isle of Wight from Horsey's death until his own in 1603; his aunt was the mother of Leicester's wife. In 1587 he was granted the wardship of Lord Paget's son and heir (*A.P.C., 1586–87*, p. 352).

106. Margin: "Sir Amias Paulet," Captain of the Isle of Jersey from 1571 until his

death in Sept. 1588, having served as ambassador to France (1577-1579) as well; he was chosen in April 1585 to provide stricter confinement for Mary, Queen of Scots.

107. Margin: "Sir Thomas Leighton"(d. 1611), Leicester's follower and Captain of the Isle of Guernsey, married to "Bess," Elizabeth (not Cecilia, as in D.N.B.), daughter of Sir Francis Knollys, in May 1578.

108. Master of the Ordnance from Apr. 1560 until his death in 1590.

109. The predecessor is Sir Edward Warner, who as Lieutenant held the Tower for Northumberland, was deprived of the office under Mary, and was restored on Elizabeth's accession. Owen Hopton, in a letter of 1588, fixed his appointment to the post at about 1570 (Ellis, *Original Letters*, 4: 67-71).

110. Margin: "Sir Rowland Heiward" (1520?-1593), clothworker, Mayor of London 1570-1571 and 1591, "probably the most impressive of the élite aldermen during the Elizabethan period" (Foster, *Politics of Stability*, p. 73).

111. Margin: "Mad Fleetwood." William Fleetwood (d. 1594) was noted chiefly as a loud Parliamentarian until, by Leicester's influence (*D.N.B.*), he became Recorder of London, 1571-1592. He was jailed in 1576 for breaking into a foreign embassy's chapel in search of recusants and was considered by Parsons to have been one of the "chiefest persecutors" of Catholics (C.R.S. 2, p. 191). See also Harris, "William Fleetwood."

112. Margin: "My Lord of Huntingdon's preparation at Ashby," i.e. Ashby de la Zouch, Leicestershire, the Earl's principal seat.

113. The Queen visited Kenilworth in 1565, 1572, and 1575; the last of these is probably the visit intended here. In 1570 it was reported that Leicester "hath many workmen at Killingworth to make his house strong, and doth furnish it with armor, munition, and all necessaries for defense" (Lodge, *Illustrations*, 1: 516); in 1581 Charles Arundell mentioned this fortification, "with brass, pieces, munition, powder, etc., proportionable as strong as the town against a day, under color of making the Queen sport with fireworks shooting, etc." (S.P. 12/151/50). See Stone, *Crisis of the Aristocracy*, pp. 220-21.

114. Margin: "Ralph Lane," presumably Sir Ralph Lane (kt. 1593, d. 1603), courtier, financial speculator, seaman, first "governor" of Virginia (1585); he was both opportunistic and often in trouble, but neither this incident nor his "harassment"is identified. The Queen's most serious illness, a near-fatal case of smallpox, came in fall 1562; at that time she had the Council swear to recognize Dudley as Protector of the realm in the event of her death. The text does not suggest that Kenilworth was yet in Dudley's possession; he received it in the following year.

115. "Astronomers": astrologers.

116. "Lightly": likely (*O.E.D.*).

117. "Sinours": sinews (*O.E.D.*).

118. "One for her Majesty": Sir Walter Mildmay, on 25 Jan. 1581 (discussed in Neale, *Elizabeth I and Her Parliaments, 1559-1581*, pp. 382-85).

119. "Enhanced before": having had their rents increased (*O.E.D.*). See, e.g., letters patent to Leicester, dated 5 Apr. 1579, gifts of land, some of them exchanges, in London and twenty counties in England and Wales (Folger Library, 2.e.5).

120. "License of alienation": exclusive right to collect a duty on the sale of crown lands.

121. The loss of Calais was a blow to English pride; in England's hands since 1347, it was taken by the French in Jan. 1558. During ensuing peace talks Philip of Spain stood by his English allies in demanding its return, but after Elizabeth's accession it was clear that, without assurances that England would remain Catholic and pro-Spanish, he would conclude a peace of his own. In Apr. 1559 the Queen's agents settled upon the Treaty of Câteau-Cambrésis, which affected to leave Calais with the French for only eight years but which was really a face-saving acknowledgement of its loss. It seems, however, to have been Cecil who was responsible for the decision to compromise, a decision that Dudley opposed (Wernham, *Before the Armada*, p. 244; D. Wilson, *Sweet Robin*, pp. 104-7).

122. War with France was concluded by a treaty negotiated under Northumberland's direction and signed on 29 March 1550, under which Boulogne was surrendered in return for four hundred thousand crowns (i.e., "upon composition"). Protector Somerset had been sent to the Tower in Oct. 1549 but was released in Feb. 1550, free but powerless until his rearrest in Oct. 1551. Early in 1550 Southampton and Arundel were superseded on the Council by Dudley's own men; the former was confined to his house (where he died in July), the latter was imprisoned.

123. "Copesman": chapman, merchant (*O.E.D.*).

124. Two MS. copyists here interpolate the phrase "as Gabriel Bleke of Gloucestershire did" (St. John's, Cambridge, MS. L.11; Folger Library MS. G.a.9), a statement supported by this from Leicester's will, July 1587: "In the mean time, after the decease of Gabriel Bleke and his wife, I do give and grant to the said Robert [his son by Lady Sheffield] all such lands and leases as I have conveyed unto me from the said Gabriel forever, and the same lands, houses, and leases to enjoy presently after the decease of the said Gabriel Bleke and his wife, now living" (Sidney Papers, 1: 72).

125. Three licenses to export eighty thousand woolen cloths, summer 1562, "an enormously lucrative concession" (D. Wilson, *Sweet Robin*, p. 132), assigned to the Merchant Adventurers company (for 6,266 pounds) on 27 Mar. 1563 (A. Kendall, *Robert Dudley*, p. 44).

126. For example, for the farm of sweet wines he received twenty-five hundred pounds per year from Thomas Smith, Customer of London (D. Wilson, *Sweet Robin*, p. 168).

127. Grant to Edward Horsey of all forfeitures due for keeping taverns or selling wine contrary to statute, with power to compound with offenders for reasonable sums, 2 Apr. 1571 (*Calendar of Patent Rolls, 1569-72*, p. 165, no. 1342). "Ordinary": tavern, inn (*O.E.D.*).

128. "Poolings," pollings: plunderings, extortions (*O.E.D.*).

129. The extent of Edmund Dudley's personal malfeasance has been a vexed question, but this passage seems a fair assessment. See Brodie, "Edmund Dudley, Minister of Henry VII"; Elton, "Henry VII: Rapacity and Remorse" and "Henry VII: a Restatement"; Cooper, "Henry VII's Last Years Reconsidered."

130. Stow, *Chronicles of England* (1580), p. 895.

131. The gentleman, as he implies, has not read Dudley's book, an interesting allegory of the ideal state but no "book of secrets." The tree's roots are love of God, justice, truth, concord, and peace; the fruits of each are honor of God, honorable dignity, worldly prosperity, tranquility, and good example. Each fruit has its "paring" (e.g., increase of virtue) and its "perilous core" (e.g., lewd enterprise), which core, with its "poignant sauce" (dread of God), becomes a corresponding virtue (e.g., noble enterprise). See *Tree of Commonwealth*, ed. Brodie.

132. "Nephew": grandson (*O.E.D.*), used often but not exclusively in this sense.

133. This pun on cancel-*cancellarius* (Chancellor) is repeated by Richard Verstegan in *Advertisement Written to a Secretary*, pp. 45–46.

134. Margin: "The Lord Treasurer," Cecil, became Chancellor of Cambridge in 1559; Leicester, of Oxford in Dec. 1564.

135. This distinction is largely true: Oxford was often considered a center of papistry, and Cambridge came to be associated with Puritanism. See Knappen, *Tudor Puritanism*, pp. 218–19; Porter, *Reformation and Reaction*, passim.

136. Leicester did use his influence at Oxford for rewarding his followers—e.g., removal of the Vice Chancellor in 1576 for refusing to admit the Earl's nomination to a doctorate—but he also attempted extensive reforms; many of his letters insist upon correction of abuses in students' apparel, deportment, and so forth. See Rosenberg, *Leicester*, pp. 132–38.

137. Dr. Walter Bayley is noted above; Martin Colepeper (or Culpepper) was Doctor of Physic at New College, and Vice Chancellor of the University in 1578.

138. Dr. John Dee (d. 1608), the most famous English astrologer, alchemist, and mathematician of his day, was patronized not only by Leicester but by many others as well, including the Queen; he was out of England from Sept. 1583 until 1589. Dr. Thomas Allen (d. 1632), mathematician and antiquary, and widely reputed a magician, left Oxford in 1570; Leicester "offered him a bishopric, but he preferred a life of retirement" (*D.N.B.*).

139. Dr. Julio is noticed in Appendix D (6). Dr. Roderigo Lopez, a Portuguese Jew, chief physician to Leicester (*ca.* 1576) and, by 1586, to the Queen, was later prosecuted on treason charges by the second Earl of Essex and executed in June 1594.

140. Margin: "At Digby's house in Warwickshire Dame Lettice lay, and some other such pieces of pleasure." This is Sir George of Coleshill, Warwick, father of the future Earl of Bristol, and known as a friend of Leicester's.

141. Phalaris, tyrant of Agrigentum in Sicily (*ca.* 560 B.C.), was remembered for his custom of roasting his enemies in a brazen bull.

142. Margin: "Poor men resisting Warwick's enclosure at North Hall were hanged for his pleasure by Leicester's authority." North Hall (or Northall, or Northaw) was one of Warwick's manors in Hertfordshire. His tenants tore down his pales in Apr. 1579; Hatton was sent to quell the disturbance, and two men were hanged as a consequence (see Victoria History, *Hertfordshire*, 4: 216).

143. The barony of Denbigh was bestowed upon Dudley on the day prior to his creation as Earl (28 Sept. 1564, *Calendar of Patent Rolls, 1563–66*, p. 178), though grants of land had been made in June 1563 (*ibid.*, *1560–63*, pp. 534–40).

144. Following the grant, "Leicester at once began to exploit his strength by demanding £1,000 down and increases in rent of £333 6s. 8d. per annum from his

tenants in return for renewable forty-year leases" (P. Williams, *Council in the Marches*, pp. 237-38).

145. Leicester received the grant of Kenilworth on 9 June 1563 (*Calendar of Patent Rolls, 1560-63*, p. 540); Stow cites the twenty-four-pound yearly value (*Chronicles*, 1580, p. 1123). The Earl is said to have invested sixty thousand pounds in improvements and to have extended its parks and chases to nearly twenty miles around (Waldman, *Elizabeth and Leicester*, p. 131).

146. This grant, which Leicester received in 1574, allowed him to take over all lands that had been encroached upon by the freeholders, which were considerable, as a tenant of the crown. Normally his profit lay in compounding for them with the present occupants.

147. Suetonius, *Nero*, sec. 32.

148. "Papers of perjury": public display, wearing a placard identifying their crimes. The gentlemen of the Lleyn peninsula were cited before a Council in the Marches that was packed with Leicestrians and were imprisoned at Ludlow Castle shortly after the 1577 verdict against their case (P. Williams, *Council in the Marches*, p. 246).

149. Leicester, to increase his revenues as Ranger of Snowden Forest from searching out concealed lands within its borders, extended its limits to extraordinary lengths, even (as above) into the Isle of Anglesey. His chief opposition was a local magnate, Sir Richard Bulkeley, who had influence with the Queen; he checked the Earl's 1576 attempts and finally won a royal proclamation, 15 Dec. 1579 (*Tudor Proclamations*, no. 644), which suspended further inquiry into titles. Leicester and the Council in the Marches harassed Bulkeley for years after, and the citizens of Beaumaris, in Anglesey, were interrogated in Feb. 1580 over "scandalous and lewd rumors" and "Welsh rhymes or libels" that "somewhat touched the Earl of Leicester in honor and credit" in the Snowden matter (Hatfield, Cecil Papers, 203/81). "The business reveals a sinister side of the Council's activities— the judging of a great lord's suit by persons who were all friendly to him"; see P. Williams, *Council in the Marches*, p. 248, also pp. 237-39, 246-47. A sympathetic overview of Dudley's dealings in North Wales appears in D. Wilson, *Sweet Robin*, pp. 170-73.

150. Leicester's building projects, including restoration of the castle and a new cathedral (begun in 1578), were indeed left unfinished (D. Wilson, *Sweet Robin*, p. 172).

151. This sentence was pronounced upon Nero by the Senate, but he anticipated its execution by committing suicide in A.D. 68 (Suetonius, *Nero*, sec. 49).

152. Suetonius, *Vitellius*, sec. 17.

153. Leandro Alberti, *Descrittione di tutta Italia* (1550), fols. 85^v-86.

154. Humphrey Ferrers (later knighted, d. 1608), of Tamworth, sheriff of Warwickshire in 1577 and 1588; a client of Leicester's (see, e.g., the Earl preferring Mr. Savage to the benefice of Walton in Ferrers's gift, Huntington Library MS. H.A.2376).

155. On the riot at Drayton Basset, see Appendix D (5).

156. On the death in 1577 of Sir Gerald Croker, his leases of two manors in Hook Norton, Oxfordshire (one of which had escheated to the crown with the attainder of Leicester's father), passed to Richard Lee, illegitimate brother of Sir Henry.

Litigation ensued between Richard and Croker's son. The above passage "suggests that the lordship of John Dudley had been regranted to his son and that he may have wished to secure a surrender of the lease through Lee" (Chambers, *Sir Henry Lee*, p. 176).

157. Greville, of Milcote, Warwickshire, cousin of Fulke the poet, was a man of Catholic connections who was in trouble all his life; in Nov. 1589 he was pressed to death for refusing to enter a plea in a murder charge. The reference here is probably to his imprisonment in early 1579 for a murderous attack upon Sir John Conway, a follower of Leicester (see Stopes, *Shakespeare's Warwickshire Contemporaries*, pp. 162–64).

158. Leicester's ally Lee became Lieutenant of the Royal Manor of Woodstock in about 1571, where his subordinate George *Whitton*, Controller and Surveyor of the Manor (a post his family had held since 1496), had become accustomed to running things after years of nonresident lieutenants. Squabbling ensued, until in late 1580 Whitton entered complaints against Lee before the Council. His expressed fears of Lee's friends at Court (*C.S.P. Domestic, Addenda, 1580-1625*, pp. 26–27) were justified, for he soon found himself in the Marshalsea prison; having made submission, however, he did *not* lose his post, which was still in his family in 1650. See Chambers, *Sir Henry Lee*, pp. 91–104.

159. Litigation over the Berkeley lands had been going on for two centuries; at this time it was pursued by the Dudleys against Henry (d. 1613), seventh Lord Berkeley, Lord Harry Howard's brother-in-law, from whom they were able to recover several manors. In Aug. 1574 Leicester persuaded the Queen to leave her itinerary and be his guest at Berkeley Castle in its lord's absence, as if it were his own (Nichols, *Progresses*, 2: 392n; Jenkins, *Elizabeth and Leicester*, p. 193).

160. See Appendix D (6).

161. Sir John of Feckenham, Justice of Chester, brother of Sir Nicholas the diplomat, was fined in 1579 and deprived of office because, it was said, of "Leicester's cunning dealing" (Camden, *Elizabeth*, 3: 33); he had tangled with the Earl in 1568–1569 over jurisdictional rights in the city of Chester, but that seems to have ended amicably. More likely he was vulnerable because of his family's recusancy and was deprived for a number of abuses of his office, one of which was resolved in Star Chamber (three cases against him, 1579, described in P. Williams, *Council in the Marches*, pp. 266–67; a fourth, *C.S.P. Domestic, 1547-80*, pp. 604ff.). He died soon after, on 22 May 1580, leaving his sons Francis, Thomas, and George; Thomas seems to have had a hand in production of the *Commonwealth*. See also Rowse, *Sir Walter Ralegh*, pp. 73–74.

162. The Giffords were near relations of Throgmorton's. John, of Chillington, Staffordshire, was one of the most heavily persecuted recusants of the time (Trimble, *Catholic Laity in Elizabethan England, passim*); one of his sons, Thomas, has been advanced as author of the *Treatise of Treasons* of 1572 (Clancy, "A Political Pamphlet," pp. 23–25); another son, Gilbert, was a priest in exile, though perhaps as early as 1584 he was an undercover agent for Walsingham; his nephew Dr. William also fled the realm and from July 1582 on was a professor at the seminary in Rheims.

163. Drury (d. 1617) and his brother Sir William were under arrest from Dec. 1559 to Oct. 1560 for an obscure plot against Dudley (*C.S.P. Spanish, 1558-67*,

p. 118; C.S.P. Foreign, 1560–61, p. 350); he was still in trouble in 1561 (C.S.P. Domestic, 1547–80, p. 110). Thereafter he enjoyed a long career at Court; though many of his family were Catholics, he was known as a Puritan and was sent to aid Amias Paulet in the custody of the Queen of Scots. Sir William was married to Sir Edward Stafford's sister.

164. "Statists": statesmen, those skilled in affairs of state (all early O.E.D. entries, dating from Sidney's borrowing of the word in 1584–1585, employ it pejoratively).

165. "Protend": portend (O.E.D.).

166. "Fautors": adherents, followers, partisans (O.E.D.).

167. 13 Elizabeth, cap. 1 (1571), in Prothero, Select Statutes.

168. Margin: "Pooley told this to Sir Robert Jermine." Robert Poley was an agent who was later involved in provoking the Babington Plot and in the death of Christopher Marlowe; in early 1585 he was in trouble for possession of a copy of the Commonwealth and was suspected by Leicester of having had a hand in it (S.P. 78/17/26). This incident, if it occurred, should be placed in summer 1579 (when the marriage was first revealed), four years prior to the earliest information known about the man; see Boas, Christopher Marlowe, chap. 8 et passim. Jermine was associated with Leicester and married his son to a daughter of the Earl's follower William Killigrew.

169. Leicester was made Constable of Windsor Castle on 23 Feb. 1562 (Calendar of Patent Rolls, 1560–63, p. 310). Neville (d. 1593) had been one of the cosigners of King Henry's will, was knighted under Northumberland (1551), and served in Court government until his death. The Marsh annotator apparently tried to verify this charge: "Sir Henry Neville himself sayeth and confesseth [in]deed that th[is is] a most impu[dent] and shameless lie."

170. Anne Knollys married Thomas West, Lord De La Warr, in 1571; her brothers, including Robert (d. 1625), usher of the Tower Mint, were wholly of Leicester's party (Naunton, Fragmenta regalia, pp. 80–82). Anne Askew was just another lady at Court (see Hatton Memoirs, p. 223). The event, if it happened, is another echo of the tense summer of 1579.

171. Margin: "I mean the noble old Earl of Pembroke," William Herbert (d. 1570), first earl of the new creation. During the most furious phase of Dudley's wooing, autumn 1560, Pembroke was almost the only Councillor to back him, and that cautiously (MacCaffrey, Shaping of the Elizabethan Regime, p. 104).

172. See 13 Elizabeth, cap. 2, V (1571). "But incredible it is what jests lewd catchers of words made amongst themselves by occasion of that clause. . . . Insomuch as I myself, being then a young man, have heard them oftentimes say that that word was inserted into the Act of purpose by Leicester, that he might one day obtrude upon the English some bastard of his, for the Queen's natural issue" (Camden, Elizabeth, 2: 29).

173. That is, Mary, Queen of Scots, "now in prison"; despite the sequence above, no such suit took place after the 1571 statute. Elizabeth suggested a Mary-Leicester match in Mar. 1563; Dudley, appearing to acquiesce in the idea, did not care for it at all (Read, Cecil, pp. 303–25).

174. Arabella (or Arbella) Stuart (1575–1615), daughter of Charles, Earl of Lennox, and Elizabeth Cavendish, daughter of the Countess of Shrewsbury. She had a

claim to the crown through Lennox's mother, the child of Margaret Tudor's second marriage. Mendoza reported this intrigue in Dec. 1582 (*C.S.P. Spanish, 1580–86*, p. 426), and in Mar. 1583 he, the Queen of Scots, and Lord Paget all showed renewed interest in it (*ibid.*, p. 451; *C.S.P. Domestic, 1581–90*, pp. 99–100); King James was still angry about it in Sept. 1584 (*C.S.P. Scots, 1584–85*, p. 318).

175. Northumberland and Edward Seymour, the Protector, were "reconciled" in spring 1550, but Seymour was executed at the former's instance in Jan. 1552. The period of coexistence between York and Edmund Beaufort, beginning in spring 1452, degenerated into the struggles that, for Somerset, ended at St. Albans in 1455.

176. Both Thomas Lord Stanley and his brother aided in Henry's victory in 1485; Thomas, created Earl of Derby, was then eased out of his position of power, but perhaps the reference should be to Sir William, executed on flimsy treason charges in Feb. 1495. Henry Stafford, Duke of Buckingham, aided Richard in June 1483 but broke into rebellion and was executed on 2 Nov. Richard Neville set Edward up in 1461, plucked him down in 1470, and lost his life to him at Barnet in 1471. Henry Percy (killed 1408), Earl of Northumberland; his brother Thomas (executed 1403), Earl of Worcester; and his son Henry Hotspur (killed 1403) helped to depose Richard II but rebelled and were killed by Henry's forces.

177. Niccolo Machiavelli, *The Prince*, chap. 3.

178. Suffolk was executed on 23 Feb. 1554 after an abortive rising meant to have been coordinated with Wyatt's Rebellion.

179. Margin: "Southhowse," Christopher Southouse, a lifetime servant of Huntingdon's; "ledger," or lieger: a resident ambassador or agent. "Hasty king": after Huntingdon's family name, Hastings.

180. To Jane, née Guildford, who died in Jan. 1555.

181. His niece, Edward IV's daughter Elizabeth, who married Henry VII on 18 Jan. 1486; his wife, Warwick's daughter Anne Neville, who died on 16 Mar. 1485.

182. Margin: "A new triumvirate between Leicester, Talbot, and the Countess of Shrewsbury"; Arabella Stuart resided with the Countess her grandmother, Bess of Hardwick, who against her husband's will conspired with her stepson Gilbert Talbot and with Leicester to effect this match.

183. Margin: "Richard of Gloucester, Anno 1 Edward V," i.e., Richard III, called the Boar from his crest.

184. William Lord Hastings helped Richard overcome his opposition in spring 1483, but on 13 June he was himself denounced before the Council, hauled from the room, and executed the same day. "The other" were executed at Pontefract (Pomfret) Castle in Yorkshire twelve days later; the notion of simultaneous executions comes from More's *History of King Richard III*, 2: 48a.

185. Margin: "Esther 5" (verses 10–13). "Duke Aman" is the biblical Haman, his rank a characteristic embellishment.

186. Ahasuerus, the biblical Persian king, is often identified as Xerxes I (reigned 486–465 B.C.); "Mardocheus" is Mordecai the Jew, Esther's cousin.

187. Actually, Warwick's father, Richard of Salisbury, was killed at Wakefield (1461), nine years before his son "put down" Edward IV.

188. "Vilipend": treat contemptuously, vilify (*O.E.D.*); as the Marsh annotator writes, "This smelleth a little of the inkhorn."

189. The enmity between Lady Essex and the Queen was notorious; Elizabeth commonly referred to her as "that She-wolf." Amadis of Gaul was the hero of a popular chivalric-romance tradition.

190. The ambitions of Lord Thomas Seymour, the Protector's brother, led to his execution without trial on 20 Mar. 1549; the common view was that the breach between him and his brother had been caused by the "devilish woman" Ann Stanhope, the Protector's wife (Camden, *Elizabeth*, p. 6; Read, *Cecil*, p. 54).

191. Again, *13 Elizabeth, cap. 1* (1571).

192. "And be it further enacted, that if any person shall during the Queen's Majesty's life in any wise affirm or maintain any right," etc. (Prothero, *Select Statutes*, p. 59).

193. Margin: "Papistical blessing."

194. Margin: "Richard going towards Jerusalem began the custom by Parliament, as Polydore noteth Anno 10 of Richard II, to declare the next heir"; Richard I named his nephew Arthur in 1190.

195. Resistance to discussion of the succession came ultimately from Elizabeth herself; presumably the *Commonwealth*'s authors knew that. The frequency with which the statute is mentioned here indicates the importance that was attached to the problem of uncertain succession at the time.

196. On 17 July 1579, as Elizabeth was rowing on the Thames with Simier, a young man named Thomas Appletree, in a nearby boat with a group of children, discharged a harquebus at random and the ball hit one of the Queen's rowers. Although clearly an accident and although Elizabeth refused to "believe that which some buzzed in her ears, that he was purposely suborned against her or Simier" (Camden, *Elizabeth*, 2: 96), the fellow was condemned to death. As he stood "very penitent" upon the gallows, Hatton arrived to read a long pardon and take the opportunity to make some pointed remarks to the crowd on its narrow escape from chaos; these were "put in print" in Stow's *Chronicles*, pp. 1199–1204.

197. Toward the end of his conspiracy trial, 25 Feb. 1585, Dr. William Parry said that he had no hope of acquittal "because he was not settled." When asked by Hatton what he had meant, he answered: "Look into your study and into your new books, and you shall find what I mean" (Holinshed, *Chronicles of England*, 4: 578), intending thereby (following the *Commonwealth*) to show that he was being convicted for his party affiliation rather than for any crime he had committed (which was most likely true). See Brooks, *Sir Christopher Hatton*, p. 242, and his letter, *Times Literary Supplement*, 26 Dec. 1942. Most writers have followed Camden's translators' garbled accounts, to the effect that Parry meant that he had not been "constant in my resolution" (*Elizabeth*, 3: 47).

198. "Puny": a novice or tyro (*O.E.D.*).

199. Complaints of the presence of foreign artisans were a familiar feature of Elizabethan life; here the common xenophobia and economic grievance is combined with implication of a deliberate political plot, as it had been in the *Treatise of Treasons* (1572), fol. 104, where there are "forty or fifty thousand strangers . . . in readiness always to be employed [by Cecil] to any sudden exploit." Significant also is the attempt here to link the Puritan communions or "prophesyings" to political subversion (see Collinson, *Elizabethan Puritan Movement*, pp. 143, 199).

200. Commynes, *Memoirs*, bk. 1, chap. 7.

201. Commynes, *Memoirs*, bk. 3, chap. 4.
202. Executed 24 Nov. 1499.
203. Margin: "The battle by Tadcaster on Palm Sunday Anno 1460," otherwise called the battle of Towton, 29 Mar. 1460/61.
204. Barnet in Hertfordshire, a Yorkist victory, 14 Apr. 1471; Tewkesbury in Gloucestershire, a Yorkist victory, 4 May of the same year.
205. Margin: "The most of Huntingdon's ancestors by whom he maketh title attainted of treason." Attainder was admitted as a bar to inheritance of lands, but whether or not it could prevent succession to the crown was a point of controversy; see Mortimer Levine, *Early Elizabethan Succession Question*, pp. 108-9, 112-13.
206. Friar Ralph Sha (Shaa, Shaw) made official statement of Richard's title at St. Paul's in London on 22 June 1483; his sermon's text was "bastard slips shall not take root," but the idea was that Edward's children were illegitimate, not Edward himself. This version follows Polydore Vergil's (1844), pp. 183-85.
207. Edwin Sands (Sandys, d. 1588), Archbishop of York (1576), was at Cambridge when Northumberland arrived in pursuit of Mary, and he wisely preached a sermon enforcing Jane Grey's title (Holinshed, 4: 110-11); Nicholas Ridley did the same in London.
208. Margin: "The line of Portugal," discussed again below.
209. Henry Tudor's claim derived from Gaunt's *eldest* son by his third wife, but the last son who left surviving issue.
210. That is, *grandson* of Edward III, by the Black Prince Edward.
211. An error; the prince's name was Edward.
212. Katherine, widow of Sir Hugh Swynford. John of Somerset's line took the surname Beaufort.
213. These titles, vigorously advanced by more pro-Spanish exiles later in the reign, may be outlined here. The Portuguese: from John of Gaunt and his wife Blanche, to their daughter Philippe, to her son Manuel Fortunatus, king of Portugal; from him the male line ended in 1578, but through his daughter Isabella, wife of the Emperor Charles V, it continued to her son Philip II of Spain (though it also included Don Antonio, Prior of Crato; and Catherine, Duchess of Braganza). The Spanish: from Gaunt and his wife Constance (daughter of Peter I of Castile), to their daughter Catherine (who married Henry III in 1397), to her daughter Isabella of Castile, to her daughter Joanna the Mad, to her son Charles V, and thence again to his son Philip II (though it also included the Duke of Parma).
214. An error. Anne was the *grand*daughter of the third Earl of March; she became his heir (1425) only after the deaths of her father and brother, the fourth and fifth Earls.
215. Another error. Anne's husband Richard (ex. 1415) was Langley's *second* son and was styled Earl of Cambridge; when his elder brother Edward, the second Duke of York, died childless at Agincourt, Anne's and Richard's son, another Richard, became heir to the dukedom. John Leslie, whom the *Commonwealth* is following here, did not make these errors.
216. Cecily (d. 1507) married John Viscount Welles, who died in 1499 without issue; Anne (d. 1511) married Thomas Howard, third Duke of Norfolk, but died without surviving issue; Katherine (d. 1527) married William Courtenay (d. 1551),

whose son, the Marquess of Exeter, was executed in 1539 and whose only grandchild, Edward Earl of Devon, died unmarried in 1556.

217. Sir Richard Pole (d. 1504) and the Countess of Salisbury (executed 1541) left, among others, Henry Lord Montagu (ex. 1538), Reginald Cardinal Pole (d. 1558), and Ursula (d. 1570), who married the son of the executed Duke of Buckingham and was Sir Edward Stafford's grandmother.

218. Lord Montagu's daughter Catherine Pole (d. 1576) married Francis Hastings (d. 1561), second Earl of Huntingdon, in 1532 and was the mother of the third Earl.

219. The best arguments against and for Richard's responsibility for these murders are P. Kendall's *Richard the Third*, appendix 1, and Charles Ross, *Richard III*, pp. 96–104.

220. Margaret, in 1507, married James IV (d. 1513); in 1514 she married the sixth Earl of Angus, who divorced her in 1527 on the grounds of a precontract.

221. This Margaret married Matthew Stuart in 1544. Their eldest son Henry Lord Darnley married the Queen of Scots in July 1565 and was murdered in Feb. 1567; he was the father of James VI. The second son Charles married Elizabeth Cavendish in 1574 (without the Queen's permission) and died in 1576.

222. Mary married Louis XII in Oct. 1514; although he died three months later and although she had married Brandon by the following May, she was referred to as "the French Queen."

223. Actually *Henry* Clifford (d. 1570), second Earl of Cumberland, who married Eleanor in 1537; George was his son by a later marriage and his successor in the earldom.

224. An annulment was granted in 1527 on grounds of a prior contract by Angus. In 1561 the canny Cecil had Thomas Randolph in Scotland lay hands upon the annulment records, which proved Lady Lennox technically a bastard and the claim of Lord Darnley her son invalid (Read, *Cecil*, p. 234); assuming that the papers were genuine, Lady Arabella's title would likewise be invalid.

225. It appears that Brandon had obtained a valid divorce from Lady Mortimer before his marriage to Anne Browne, who died before his 1515 marriage to Mary Tudor; a papal bull of 1528 declaring the legitimacy of his children had cited a decree by the proper authorities. See Levine, *Succession Question*, pp. 126–36.

226. That only the *Commonwealth*, with its Howard-Fitzalan ties, raises this issue suggests that it is rather a family grudge than a legal objection. Henry Grey's father had contracted his children to those of the eleventh Earl of Arundel (the twelfth Earl did marry Grey's sister), but when Brandon married Grey (then his ward) to his own daughter Frances in 1533, Catherine Fitzalan's interest must surely have been resolved. See Levine, *Succession Question*, pp. 137–38.

227. Catherine was married, or more likely betrothed, to Henry Herbert in May 1553; the evidence seems to indicate that they were later divorced, probably in early 1554. See Levine, *Succession Question*, pp. 138–46.

228. In Aug. 1561 Catherine was discovered to be pregnant by Edward Seymour, Earl of Hertford; both were imprisoned, and the Queen ordered Archbishop Parker to head a commission investigating their claim to have been married in the previous autumn. His verdict was against them, but this was probably an opinion commissioned in advance by Elizabeth. Edward Lord Beauchamp was born to

Catherine in the Tower on 21 Sept. 1561; his brother Thomas, likewise in the Tower, on 10 Feb. 1563. See Levine, *Succession Question*, pp. 15–29.

229. Here begins the first passage quoted by Sir John Harington.

230. The validity of this and the following arguments (rule of thirds, tenant by courtesy, division among daughters, and executors) is discussed in Levine, *Succession Question*, pp. 99–125.

231. Virtually all of the arguments on the preceding and following pages are paraphrased from the Bishop of Ross John Leslie's much fuller *Defense of the Honor of . . . Mary* (or from the 1584 reprint of its succession section, *A Treatise Touching the Right*). This whole passage concerning the crown as a corporation, however, is taken *ad verbum* (*Defense*, fols. 68ᵛ–69; *Treatise*, fols. 29ᵛ–30). The standard work on this idea is Kantorowicz, *King's Two Bodies* (1957).

232. Margin: "Flores Hist. An. 1066," an error for Matthew of Westminster's *Flores historiarum*, 1057 (1: 543); this must be a reference to Matthew's book, of which there were several editions in the sixteenth century, rather than to Roger of Wendover's, of which there were none. The error derives from a misleading arrangement of correct references in Leslie (*Defense*, fol. 76; *Treatise*, fol. 33ᵛ); the inference is that the *Commonwealth*'s references are taken, not from the works cited, but from Leslie. All of Leslie's complicated legal citations, however, have been omitted.

233. "Bretaigne": Brittany.

234. Margin: "Polydore, lib. 15. *Flores historiarum*, 1208." In Matthew's *Flores* the 1208 entry records only the barons' accusation concerning Arthur's death (2: 108), and the murder, reported as current rumor, is under A.D. 1202 (2: 98–99).

235. Polydore Vergil, *Anglica historia* (1950), 113–14 notes, *sub* 1498. The annotator of the Marsh copy speaks tellingly to this point: " . . . and if the king should say so it were strange that a word of the king should bind the crown which a maxima of the law (as he sayeth) cannot do."

236. Mary's minister Maitland of Lethington wrote to Cecil on 4 Jan. 1566, urging this argument squeamishly: "To that you know for answer what may be said by any English patron of my mistress' cause, although I being a Scot will not affirm the same, that there ariseth a question amongst you whether the realm of Scotland be forth of the homage and 'legiance of England. And heretofore you have in sundry proclamations . . . and in sundry books at several times labored much to prove the homage and fealty of Scotland to England. . . . The argument [is] fitter for your assertion than mine" (Collier, *Egerton Papers*, p. 43).

237. On several occasions King James sued to be admitted to his Lennox patrimony in England, presumably in an attempt to establish a precedent for foreign inheritance. In 1578 his agents claimed that "in ancient time" Scottish kings had "succeeded without question by right of inheritance to lands in England" (Camden, *Elizabeth*, 2: 91).

238. Here ends the first passage quoted by Harington, *Tract on the Succession*, pp. 55–61.

239. For discussion of the vexing problems presented by this will, see Levine, *Succession Question*, chap. 9.

240. Leslie, whom the *Commonwealth* is following, had seriously advanced this

argument that the gentleman mentions (*Defense*, fols. 96–96ᵛ; *Treatise*, fols. 46ᵛ–47); he tried to prove that no such will could have been extant in 1553 or Dudley would not have needed Edward VI's letters patent, whereas of course the Duke was concerned with bypassing not only the prior line of Scotland but also Mary Tudor herself. Thus the *Commonwealth* corrects this flaw in the Marian case without mentioning Leslie's error.

241. See the acts *28 Henry VIII, cap. 7* (1536) and *35 Henry VIII, cap. 1* (1543).

242. Lady Frances (d. 1559), after the death of the Duke of Suffolk in 1554, married her servant Stokes (d. 1585), by whom she had no further children.

243. The will's enrollment in Chancery was defaced in about 1553 (see below). The will itself was widely thought to have disappeared; even John Hales ("Declaration of the Succession," 1563), to whose purpose its existence was essential, lamented its loss and built his case without it. The original does exist and was examined in 1566 by members of the Privy Council (Axton, "Influence of Edmund Plowden's Succession Treatise," pp. 223–24). Although controversy has continued for some time (see A. F. Pollard, *England under the Protector Somerset*, pp. 3–7; and L. Smith, "Last Will and Testament of Henry VIII"), it now seems likely that both will and signature are valid (Levine, "Last Will and Testament of Henry VIII," and *Succession Question*, pp. 156–57; Scarisbrick, *Henry VIII*, pp. 491–94).

244. Gates, Privy Councillor and Chancellor of the Duchy of Lancaster, was a creature of Northumberland's who perished with the Duke in 1553. His name heads the list of signatures to the will.

245. William Lord Paget (d. 1563), father of Arundell's friend, was Secretary of State under Henry and Privy Councillor under Mary. This incident, although it passed current among the controversialists, seems otherwise unconfirmed; the great lawyer Plowden, however, claimed to have been present and said that Sir Henry Neville could prove that it had occurred (Jordan, *Edward VI: the Young King*, p. 55n).

246. Montague (d. 1556), ancestor of the Dukes of Manchester, was a Councillor and Chief Justice of King's Bench (1539–1545) and Common Pleas (1545–1554), whose mother was a Dudley and who was deprived of office after Northumberland's fall.

247. William Clerc (Clerk, Clark) was one of three men (Gates was another) who had custody of the king's dry-stamp.

248. This book is unidentified; as the major Suffolk claimant had died in Jan. 1568, one would not expect to find a Suffolk tract in 1569 or 1570. It may be the "poisoned pestiferous pamphlet" against Mary's "claim and interest" mentioned by Leslie in 1569 as cast abroad the previous July (*Defense*, sig. *iiᵛ), which in turn may refer to George Buchanan's anti-Marian "Book of Articles," June 1568.

249. Although Thomas Wilson, in his *State of England A.D. 1600*, shows that he was aware of other books on the succession, his discussion is drawn directly from the *Commonwealth*. From it he lifts *ad verbum* this entire passage (beginning "And sithence that time . . ."), though he adds the phrase "by the means of some in ye company ('tis thought the Earl of Leicester), it took not effect" (pp. 8–9). That this meeting occurred is not improbable; given the participants, it sounds very like the Feb. 1569 attempt to unseat Cecil (see Read, *Cecil*, pp. 442–43).

250. Here begins the second passage quoted by Harington.
251. Margin: "The Dudleys."
252. Here ends the second passage quoted by Harington, *Tract on the Succession*, pp. 61-62. Ironically, when Navarre did succeed as Henri IV (1589), he was forced to convert to Catholicism (1594) before he could receive his kingdom in some quiet.
253. James (now aged eighteen) was being carefully watched for his religious inclinations from all over Europe; he seems to have shown himself Protestant to the English government and Catholic to the Catholic powers.
254. For similar remarks see Camden, *Elizabeth*, 3: 21; on the tenor of these pulpit attacks see Willson, *King James VI and I*, pp. 36-50. The contemporary annotator of the Marsh's copy says of this: "We know all this [to] be a suborned disco[urse] devised [by] the young [king] his licentious minions . . . of purp[ose] to shadow their bloody and pestilent proceedings against the soundest and best affected ministers of the realm, that they might the more easily draw their neck from the yoke of that Christian [religion] which hath been [now] established so long."
255. Patrick Adamson (1537-1592), Archbishop of St. Andrews, was a vigorous enemy of the Presbyterian Kirk; says the Marsh annotator, "Tis a merry world when you fall a-praising him. . . . It behooved this good Sir Patrick to take this course, to [tr]y his time, [and] to make his most advantage of the young king's unbridled licentiousness, for otherwise he might happen to have [los]t his Arch-[episcop]acy and have proved but a [poo]r and beggarly [mas]ter." Adamson arrived in London on 30 Nov. 1583 (a few days after Arundell had fled the realm), ostensibly on his way into France but actually to seek further aid for James from the Queen; he returned to Scotland in May.
256. Theodore Beza (d. 1605), Calvin's successor as head of the church of Geneva.
257. Henry Fitzalan (d. Feb. 1580), twelfth (and last) Earl of Arundel of his line; his second wife was Charles Arundell's aunt and his daughter and heir in her issue, Mary (d. 1557), was the Duke of Norfolk's first wife; their son Philip succeeded in the title.
258. The seat of the Marquess of Winchester, where the royal progress was stopped in August 1569 (Nichols, *Progresses*, 1: 254).
259. Similarly, in 1569 Leicester wrote (and Pembroke also signed) a letter to the Queen of Scots as part of the negotiation for Norfolk's marriage to her. When the plot had fallen apart and Norfolk was under arrest, Leicester sent to him secretly and begged him to contrive to get the letter back; Norfolk, however, merely requested that Mary "would not let it come to light to my Lord of Leicester's hurt, because the whole letter was his own handwriting, marry, yet I wished her to keep it still for all chances" (Norfolk's confession, *C.S.P. Scots, 1571-74*, p. 40). It appears from her secretary's notes of Nov. 1584 that fifteen years later she kept it still, for all chances (*ibid., 1584-85*, p. 390).
260. Norfolk was finally executed on 2 June 1572, but the events described here occurred in Sept. and Oct. 1569. That this account of Norfolk's fall is not so tendentious as it sounds is borne out by the conclusions of modern historians, at least insofar as Leicester moved nimbly enough at the last to save his own skin; see, e.g.,

Williams, *Thomas Howard*, chaps. 9-13; Read, *Cecil*, pp. 440-52; also Camden, *Elizabeth*, 1: 127-32, and Norfolk's confession, *C.S.P. Scots, 1571-74*, pp. 32-40. A partisan account of his execution is contained in the "Letter of Estate," pp. 25-26.

261. When the unbalanced John Somerville was taken in Oct. 1583 for planning to kill the Queen, his father-in-law Edward Arden of Park Hall, Arden's wife and daughter, and Father Hugh Hall were also arrested. The women were pardoned, and Hall became a government spy, but on 16 Dec. Somerville hanged himself in Newgate prison, and the following day Arden was executed, the victim, it was said, of Leicester's malice (because he had slandered Lady Essex and refused the Earl's livery, says Camden, *Elizabeth*, 3: 28; because he had given refuge to Fr. Campion, according to Parsons, C.R.S. 4, p. 115, and C.R.S. 39, pp. 188-89). Hall was an expert gardener and had worked in that and in a spiritual capacity for the Catholics Lord Windsor and Sir John Throgmorton; in the early 1580s he was landscaping Hatton's new house at Holdenby. Hatton was widely considered a secret Catholic and probably knew that Hall was a priest, but there is no sign that Leicester devised to entrap him. See Brooks, *Hatton*, pp. 61, 216, 257-58; Read, *Walsingham*, 2: 381n. Sir Charles Cavendish was one of the Countess of Shrewsbury's sons and was attached to Leicester, but his role in this affair is unknown.

262. Henry Unton (or Umpton, knighted 1586, d. 1596), later ambassador to France, was a follower of Hatton (Brooks, *Hatton*, p. 259). When in early 1583 his brother Edward was imprisoned by the Inquisition at Milan, he rushed to Lyons to negotiate his ransom while Leicester and Hatton threatened to have Mendoza imprisoned in reprisal (*C.S.P. Spanish, 1580-86*, p. 443). Solomon Aldred (d. 1592), an English tailor living in Lyons and soon to become an agent for Walsingham (Hicks, "Elizabethan Propagandist"), came forward to act as go-between; Parsons claims that Aldred dealt directly with Hatton (C.R.S. 2, p. 206). Edward Unton was released in the following year and died in 1589 (*D.N.B.*). No trace has been found of the letters cited here.

263. From 1575, when Cockyn's confession revealed the complicity of his servants in furthering Mary's correspondence, the Earl was considered too lenient in his commission (Read, *Walsingham*, 2: 354-55). When in late 1583 his marital troubles erupted, his wife ("his nearest in bed"; his nearest "in blood" is his son Gilbert) spread scandals concerning his behavior with Mary (Mary believed the Walsingham faction had put the Countess up to it; *C.S.P. Scots, 1584-85*, p. 5), and those who had wished for greater severity seized upon these rumors in order to straiten her captivity. In Aug. 1584 Shrewsbury was permitted to come up to London to clear himself, and although Elizabeth expressed her confidence in him, Mary was removed to stricter keepers, first Sir Ralph Sadler, then in Apr. 1585 the stern Amias Paulet.

264. That is, the first nobleman of his line, an upstart.

265. Still another allusion reflecting a deep second-generation grievance over the failure of the Protector's party. Arundel was arrested upon Somerset's fall (Oct. 1551), along with Charles Arundell's father; he was transferred to the Tower in Nov. and not released until Dec. 1552.

266. This anecdote has been borrowed but applied to Leicester and Philip Howard, the next Earl of Arundel, by the author of the "Letter of Estate" (p. 31).

267. Confirming this account, see Stow, *Chronicles of England*, p. 1065. "Palfrey" was usually employed of a small, gentle horse used by ladies, hence doubly contemptuous here.
268. Leicester was appointed Chamberlain of the County Palatine of Chester in 1565.
269. Compare "*Le fleuve passé le sainct oublié*: Prov. The danger past our vows are soon forgotten" (Cotgrave's *Dictionarie*, *sub* "Sainct").
270. Frances (d. 1598) was Lady Sheffield's sister; in 1573 she was "very far in love" with Leicester (*Hatton Memoirs*, p. 23), though a few years later she married the Earl of Hertford.
271. The Countess died 23 Sept. 1576.
272. Mary's supporters liked Shrewsbury because he was a lenient man and because as long as she was in his custody they were able to find means of communicating with her. When the opposition had sufficiently disgraced him, Mary was indeed placed in stricter confinement (Jan. 1585) and her correspondence was cut off for a year. It was allowed to resume, in Jan. 1586, only when Walsingham was ready to have it done his own way, the results of which appeared when she was executed in Feb. 1587.
273. "Packs": intrigues, plots (*O.E.D.*).
274. "Admiration": wonder, astonishment (*O.E.D.*); not "approval."
275. "Bruitling," from "bruit": noise, clamor (*O.E.D.*).
276. "Foruscites": from the Italian *fuoruscito*: outlaw, exile.
277. That is, Poland (under the tolerant Stephen Bathory) and Bohemia. Later events proved these examples to have been based on very insecure ground.
278. The most recent attempt at peace between the Huguenots and the militant Catholics of the "Holy League" in France had been the Treaty of Fleix, Nov. 1580; it, like its predecessors, was doomed, chiefly through the "will and inclination" of the Guise faction.
279. The Spanish, like the English, had their propaganda aimed at convincing the world of their lenity toward dissenters; whether this passage is a part of that propaganda or its victim would be difficult to determine.
280. "Familians," i.e., the Family of Love, a quasi-Anabaptist sect founded in the Low Countries by Hendrik Niklas, prosecution of which in England reached something of a peak in 1579–1580.
281. Cicero, as consul, suppressed the revolt of Lucius Sergius Catilina in 63 B.C.
282. Diodorus Siculus, 16.93–94; Plutarch, *Alexander*, 10.4.
283. Gaveston (executed 1312), Earl of Cornwall; and later Hugh Despenser (ex. 1326), Earl of Winchester; and his son Sir Hugh (ex. 1326) were favorites of Edward II. De Vere (d. 1392), Earl of Oxford, Marquess then Duke of Ireland; and Mowbray (d. 1400), Duke of Norfolk, favorites of Richard II.
284. "Instinct": instigation, prompting (*O.E.D.*).
285. Margin: "Polydore, lib. 23, *Historia Anglica*." Humphrey of Gloucester died in Feb. 1447, probably of a stroke, ten days after he was arrested at the instance of William de la Pole, then Marquess of Suffolk. Most of Polydore Vergil's twenty-third book exhibits the general sense of Suffolk as the cause of calamity, but the point is not explicitly made.

LEICESTER'S COMMONWEALTH 221

286. Margin: "Anno 30 of King Henry VI," an error (which follows Polydore Vergil's implied sequence of events [1844, pp. 82–83]) for Anno 27. Suffolk was Margaret's chief ally, but when he was finally brought up on all manner of charges, she had her husband banish him for five years by royal prerogative (thereby forestalling a verdict). He departed on 30 Apr. 1450 but was intercepted in Dover Strait and beheaded by angry subjects on 3 May.

287. Despite this rather threatening reference to the social contract, the *Commonwealth* is based upon thoroughly legitimist assumptions. Leslie mentions the same idea but discusses at great length why "the world was for the most part constrained to repudiate election" (*Defense*, fol. 51v); Mary is the most qualified candidate for the succession, he says, "but now I claim nothing for the worthiness of the person, which God forbid should be anything prejudicial to the just title of others; if most open and manifest right, justice, and title do not concur with the worthiness of the person, then let the praise and worthiness remain where it is, and the right where God and the law hath placed it" (fol. 54v).

288. Margin: "Cicero, in Officio" (*De Officiis*, 2: 23); in W. Miller's translation, "Fear is but a poor safeguard of lasting power" (Loeb Classical Library, p. 191).

289. The figure of St. George, suspended from the collar of the Order of the Garter (which Dudley received in 1559).

290. Appended to the 1584 edition to make up the pages is a Latin quotation, omitted here, followed by this English translation.

APPENDIX A

Printed and Manuscript Forms of Leicester's Commonwealth

PRINTED FORMS

The 1584 quarto first edition of *Leicester's Commonwealth*[1] has the following title page, all of which is set within an ornamental border except the date at the end, which is set into an ornamental base:

THE/ COPIE OF A/ *LETER, WRYTEN BY A/* MASTER OF ARTE OF CAMBRIGE,/ TO HIS FRIEND IN LONDON, CON-/ cerning some talke past of late betwen two wor-/ shipful and graue men, about the present state, and/ some procedinges of the Erle of Leycester and/ his friendes in England./ *CONCEYVED, SPOKEN/ and publyshed, wyth most earnest protes-/ tation of al duetyful good wyl and affe-/ ction, towardes her most excellent Ma./ and the Realm, for whose good onely it is/ made common to many./* Iob. Cap. 20. Vers. 27./ Reuelabunt coeli iniquitatem eius, & terra confurget/ aduersus eum./ The heauens shal reueile the wicked mans iniqui-/ tie, and the earth shal stand vp to beare witnes/ agaynst hym./ ANNO M. D. LXXXIIII.

The present text has been prepared from a collation of nine copies of the 1584 edition, namely, those in the Folger Shakespeare Library; the Bodleian Library, Oxford; the Yale and Cambridge University Libraries; the Libraries of the Universities of London and of Durham; the Archbishop Marsh's Library, Dublin; and the two in the British Library. There are only a handful more extant that have not been consulted. Only three variant readings have emerged from these mentioned, none of them of any consequence:

1. On page 112 above, for the phrase "*so that it* redounded," one copy has "*which* redounded" (Marsh's).
2. On page 126, for "no *man* durst accuse," two have "no *men*" (London and Durham).
3. In the scriptural quotation at the end of the text, for "fire that neede*th no* kindling," one has "fire that neede *have* kindling" (Yale).

In 1585 a French translation appeared entitled *Discours de la vie abominable, ruses, trahisons . . . le my Lorde de Lecestre*, which evidently emanated from the same Paris-based group of men. It follows its original very closely but appends twenty-two pages of additional material, discussed and printed here (see Appendix B) in a contemporary retranslation into English.[2] The English original appeared in several forms in London in 1641. There was a quarto version that differs in no substantial way from the first edition: *Leicester's Commonwealth: Conceived, Spoken and Published with Most Earnest Protestation of All Dutiful Goodwill and Affection towards This Realm*.[3] There was also, similarly faithful to the original, an octavo with the same title, which appeared both by itself and (under a cancel title page) with the long poem "Leicester's Ghost" appended in abridged form.[4] And there was a sixteen-page quarto version, *Leicester's Commonwealth Fully Epitomiz'd*, "contracted in a most brief, exact, and compendious way with the full sense and whole meaning of the former book, every fragment of sense being interposed."[5]

Just why the book should have been reprinted in 1641 is unclear; the "fully epitomiz'd" version even seems like an attempt to capitalize upon a hot market. J. H. M. Salmon feels that it was one of many books "approving resistance" that were reprinted just before the Civil War,[6] but this seems unlikely since while the *Commonwealth* may imply a need for resistance, all that it approves of is legal retribution against Leicester through Elizabeth's courts of law. In "Fully Epitomiz'd" a curious addition has been made: "But it is very strange to see *what a contemner of the Prerogatives of England he is, and* how little account he maketh of all the ancient nobility of our realm"[7]— perhaps suggesting that the editor was rather a royalist than otherwise. Derek Wilson suggests that the republication was connected with the trial of the Earl of Strafford, another royal favorite whom many believed the realm could spare,[8] but the book seems to have appeared some months after Wentworth's execution in May. Dr. Thomas Clancy's suggestion (letter 10 September 1970) is the most plausible one, that with the weakening of controls upon printing in 1640 and 1641, the public's taste for "racy reading" was here being gratified. And "Fully Epitomiz'd" bears him out in this, for of all the deletions there undertaken, scarcely one salacious detail of the Earl's crimes has been omitted. In any case, the revival of interest in the tract caused offense in some quarters. On 13 October 1641, Sir Edward Nicholas, clerk of the Privy Council, wrote to Bourne and Parker, wardens of the Company of Stationers:

> Sirs, I hear there is now printing at one [John] Dawson's, a printer in Thames Street, a book called *Leicester's Commonwealth*, which I am told is very scandalous to divers of the Lords' ancestors, and a book unfit to be divulged. It is one [William] Sheares that joins with Dawson in the printing of it. I pray give order forthwith to stay the printing or dispersing of any of those books until the Lords of Parliament or the Lords of the Privy Council shall meet, which will be Wednesday next. [S.P. 16/484/75.]

The *Commonwealth* was reissued again several times in the early eighteenth century by Dr. James Drake. He claimed, on the title page of the 1706 edition, that he was using "an Old Manuscript never Printed," and he may have been, but more likely he was using as copytext one of the 1641 reprints; he almost certainly was not using the 1584 first edition.[9] In 1904, the librarian of the Lambeth Palace Library, F. J. Burgoyne, brought out an unannotated reprint of the 1641 quarto (L.968), which he entitled *History of Queen Elizabeth, Amy Robsart, and the Earl of Leicester*. Two very brief extracts also appeared in *British Pamphleteers*, edited by George Orwell and Reginald Reynolds (1 [1948]: 36–39). And recently the Scolar Press has issued an unannotated facsimile reproduction of the 1584 edition (the Cambridge University copy) in its English Recusant Literature series (no. 192). These represent the printed forms that the *Commonwealth* has taken to the present day.

MANUSCRIPT FORMS

As the 1584 printed text began to grow scarce through government efforts to limit its circulation, a great many copies were made of it by hand and others were made from these. The number of such manuscripts surviving should suffice to demonstrate the great interest aroused by the book in its own time; there are now several times more such texts extant than there are printed copies. Of the fifty-eight manuscripts related to the *Commonwealth* that have been studied for the present edition, only the "Letter of Estate," discussed hereafter, is in any way remarkable. Despite speculation in the past about some of them having been early drafts, all of the others turn out to be derived from the printed edition, copied either directly from it or from an intervening manuscript; each of them contains variants that are plausible misreadings of the original and which at the same time introduce errors of fact or sense into the text. Of the vast number of variant readings, nearly all are merely scribal errors or conjectures; thus, "one Gates" becomes "John Gates," "Bald" Buttler becomes "Baldwin," in the same way that Cardinal Châtillon becomes "Charlion." There are a few instances of significant interpolation, however, such as the addition of Gabriel Bleke's name and the marginal account of the Drayton Basset riot, and these have been recorded in the annotations. The following is a list of the manuscripts studied for this edition (it appears that I have not seen only about five known manuscripts):[10]

1. *Complete*. The first category includes all those manuscripts that represent more or less successful attempts at full and accurate transcription of the 1584 edition and which have survived substantially undamaged (forty-four MSS.):

British Library, Harleian MSS. 405, 557, 2245, 2290, 4020, 4282, 6021.
British Library, Lansdowne MS. 265.
British Library, Stowe MSS. 156, 270, 271.
British Library, Hargrave MS. 311.
British Library, Sloane MSS. 1303, 1566, 3273.
British Library, Additional MSS. 6130, 33,739.
Cambridge University Library MSS. Ff.2.3, Gg.2.28, Ii.5.1., Mm.4.33, Mm. 6.33.
Cambridge, Trinity College MSS. R.5.9, R.5.18.
Cambridge, St. John's College MSS. L.11, S.46.
Cambridge, Emmanuel College MS. 1.3.28.

Oxford University, Bodleian Library, Additional MS. A93.
Oxford, Exeter College MS. 166.
Trinity College, Dublin, MSS. 480, 481, 483.
University of Kent at Canterbury Library.
Inner Temple Library, Petyt MS. 538 (v.45, no.8).
Pierpont Morgan MS. MA 1475.
Folger Shakespeare Library MSS. G.a.7, G.a.8, G.b.11, G.b.13, V.b.41.
Huntington Library MSS. HM 90, HM 267, EL 1161.
Harvard University Library, fMS. 1121.

2. *Imperfect*. The second category includes those that were intended to be full and accurate transcriptions but which have been substantially damaged through time (six MSS.):
British Library, Harleian MS. 7582.
British Library, Lansdowne MS. 215.
Cambridge University Library MS. Mm.6.63.
Yale University Library, Osborne Collection, MS. f.a.3.
Folger Shakespeare Library MS. G.a.9.
Alnwick Castle, Northumberland[11]

3. *Incomplete*. The third category includes all those that are largely only paraphrases or summaries of the full text or that reveal deliberate omission of substantial portions (five MSS.):
Cambridge University Library MS. Ii.4.33.
Oxford University, Bodleian Library, Jones MS. 32.
Trinity College, Dublin, MS. 482.
Pierpont Morgan MS. MA 662.
Folger Shakespeare Library MS. G.b.12.

4. *Extracts*. The fourth category includes those that are listed in their respective catalogues as copies of the *Commonwealth* but which actually are only brief collections of passages drawn from it (two MSS.):
British Library, Hargrave MS. 168 (fols. 395–403).
British Library, Sloane MS. 874 ("The Earl of Derby's Historical Collections," fols. 7–12v).

THE "LETTER OF ESTATE"

One related manuscript requires special notice. The "Letter of Estate" (S.P. 15/28/113, fols. 369–88v) was written, apparently in

APPENDICES WITH RELATED NOTES 227

1585, by an anonymous ill-wisher of Leicester who leaned heavily upon *Leicester's Commonwealth* in form and content but who wrote independently of the refugee courtiers for his own purposes, with several new charges. Confusion has been caused, however, by the fact that several scholars have mistaken the "Letter" for an early draft of the *Commonwealth*. A reconstructed text of the badly damaged manuscript, with a discussion of its circumstances, appears in D. C. Peck, " 'The Letter of Estate': An Elizabethan Libel," *Notes and Queries*, n.s. 28 (1981): 21-35.

NOTES TO APPENDIX A

1. *S.T.C.* 19399 (*sub* "Parsons"); in the revised edition of *S.T.C.* it will have the number 5742.9. In Allison and Rogers's *Catalogue of Catholic Books*, it is no. 261.
2. There was also a Latin adaptation by Julius Briegerus, the *Flores Calvinistici*, falsely imprinted Naples, in early 1586.
3. Wing, *Short-Title Catalogue* . . . *1641-1700*, 2: L.968.
4. *Ibid.* L.969. "Leicester's Ghost," a rhyme-royal complaint in the manner of the *Mirror for Magistrates*, was written by Thomas Rogers of Bryanstone in about 1605, largely paraphrased from the *Commonwealth*. The abridgement appended to L.969 also appeared separately in quarto in 1641 (Wing, L.970), but the original manuscript has been edited for the Renaissance English Text Society (vol. 4), by Franklin B. Williams, Jr. See also Bowers, "Kyd's Pedringano," pp. 248-49, and F. Williams's article, "Leicester's Ghost," which contains a full bibliographic analysis of the 1641 editions.
5. Wing, 2: L.969A. The quotation is from the title page. Unlike the 1584 edition and the other 1641 versions, this text seems to have become very rare, but has been reprinted in *Harleian Miscellany*, 4: 576-83.
6. Salmon, *French Religious Wars in English Political Thought*, p. 82.
7. Wing, 2: L.969A, p. 14; *Leicester's Commonwealth*, p. 174 above.
8. D. Wilson, *Sweet Robin*, p. 267.
9. Drake, *Secret Memoirs of Robert Dudley* and *Perfect Picture of a Favorite*. Reprinted as *The Memoirs of Robert Dudley*, as *Collectanea adamantaea*, no. 24, in four volumes (privately printed, 350 copies, 1887-1888).
10. It should be pointed out that many of these are listed in their respective catalogues under the name Robert Parsons.
11. As published by Burgoyne, *Collotype Facsimile and Type Transcript of an Elizabethan Manuscript Preserved at Alnwick Castle, Northumberland*.

APPENDIX B

The French Translation, 1585, and Its Addition

On 30 March 1585 Sir Edward Stafford reported from Paris that he had received word of the appearance of a French translation of *Leicester's Commonwealth* (the relevant letters are printed in Appendix E). He suggested that it had been printed in Rheims, home of Dr. Allen's seminary, though the exile community was asserting that it had been done at Cologne (both are unlikely), and he indicated that Thomas Throgmorton had been engaged in translating it until he had stopped him. Throgmorton may well have been its translator; at least, as Mendoza informed Philip II on 1 June, it was certainly done by an Englishman.[1]

Entitled the *Discours de la vie abominable . . . le my Lorde de Lecestre*, the bulk of the work is a close and accurate translation of the entire *Commonwealth* (marred only by the fact that the compositor has worked havoc upon the proper names). Prefaced to it, however, is an allegorical emblem (apparently borrowed from another source), with a rather dull poem explaining it, along with several dedicatory verses. At the end there is affixed what Stafford called a "villainous" and a "filthy addition," which adds further charges against the Earl, at least one of which is indeed filthy. Stafford was certain that the matter for the addition had been sent out of England, and though that may or may not be true, certainly it displays the same detailed acquaintance with Leicester and his associates that the *Commonwealth* does. Although the tone is rather more sprightly than the *Commonwealth*'s, in the absence of other evidence, we are safe in assuming that the same men were responsible for both publications.

A few points are worth remarking about the addition: first, it is clearly aimed at a French audience (why Stafford should have been so sure that it was intended for an English one is not at all clear); second, its author considers it an updating, one of a planned series; third, it is purely defamatory, with none of the ancillary concerns for toleration and the succession found in the book itself; fourth, it includes an intensified attack upon the Puritans and a stronger, though rather transparent, effort to suggest divisions between the Puritans and Leicester their leader; and fifth, it contains the *Commonwealth*'s only direct allusion to members of the Catholic Court party, that is, to Lord Harry Howard and Charles Arundell (as well as to the Earls of Arundel and Southampton)—this impersonal mention, and its mistaking "Sir Robert" for Sir Edward Stafford, may have been intended as smokescreen.

The French publication can be seen in the British Library (10806.a.10). The text for this English version of *La vie*'s addition is that of a contemporary retranslation attached to a manuscript copy of the *Commonwealth* (not of *La vie*), Exeter College, Oxford, MS. 166 (pp. 203-26). It is apparently a retranslation of the printed French, not the (hypothetical) English original, and the handwriting is unfamiliar. The spelling and punctuation have been modernized.

"THE 1585 ADDITION"

An Addition of the Translator, in which are declared many enormous and unchristian acts committed by the said Earl of Leicester, of which there hath been new advertisement and knowledge day by day.

The abominable and wretched life of this monstrous Earl is so plainly set forth, declared, and deciphered in the precedent discourse and conference that it may seem to thee a thing right strange (gentle reader) that any man should be able to add any more. But the sea or gulf of this man's sins is so bottomless that it is a thing impossible to sound the depth of it, and his life so brutish and the injuries he hath done to all manner of people are such and so great in number that it is very difficult to take perfect notice of them without making as it were a general assembly of all the people of England, to hear what each man can allege in particular. Wherefore all that we can conveniently do about this business is nothing else but (for the better beautifying and more perfecting the story of his life) to add from day to day such his actions as the time shall discover unto us. In which, as I have done mine endeavor in this my translation and additions, so others as I understand will perform shortly in setting out this book both in Latin and Italian, as soon as they can receive more large advertisement from England, from whence there is already gathered, as I hear, a good quantity that shall be augmented from more to more. For his Lordship taketh so good a course herein that writers shall never want matter, he being as it were so drunk in the hateful and abominable pleasures of this life that he doth every day disgorge himself of so huge a surfeit of sin and vomiteth up such loathsome filth in such quantity and variety that he giveth occasion more than enough to all tongues to speak, all pens to write, and all the world to wonder. But to the end I may stay you no longer in this proem, and that you may enter into the matter, I will propound in the first place (the rather to gratify the French readers, and to make them understand what good affection this good lord beareth to the nation) how traitorously he behaved himself in Flanders toward Monsieur, son and brother of the Most Christian Kings, which I know will carry so good a taste that it will pass current over all France for an act of a very knave.

Now then, when after great long consultation upon the treaty of marriage between Monsieur and the Queen of England it was in fine determined and concluded to turn all that business into an enterprise of the Low Countries, this good apostle-like Earl, finding in his own conceit his credit to be greatly diminished, his glory obscured, and all the grace of his future royalty like to be reversed by the too long stay of his Highness in England, he showed himself so inclining to this voyage of Flanders that he made offer of all his *devoir* and service for the advancement of the enterprise, and forthwith he presenteth himself to Monsieur, offering to serve him and conduct him in person to the said countries, promising with oaths and protestations (a thing which he useth of custom when he means least faith) so to deal with the Prince of Orange that his Highness should obtain of him what he listed and upon what conditions he pleased, so far forth as Monsieur, thinking this had proceeded of a good affection and sincere mind, accepted his offer and took him with him when he went. But being arrived at Antwerp, this good Earl (calling to mind, I trow, the liberal promises he had made by vows and oaths) showed himself so desirous to acquit him toward his Highness and so eager to do him some acceptable service that not enduring to wait the opportunity to do it himself he dispatched with all diligence Mr. Philip Sidney, his nephew, to the Prince of Orange, and why, trow you? Certainly for no other end but to stir and provoke the Prince against his Highness and the French, and to will him to take good heed to Monsieur's proceedings among them, and above all to teach him this lesson: that he never suffer any lords to grow so great in the country but that he leave it still in his own power to put them beside the seat when himself shall think good; lo, the sum of his nephew's message to the Prince of Orange, which he did full diligently, following the command of his uncle, and adding matters very reproachful of his own head, to derogate from the great virtue and honor of his Highness, as the Prince of Orange himself confessed after to Monsieur, who telling it to some of his friends imprinted it so deeply in the hearts of many as they will never forget it if opportunity will serve of revenge.[2]

Now (gentle reader) I refer me to thy judgment if ever any prince of the estate and calling of Monsieur were more traitorously handled by such a petty companion (for he was no better in regard of so great a prince). Considering specially how well his Highness had deserved of all the English nation, which (for better discovering the wickedness of this monster) I will make you understand in a few words.

Monsieur, having weighed and considered with himself the near neighborhood of the two realms of England and France and the calamity that had often come to both of them by means of wars most bloody, and the commodity like to come hereafter and already come by means of the peace and unity that they have held a good while together, was so moved in mind to do his uttermost endeavor to tie and join them with an undissolvable knot of amity that he made a motion of marriage between the Queen and him, as well by his ambassadors as himself in person, passing into England, nor making any doubt (for the benefit of the two flourishing realms) to venture himself to the danger and hazard of a journey so long and perilous, without being accompanied either of his accustomed train, either of his usual guard for his person, showing more than sufficiently by that one act how firmly he trusted in the good faith of the Queen and in the good mind of her people; from which I dare be bold to say the Queen of England had more honor in the conceit of the world than in any one affair that ever she dealt in with any prince beside whatsoever. Which her Majesty (for I speak it to her honor) with all her principal nobility[3] of the country seemed to have very good consideration of, in giving his Highness such honorable entertainment as so noble a prince, making offer so liberal of his amity and alliance, did well deserve. For there was not a man of honor and mark in all the country that was not well apaid and glad of this goodly alliance, setting aside only this monster and his complices, who having long since cast in his mind how to make the crown one day fall on his head, as in the precedent conference hath been plainly declared, and foreseeing the annihilating of all his complots and designments if such a marriage and alliance should take effect, he opposed himself by all the means and secret practices that he could devise, disguising notwithstanding and covering (as much as was possible) all his devices and appointments with all kind deceits, dissembling, lying, and flattering, showing so good a countenance to Monsieur as Judas did when he kissed his master, yet so as elsewhere his instruments and fuelers[4] (the Puritans and others) murmured and grudged, scattering infamous libels and babbling and preaching in open pulpit against his Highness and all the French, and himself with his complices consulting and concluding among themselves to rebel openly in case the marriage should take effect. And (which is more) his malice to Monsieur was so great and his hate so irreconcilable that after, when he had no cause at all to mistrust the marriage, his Highness being now departed out of England (as hath been said), he ceased not for all that to show the fruits of a cruel and malicious heart, seeking all occasions and means under color of promised fidelity and service to avert and alienate from his Highness the hearts of his honorable friends, not respecting either the affiance Monsieur had in him, either the commandment of the Queen his mistress, either his own promises confirmed with infinite oaths and protestations. Now then, regard and behold, friendly readers, with the eyes of your understanding another Catiline, excessive in ambition, in malice more than monstrous, traitorous beyond measure, perjured afore the face of God, and therefore worthily odious to all the world.

But you will say to me (perhap) that this good Earl, being not furnished with honesty and sincerity more than he should necessarily bestow and employ in favor of his own kinsfolks and friends of his own country, had great reason not to be too prodigal of the same to Monsieur, being a stranger and a foreigner.

But if peradventure it will be proved that he showed himself no less faithless to his friends than malicious to his enemies, nor less ingrateful to his kin than dissembling and false to strangers, I think you will make no great difficulty to conclude with me that he is the [most] monstrous man that lives on the earth, of which I will make you most plain demonstration by this example. It came to pass that Sir Henry Sidney, father of the Sidney that we spake of before and brother-in-law to this good Earl (as having married his sister) and one of the Queen's Privy Council as well as himself, being informed of the many extortions, usuries, oppressions, frauds, and other enormities committed by one Scory, pretended Bishop of Hereford[5] (an old apostata and renegade monk, and one that hath of long time done more slander than service to the church of England), and being, as I say, moved with an honest zeal of justice, exhibited a bill in the Star Chamber against the said Scory of all those his misdemeanors, not doubting, considering the greatness and honorableness of that court, that justice would speedily have his course against a transgressor so very manifest.

But the affair had this issue, that albeit Sir Henry Sidney employed all his credit and all his friends to the following of this matter, yet notwithstanding this good Earl his brother-in-law handled the matter so finely with the Queen (whose eyes he blinded no doubt with some honest pretence) that by her express commandment the matter was taken quite out of the Star Chamber and the deciding thereof referred to certain other bishops who were made judges and arbitrators, with other ministers, companions, and brothers in Christ of the said party accused, which judges having a great zeal to the house of the Lord judged it necessary to wink at and bear somewhat with the infirmity of their frail brother, for fear of slandering the gospel. In such sort that the matter was huddled up I know not how among themselves, but this I know well, that the Apostata was sent home again without any notable punishment.[6] But if you have a desire to know what moved this Earl so willfully to oppose himself against his brother-in-law in the favor of so detestable a villain and in a cause so wicked and injust, sure to answer you in a word, *Quid non mortalia pectora cogis, Auri sacra fames,* O detestable famine of gold, what canst not thou enforce man unto?[7] For Scory handled his matter and pleaded his case so well and wisely that the Countess of Leicester was assaulted with some thousands of angels,[8] which she, poor lady, finding herself too weak to resist so great an army so well ranged in battle [ar]ray and making so fair a muster, did not only yield herself prisoner without making any resistance, but also gave notice to her Robin of the great forces of the enemy. She also won him without great difficulty to yield himself a slave with her to the same fortune. Which was no great marvel, seeing his hap daily to be such that how valiant and brave soever he shows himself in other matters, yet when he must try it hand to hand in close lists with any bribe of gold or other gift he hath straight fought craven and shamefully yielded without stroke striking, as you see plainly in this example, the whole process whereof was revealed by the bishop's own son. Neither must you marvel that I call him his son, for the ministry of England is not barren nor idle, nay which is more (thanks be to God) they have in the name of the Lord begotten good store of children and increased and multiplied exceedingly. But as I said unto you, this young bishop, or at the least son and heir of a bishop, being come to the city of London with the reverend prelate his father, told to one of his friends that they had brought with them more money (to clear and level those accounts with the Countess of Leicester as I told you before) than would have served him to have played away at dice and cards as they say (his whole rest) in seven year. Out of which words they that knew the humor and disposition of this good priest's son might easily guess that the sum was not small, for I assure you that this is so gentle a companion, and (praise be to the Lord) so brave and gallant a gamester at dice and cards and other exercises of base mystery as the ministry of England hath not bred the like this great while.⁹

But to come to the last act of this comedy, my good Lord of Leicester, failing somewhat in the managing of this matter, did not carry it so cleanly but that it came to be discovered and so made known to his brother-in-law Sir Henry Sidney and his friends, namely the Earl of Pembroke, son-in-law of the said Sidney and consequently nephew by marriage of the Earl of Leicester, who took this matter in so evil part as not being able otherwise to dissemble it he told this great Lord his uncle in plain terms that if by his means the course of justice was impeached and hindered in this matter of the bishop (as many would judge it was), it was a plain sign he had neither honor nor honesty; in so much as this good Lord, finding himself taken so tardy nor knowing of what wood to make his shafts, found out a very ready way to maintain his credit by heaping up sin upon sin and masking this corruption of his under the veil of perjury, denying the facts with great oaths and protestations. All which false and feigned words could not so satisfy his said nephew but that he said after to one of his friends that his uncle was a very beast, treacherous to his kin and unthankful to his friends, "by whose alliance" (said he) "I have spent and impaired my state to the value of twenty thousand pound, without ever receiving at his hand honor, advancement, or any other pleasure," which words, coming from the mouth of a personage so honorable and so near allied to this Earl as is the Earl of Pembroke, seemeth to me to be of sufficient weight to aver the assertion or conclusion before recited, namely that this monster of a man is no less unfaithful and false to his kinsfolk and friends than to strangers and others that belong not to him, as shall appear yet more plainly in the discourse ensuing, wherein I will declare another notable prank.

There was a certain man named Appleyard,[10] a gentleman of good calling and brother of this man's first wife (but, that notwithstanding, one of the instruments employed to work her death, as in the precedent conference is more plainly declared),[11] which Appleyard by the just judgment of God ran so far into debt that not any way knowing how to escape the hands of his creditors and the law was constrained for remedy to have recourse to the aid and favor of this Earl his brother-in-law, who being content to relieve his necessity herein (but so as it might be without any cost of his own) solicited another of his favorites named George Darcy (a gentleman of an honorable house)[12] to do so much at his request in favor of his companion Appleyard to be his surety and give his band for him, promising Darcy of his honor to save him harmless and indemnified for all forfeitures that by law he should incur in this dealing.

Darcy, trusting in the word and honor of so great a monarch as this great Lord his good master, made no great scruple to perform it and indeed became bound to the creditors of Appleyard, who not being satisfied nor discharged of the part of the said Appleyard according to his promise, commenced their suit against Darcy, constraining him for the payment thereof to sell all his patrimony that his father had left him, and all of it not being sufficient for the entire payment they caused him to [be] kept in prison for the rest, in manner that the poor gentleman was driven to stay a good while in prison, spoiled of his goods and liberty, calling continually on this good Lord his master by the solicitation of his friends and beseeching his Lordship with all humility to have consideration of his poor estate, and if the commiseration of his present calamity or respect of his past service were not sufficient to move him to compassion of his distressed state, yet at the least it might please his Lordship to do somewhat for him for his own honor's sake, which he had engaged to him so deeply for his indemnity.

But this good Earl, that had brought him to this so pitiful estate as you have heard, made so little reckoning whether he sank or swam that he was content to hear all these complaints without any compassion and to behold his ruin without any remorse, leaving him at the mercy of his creditors and so quite forsaking him at so great an extremity and final ruin. As the poor gentleman feels too well at this day (if he yet live), leaving an insupportable grief in the minds of his friends, a scorn of his family, and an example in himself to all the world and most evident witness of the ungratitude, falsehood, and most barbarous usage of this monster.

But in this we may very well consider the just judgment of God. This Darcy, having been at some other time an instrument of the wickedness of this monster, found him in the end the only motive and author of his ruin. For you must understand that about the beginning of the reign of her Majesty that now reigneth in England, the Duke of Swethland (and after king of the same country) came into England in person to demand her Highness in marriage. But our Earl that shot at the same mark, thinking the presence of so great a competitor to be too great a dis[ad]vantage to himself, could by no means endure it, and for that cause thought it expedient to procure him an answer not only very short but very sharp, namely as should prick him to the very heart and should send him back again in far greater haste than he came.

For he appointed with himself to cause him to be massacred, and giving the matter in charge to Darcy he associated to him in this enterprise the forenamed Appleyard, who taking upon them to have done it had also surely effected it (as Darcy afterward confessed to divers) if the Duke had not surceased his suit and hasted from England with great diligence.[13]

Now consider I beseech you a while, friendly readers, first the barbarous ingratitude of this Earl, that made no scruple at all utterly to overthrow a gentleman that had dedicated his goods, his soul, and life, and whole service to him. Then consider the justice of God in punishment of this Darcy by the same man in favor of whom he had so grievously offended. And last of all mark how after these discourses of his treachery, falsehood, oppressions, rapines, and perjury we be come as it were by due course by degrees to touch his bloody practices of murder. Of which sith occasion so well serves of our present purpose I will yet bring you as briefly as I can certain examples most notable and manifest. It is a thing well known and spread over all the Court that my Lady Stafford, wife of Sir Robert Stafford,[14] having observed and noted divers most abominable disorders and enormities of this good Earl, and doubting in her heart that if speedy redress were not had thereof all the world would cry out of it to the great slander and reproach of all the Court, complained one day to the Queen, of which this my good Lord being advertised very speedily and imagining belike in his mind that this complaint proceeded of the abundance of some melancholic humor in her, and moved with a brotherly charity, judged that this humor offending should be well purged, and to this end gave in charge to one George Vaux, his yeoman of his bottles, to provide with all diligence that some drugs might be had fit for such operation. Who belike, not taking good heed to the confection of the potion, instead of Elleborum[15] took a quantity of Regal,[16] and the less to offend the weak and delicate stomach of the lady (who perhaps could not well brook the force of so strong a medicine if she should know of it) he espied an opportunity and a fit commodious hour for her to take it unwittingly. For spying her one day passing by the place where my Lord's bottles stood that were in his charge, he presented her with a cup of my Lord's wine under a color of courtesy, which the good lady, not dreaming of any malice, refused not but took a good draught, which was the dearest draught that ever she drank in her life, for the poor lady had no sooner swallowed down this good wine of my Lord's but that she was immediately after swollen and as it were leprous; in such sort that albeit by the great goodness of God she escaped death, yet notwithstanding, all the world might easily see that she had been poisoned, although the said lady neither then nor after (such was and yet is the greatness of the Earl) could have any redress or amends of so great and unsupportable an injury. Yet notwithstanding, this ill happened to this lady brought yet both to herself and others this good: to take better heed hereafter how they come to such bargains to come so near to my Lord's bottles or to taste of his Lordship's wine anymore.[17]

Furthermore his Lordship's bloody practices about Monsieur Simiers when he dealt for Monsieur in England are evident and most plain, not only by that that is before recited in the precedent conference but that also that he would have practiced with Mr. Fairfax [Fervaques] to assault him in the open street as he was going to the Royal Exchange, under pretense of an old quarrel that was between them; and to this end he promised him the aid and assistance of all his hewsters and murderers, of which he entertains no small number to serve him at all assays.

But God (that by his providence overthrows the purposes of the wicked) suffered this to come to the knowledge of the Queen, who calling Leicester to her in presence of divers of her Council and great lords made him there a knight of the new order for this his new practice, giving him goodly titles of murderer, traitor, and villain, and protesting of her honor that if Simiers should leese but one drop of his blood his Lordship should be hang[ed] like a knave as he was, which words did so cool and abate the courage of this brave knight that that which he had so wickedly plotted passed no farther, although the stay was not in himself, whose wicked meaning was sufficiently declared in this matter long before.[18]

Unto this practice we may also add another no less traitorous, murderous, and mischievous than those that are above mentioned. Namely how he would have set one Captain Moffett to kill the Earl of Westmoreland in Flanders where he served the King of Spain. But the Captain, not willing to commit such an act, discovered it to the Earl and purchased thereby the immortal hate and disgrace of the said Leicester, which he knowing to be so bloody and his revenge so unmerciful and unmeasurable durst not return into England his country, but liveth abroad in exile and shall be constrained so to do till it shall please God to confound and take away this bloody butcher out of the world.[19]

Now I beseech thee (gentle reader) again to consider if ever thou have heard of a more notorious murdering villain than this, or if thou canst not liken him to Timon or to a *misanthropos* (a hater of mankind),[20] without pity, without religion, without all humanity. Neither is it unlikely that being so daily accustomed as he is to all villainies and murders that all sense of human nature is extinguished in him, and that he is transformed into a substance or mass of sin. Yes, certain, the likelihood is very great and yet notwithstanding, this good gentleman is not only very zealous forsooth of the gospel but also the very primate, head, and protector of the purest gospellers and preachers (I mean the Puritans) of this present time; and sure it stands with very good reason, for there is such an analogy and proportion between the members and the head, and their sympathy in nature and quality suiteth so well the one to the other, that we may well say of them the common proverb *Dignum patella operculum*,[21] that is a fit cover for such a dish, or like master like man; for as touching him you have already heard what he is, and to prove to you what companions these his brethren the Puritans are it shall suffice to show his Lordship's opinion of them. You must know therefore that he having caused a certain number of these Puritan ministers [to assemble] one day in his chamber, as he useth to do ordinarily once or twice in the week, when they had after their manner prophesied, catechized, disputed, and preached, he said after to one of his friends (in good sadness) that they were knaves and villains and caitiffs, "although," he said, "I am constrained to use their aid." Lo, hear the testimony of this good Earl touching his brethren, in which you may be bold to believe him of his word, although I do not wish you in other matters to believe his oath, and herein you must note certain points. First, what good apostles these his new evangelists are whom in show of the world he will seem so greatly to reverence and as it were adore. Secondly, what agreeableness there is between a head so monstrous and a body so prodigious and villainous as he himself confesseth his ministers and Puritans to be. And lastly, one may see manifestly, whatsoever he pretends in outward appearance, that indeed he hath no religion at all, but is rather a very miscreant and atheist, serving his turn only of the pretext of this new religion, to make his matter the better, that is to say, to strengthen himself by mean of a faction and by that means to advance his plots and appointments of his future kingdom, when the hour and opportunity shall serve him. But concerning his atheism and impiety, though his own confession may suffice us in this case, yet to show it as clear as the sun itself I will bring you yet one other example, of one notable villainy of his and an act of a mere atheist, passing all I have yet recited, the which act was revealed by Robert Christmas, sometimes one of his minions and favorites,[22] who being by the just judgment of God fallen in misery and calamity and having lost his living and all his credit was constrained to pass many wretched years in prison, where lamenting himself one day of his fortune to one of his friends that came to visit him did impute all his misfortune to the just judgment of God for his furthering in times past many of this Earl's villainies, and specially for having so long concealed this execrable wickedness which I am about to tell you, the story whereof is thus.

This gallant Earl being greatly in love with a lady (whose name I will spare for her honor) and not finding himself so far in her good grace and favor as he desired, to accomplish his disordinate appetite he went to one of his she-friends and special counsellors, marvellous well seen in such affairs, called Mother Davis [or Davies], a famous and notable sorceress abiding as then beyond the river of Thames over against Paul's. For you must understand that his Lordship is furnished of all sorts of counsellors and fit instruments for all exploits, for he employeth some for bawdry, others for rapines and extortions, and some for conjuring, enchanting, and sorcery, by whose aid he daily effecteth such marvellous matters that he seemeth to the judgment of every man to be omnipotent in doing all mischief. But to prosecute my former matter and the course of my story, this great matron Mother Davis knowing well that this good companion was no novice or prentice in such affairs nor so conscionable as to make a scruple of small matters, nay further, knowing him to be so hardy a knight that for a need he would leap frankly over the very mountains of iniquity, she made no bones of the matter to ordain him a receipt for his mistress, a receipt I say drawn from the very dregs and sink of sorcery, namely such a one as in my opinion there is not a heart of any Christian man (except his) that could once abide to hear it spoken, so far would it be from one to put an act so horrible in execution.

For the most accursed beast appointed him to take young martins out of their nest and cause them to be distilled with some of his own nature or seed and certain other herbs and drugs mentioned in the said receipt, and having drawn forth no doubt some precious liquor out of these filthy simples he caused the lady to drink of the same. O accursed impiety and unworthy the ears of a Christian, yet fit enough for such a sorceress as she is, such an old witch whose profession is no other than to consecrate herself body and soul to the service of the devil. But this is a thing marvellous and fearful, that a Christian lord, such a one as Leicester nameth himself, that is to say the protector and patron of so pure a gospel, would offer himself an executor of so damnable a practice, coming from the mouth most venomous of so wicked a sorceress, inducing him not only to be partaker of the sorcery but also to commit a sodomitical act against his own [human] nature. But will you know the reason, at the least in mine opinion? I believe he had heard of certain heretics in times past that were wont to sprinkle the beastly sacrifices they offered with their own seed, and for this cause thinking it would derogate much from his absolute puissance if such petty companions should excel him in any kind of vice he made no difficulty to practice this goodly conclusion of sorcery, and so well he effected it that within a few days he made the lady drink this villainous and odious liquor in certain wine that was presented her, an act not only abominable afore God, injurious to his own nature, but also traitorous and disloyal toward the lady his mistress, to whose service he did owe all loyalty, yea and his very life, for divers respects which I may not utter for not discovering her name, which I will not do for the honor I bear her, greatly lamenting her ill fortune that being so great a lady as she is she should be notwithstanding so unlucky to be drenched with such a cup so unpleasant, not fit for a dog, to be drawn to affect a vessel so foul and unsavory as is the villainous, filthy, and brutish corpse of this monster of a man. But fearing (friendly reader) that by making thee taste so filthy a dish I may offend your stomach, as I have in part before this offended mine own, I now cease to search this matter any farther, being indeed astonished at his wickedness, and detesting all his villainies, and having a horror of his loathsome life, which he hath led a long time, saucing it with all sorts of beastliness.

Having therefore sufficiently declared his honesty by these particularities, or rather deductions, I approach now to the end of my discourse, omitting very many exploits achieved by this brave Earl, the which in their own nature are odious and would be esteemed in other men monstrous, though in his Lordship they can be counted but *peccadilia*, little faults, in regard of other more wicked villainies with which he is replenished. Wherefore I will pass over to speak at large of his endeavor that he hath ever used to sow and nourish debate and contention between the great lords of England and their wives, in which he alway showed himself a good practicer and very diligent, knowing that according to the Italian proverb, *Nel mare turbato guadagna il pescatore*, in a troubled water the fisher gains most.[23] Although to say true, his Lordship hath not always gained much at this play, but hath oftentime so fished that instead of a fish he hath taken a frog,[24] and at sometime lost both hook and line and pain and honor and all. And of his such practices I could bring you many examples, as that of the Earl of Arundel and his lady, between whom he sought all means to nourish discord, hoping by that means to subvert the greatest and most honorable family of England.[25] The same he attempted between the Earl of Oxford and his lady, daughter of the Lord Treasurer of England, and all for an old grudge he bare to her father the said Lord Treasurer.[26] The like he sought to do between the Earl of Southampton and the Countess, thinking by so doing to satisfy his appetite and fond lust, although he was frustrated of his intent therein.[27] But among all his other practices that which he brought to pass between the Earl of Shrewsbury and his pretended wife is worthy to be noted, whom he so bravely brought about (playing his own part then of the very Earl of Leicester in person) that he induced the good dame to accuse her husband of high treason, thinking by this means to take out of his hands his most honorable prisoner the Queen of Scots, and to give her in keeping to one of his creatures, to be able thereby to command the life of the said afflicted princess at his pleasure.[28] Of all which examples alleged I could (I say) make you a discourse in particular, if I did not think them to be fit to pass over as matter of little weight in respect of others before mentioned. Also I will say nothing of his dissimulation and deceit that he useth commonly in matter of law and justice, writing his letters contrary one to the other, one openly in favor of the suitor (to whom he pretendeth to desire to pleasure), another secretly in favor of the adverse part, as my Lord Chief Justice of England and the Queen's Attorney General can tell very well and have oftentimes confessed.[29] Neither will I now speak (partly for the reason before alleged and partly because I am not yet sufficiently advertised of the matter) of his malicious and violent persecuting of my Lord Harry Howard, brother to the Duke of Norfolk, and of Mr. Charles Arundell, the Queen's near kinsman and sometime in great reputation and credit with her, being two personages honorable in divers degrees and much favored and esteemed in Court, and yet he keepeth one of them as I am informed in prison, and hath constrained the other to leave his country and to live an exile to maintain his liberty.

 I overpass I say all these things here with silence, and many other, for the cause aforesaid and for avoiding of tediousness, contenting myself that I have already discovered in this brief addition his treason and falsehood toward the person of so great a prince as the king's brother Monsieur was, that I have laid before your eyes his foul ingratitude toward his own friends, his barbarous and inhuman dealing toward his kinsfolk, his oppressions, corruptions, perjuries, murderous practices, sorceries, sin against nature, and flat atheism. For the plainer demonstration of whose excess[es] and enormities I have painted him out in all his colors, and I have proved him a gentleman perfect in all knavery, so as his Lordship needs not give place to any man whatever he be in all kind of lewdness, yea that he deserveth to bear away the prize due to the chief hangman on the earth, and for this I believe that ere long he shall be by common consent of all villians of the world judged and reputed worthy to carry the scepter and to be commander among them, which if it come to pass it may be some satisfaction to his ambitious humor, which never aimeth at other mark than crowns and kingdoms.

But to end this discourse, you see that I have already acquitted my promise to the reader and showed my goodwill to this good Earl, so as I think I am not one halfpenny in his debt, now I will take my leave of his Lordship without kissing his hands till [the] time they be better washed with tears of repentance, having been in times past so defiled with blood and with all sorts of filthiness and of wickedness.

NOTES TO APPENDIX B

1. *C.S.P. Spanish, 1580-86*, p. 538.
2. During Anjou's second visit to England (Nov. 1581-Feb. 1582), his courtship, though prominent in gossip, had given way to an attempt to secure financial aid for his ventures in the Low Countries. Leicester's party, which urged English support of the Dutch rebels against Spain, began to back his cause in hopes that Elizabeth would, by aiding Anjou, aid their Dutch friends as well. Thus Leicester and Walsingham became more amiable toward him, feigning support of his marriage. When Anjou left on 7 Feb., he was given not only money but also an English entourage including Leicester and over one hundred gentlemen, in order to lend prestige as he began his new regime. William Prince of Orange met the party at Flushing, where he was introduced to Leicester by Philip Sidney, with whom he had been acquainted since 1577. On 19 Feb. the party entered Antwerp in state, where Leicester's presence gained some acceptance of Anjou as figurehead sover-

eign. The Earl, however, was striving to undermine Anjou and (probably with Elizabeth's sanction) was warning Orange to keep the unreliable Frenchman in check. In the following Jan. Anjou made his inept attempt to take real power by force and was expelled from the Netherlands for good. See Read, *Walsingham*, 2: 89-103, and for their arrival in Antwerp, Holinshed, 4: 460-87.

3. Literally, "all the ancient and principal nobility."

4. Literally, *boutefeux*: "one who kindles feuds and discontents" (Dr. Johnson's *Dictionary*).

5. John Scory, an ex-Dominican monk, Protestant Bishop of Rochester (1551) and of Chichester (1552), Marian exile, Bishop of Hereford until his death on 25 or 26 June 1585.

6. Scory was notoriously avaricious. In 1582 Sidney, as Lord President of the Council in the Marches, began investigations into his dealings, and on 20 Nov. the Bishop sent his son Sylvan to Court to seek intervention in his behalf (Strype, *Annals of the Reformation*, vol. 3, part 1, pp. 171-72). Sylvan returned to him with promises of help from Walsingham (Bp. Scory to Walsingham, 3 Feb. 1583, S.P. 12/158/55), but Sidney persisted, and by June the old man had come to London, accusing Sidney of malfeasance and requesting of Burghley that he "be either exempted from [Sidney's] authority, to answer in the courts there at Westminster" or else translated to another see. Sometime later, with the matter apparently unresolved, he returned home, complaining of the existence in his district of rumors that whilst in London he had been imprisoned and that he "must with six bishops make a purgation" (*ibid.*, p. 174); whether his case was really heard by six bishops is not known, nor is there evidence of Leicester's involvement.

7. Virgil, *Aeneid*, bk. 3, line 56.

8. The conventional pun: angels as heavenly beings and as the gold coin with the Archangel Michael as its device.

9. In Jan. 1584 a spy reported that Sylvan Scory was haunting the French ambassador's house and saying that "if his father were dead and his goods sold, he would not tarry" in crossing the seas. Upon his father's death in June 1585, Sylvan burst into the house (even as the old man was dying), yelling, "All is mine, all is mine, where is my sword, where is my sword," and, with eight or nine "ruffians and roisters," forcibly ejected his mother and his brother-in-law Giles Allen, and began selling off the Bishop's goods. Allen begged the Privy Council to act in the matter, and in his petition he pointed out the need for haste, "for the body of the dead remaineth yet unburied" (S.P. 12/180/1). Sylvan thereupon appealed to Leicester for help but was arrested anyway and brought up to London; on 27 July he wrote again, asking that the Earl prevent the matter from coming before the Council because it would be "most tedious and brabbling" to their Lordships and because he could assure them that in the end he would win the case anyway, even though his mother had stolen all his evidence. He mentioned that all those helping his mother were "most arrant Papists" (S.P. 12/180/49). At an earlier examination, 12 Feb. 1585, Scory had testified, among other things, that he had never read *Leicester's Commonwealth*, that whilst abroad he had known Morgan and Throgmorton but not well, that he had consorted with Mendoza but only for reasons of private gratitude, not treason, and that he had been the means of making Mendoza

and Leicester friends by inviting them to dinner at Mr. Customer Smith's! (S.P. 12/176/53.) By 10 Jan. 1586 Scory was serving in the Low Countries as a horseman, was later a Member of Parliament, and seems to have died in 1617. He is noted in John Aubrey's *Brief Lives*, pp. 269-70.

10. John Appleyard was half brother of Amy Robsart; during the 1560s Leicester gained several offices for him and "procured him to be made sheriff of Norfolk and Suffolk" (in 1559), but he felt he had received only "fair promises," and in 1567 they fell out. He believed that Horsey and Christmas had incensed the Earl against him and that his only fault had been to press Leicester for leave to reopen his sister's case—since he claimed to have reason to think that murder could be proved. In early 1567 Appleyard was approached by someone to join a plot to accuse Leicester of her death, and he was heard asserting "that he had for the Earl's sake covered the murder of his sister" (according to Blount's report to Leicester, the suborners were Norfolk, Sussex, and Heneage). After a stay in the Fleet, he made submission in May after having been shown a copy of the coroner's verdict of accidental death (all from H.M.C. Salisbury MSS., 1: 345-46, 349-52). In May 1570 he led an insurrection in Norfolk aimed at freeing the Duke of Norfolk from the Tower; in late Aug. he and three others were condemned to death (letter, 31 Aug. 1570, Lodge, *Illustrations*, 1: 512-13; John Jerningham's pardon, 28 June 1571, *Calendar of Patent Rolls, 1569-72*, p. 165). In May 1574, after four years in Norwich Castle, he was removed to house arrest and apparently died not long after.

11. The French is less ambiguous; it is her death, not Appleyard's involvement, that is discussed in the *Commonwealth*.

12. This George Darcy is unidentified, as are his troubles. In 1581 Charles Arundell wrote to a Mr. Darcy, warning him to beware of "false supporters and rotten staves" (S.P. 12/151/56).

13. This allegation is unconfirmed elsewhere. The Duke of Sweden (later Eric XIV) never came into England; he attempted the journey in Aug. 1560 and was expected again in autumn 1561. The reference may be to his brother John Duke of Finland, who pursued Eric's suit by proxy from autumn 1559 to the following spring. This tale is at variance with the *Commonwealth*'s version of the Swedish suit.

14. This is Douglass Howard, formerly Lady Sheffield, wife of Sir *Edward* Stafford.

15. Hellebore, a medicinal herb. The MS.'s margin note states that "one is an herb called sentuary, the other a poisoning herb called wolfwort," i.e., wolfbane.

16. Literally, "Reagal," probably red arsenic, often called realgar.

17. Lady Sheffield swore, in Star Chamber testimony of 1604-1605, that Leicester had tried to poison her as a consequence of her refusal to disclaim his marriage to her (Hawarde, *Reportes*, p. 199); there is no independent confirmation. Possibly in deference to her reputation in the French Court, the author here retails her version of the poisoning while suppressing its origin in her relationship with Leicester. Little is known of George Vaux, merely that he was one of Leicester's servants (e.g., Huntington Library MS. EL 6206 B, fol. 63).

18. Fervaques, on instructions of the Queen of Navarre, had been instrumental in alienating Anjou from his agent Simier (the "old quarrel" mentioned). When Anjou arrived in England in Nov. 1581, he had Fervaques in his entourage; Simier

followed, ostensibly to challenge Fervaques to the field, actually to report Anjou's progress to the French king. In mid Dec. Fervaques accepted Simier's challenge, then, apparently with Leicester's connivance, endeavored to have Simier attacked by assassins on the London Exchange. Simier escaped and informed the Queen, who rebuked Leicester severely and forbade anyone to harm Simier. Fervaques, convinced that Simier had been warned in advance, pursued the supposed informant, one Lafin, with his dagger drawn, right into the Queen's presence and found himself sequestered from coming to Court. Most available evidence is in H.M.S. Salisbury MSS., 2: 463, 470–73 *et passim* and H.M.C. Rutland MSS., 1: 131, plausibly reconstructed by M. Hume in *Courtships of Queen Elizabeth*, pp. 276–79. The Exeter translator has erroneously anglicized Fervaques to "Fairfax."

19. In Jan. 1575 Thomas Moffett arrived in Antwerp with a plan, not to kill, but to abduct Westmoreland away to England (as Dr. Story had been in 1570) and with letters (supposedly instructions) bearing Leicester's seal. The English ambassador to France, Dr. Wilson (then in Antwerp), referred him to Edward Woodshaw, a Catholic refugee who was an informant for Lord Burghley. On 26 Jan., before proceeding with the plan, Woodshaw wrote to Burghley asking his and Leicester's direct sanction, as he had doubts about Moffett. On 19 Feb. he wrote again to accuse Moffett of treachery: He said that Moffett had told Westmoreland of the plan and that together they had devised a counterplan to deceive Leicester of the thousand pounds promised for the abduction, and he asked that Leicester have Moffett sent for home and kept a close prisoner. Burghley passed Woodshaw's news on to Leicester, who replied on 27 Feb. that "Moffett is playing the varlet" and that he would try to have him brought back to England (all from H.M.C. Salisbury MSS., 2: 86–93). Whether such a plan originated with Leicester or with the exiles, to discredit the Earl or to trap Woodshaw, is open to question. On 16 Oct. 1594, Sir Edward and Lady Stafford were seeking to gain favorable treatment for "old Captain Moffett" in Newgate prison, apparently successfully (cited in *Miscellanea Genealogica et Heraldica*, n.s. 3 [1880], p. 369, with inaccurate reference).

20. Timon, fifth-century Athenian, proverbial misanthrope; see Plutarch's *Life of Antony* (translated into English by Thomas North, 1579) and Lucian's *Timon* (translated into French by Filbert Bretin, 1582). "Misanthropos" is in Greek characters in both the French edition and the Exeter manuscript.

21. Proverb, from Saint Jerome, *Selected Letters*, no. 1, section 7.

22. Christmas had been a servant of Leicester's since at least June 1566 (S.P. 15/13/5); Leicester was once tasked by a Puritan writer for keeping him on, as he and a few others "were sinners above all men in England" (British Library, Harleian MS. 419, fol. 162). In 1581 Arundell included him in his attacks upon Oxford and Leicester (S.P. 12/151/50).

23. A proverb also used by Richard Grafton (*Chronicle*), Sidney (*Arcadia*), Samuel Daniel (*Civil Wars*), and Bishop Hall. See the *Oxford Dictionary of English Proverbs*, pp. 207–8.

24. Another proverb (*Oxford Dictionary*, p. 205).

25. That is, the Howards. Philip, Earl of Arundel (after 1580), the Duke of Norfolk's son, had been married in 1569 at the age of twelve to Ann Dacres, also twelve. After leaving Cambridge in 1576, he came to Court, where he lived ex-

travagantly while his wife remained in the country. Under the influence of his uncle Lord Harry, he moved in the circles of the Catholic Court party, though not yet himself a Catholic. As that group's fortunes fell after 1580, he rejoined his wife and openly professed her religion, for which they both suffered accordingly. In his later, more serious troubles (beginning in 1583 and ending with his capital sentence for treason in 1589 and his death in the Tower on 19 Oct. 1595), he accounted Leicester his chief enemy, but there is no evidence of Leicester's having sowed discord in his marriage. On his life, see English Martyrs 2, C.R.S. 21 (1919).

26. Oxford married Anne Cecil, the daughter of his guardian Lord Burghley, on 19 Dec. 1571. After his return from Europe in 1576 he did put his wife aside, accusing her of adultery. He was not reconciled to her until 1582, shortly before her death. There is no evidence of Leicester's responsibility in this matter, but the reference may be to the events of 1580 when Oxford defected to Leicester's party.

27. Henry Wriothesley, second Earl of Southampton, was a Catholic who spent eighteen months in the Tower at the time of Norfolk's treason (and was accused of having charged Leicester with being the cause of the Duke's death, H.M.C. Salisbury MSS., 2: 21). In about 1577 Southampton accused his wife, Mary née Browne, of incontinence with a servant, and in early 1580 he put her away for this reason. She blamed his servant Dymock for having turned him against her; Fr. Parsons blamed Charles Paget (C.R.S. 2, p. 183). At his death on 4 Oct. 1581, the Earl left a will grossly unfair to his wife and children, and ten days later (and several times after) she appealed to her friend and kinsman Leicester for help in circumventing it, which he supplied. (The best account is Akrigg, *Shakespeare and the Earl of Southampton*, pp. 12–19.) The only evidence of Leicester's having created discord appears in one of the widow's letters to him: "Ten thousand times have I remembered your speeches to me full often touching the disposition of the man [her husband]. I think I shall hold you for more than half a prophet" (printed in Stopes, *Life of Henry, Third Earl of Southampton*, p. 9).

28. In late 1583 the Countess of Shrewsbury and her sons William and Charles Cavendish spread rumors that her husband had been guilty of adultery with his prisoner the Queen of Scots. Queen Mary protested to Elizabeth in Dec., and in Jan. she accused Leicester and Walsingham of having been behind it all (*C.S.P. Scots, 1584–85*, p. 5). In Sept. 1584 Elizabeth acquitted Shrewsbury of all blame, and in Nov. the Countess and her sons were examined by the Council over their actions (the Earl brought suit for defamation against the sons in Jan. 1586), but because of the scandal, by late Aug. 1584 the Earl, to the chagrin of Mary's supporters, had already been relieved of his charge. A coherent account is in E. Williams, *Bess of Hardwick*, chaps. 13–15, though the reconstruction of the Countess's motives, pp. 159–61, must be regarded as fanciful.

29. The margin identifies Sir Christopher Wray (1524–1592), Chief Justice of the Queen's Bench from 1574 until his death, and Mr. (later Sir) John Popham, Attorney General from 1581 to 1592 (Chief Justice until his death in 1607).

APPENDIX C

Sidney's
Defense of Leicester

Among the various official responses to *Leicester's Commonwealth*, there was one important unofficial one. Sometime during the winter of 1584–1585 a copy came into the hands of Sir Philip Sidney, who undertook to reply to the attack against his uncle in his so-called *Defense of Leicester*.[1] The haste with which he worked is obvious both from the state of his drafts, which survive, and from the rather hectic array of often half-completed thoughts in the argument itself. Clearly his efforts were at first intended for publication, but in fact they never saw print, nor were they very much circulated in manuscript. The reasons for this forbearance should not be far to seek. Had Leicester had a chance to see Sidney's tract, he would doubtless have considered its particular strategies more harmful than helpful to his cause, and he would probably have preferred to avoid public debates over the pros and cons of criminal allegations against him. What Leicester needed, and what he got, was a testimony of categorical innocence from the Queen, not vehement rhetoric and thrown gauntlets from his own partisans.

Nevertheless, though obviously among his less distinguished works, Sidney's essay is worthy of more credit than it is usually given. It is customary to fault the *Defense* on the grounds that it evades direct rebuttal of the substantial allegations about the Earl, and thus "gives no picture of Leicester the man to set against the vivid and detailed characterization of the libeller,"[2] and that instead it dwells entirely upon the Earl's noble lineage, which was of course Sidney's own lineage, whereas the charge of "want of gentry" had been an extremely minor part of the *Commonwealth*'s attack. This assessment is largely just, but it requires three qualifications that are not so customarily made. First, vindicating the Earl of specific charges would in most cases have been impossible since the form in which they are often made does not admit of positive evidence to the contrary. All that any defender could have done was merely to assert (not prove) that, however circumstances appeared, the Earl had no malicious intentions and then attempt to impugn whatever evidence had been adduced to show that he had. The first of these Sir Philip does in the only way he can, by formally testifying "that I could never find in the Earl of Leicester any one motion or inclination toward any such pretended conceit," and the second he does too, and very well, by ridiculing the *kind* of evidence being used by his opponent: "Such a gentlewoman spake of a matter no less than treason; belike she whispered, yet he heard her," and so on.

Second, Sidney, realizing (as we have seen) that he cannot address particular libellous allegations, attempts instead the next best thing, a largely independent counterattack upon libels and libellers in general. It must be acknowledged that he does a good job of this as well. Of libels he reminds us that anything can be said and anyone traduced by an anonymous writer, that virtually anything can by innuendo be made to look suspicious, that the enmity of certain parties can often be a kind of praise.[3] Of the *Commonwealth* in particular he undertakes a critique that makes up as astute a commentary on the book's flaws as has appeared anywhere. His isolation of its implausible kinds of evidence, such as overheard secrets, we have already noticed. He recognizes that the *Commonwealth*'s authors, whatever they protest to the contrary, are being less than candid in their professions of loyalty to the Queen, and he seems to recognize (as had Elizabeth herself) the derogation of the Queen implicit in the allegations about her trusted favorite. Furthermore, Sidney puts his finger squarely upon the weaknesses of the *Commonwealth*'s defamation—that by adopting a rhetoric "all still so upon the superlative," it raises its villain well out of the realm of plausibility, and that by inventing "a whole dictionary of slanders" against him, it creates inconsistencies that cannot easily be resolved, ending with a man who is both potent and abject, well friended and friendless, physically debilitated and luxurious, cowardly and reckless—"the devil's roll of complaints" against all mankind, laid at the door of only one man.

The third qualification to be made concerns Sidney's exposition of the Dudley lineage. The customary appraisal argues that Sir Philip unwisely shifts his defense from the moral allegations to the very minor problem of Leicester's, and Sidney's own, ancestry, but that having done so, he makes a "comparative success" of it. In fact, he does not make very much of a success of it; he is not being entirely straightforward when he dismisses the telling objection that the most impressive Dudley connections accrue only through females, nor is he when he demonstrates at length the ancient nobility of the Suttons of Dudley, since the issue was precisely whether the Dudleys were lawfully related to that house at all. And when at last he considers the point upon which debate had fixed, the status of John Dudley of Atherington, he loftily characterizes the facts as well known to everyone yet calls the man Piers instead of John. But when we imply that Sir Philip shifted his defense to the Dudley lineage merely because Leicester was otherwise indefensible or because his own injured family pride had distracted him, we may partially misunderstand his intentions and do him some disservice. It is true that he defends the Earl in general terms and that he tries to invalidate the effect of the entire libel, but toward the end of his essay he indicates that the matter of ancestry had been his primary topic from the start and that he had undertaken to write, not because Dudley's lineage had been questioned, which incidentally involved his own, but precisely because his own honor had been touched. It is quite possible that he did not set out to exculpate his uncle squarely, then through some peculiar aristocratic sensitivity become sidetracked by an imagined insult to himself; but rather he may have intended from the outset to defend his own family honor, as he may have felt required in honor to do. Characteristically of the young chevalier, he ends his essay with an absurdly inappropriate challenge to a duel.

I have taken the text of Sidney's *Defense* from photocopies of the holograph drafts in the Pierpont Morgan Library, relying very heavily upon the excellent edition by Katherine Duncan-Jones in Sidney, *Miscellaneous Prose of Sir Philip Sidney*, pp. 129–41.

Defense of Leicester

Of late there hath been printed a book in form of dialogue to the defaming of the Earl of Leicester, full of the most vile reproaches which a wit used to wicked and filthy thoughts can imagine; in such manner, truly, that if the author had as well feigned new names as he doth new matters, a man might well have thought his only meaning had been to have given a lively picture of the uttermost degree of railing. A thing contemptible in the doer, as proceeding from a base and wretched tongue, and such a tongue as in the speaking dares not speak his own name; odious to all estates, since no man bears a name; of which name, how unfitly soever to the person, by an impudent liar, anything may not be spoken, by all good laws sharply punished, and by all evil companies like a poisonous serpent avoided. But to the Earl himself, in the eyes of any men who with clear judgments can value things, a true and sound honor grows out of these dishonorable falsehoods, since he may justly say as a worthy senator of Rome once in like case did,[4] that no man these twenty years hath borne a hateful heart to this estate, but that at the same time he hath showed his enmity to this Earl, testifying thereby that his faith is so linked to her Majesty's service, that who goes about to undermine the one, resolves withal to overthrow the other. For it is not now first that evil contented and evil minded persons, before the occasion be ripe for them to show their hate against the prince, do first vomit it out against his counsellors. Nay, certainly, so stale a device it is as it is to be marvelled that so fine wits, whose inventions a fugitive fortune hath sharpened and the air of Italy perchance purified,[5] can light upon no gallanter way than the ordinary pretext of the very clownish[6] rebellions. And yet that this is their plot of late, by name first to publish something against the Earl of Leicester, and after when time served against the Queen's Majesty, by some of their own intercepted discourses is made too manifest.[7] He himself in some places brings in the example of Gaveston, Earl of Cornwall, Robert Vere, Duke of Ireland, and De la Pole, Duke of Suffolk.[8] It is not my purpose to defend them, but I would fain know whether they that persecuted those councillors, when they had had their will in ruining them, whether their rage ceased before they had as well destroyed the kings themselves, Edward and Richard II and Henry VI. The old tale testifieth that the wolves that mean to destroy the flock hate most the truest and valiantest dogs. Therefore, the more the filthy impostume of their wolfish malice breaks forth, the more undoubtedly doth it raise this well deserved glory to the Earl, that who hates England and the Queen must also withal hate the Earl of Leicester.

And as for the libel itself, such is it as neither in respect of the writer nor matter written can move, I think, the lightest wits to give thereto credit to the discredit of so worthy a person. For the writer (whom in truth I know not, and, loth to fail, am not willing to guess at) shows yet well enough of what kennel he is, that dares not testify his own writings with his own name. And which is more base (if anything can be more base than a defamatory libeller) he counterfeits himself in all the treatise a Protestant, when any man which with half an eye may easily see he is of the other party; which filthy dissimulation if few honest men of that religion will use to the helping of themselves, of how many carats of honesty is this man, that useth it as much as his poor power can to the harm of another? And lastly, evident enough it is to any man that reads it what poison he means to her Majesty, in how golden a cup soever he dress it.

For the matter written, so full of horrible villainies as no good heart will think possible to enter into any creature, much less to be likely in so noble and well known a man as he is, only thus accused to be by the railing oratory of a nameless libeller. Perchance he had read the rule of that sycophant, that one should backbite boldly, for though the bite were healed, yet the scar would remain. But sure that schoolmaster of his would more cunningly have carried it, leaving some shadows of good, or at least leaving out some evil, that his treatise might have carried some probable show of it. For as reasonable commendation wins belief, and excessive gets only the praiser the title of a flatterer, so much more in this far worse degree of lying it may well rebound upon himself the vile reproach of a railer, but never can sink into any good mind. The suspicion of any such unspeakable mischiefs, especially it being every man's case even from the meanest to the highest, whereof we daily see odious examples, that even of the great princes the dear riches of good name are sought in such sort to be picked away by such night thieves. For through the whole book, what is it else but such a bundle of railings as if it came from the mouth of some half-drunk scold in a tavern, not regarding, while evil were spoken, what was fit for the person of whom the railing was, so the words were fit for the person of an outrageous railer? Dissimulation, hypocrisy, adultery, falsehood, treachery, poison, rebellion, treason, cowardice, atheism, and what not, and all still so upon the superlative that it was no marvel though the good lawyer he speaks of made many a cross to keep him from such a father of lies. And in many excellent gifts passing all shameless scolds, in one he passeth himself, with an unheard of impudence bringing persons yet alive to speak such things which they are ready to depose upon their salvation never came in their thoughts. Such a gentlewoman spake of a matter no less than treason; belike she whispered, yet he heard her. Such two knights spake together of things not fit to call witnesses to, yet this ass's ears were so long that he heard them.[9] And yet see, his good nature all this while would never reveal them till now, for secrecy sake, he puts them forth in print. Certainly, such a quality in a railer as I think never was heard of, to name persons alive as not only can but do disprove his falsehoods, and yet with such familiarity to name them, without he learned it of Pace, the Duke of Norfolk's fool;[10] for he when he had used his tongue as this heir of his hath done his pen, of the noblest persons, sometimes of the Duke himself, the next that came fitly in this way, he would say he had told it him of abundance of charity, not only to slander but to make bait.[11] What therefore can be said to such a man? Or who lives there, even Christ himself, but that so stinking a breath may blow infamy upon? Who hath a father by whose death the son inherits, but such a nameless historian may say his son poisoned him? Where may two talk together, but such a spirit of revelation may surmise they spake of treason? What need more? Or why so much? As though I doubted that any would build belief upon such a dirty seat. Only when he, to borrow a little of his inkhorn, when he plays the "statist,"[12] wringing very unluckily some of Machiavel's axioms to serve his purpose, then indeed he triumphs. Why, then, the Earl of

Leicester means and plots to become king himself; but first to rebel from the prince to whom he is most bound and of whom he only dependeth; and then to make the Earl of Huntingdon king; and then to put him down, and then to make himself. Certainly, Sir, you shoot fair. I think no man that hath wit and power to pronounce this word "England" but will pity a sycophant so weak in his own faculty. But of the Earl of Huntingdon, as I think, all indifferent men will clear him from any such foolish and wicked intent of rebellion. So I protest, before the Majesty of God, who will confound all liars, and before the world, to whom effects and events will witness my truth, that I could never find in the Earl of Leicester any one motion or inclination toward any such pretended conceit in the Earl of Huntingdon. I say no whit further. For as for the present, or for drawing it to himself, I think no devil so wicked nor no idiot so simple as to conjecture. And yet, being to him as I am, I think I should have some air of that which this gentle libel-maker doth so particularly and piecemeal understand. And I do know the Earls of Warwick, of Pembroke, my father and all the rest he names there will answer the like. And yet such matters cannot be undertaken without good friends, nor good friends be kept without knowing something. But the Earl's mind hath ever been to serve only, and truly, setting aside all hopes, all fears, his mistress by undoubted right Queen of England, and most worthy to be the queen of her royal excellencies, and most worthy to be his queen, having restored his overthrown house and brought him to this case that curs, for only envy, bark at. And this his mind is not only (though chiefly) for faith, knit in conscience and honor, nor only (though greatly) for gratefulness, where all men know how much he is bound, but even partly for wisdom's sake, knowing by all old lessons and examples that how welcome soever treasons be, traitors to all wise princes are odious, and that, as Matius answered Tully, who wrate to him how he was blamed for showing himself so constant a friend to Caesar, that he doubted not even they that blamed him would rather choose such friends as he was than such as they were.[13] For wise princes well know that these violent discontentments grow out of the party's wicked humors, as in sick folk that think with change of places to ease their evil, which indeed is inward, and whom nor this prince nor that prince can satisfy, but such as are led by their fancies; that is to say, who lean to be princes.

But this gentle libel-maker, because he would make an evident proof of an unquenchable malice, desperate impudency, and falsehood which never knew blushing, is not content with a whole dictionary of slanders upon these persons living, but as if he would rake up the bones of the dead, with so apparent falsehoods toucheth their houses as if he had been afeard else he should not have been straight found in that wherein he so greatly labors to excel. First, for Hastings he saith the Lord Hastings conspired the death of his master King Edward's sons. Let any man but read the excellent treatise of Sir Thomas More, compare but his words with this libel-maker's, and then judge him if he who in a thing so long since printed and, as any man may see by other of his allegations, of him diligently read, hath the face to write so directly contrary;[14] not caring as it seems though a hundred thousand find his falsehood, so some dozen that never read Sir Thomas More's words may be carried to believe his horrible slanders of a nobleman so long ago dead. I set down the words of both, because by this one lively comparison the face of his falsehood may be the better set forth. And who then can doubt but he that lies in a thing which with one look is found a lie, what he will do where yet there is though as much falsehood yet no so easy disproof?

Now to the Dudleys such is his bounty that when he hath poured out all his flood of scolding eloquence, he saith they are no gentlemen, affirming that John, Duke of Northumberland was not born so.[15] In truth, if I should have studied with myself of all points of false invective which a poisonous tongue could have spit out against that Duke, yet would it never have come into my head of all other things that any man would have objected want of gentry unto him. But this fellow doth like him who, when he had shot off all his railing quiver, called one cuckold that was never married, because he would not be in debt to any one evil word.

I am a Dudley in blood, that Duke's daughter's son, and do acknowledge, though in all truth I may justly affirm that I am by my father's side of ancient and always well esteemed and well matched gentry, yet I do acknowledge, I say, that my chiefest honor is to be a Dudley, and truly am glad to have cause to set forth the nobility of that blood whereof I am descended, which but upon so just cause without vainglory could not have been uttered, since no man but this fellow of invincible shamelessness would ever have called so palpable a matter in question. In one place of his book he greatly extolleth the great nobility of the house of Talbot, and truly with good cause, there being as I think not in Europe a subject house which hath joined longer continuance of nobility with men of greater service and loyalty. And yet this Duke's own grandmother, whose blood he makes so base, was a Talbot, daughter and sole heir to the Viscount of Lisle, even he the same man who, when he might have saved himself, chose rather manifest death than to abandon his father, that most noble Talbot, Earl of Shrewsbury, of whom the histories of that time make so honorable mention.[16] The house of Grey is well known; to no house in England in great continuance of honor, and for number of great houses sprung of it, to be matched to none, but by the noble house of Neville. His mother was a right Grey, and a sole inheritrix of that Grey.[17] Of the house of Warwick, which ever strave with the great house of Arundel which should be the first earl of England, he was likewise so descended as that justly the honor of the house remained chiefly upon him, being the only heir to the eldest daughter and one of the heirs to that famous Beauchamp, Earl of Warwick, that was Regent of France. And although Richard Neville, who married the youngest sister, because she was of the whole blood to him that was called Duke of Warwick, by a point in our law carried away the inheritance, and so also, I know not by what right, the title, yet in law of heraldry and descents, which doth not consider those quiddities of our law, it is most certain that the honor of the blood remained upon him chiefly, who came of the eldest daughter.[18] And more undoubtedly is it to be said of the house of Berkeley, which is affirmed to be descended lineally from a king of Denmark, but hath ever been one of the best houses in England. And this Duke[19] was the only heir general to that house, which the house of Berkeley doth not deny, howsoever as sometimes it falls out between brothers there be question for land between them.[20] Many other houses might herein be mentioned, but I name these, because England can boast of no nobler, and because all these bloods so remained in him that he, as heir, might if he had listed have used their arms and name, as in old time they used in England and do daily both in Spain, France, and Italy. So that I think it would seem as great news as if they came from the Indies, that he who by right of blood, and so accepted, was the ancientest viscount of England, heir in blood and arms to the first or second earl of England, in blood of inheritance a Grey, a Talbot, a Beauchamp, a Berkeley, a Lisle, should be doubted to be a gentleman. But he will say these great honors came to him by his mother. For these, I do not deny they came so, and that the mother being an heir hath been in all ages and countries sufficient to nobilitate is so manifest that even from the Roman time to modern times in such case they might, if they listed, and so often did, use their mother's name; and that Augustus Caesar had both name and empire of Caesar only by his mother's right, and so both mother's. But I will claim no such privilege. Let the singular nobility of his mother nothing avail him, if his father's blood were not in all respects worthy to match with hers, if ancient, undoubted and untouched nobility be worthy to match with the most honorable house that can be. This house, therefore, of Dudley, which in despite of all shamelessness he so doth deprave, is at this day a peer, as we term it, of the realm, a baron, and, as all Englishmen know, a Lord of the Parliament, and so a companion both in marriage, Parliament, and trial to the greatest duke that England can bear. So hath it been ever esteemed, and so in the constitutions of all our laws and ordinances is it always reputed. Dudley house is so to this day and thus it hath been time out of mind. In Harry V's time the Lord Dudley was his Lord Steward, and did that pitiful office in bringing home, as the chief mourner, his victorious master's dead body, as who goes but to Westminster in the church may see.

I think if we consider together the time, which was of England the most flourishing, and the king he served, who of all English kings was most puissant, and the office he bare, which was in effect as great as an English subject could have, it would seem very strange, so that Lord Dudley if he could out of his grave hear this fellow make question whether his lawful posterity from father to son should be gentlemen or no.[21] But though he only had been sufficient to erect nobility to his successors, bringing, as the Romans termed it, so noble an image into the house, yet did he but receive his nobility from his ancestors, who had been lords of that very seignory of Dudley Castle many descents before, even from King Richard I ['s] time, at which time Sir Richard Sutton married the daughter and heir of the Lord Dudley; since which time, all descended of him, as diverse branches there be, left the name of Sutton and have all been called Dudleys, which is now above four hundred years since, and both those houses of Sutton and Dudley having been before that time of great nobility. And that Sutton was a man of great honor and estimation that very match witnesseth sufficiently, it being a dainty thing in that time that one of Saxon blood, as Sutton's name testifieth he was, should match with such an inheritrix as Dudley was; the like example whereof I remember none but the great house of Raby, who matched with Neville, who of that match, as the Suttons were called Dudleys, so did they ever since take the name of Neville. So as of a house, which these four hundred years have been still owners of one seignory, the very place itself to any that sees it witnessing, such as for any other I know in England none but the noble house of Stafford hath the like, considering the name of the house, the length of time it hath been possessed, the goodliness of the seat, with pleasures and royalties about it, so as I think any that will not swear themselves brothers to a reproachful tongue will judge of his other slander by this, most manifest, since all the world may see he speaks against his own knowledge. For if either the house of Dudley had been great anciently and now extinguished, or now great and not continued from old time, or that they had been unentitled gentlemen, so as men must not needs have taken knowledge of them, yet there might have been cast some veil over his untruth. But in a house now noble, long since noble, with a nobility never interrupted, seated in a place which they have each father and each son continually owned, what should be said but that this fellow desires to be known suitable: having an untrue heart, he will become it with an untrue tongue.

But perchance he will seem to doubt: for what will he not doubt who will affirm that which beyond all doubt is false, whether my great grandfather, Edmund Dudley, were of the Lord Dudley's house or no. Certainly he might in conscience and good manners, if so he did doubt, have made some distinction between the two houses, and not in all places have made so contemptible mention of that name of Dudley, which is borne by another peer of the realm.[22] And even of charity sake he should have bestowed some father upon Edmund Dudley, and not leave him not only ungentled but fatherless. A railing writer extant against Octavius Augustus saith his grandfather was a silversmith;[23] another Italian, against Hugh Capet, though with most absurd falsehood, saith his father was a butcher. Of divers of the best houses of England there have been such foolish dreams, that one was a farrier's son, another a shoemaker's, another a milliner's, another a fiddler's—foolish lies, and by any that ever tasted any antiquities known to be so. Yet those houses had luck to meet with honester railers, for they were not left fatherless clean, they descended from somebody, but we, as if we were Deucalion's brood new made out of stones, have left us no ancestors from whence we are come. But alas, good railer, you saw the proofs were clear, and therefore even for honesty sake were contented to omit them. For if either there had been difference of name or difference of arms between them, or if, though in name and arms they agreed, yet if there had been many descents fallen since the separating of those branches —as we see in many ancient houses it so falls out as they are uncertain whether came out of other—then, I say, yet a valiant railer may venture upon a thing where, because there is not an absolute certainty, there may be some possibility to escape. But in this case, where not only name and arms, with only that difference which acknowledgeth our house to be of the younger brother, but such nearness of blood as that Edmund Dudley's was no further off than son to the younger brother of the same Lord Dudley, and so as he was to be Lord Dudley if the Lord Dudley had died without heirs, and by the German and Italian manner himself was to have been also called Lord Dudley, that his father being called Piers Dudley, married to the daughter and heir of Bramshot in Sussex, it was the only descent between him and the Lord Dudley who was his grandfather, his great grandfather being that noble Lord Dudley whom before I mentioned.[24] And no man need doubt that this writer doth not only know the truths hereof, but the proofs of this truth, this Piers, Edmund's father, being buried at Arundel Castle, who married Bramshot and left that land to Edmund, and so to the Duke in Sussex, which after the Duke sold, by confiscation came to the crown. This tomb any man at Arundel Castle may see. This Bramshot land I name, a thing not in the air, but which any man by the ordinary course of those things may soon know, whether such land did not succeed unto Edmund from his father. So as where is this inheritance of land and monuments in churches and the persons themselves little more than in man's memory, truly this libeller deserves many thanks, that with his impudent falsehood hath given occasion to set down so manifest a truth.

As to the Dudleys, he deals much harder withal, but no whit truer. But therein, I must confess, I cannot allege his uncharitable triumphing upon the calamities fallen to that house; though they might well be challenged of any writer of whom any honesty were to be expected. But God forbid I should find fault with that, since in all his book there is scarce any one truth else. But our house received such an overthrow, and hath none else in England done? so I will not seek to wash away that dishonor with other honorable tears. I would this island were not so full of such examples. And I think, indeed, this writer, if he were known, might in conscience clear his ancestors of any such disgraces; they were too low in the mud to be so thunderstricken. But this I may justly and boldly affirm: let the last fault of the Duke be buried.[25]

And in good faith, now I have so far touched there, as any man that list to know a truth—if at least there be any that can doubt thereof—may straight be satisfied, I do not mean to give any man's eyes or ears such a surfeit as by answering to repeat his filthy falsehoods, so contrary to themselves as may well show how ill lies can be built with any uniformity. The same man in the beginning of the book was so potent, to use his term, that the Queen had cause to fear him; the same man in the end thereof so abject as any man might tread on him; the same man so unfriendly as no man could love him; the same man so supported by friends that Court and country were full of them; the same man extremely weak of body, and infinitely luxurious; the same man a dastard to fear anything, the same man so venturous as to undertake, having no more title, such a matter that Hercules himself would be afraid to do, if he were here among us.[26] In sum, in one the same man all the faults that in all the most contrary-humoured men in the world can remain, that sure I think he hath read the devil's roll of complaints which he means to put up against mankind, or else he could never have been acquainted with so many wretched mischiefs.

But hard it were, if every goose quill could any way blot the honor of an Earl of Leicester, written in the hearts of so many men through Europe. Neither, for me, shall ever so worthy a man's name be brought to be made a question, where there is only such a nameless and shameless opposer.

But because that thou, the writer hereof, dost most falsely lay want of gentry to my dead ancestors, I have to the world thought good to say a little, which I will assure any that list to seek shall find confirmed, with much more. But to thee I say, thou therein liest in thy throat, which I will be ready to justify upon thee in any place of Europe where thou wilt assign me a free place of coming, as within three months after the publishing hereof I may understand thy mind. And as, till thou hast proved this, in all construction of virtue and honor all the shame thou hast spoken is thine own, the right reward of an evil-tongued schelm,[27] as the Germans especially call such people. So again, in any place whereto thou wilt call me, provided that the place be such as a servant of the Queen's may have free access unto, if I do not, having my life and liberty, prove this upon thee, I am content that this lie I have given thee return to my perpetual infamy. And this which I write I would send to thine own hands if I knew thee. But I trust it cannot be intended that he should be ignorant of this, printed in London, who knows the very whisperings of the Privy Chamber. I will make dainty of no baseness in thee, that art indeed the writer of this book.[28] And from the date of this writing, imprinted and published, I will three months expect thine answer.

NOTES TO APPENDIX C

1. There is little doubt that it was to the English edition that Sidney was responding, rather than to the French translation of spring 1585, since the latter's addition levels charges against Sidney himself, about which he is silent and would not have been had he seen them.
2. Katherine Duncan-Jones, in Sidney, *Miscellaneous Prose of Sir Philip Sidney*, p. 127.
3. This last was the main theme of Alberico Gentili's 1585 defense of the Earl, included in his dedication to Sidney of *De legationibus tres libri*, (2: v).
4. Cicero, Second Philippic, sec. 1 (*Philippics*, p. 65).
5. Sidney, though he guesses wrongly about Italy, correctly understands his adversaries to be Catholic exiles.
6. "Clownish": rude, awkward, ignorant (*O.E.D.*).
7. Probably a reference to the invasion plans captured with Fr. Creighton on 4 Sept. 1584, which described "infamous and slanderous libels" already written and ready to be published against Elizabeth herself (Knox, *Allen*, pp. 428, 430).
8. See *Leicester's Commonwealth*, notes 283 and 286. As Duncan-Jones points out, conceding an association between Leicester and these villains is probably not very wise of Sidney.
9. Midas's ass's ears were proverbial, from Ovid, *Metamorphoses*, bk. 11 (lines 194–216 in Golding's 1567 translation).
10. John Pace (d. 1590), a professional jester first with the third Duke of Norfolk (*ca.* 1545), later with Elizabeth's Court.
11. "Make bait": create trouble (literally "to set dogs on") (*O.E.D.*).
12. "Statist": one skilled in affairs of state. The *O.E.D.* credits this passage as the first use of the word, but as Sidney indicates, he borrows it from the *Commonwealth*.
13. Gaius Matius to Cicero, 43 B.C. (Cicero, *Letters*, 2: 511).
14. In this attempt to impugn the *Commonwealth*'s use of history, Sidney is in error on both counts. The tract does not say that Hastings conspired the death of Edward's sons, only that he helped the Protector eliminate their "friends and kinsmen," which allegation More's *History of King Richard III* clearly confirms (2: 48a).
15. The *Commonwealth* had not asserted that the Dudleys were not gentlemen, only that they were lately risen into the peerage.
16. John Talbot, first Earl of Shrewsbury, commander of the army in France, was killed with his younger son, John Viscount Lisle, in 1453.
17. Edward Grey (d. 1492) married the heiress of Viscount Lisle; his daughter and heiress in her issue married Edmund Dudley, Leicester's grandfather.
18. Richard Beauchamp (d. 1439) had three daughters by his first wife, of which Margaret, wife of the forementioned Shrewsbury, was the eldest; his son Henry (d. 1446), by his second wife, succeeded in his title, which then devolved upon Neville, who had married Henry's younger sister.
19. Northumberland, Leicester's father.

20. Sidney alludes to the suits being brought by the Dudleys against the Lord of Berkeley, as charged in the *Commonwealth*. Thomas, fifth Lord Berkeley, died in 1417, leaving only his daughter, who married the forenamed Richard Beauchamp, and the son of his brother James; from this son, James, first Lord Berkeley, the Elizabethan Berkeleys (who did deny the Dudley claim) were directly descended.

21. Sidney is being disingenuous. No one impugned the nobility of the Suttons of Dudley; the question was whether Leicester's family was indeed connected to that house at all.

22. The main line of the Suttons of Dudley was represented by Edward, the fourth Lord of Dudley Castle, who died in July 1586.

23. Duncan-Jones identifies Lucas Gauricus, *De vera nobilitate*, *Opera omnia* (Basel, 1572), 2: 1882.

24. This was precisely the point raised by Leicester's detractors, whether John Dudley (d. 1510) of Atherington, Sussex, who married the Bramshot heiress and was father of Edmund, had indeed been a younger son of John Sutton, the first Lord Dudley, as claimed in the Dudley genealogies (e.g., British Library, Lansdowne MS. 775, fol. 1ᵛ). It is now generally accepted that he was, though Sidney's mistaking the man's forename may indicate how little was known of him.

25. Sidney is alluding to the failure of Northumberland's *coup d'état*. His point seems unfortunately to be that "anybody who is anybody" has been executed for treason.

26. That is, undertake to win the crown for himself.

27. "Schelm": rascal (*O.E.D.*, citing this passage as first use).

28. A gentleman need not ordinarily fight a duel with a common person, but Sidney graciously offers to make an exception.

APPENDIX D

Further Notes

1. The Death of Amy Robsart

This is the earliest extant printed expression of the rumors concerning Amy's death. Dudley married Amy Robsart in 1550, but after Elizabeth's accession he spent most of his time at Court, in obvious flirtation with the Queen. Amy seems always to have been on good terms with her husband but lived abroad in the country, and in summer 1560 she was residing at Cumnor in Berkshire, the home of Dudley's man Anthony Forster. On Sunday, 8 September, she insisted that all of her attendants go to a nearby fair at Abingdon, and upon their return she was found at the foot of a set of stairs with a broken neck. (Richard Verney, or Varney, was a dependent of Dudley's, but there is no sign of his having been present.) Dudley's man Thomas Blount arrived immediately upon the scene; five of his and Dudley's letters back and forth survive in copies,[1] and in them, although Dudley evinced no grief whatever and expressed concern only for his reputation (wishing devoutly that "this mischance had not happened to me"), he repeatedly commanded Blount to be certain that the coroner's jury searched out the full truth of the matter, "whether it happened by evil chance or by villainy," because otherwise "I have no way to purge myself of the malicious talk that I know the wicked world will use." Blount himself seems to have believed Amy "had a strange mind in her," that is, that she had committed suicide. While investigation was progressing, Lord Robert was sent away from Court.

After initial suspicion of Forster, the jury found "death by mischance." This may be correct (there is no hard evidence that it is not),[2] or it may be a tactful way of acknowledging a suicide. Indeed, suicide seems to me more likely; Amy apparently had been suffering for some years from cancer of the breast, and would naturally have been despondent, and so her ladies reported of her—praying "God to deliver her from desperation" (Adlard, p. 36)—and she seems to have been adamant that she be left alone on that day. Quite possibly her illness, with her husband's manifest neglect and with the country alive with gossip of his romance with the Queen, drove her to despair.[3] From what kind of stairs she fell is unknown, and it would make a difference; tumbling down a few steps is for obvious reasons an uncommon method of suicide, whereas throwing oneself from the head of a stairwell is said to be psychologically consistent with her presumed state of mind. On the other hand, Ian Aird has argued from medical evidence that the facts suggest spontaneous collapse of the cervical spine as a consequence of cancer, and this view is finding some support.[4] Murder, either by Dudley or another, though possible, is the least likely alternative.

As Dudley had foreseen, a flurry of scandal instantly arose. The Spanish ambassador, De Quadra, wrote on 11 September that before her death Cecil had told him "that Robert was thinking of killing his wife, who was publicly announced to be ill, although she was quite well, and would take very good care they did not poison her," adding that "the next day the Queen told me that Robert's wife was dead or nearly so, and asked me not to say anything about it."[5] Whether he intended it to be understood from this temporal ambiguity that Elizabeth had spoken this prior to Amy's death seems impossible now to resolve, though much ink has been spilled on the question. On the eighteenth the preacher Thomas Lever wrote to Cecil from Coventry, reporting "grievous and dangerous suspicion and muttering" in his country and pleading that the truth be found out and made public.[6] Ambassador Throgmorton was appalled by what he heard in Paris: "Some let not to say what religion is this, that a subject shall kill his wife and the prince not only bear withal but marry with him."[7] In many of his letters from this autumn, the ambassador laments the state of the Queen's reputation and its effect upon his diplomacy, but when his secretary, Robert Jones, spoke to

Elizabeth personally about it, "she laughed, and . . . told me that the matter had been tried in the country and found to be contrary to that which was reported, saying that [Dudley] was then in the Court, and none of his at the attempt at his wife's house, and that it fell out as should neither touch his honesty nor her honor."[8] Although Robert had taken pains to see that John Appleyard and others of his wife's family were summoned to oversee the investigation lest there remain any doubts, seven years later Appleyard was saying that "he had for the Earl's sake covered the murder of his sister."[9]

A less circumstantial account of Amy's "murder" appears in Peck, "Letter of Estate" (pp. 27-28).

2. THE DEATH OF THE EARL OF ESSEX

Walter Devereux, first Earl of Essex, went into Ulster with a military force in 1573. His wife Lettice Knollys was involved with Leicester, at first as early as 1565 and then again in her husband's absence, as (probably) during the Kenilworth festivities of 1575; she married him in 1578. Whether Essex sought revenge upon Leicester "for begetting his wife with child in his absence" may be doubted, but they were hostile toward one another, and this may have been part of the reason; on 5 December 1575, Antonio de Guaras wrote from London, during Essex's return, that "as the thing is publicly talked about in the streets there is no objection to my writing openly about the great enmity which exists between the Earl of Leicester and the Earl of Essex, in consequence, it is said, of the fact that whilst Essex was in Ireland his wife had two children by Leicester."[10] Essex's Irish failures brought him home in 1575, but he was soon forced to go back, largely, according to Camden, because of Leicester's influence in Council (*Elizabeth*, 2:80). In late summer 1576 he was in Dublin, preparing to come home again; there he became ill and, after three weeks' languishing, died on 22 September.

On 13 September Essex wrote to Richard Broughton: "The last day of the same month [August] a disease took me and Hunnis my boy and a third person to whom I drank, which maketh me suspect of some evil received in my drink. . . . My page [was] extremely ill also, but now of late that he is recovered."¹¹ Shortly after his death his chaplain, T. Knell, reported the event, adding that

> the yeoman of his cellar [Rowland Crompton] by certain words by him [Essex] spoken was of some suspected in his wine to have given him somewhat. . . . Some said that as many as drank with him that night were paid, as certain gentlewomen which also had the lask [diarrhea], which whether they had or not I am uncertain. [But Hunnis, his Lordship's taster, was indeed ill,] yet the suspicion of Crompton the yeoman of his cellar was so far from my Lord as by no means he said he would think it is him. . . . He said he thought some other of Ireland had done it, but none of his own house.¹²

Essex's "third person" and Knell's "certain gentlewomen" both refer, as only the *Commonwealth* indicates, to Alice Draycot. In a letter of 13 September 1576, hitherto unnoticed, Robert and Margaret Bysse and Cicely Fagan wrote from Dublin to their aunt, Mary Draycot, consoling her on the recent death of her daughter; they mention no suspicion of foul play but apologize "that we were not at her burying, for she was buried before we knew of any death."¹³

The Lord Deputy, Leicester's brother-in-law Sidney, reported to Walsingham on 20 October that he had found no evidence of poison, but that there were malicious rumors abroad "that arose by some words spoken by him," rumors especially concerning Crompton.¹⁴ On 4 February 1577 he wrote to Leicester himself: "I trust I have satisfied you and others touching the false bruit of the Earl of Essex's poisoning. I would have made Knell retract his foolish speech, but God prevented me, he dying of the same disease as the Earl, which was most certainly a mere flux [dysentery]. . . . If the Earl had lived, you should have found him as violent an enemy as his heart would have served him."¹⁵ Four days later the Lord Chancellor of Ireland, William Gerrard, sent to Walsingham the notes of his investigations into "the malicious bruits of the Earl of Essex his poisoning,"¹⁶ but rumors continued to circulate widely; for example, in an anonymous eulogy to Essex's deathbed piety (one of many that survive), the writer asserts quite positively that he had died of *dysenteria* but adds, " . . . or whether it were of any other accident the living God both knoweth and will revenge it."¹⁷

Henry Sidney, despite his obvious connection with Leicester's interests, was apparently a man of very great honesty, and in the absence of harder evidence than we now have, his report should be believed. The symptoms described by him and others could suggest poison but accord just as well with dysentery or typhoid fever, and there is no strong reason to doubt this judgment.

Another account of Essex's murder appears in Peck, "Letter of Estate" (pp. 28-29).

3. LEICESTER AND THE LADY SHEFFIELD

By family tradition, Leicester first met Douglass Howard, wife of John Lord Sheffield, when the Queen's progress was stopped at nearby Belvoir Castle in 1565.[18] Their affair seems to have begun soon after her husband's death in 1568; Conyers Read discusses a love letter (of a sort) from Leicester probably to Douglass, which letter he dates 1573 and which seems to imply a history of some years in their liaison.[19] When in 1603 her son by Leicester attempted to prove his legitimacy in the ecclesiastical courts, the Earl's widow Lettice Knollys brought a countersuit for conspiracy in Star Chamber, on which occasion Douglass testified to her own version of the relationship.[20] She said that she had been formally contracted to the Earl in 1571; at what seems to have been the occasion of a pregnancy, he married her (she says) in May 1573 at Esher in Surrey, in the presence of Sir Edward Horsey and Dr. Julio, among others. Leicester, in fear of the Queen's wrath, insisted upon secrecy. Also in May 1573, Court gossip was noticing that Douglass and her sister Frances were "very far in love" with Leicester, "as they have been long," and were "at great wars together" over him.[21]

The boy Robert ("Robin") was born on 7 August 1574, with Warwick and Sir Henry Lee godfathers by proxy. Later, after their separation, Leicester got the boy away from his mother, had him brought up at his kinsman John Dudley's house at Stoke Newington (as the *Commonwealth* says), and in 1588 enrolled him in Oxford as *filius comiti* (son of an earl); he provided generously for the boy in his will (but scrupulously referred to him as his "base son"), making him some nine important bequests.[22] When young Robert's attempt to gain his patrimony was removed to Star Chamber, he was acquitted (on 10 May 1605) of the conspiracy charge that had been brought there,[23] but his witnesses were fined for perjury and the documents in the case were impounded to prevent their being used again, which amounts (if not to a legal judgment) to a statement of the court's opinion of his claim. Soon afterward he deserted his wife and left for a brilliant career on the continent, where he died in 1649.[24] In 1644 his wife was made Duchess of Northumberland by Charles I, a formal recognition of his legitimacy but, in the circumstances, not a very meaningful one.[25]

Whether or not there was another child born, a daughter, as the *Commonwealth* asserts, is open to question. Her existence has been widely assumed; for example, she has been advanced in identification of Spenser's allegorical "Dido."[26] When in the 1605 trial one of the witnesses insisted upon the fact of her birth, Lord Henry Howard (then Earl of Northampton) stepped forward and denied it in Lady Sheffield's name.[27] It seems likely, however, that there was such a child, the occasion for whatever "marriage" occurred in May 1573; but since she appears nowhere thereafter, she probably died early.

In 1575 or 1576 Leicester, having tired of Lady Sheffield, began or renewed his courtship of Lady Essex. According to Douglass, the Earl offered her seven hundred pounds to disclaim their marriage, and when she refused, he tried to poison her. On 21 September 1578 he married Lady Essex, and on 29 November 1579 Douglass married Edward Stafford, "for her safety," she said.[28] Stafford later testified (just before his death in 1605) that the Queen had promised Douglass that if there were a provable contract between Douglass and Leicester "she would make him make up her honor with a marriage or rot in the Tower" but that Douglass had been forced to answer that she had trusted the Earl too much to insist upon anything in writing.[29] Both the Queen and the Earl of Sussex seem to have been ready to intervene on her behalf, but in the absence of any evidence at that time the matter was dropped and Douglass tacitly confessed her unmarried status by proceeding with her marriage to Stafford. Thus we can safely conclude that although the Earl acted in bad faith and although Douglass justly believed she had been wronged, and although there may have been a contract and a wedding ceremony of some sort (designed to put her mind at rest), there had probably been no authentic marriage registered in law. The contradiction between her belief that she was already married and her having wedded Stafford, with her failure to make a better case in 1579, when the Queen and Leicester's enemies would have been delighted to help her obtain justice, make her assertions seem rather the desperate fictions of a compromised woman. Derek Wilson has recently made a case for believing the marriage to have been genuine,[30] but it is unconvincing. Lady Sheffield died in December 1608.[31]

4. ANNE VAVASOUR

The *Commonwealth*'s animus against this lady provides another link between the book and the Catholic courtier's fortunes in the years 1579–1581. Anne Vavasour, daughter of Henry of Copmanthorpe, Yorkshire, came to Court (evidently at fifteen) in 1580. She was kinswoman to Charles Arundell, Lord Harry Howard, and Lord Paget, and whilst there she moved in Howard circles, under the care of other relatives, the Knyvetts, and especially her aunt, widow of Paget's brother Lord Henry. In summer 1580 she was being amorously pursued by the Earl of Oxford, which called forth from Walter Raleigh his sterling little poem of brotherly advice to her, "Many desire, but few or none deserve."[32] The advice was in vain, however, for in late summer she became pregnant by Oxford ("leavings of another man"), who (according to Lord Howard) immediately made plans to carry her over the sea and, though he was already wed to Burghley's daughter, there to marry her.[33] In December 1580 Oxford betrayed his friends in the Howard circle and joined the Earl of Leicester; Anne (or her brother) brought Oxford and Arundell together, Arundell says, so that the Earl might suborn him to corroborate his story.[34] When Arundell and Howard were placed in the confinement in which for ten months they remained, Oxford too was imprisoned, only to be released soon afterward and (in Arundell's words) to go "grazing in the pastures, up and down the town."[35] But then in March Anne's baby arrived, and directly it was delivered she was sent to the Tower; Oxford seems to have tried to flee the realm, but he too ended up in the Tower.[36] On 8 June he was released but remained under house arrest for some while longer, the Queen being reluctant to free him until he had confronted Howard and Arundell.[37]

As a consequence of all this, Oxford was forbidden the Court for two years more, during which time street battles continued between Oxford and Anne's kinsmen. He was dangerously hurt in a fight with Thomas Knyvett in March 1582; servants of Oxford and the Knyvetts fought in June; later in June Thomas Knyvett himself was attacked, and again in July 1582, when he killed one man in self-defense; in March 1583 one of Oxford's men killed one of Knyvett's, and as late as January 1585 the Earl was challenged to a duel by Anne's brother Thomas.[38] Arundell, of course, hated Oxford, and sometime in 1581 he wrote a letter (apparently) to Anne lamenting her "disgrace and banishment" and counselling her to "pluck up your courage . . . and think that God hath not forgotten you."[39] Nevertheless, despite his goodwill at that time and her relatives' indignation in her behalf, Anne soon forsook her friends by becoming the mistress of Leicester's ally Sir Henry Lee (thereby displacing Lee's much-ignored wife, Lord Paget's sister); in about 1585 her brother Thomas, instead of joining his relatives at Court, took service under the Earl of Leicester. Whether or not Anne Vavasour was really "attempted" by Leicester as the *Commonwealth* asserts, her presence here in such contemptuous mention reflects her defection to his party.[40]

5. THE DRAYTON BASSET RIOT

This problem has been studied in some detail, but the main facts can be outlined here.[41] William Robinson died "in the Queen's service" on 12 July 1563, and so quite likely he had served with Warwick at Newhaven as asserted. Thomas, his eldest son, inherited the manor of Drayton Basset in Staffordshire but ran into financial difficulties and in about 1576 alienated Drayton and other properties to one Richard Paramore, a merchant and land speculator from London. Robinson's friends maintained the manor merely to have been mortgaged on a seven-hundred-pound loan for which payment was not yet due, and Paramore had to have Thomas's brother John evicted by an injunction from the Court of Exchequer.

John Robinson was determined to pursue the matter, and violence broke out in June 1578, continuing intermittently throughout the summer. On 2 September, Thomas and John Robinson, supported by Walter Harcourt (knighted 1591, d. 1608) of Stanton Harcourt and Ellenhall (who had married their sister Dorothy), several other Harcourts, and as many as a hundred gentlemen and servants from the neighborhood, conducted a raid upon the house, drove off Paramore's agents, and fortified their position. Paramore sought the aid of Humphrey Ferrers, a leading citizen of nearby Tamworth and a client of the Earl of Leicester's. Ferrers and Sir George Digby summoned a posse and assaulted the house, and in the ensuing skirmish one of Ferrers's servants, Tristram Warde, was killed by John Robinson himself. Ferrers then rode up to London and complained to the government, but when the Lords Dudley and Stafford, acting on Privy Council orders of 14 September, arrived to restore order, they too were resisted. By the twenty-ninth, however, the rioters had surrendered or been taken, for on that date the chief among them were committed to the Fleet prison. Interrogations began, under Recorder William Fleetwood, not only of the participants but also of some of the local gentry (including Edward Arden and Sir Francis Willoughby), who were suspected of having materially supported the rioters. Thomas Lord Paget was reported to be working at Court to have the whole proceedings quashed as expensive and unnecessary.

The case against the rioters was heard in Star Chamber, and by October 1580 Harcourt and at least some of the others had been fined and released.[42] John Robinson testified that he had resisted Ferrers's demands because the only authority the man had had was "a letter of attorney . . . from my Lord of Leicester to enter into the said manor of Drayton Basset to my Lord of Leicester's own use." His defense in the charge of having killed Warde was that Warde was slain "by some of his own company that came with him," a version echoed elsewhere as well.[43] We cannot be certain that John Robinson was indeed sentenced to death, but there is reason to believe that he was; the margin note of one of the manuscript copies of *Leicester's Commonwealth* corrects the error in the printed edition in terms that suggest a firsthand knowledge: "Here is a mistaking, for it was not Thomas Robinson, the owner of the land, that was thus condemned, but his brother."[44]

A letter survives, written by Leicester to Ferrers at the height of the row (14 September), in which the Earl instructed his "loving servant" to guard his interests zealously, "as a matter that toucheth both your honesty and mine honor."[45] Eventually the manor did come into Leicester's hands; Paramore seems to have assigned his interest to the Earl in 1580 "in consideration of a great sum of money," and in 1581 Leicester travelled into Staffordshire to look the property over.[46] He bequeathed Drayton Basset to his wife in his will dated 1587, and although litigation over the title continued between Thomas Robinson and the Earl's widow after Leicester's death in 1588, the Countess died in residence there in 1634.

We are still unable to determine whether Leicester was guilty of the *Commonwealth*'s accusations against him; we may assume not entirely so. We do know that there was a violent incident over Drayton Basset, that the Earl was involved in it in some measure, and that he eventually fetched up with the title. We also know that the growing presence of his interests in the midlands seems to have been widely resented by the local population and that this incident seems to have been understood as another step in Leicester's encroachments in the region. In any case, the *Commonwealth*'s allegations are by no means far-fetched.

6. Dr. Julio and the Suspension of Archbishop Grindal

Archbishop Edmund Grindal's removal from his duties in June 1577 resulted from his refusal of the Queen's order that he suppress the Puritanical "prophesyings"; he remained suspended until his death in July 1583.[47] Contemporary rumor attributed his disgrace, however, to the fact that "he had condemned an unlawful marriage of Julio . . . with another man's wife, while Leicester in vain opposed against his proceeding therein."[48] Dr. Julio (born Guilio Borgarucci) was a Protestant who, having returned with the Earl of

Warwick from Le Havre, had entered Leicester's service in about 1563; in September 1573 he was taken on as physician to the royal household, in which post he seems to have died in about 1581. He was often alluded to as the type of the "Italian poisoner"; for example, Webster, in his play *The White Devil* (1612), has the evil Duke Brachiano employ a "Dr. Julio" to poison his wife. At one point in his career he was brought up for having married a woman already wed, but the matter received favor from Dr. Valentine Dale, then Master of Requests.[49] Sir William Cordell, Master of the Rolls, reopened it in 1573, and finally in late 1576 the case came before Grindal.

On 4 December 1576 Julio wrote the following letter to the Earl of Leicester, in which he seems to ask for extraordinary favor:

> My singular good Lord. I do understand by my proctor and other my lawyers of the hard dealing of Dr. [Thomas] Yale, who now fulfilleth as much as he signified unto me by Thomas of Denbigh my man, how the Archbishop of Canterbury had sworn I should never obtain this gentlewoman I have married, nor enjoy her. For the said Dr. Yale will not admit my witnesses to be examined but in such sort as seemeth to be *contra jus gentium* and hath not been used, as by certain articles which I have drawn shall the more at large appear unto your honor, and besides this he doth also publish decrees against his own former proceedings in my great prejudice, whereupon my learned counsel do wish me to appeal unto her Highness, whom it may please your honor to entreat to be so good and gracious to me that with her Majesty's favor I may have justice done me, and that my matter may be committed to such as neither be allied, affectioned, or suspected by either parties, to the intent that equity and justice may take place and that I be not precipitated in law or condemned *in dicta causa*, as mine unnatural adversaries do put in ure, whereby such as should allow of good doings and good intents do seem publicly to overturn all the good considerations of conscience and course of right and justice, as my learned men, being as they do term it at their wit's end to see such partialities, have signified unto me. Thus I shall have cause not only to pray to God for her Majesty's good health and prosperous long life, but also I shall accompt this for a singular benefit among a great many that your honor of your goodness hath bestowed upon me. From Brudges, the 4 of December 1576. Your honor's faithful servant during life, Guilio Borgarucci.[50]

Leicester apparently approached the Archbishop on behalf of his client, but (according to Strype) "notwithstanding the Earl's solicitation, he was not to be swayed contrary to his judgment and conscience," and he rendered a decision against Julio. Leicester appears certainly to have supported Grindal in the matter of the prophesyings, but nevertheless it is possible, if unlikely, that there was more connection between Julio's troubles and the fall of the Archbishop than we might otherwise recognize. Professor Collinson has found a letter from Burghley to Walsingham, dated 31 May 1577 (that is, when there was a question whether the Queen might attempt to have Grindal removed altogether), which at least indicates that Julio was somehow involved in the Archbishop's difficulties in ways that made Cecil uneasy:

> In the evening [Burghley says] after that we had delivered to the Archbishop her Majesty's message, I understood that Mr. Julio had that morning told a doctor of the law what should be done. So as I see he was more of her Majesty's counsel than two or three that are of present counsel. These proceedings cannot but irritate our merciful God, [and I hope that] He shall show mercy to his afflicted church. . . . I think the persons appointed to consult for deprivation of the Archbishop shall be much troubled to find a precedent.[51]

It will be observed that the *Commonwealth* inverts the usual story, supposing that it was Julio's bigamy and not his wife's that was in question.

NOTES TO APPENDIX D

1. In the Pepys MSS., Magdalene College, Cambridge, printed in Adlard, *Amye Robsart*, pp. 32–41.
2. Thus the sensible argument by Gairdner, "Death of Amy Robsart."
3. Neale agrees, *Queen Elizabeth I*, p. 87.
4. Aird, "Death of Amy Robsart"; N. Williams, *Elizabeth I*, p. 112.
5. *C.S.P. Spanish, 1558–67*, p. 175.
6. Haynes, *Collection of State Papers*, p. 362.
7. *C.S.P. Foreign, 1560–61*, p. 439.
8. Jones to Throgmorton, 30 Nov. 1560, Hardwicke State Papers, 1: 165. "The attempt" seems an odd phrase for the Queen to have used.
9. H.M.C. Salisbury MSS., 1: 351; see Appendix B, note 10. An intelligent discussion of the whole affair is found in D. Wilson, *Sweet Robin*, chap. 7.

10. *C.S.P. Spanish, 1568–79*, p. 511.
11. Malden, *Devereux Papers*, pp. 3–4. "Some evil" may imply suspicion of poison but may merely mean "some harm."
12. Ibid., p. 11.
13. This letter is tucked loose into a manuscript copy of the *Commonwealth* once owned by the Draycot family, Emmanuel College, Cambridge, MS. I.3.28. Folded with it is a conventional but affectionate verse letter to Mistress Alice Draycot, originally accompanying the gift of a devotional book, which seems almost certainly to be signed with a stylized "W. E.," i.e., Walter of Essex (though the college library catalogue records it as "Y. F.").
14. Sidney Papers, 1: 140–42.
15. H.M.C. Penshurst MSS., 2: 51.
16. S.P. 63/57/16.
17. British Library, Harleian MS. 293. no. 72, fol. 115.
18. Holles, *Memorials of the Holles Family*, p. 70. There is no confirmation of the Queen's having been at Belvoir at this time. Douglass (*ca.* 1545–1608), daughter of Lord William Howard of Effingham (and sister of Lord Charles, the admiral), styled herself Lady Sheffield to the end of her life, despite her marriage to Stafford.
19. See Read, "Letter from Robert, Earl of Leicester, to a Lady."
20. The best printed accounts are Warner's introduction, *Voyage of Robert Dudley*, pp. xxxix–xlvi, and Hawarde's *Reportes*, pp. 169–70, 198–213.
21. Gilbert Talbot to Shrewsbury, Lodge's *Illustrations*, 2: 17.
22. The will is printed in Sidney Papers, 1: 70–75.
23. Hawarde, *Reportes*, p. 212.
24. See Lee, *Son of Leicester*.
25. The letters patent, Jebb, *Life of . . . Leicester*, appendix 13.
26. Higginson, *Spenser's Shepherd's Calendar*, pp. 238–42.
27. Hawarde, *Reportes*, pp. 208–9.
28. Ibid., p. 199.
29. Warner, *Voyage of Robert Dudley*, p. xlv.
30. D. Wilson, *Sweet Robin*, pp. 207–9 and notes.
31. An abstract of her will is printed in *Miscellanea Genealogica et Heraldica*, n.s. 3 (1880): 369–70.
32. Peck, "Raleigh, Sidney, Oxford, and the Catholics, 1579," p. 431.
33. S.P. 12/15/57.
34. S.P. 15/27A/46.
35. S.P. 12/151/53.
36. Walsingham to Huntingdon, 23 Mar. 1581, H.M.C. Hastings MSS., 2: 29.
37. *A.P.C., 1581–82*, p. 74; Walsingham to Burghley, 14 July 1581 (S.P. 12/149/69).
38. See Chambers, *Sir Henry Lee*, pp. 150–62 (which reproduces a portrait of Anne Vavasour).
39. S.P. 12/151/51.
40. The best account of Anne Vavasour and her relations with Oxford is Bennett, "Oxford and *Endimion*."

41. Peck, "Earl of Leicester and the Riot at Drayton Basset, 1578," including references not provided here.
42. See interrogations and answers in Star Chamber records, Public Record Office, STAC 5/A.4/26, A.24/25, A.25/14, A.26/7, A.30/27, A.54/5.
43. *Ibid.*, STAC 5/A.4/26. The unknown copyist who made the MS. of *Leicester's Commonwealth* now in the library of St. John's College, Cambridge (MS. L.11), added a marginalium: "There was a man slain, but Leicester caused one of his own side to shoot a piece amongst his own men, and so one being slain it was said he was slain from Robinson's side."
44. British Library, Lansdowne MS. 265, fol. 41.
45. Pierpont Morgan Library, MS. M.A. 134b, no. 141.
46. "A brief of the title of the Countess of Leicester to the manor of Drayton Basset," British Library, Lansdowne MS. 62, item 53, fol. 127; I am indebted to Dr. P. R. Roberts for this reference. Leicester to Huntingdon, 26 May 1581, Huntington Library MS. H.A. 2377.
47. See Collinson, "Downfall of Archbishop Grindal," and his *Elizabethan Puritan Movement*, pp. 191–98.
48. Camden, *Elizabeth*, 3: 26; see also Harington, *Nugae antiquae*, 2: 18–20.
49. John Strype, *History of the Life . . . of Edmund Grindal*, pp. 334–35.
50. British Library, Cotton MSS., Titus B. VII, fol. 36.
51. British Library, Additional MS. 5935, fol. 68; Collinson, "Downfall of Archbishop Grindal," p. 46.

APPENDIX E

Related Documents

1. THE QUEEN'S PROCLAMATION

Shortly after the *Commonwealth*'s appearance, official action was taken toward its suppression. On 12 October 1584 a royal proclamation was issued from Hampton Court, apparently directed against *Leicester's Commonwealth*, Allen's *Defence*, and Leslie's *Treatise Touching the Right*. The present text is based on *S.T.C.* 8146 (Folger Library 256); see also Hughes and Larkin, *Tudor Royal Proclamations*, no. 672.

The Queen's Most Excellent Majesty, being given to understand that divers false, slanderous, wicked, seditious, and traitorous books and libels are covertly and in secret manner dispersed through this realm by divers seditious and traitorous persons, tending not only to the defacing of true religion now established within these her Highness' dominions, but also most traitorously and injuriously to slander the present most happy and quiet government with cruelty and extraordinary manner of proceedings in the due execution of justice, and withal most detestably and slanderously to reproach her most renowned and dear father, the dishonor or note whereof doth and cannot but touch herself as near as her Highness' own life, and so she taketh it. In some of which their most shameful, infamous, and detestable libels they go about to reproach, dishonor, and touch with abominable lies (as is well known to the whole realm) not only many of her most trusty and faithful councillors but also her Highness' judges and ministers of the law, greatly touching thereby her Highness' self in her regal and kingly office, as making choice of men of want both of justice, care, and other sufficiency to serve her Highness and the commonweal. And further, in the said books and libels they use all the means, drifts and false persuasions they can devise or imagine to advance such pretended titles as consequently must be most dangerous and prejudicial to the safety of her Highness' person and state (which the Lord long preserve).

Her Highness, foreseeing that the authors and dispersers of the said books and libels do by these wicked and indirect means seek most traitorously to render and make both her Highness and her most gracious government odious and hateful both abroad and at home, and having of late found, by plain and manifest means and proofs, that their purpose and chief intent to bring in obloquy and hatred her Majesty's principal noblemen, councillors, judges, and ministers of justice is as much as in them lieth to slander, impeach, and deface her Majesty's most happy government, and thereupon to breed some troubles within this realm, whereby their unnatural, devilish, and traitorous practices both against her Majesty their natural sovereign and the realm their own native country may take their desired effect, hath therefore thought meet that some order should be presently taken for the preventing and suppressing of such mischiefs as otherwise through ignorance of the truth might ensue thereby.

And therefore her Highness doth by this her Majesty's proclamation straightly charge and command that all such persons to whose hands any of the said books or libels either hath come or shall hereafter at any time come, do presently with all convenient speed, without showing the same to any person, deliver it to some one of her Highness' Privy Council if any such be within twenty miles, and if it be above that distance of miles from the Court, then to the *custos rotulorum* or to his deputy of the same shire where the party shall be that hath or shall have any such book or libel, and the same *custos rotulorum* or his deputy to whose hands any such book or libel shall come shall presently and safely send the same to the lords of her Majesty's most honorable Privy Council. And lest that any evil-disposed and affected person should maliciously and undutifully make any wrong or sinister construction of this her Majesty's meaning towards such as, moved with that duty and reverence that appertaineth, shall make delivery of any the said books and libels, her Highness' pleasure is, and so doth hereby signify to all her loving subjects, that they nor any of them shall be molested, impeached, or troubled for the having or receiving of any of the said books or libels, so as they do deliver the same according to the tenor and true meaning of this present proclamation, and so as it do appear that they have been no setters forth, dispersers, maintainers, or authors of any of the said books or libels. And in case any of the said parties that either hath or at any time hereafter shall have any of the said books or libels shall not make delivery thereof in sort as is before specified, then her Highness' further pleasure and express commandment is that the party or parties so offending shall be committed to prison, there to remain without bail or mainprize until order shall be taken by the lords of her Majesty's Privy Council for the proceeding against such offenders for such their offense, according to the nature and quality of the said offense.

And her Majesty's further pleasure is that all merchants, masters of ships, officers of ports, or any other that shall be bringer into this realm of any the said seditious books or libels or a disperser of the same, or shall hereafter be any way privy to the making, bringing in, or dispersing of them or any of them, and shall not immediately discover such offender or offenders to the next justice of the peace where such offense shall be committed (whereby the offenders may be apprehended and brought to be forthcoming to receive such punishment as his said offense shall deserve), that then such person or persons so offending shall be committed to prison, there to remain without bail or mainprize as aforesaid, until he be proceeded on according to justice.

And for the better execution of the said proclamation, her Majesty is pleased that all such persons as shall detect any of the said offenders, whereby they may be forthcoming to receive condign punishment according to their demerits, shall have the moiety of such forfeitures and penalties as shall be laid or inflicted upon such offenders so by them detected for such their offenses. And in case any mayor, justice of peace, or other public and inferior officer shall be found remiss in the due execution of the said proclamation, that then the said party or parties so offending shall also be produced before the said lords to receive punishment for that contempt and remissness used in that behalf in such sort as shall appertain to the nature and quality of the same offense.

2. THE SCOTTISH PROCLAMATION

Nothing is known about the process by which King James was induced to contribute his authority to suppression of the *Commonwealth*, nor is there other evidence of the book's circulation in Scotland. The proclamation of 16 February 1585 is known only in a contemporary copy now in the British Library (Additional MS. 31,897, fol. 9). The handwriting is extremely difficult to read, the text heavily abbreviated and in good part in dialect, and therefore the following modernized transcript is incomplete and not altogether reliable. Illegible words are noted by ellipses.

> James, by the grace of God King of Scots, to our . . . messengers, our sheriffs in that part . . . . . . and sundrily specially . . . , greeting.
> Forasmuch as we are credibly informed that there are divers slanderous and infamous books privily brought in and publicly dispersed in

sundry hands within our realm, full of ignominious and reproachful calumnies devised and set out by some seditious persons of purpose to obscure so far as in them lies the honor and reputation of our right trusty and right well-beloved cousin the Earl of Leicester and others, counsellors of our dearest sister and cousin the Queen of England. And remembering how in the time of our captivity at Ruthven, the very like was published and set out upon our right trusty cousin and counsellor James, Earl of Arran, our chancellor, only to move our subjects to insurrection and rebellion against us, howsoever the same appeared always to respect our own person, as the . . . do the person of our dearest sister, . . . under that prolept[?] and undoubted alteration which they mean and wish to her estate and country[?]. And . . . understanding in what commendation all princes ought to have the honor of all foreign princes, specially with these with whom they are [brought?] up in mutual friendship as we are with our dearest sister, with whom God in religion, nature in blood, and an . . . [disjoined?] as the rest of the . . . in habitation has willingly received[?] us and . . . united and concerned us in an inviolable[?] and steadfast amity, respecting that with all the particular goodwill and lawful friendship borne to us and uttered to our messengers and [shryvalties?] at all times by our said trusty cousin.
. . . . Therefore and we . . . .
. . . by open proclamation at the . . . . of East Sterling, Perth, Dundee, and various our . . . . . . made and given all and sundry our lieges and subjects who . . . . or . . . to hereafter receive any of the said reproachful books entitled A Letter of Estate Written by a Scholar in Cambridge, that they immediately without all delay bring . . . and deliver the same to our secretary to be cancelled and destroyed as ignominious and infamous under the pains that are in our act of Parliament made about the reading and concealing of slanderous and infamous libels against us, our progenitors[?], and council[?] . . .
. . . to . . . if any of the said books may be verified to have been in any of their possessions the time of this our proclamation and the same be not immediately and with all diligence[?] . . . and delivered as said . . . , the said penalty shalbe executed upon them, their lands and goods, with all . . . and . . . .
. . . . under our signet and subscribed with our hand at Holyrood House, the xvi of February, ... year 1584 [i.e., 1585].

3. THE PRIVY COUNCIL LETTER

Concerned by continued circulation of *Leicester's Commonwealth*, in June 1585 the government wrote to the officials of London and various counties (perhaps all) demanding stricter suppression of the tract and testifying in its own and the Queen's name to Leicester's innocence and good service. The letter's astute interpretation of the *Commonwealth*'s implications speaks for itself. The text is from S.P. 12/179/44 and 45, the former of which is endorsed by Lord Burghley as "a copy of a letter written by her Majesty's commandment to the Mayor of London, in defense of the Earl of Leicester" and dated 20 (or 26?) June 1585 (in no. 45 the date is left blank). There are virtually identical letters to Lord Strange, the Bishop of Chester, and the Justices of Lancashire and Cheshire, dated 20 June 1585 (printed in Peck, *Desiderata Curiosa*, 1: iv, 45), to the Council in the Marches of Wales, 20 June (H.M.C. Hereford MSS., 13th report, appendix, part 4, p. 332), and to the Justices of Surrey, 20 June (Kempe, *Loseley Manuscripts*, p. 492).

> After our very hearty commendations. Upon intelligence given to her Majesty in October last past of certain seditious and traitorous books and libels covertly spread and scattered abroad in sundry parts of her realms and dominions, it pleased her Highness to publish proclamations throughout the realm for the suppressing of the same and due punishment of the authors, spreaders abroad, and detainers of them, in such sort and form as in the said proclamation is more at large contained. Sithence which time notwithstanding her Highness hath certainly known that the very same and divers other such like most slanderous, shameful, and devilish books and libels have been continually spread abroad and kept by disobedient persons, to the manifest contempt of her Majesty's regal and sovereign authority, and namely among the rest one most infamous, containing slanderous and hateful matter against our very good lord the Earl of Leicester, one of her principal noblemen and chief councillors of estate, of which most malicious and wicked imputations her Majesty in her own clear knowledge doth declare and testify his innocence to all the world, and to that effect hath written her gracious letters signed with her own hand to the Lord Mayor, sheriffs, and aldermen of London, where it was likely these books would chiefly be cast abroad. We therefore, to follow the course taken by her Majesty, and knowing manifestly the wickedness and falsehood of these slanderous devices against the said Earl, have thought good to notify her further pleasure and our own consciences to you in this case. First that as in truth her Majesty hath noted great negligence and remissness in the former execution of her commandment, for as much as the said seditious libels

have been suffered since that time to be dispersed and spread abroad and kept by contemptuous persons without severe and due punishment inflicted for the same, so now upon the second charge and admonition given unto you, she verily looketh for the most strict and precise observation thereof in the sharpest manner that may be devised, testifying in her conscience before God unto you that her Highness not only knoweth in assured certainty the libels and books against the said Earl to be most malicious, false, and slanderous, and such as none but the devil himself could deem to be true, but also thinketh the same to have proceeded of the fullness of malice, subtly contrived to the note and discredit of her princely government over this realm, as though her Majesty should have failed in good judgment and discretion in the choice of so principal a councillor about her, or be without taste or care of all justice and conscience in suffering such heinous and monstrous crimes (as by the said libels and books be infamously imputed) to pass unpunished, or finally at the least to want either good will, ability, or courage (if she knew these enormities were true) to call any subject of hers whatsoever to render sharp accompt for them, according to the force and effect of laws. All which defects (God be thanked) we and all good subjects to our unspeakable comforts do know and have found to be far from the nature and virtue of her most excellent Majesty. And of the other side, both her Highness, of her certain knowledge, and we, to do his Lordship but right of our sincere consciences, must needs affirm these strange and abominable crimes to be raised of a wicked and venomous malice against the said Earl, of whose good service, sincerity of religion, and all other faithful dealings towards her Majesty and the realm we have had long and true experience. Which things considered, and withal knowing it an usual trade of traitorous minds, when they would render the princes' government odious, to detract and bring out of credit the principal persons about them, her Highness, taking the abuse to be offered to her own self, hath commanded us to notify the same unto you, to the end that knowing her good pleasure you may proceed therein as in a matter highly touching her own estate and honor. And therefore we wish and require you to have regard thereof accordingly, that the former negligence and remissness showed in the execution of her Majesty's commandment may be amended by the diligence and severity that shall be hereafter used. Which amendment and carefulness in this cause chiefly her Highness assuredly looketh for, and will call for accompt at your hands. And so bid you heartily farewell. From the Court at Greenwich the [20] of June 1585. Your very loving friends, T. Bromley, W. Burghley, Geo. Shrewsbury, H. Derby, F. Bedford, C. Howard, J. Hunsdon, F. Knollys, H. Sidney, Chr. Hatton, Fr. Walsingham, Wal. Mildmay.

APPENDICES WITH RELATED NOTES 285

4. CORRESPONDENCE

a. Stafford to Walsingham, Paris, 24 August 1584, reporting the appearance there of Allen's *Defence* and perhaps the *Commonwealth* (extract; Murdin, *State Papers*, pp. 418-19).

> The books to answer the True Execution of Justice in England, which I have long agone written to you were adoing, are now come out. I have sent you one of them; it is of Doctor Allen's or [Dr. William] Nicholson's doing, printed, as I hear, at Rheims, though they say in Germany, marvellous closely kept here from selling, not to be had for money, as this bearer can tell you. I was fain to recover them I have by some of their own faction, of whom I have divers things. He assureth me that at this hour there are two companies of them gone into England, two hundred in a company, to land some of them westward, some by the long seas. There is in my opinion no speaking to have them called in, for divers reasons, the one, because they are very secretly sold, the other, because they will take an advantage of it, and make men believe it is because we are touched to the quick.

b. Walsingham to Leicester, Barnelms, 29 September 1584, reporting confiscation of copies of the *Commonwealth* (*in extenso*; British Library, Cotton MSS., Titus B. VII, fols. 10-10^v, printed by Leslie Hotson, "Who Wrote 'Leicester's Commonwealth,'" pp. 481-83).

> My very good lord, yesterday I received from the Lord Mayor [Osborne] enclosed in a letter a printed libel against your Lordship, the most malicious written thing that ever was penned sithence the beginning of the world. The author thereof is Morgan, the Queen of Scots' agent in France, and as I gather by the course[1] thereof he hath been assisted therein by the Lord Paget, Charles Arundell, and [William] Tresham. About a three years past I had notice given unto me in secret sort of such an intent, with a meaning also to reach higher, as appeareth by the Italian plot found about Creighton the Scot Jesuit, and therefore if her Majesty shall be drawn by some fautor[2] of this wicked and devilish course to allow thereof the mischief like to ensue thereby will in the end reach to herself, when the time shall serve fit for the purpose. There is no good or honest man (and though he were your Lordship's mortal enemy) that doth not condemn this treacherous manner of dealing.
> I mean with the leave of God to be at the Court by tomorrow at noon; I would be glad to know your Lordship's mind what course you could like I should hold with her Majesty, as also what order you think meet to

be taken with the bringer over [Ralph Emerson] of the said books. It shall be very meet that both honest and wise men be appointed to examine him. For the mean time I have given straight charge to the Lord Mayor to see him kept for all conference by placing some honest trusty person to attend on him until he be thoroughly examined. I have also sent for the books that were found about him, which I will see strictly kept as they may not be dispersed. It behooveth us, considering the malice of this time, to walk very warily in our callings. And so I most humbly take my leave, at Barnelms, the 29th of September 1584.

c. Stafford to Walsingham, Paris, 29 October 1584, reporting attempts to trace the *Commonwealth* (*in extenso*; S.P. 78/12/105).

Sir, the Englishman that I desired Mr. Robert Cecil to tell you that arrived at the Spanish ambassador's out of England at the same instant that he [Cecil] departed, was the next day dispatched to Rouen back again and is looked for here again within eight days. He carrieth here a counterfeit name, I am sure; he calleth himself Stinter. At his return I will hearken more after him. Besides some other matters of importance that he brought with him (as I hear) he brought with him three or four of those books that are made again[st] a great councillor in England, as you know, for afore his coming I made as diligent a search as I could and could hear of none, and I know it for certainty that the Papists in the town themselves sought very narrowly for it, and [it] was not to be gotten, but since I know where two of them be, but very closely kept. There goeth a bruit among them that there were either three or four hundred of them taken in one port in England. I have done what I can to know where they were printed, but far as I can by any means find or hear, they themselves say in England or in Flanders, which I think to be true, for it hardly can be done either at Rouen or here but I should know of it, especially for this place I think I durst assure myself.

d. Robert Parsons to Alfonso Agazzari, Rouen, 13 December 1584 (extract). This letter records Parsons's version of the *Commonwealth*'s arrival in England, based upon rumors he had heard concerning it; it seems certain that in fact he knew more at first hand about the book than he here reveals. The tale of Burghley's trick played upon Leicester is no doubt spurious, but may be seen in light of Walsingham's fear (above) that there were some in the Court who might draw the Queen to "allow" of the book. The Latin original is in the Jesuit archives in Rome; the translation here is by Father Leo Hicks, as printed in "Growth of a Myth," pp. 98-99.

> The Earl of Leicester is hostile to the Treasurer, who is reputed to have written that Justitia Britannica.[3] When, then, he had received and read the reply to it, he presented a copy to the Queen, asserting that Cecil had acted rashly, since by his inept and inopportune pamphlet he had given occasion for this reply which would do great harm to their cause.
> This action of Leicester Cecil took in very bad part, but soon had opportunity of paying him back in his own coin. For a few days later there appeared a book in English, written, so it seems, by a Protestant, in which in very sober style are revealed all the vices of the Puritans, but chiefly those of Leicester: his ambition, his tyranny, his crimes and treasons against the country and the Queen, his whole manner of life and utter knavery. Five or six hundred copies of the book fell into the hands of the officials whose business it is to search out such works, and in the absence of Leicester were sent to Cecil as the leading member of the Queen's Council. But far from suppressing the copies, Cecil immediately distributed them to many and handed one copy to the Queen herself. She was the last person in the world that Leicester wanted to see the book and he was nearly beside himself with vexation at it.
> It is extraordinary, so it is reported, how eagerly the book is thumbed in England. Some offer twenty pounds for a copy and twenty crowns for a loan of one for three or four hours, so exceedingly detested by all is the Earl. Certainly, the book has remarkable things to say about him and his partisans. I only wish you were able to read it; you would be astounded. Copies were very hard to come by in these parts till our friends came from England. From them I obtained a copy and have wanted to send it to you, that you may present it to the Bishop of St. Asaph.

e. Stafford to Walsingham, Paris, 30 March 1585, reporting the appearance of the *Commonwealth*'s French translation, *Discours de la vie abominable* (*in extenso*; S.P. 78/13/86). The words in italics are from cipher.

> Sir, I thought it convenient having this gentleman a convenient bearer to write to your honor of [a] thing which is here coming out and as I take it is printed at Rheims, though it be given out to be done at Cologne, which is the book again[st] *the Earl of Leicester* newly translated into French with a very villainous addition, as I hear, both in the former part and the hinter part of it. It is not yet come hither nor as yet looked for to be here

these three or four days. I thought good by this bearer to send you word of it in time because as you think good you may give watch for the suppressing of them at their landing. For no doubt of it, they will be sent over, and [it] is determined among them to have all the means that can be and the device[?] to bring it to the sight of *the Queen*. I am in a peck of troubles what to do in it, for to complain of it were to have the matter more to be divulged abroad and to [be] more looked into and marked when it shall be seen to stir in, and especially by me because my nearest[4] have a touch in it, which though between God and *Leicester's* conscience and almost in the opinion of most Englishmen her conscience be no farther touched than an honorable intent and a weak woman deceived, yet when it cometh to French heads' standings, who can neither speak nor think well of any, I doubt how they will interpret anything. And therefore if by any device I could devise to have it suppressed I would do it, but their malice to *Leicester* is such as all the world together shall not have credit to do it but by [official] complaint, which in my opinion is the worst way, and therefore for my part, though I be touched in it, others that touch me being touched in it, till I hear your farther opinion I do not mean at all to stir in it, but in making no accompt of it make all things in it to be thought a jest, as the Queen Mother [Catherine de Medici] hath done in all things touching her that have been set out, which hath made them die the sooner and little accompt made of them. There be in this town of our good people here that to curry favor with me have made it be told me that the matter touching my friends [*sic*] is so slightly urged and in that sort and not named as that I shall have no cause to be offended,[5] but if it light in my lot and may come to know who is the doer of it, as I shall I doubt not, I will not leave to light upon [him] when he shall not be aware of it, perchance so that he shall feel of it. For I am not such a baby but that I know well enough that, though the names be either left out or the matter colored in the French, there be enough that have read the English and know the parties, that can take pains to gloss and interpret the text. I think the book is not put into French to be kept under a bushel, and though they were so geason[6] I doubt not but to receive of the first that do come. And if you command me I will send you [one] of them, for else I will not, for I cannot tell how it will be taken, and I would be sorry to give cause to have anything evil taken. Two things have hindered me to write to *Leicester* of it, the one that I have no cipher, the other [that] I would be loth to do anything subject to bad interpretation, and therefore I leave it to you to do in it as you shall think best. I have kept it from the beginning that the other came out from translating here, for [Thomas] Throgmorton was even then in hand with it, and by means that I found left it off, and ever since it hath slept, and is but now of a sudden gushed out. I am very certainly advertised that the matter of the addition is come out of England, and from thence very earnestly pressed the translating and the setting out of it afresh. I pray God my friend be not laid up again when that it shall come to *her* ear, which yet is not, for I can assure you that the melancholy of the fear of the misinterpretation of the first, contrary to the desert of *her* conscience, was the cause of the last sickness that was so long and almost of life, as in truth I was a good while greatly afraid of. Thus beseeching you to send me your mind and what in this you will command me, and desiring you for my sake to be as good to this bearer as you may, I commit your honor to God.

f. Stafford to Lord Burghley, Paris, 30 March 1585 (*in extenso*; S.P. 78/13/87).

My very good Lord, I have sent Mr. Secretary word that the book again[st] *Leicester* is come out again translated into French, with a very filthy addition, because there may order be given that they may be stayed at their coming over. They be not arrived to this town, but they are looked for every day. I am in a peck of troubles how to govern myself about the staying or complaining against the publishing of them. For first it is a particular man's case, and whether in that being a public person I may speak in it or no I know not, and besides whether making an open show to make accompt of it will do rather more harm or good to the conceit in men's judgments of it it is doubtful. For my part, though there be there touched in it [those] that I would be sorry in men's opinion there should be conceit had of, that of their conscience cannot accuse them of in the worst sort, yet for my part I rather think it better to let it alone as a thing that we make no accompt of, than by speaking of it or against it to make [them] think that a galled horse where he is touched will wince. And so I think is the way soon to make it little accompt to be made of and so die. It is marvellous suddenly come out, for I stayed it once here when I knew it was adoing and by whom, but now it is suddenly gushed out. They give out it is done at Cologne, but for my part I think it done either at Rheims or Eu. I shall [I] think ere long know of it. If your Lordship will command me, I will send you one as soon as any doth come, but else I will not, for *Leicester* is ever subject to take not well that which cometh from me, though I give no cause, and therefore I fear also the like in this, though for my friend I have as much interest against this as he. Thus I [etc.].

g. Stafford to Burghley, Paris, 10 April 1585 (*in extenso*; S.P. 78/13/99).

My very good Lord, by the copies of these two letters to Mr. Secretary your Lordship shall see all I can write. *William Waad* need carry with him one of the *books against Leicester*, which maketh me bold to send you one, which I have packeted up in a box as some other token.[7] I pray your Lordship let it be kept to yourself, for though I mean no harm I know not how things coming from me that way will be taken.

h. Stafford to Walsingham, Paris, 20 January 1586, defending himself and his secretary, Lilly (*in extenso*; S.P. 78/15/15).

Sir, Mr. Stallings at his arrival this morning both gave me a letter of your honor writ to me of your own hand; by them I perceived that you took otherwise my meaning in my last about Lilly and Michael[8] than I meant it. For truly, Sir, though I writ that I must be fain to seek some other course to make known unto her Majesty (if you would not favor me to do it) that she had no cause to be offended with me for keeping of Lilly after her commandment to me to put him away, because indeed you in her name did command me the contrary, which was to keep him and to make no show to him of anything, yet your honor doth know that as long as it since I never writ to anybody of it but to yourself, and desired you that I might be beholding to nobody but to you for it; if for this you had cause to be offended with me, I leave it to you to judge. If withal I did write unto you that which I do hear and see every day here what is said and conceived among ambassadors and others of no small quality to my disgrace, you might think whether I had cause to grieve, and in truth you must pardon me, Sir, if I must needs write this to you, that it had been a greater show of some respect the more to the place I am employed in if there had been men known for faults fit not to be kept it could have pleased you to have written to me privately the cause why it was not fit I should keep them, that I myself thereupon might have put them away, than to have kept [them] away from me as though I had had neither honesty, reason, nor discretion to have done it myself upon any just cause.

Therefore I most humbly beseech your honor to think nothing in me if I mean somewhat earnest in this, for all the wealth I have is my desire to live in good opinion and reputation, and anything that toucheth that truly I must confess doth gall me; if in that case I deal plainly with those that be my honorable good friends, I pray you think better of a man that dealeth plainly than of him that keepeth in his stomach everything dissemblingly. The one's friendship is not worth a point when it cometh to the touchstone, the other a man may be assured of at all assays. I pray you, Sir, take me in the number of the last, and hold yourself as assured that where I profess friendship I will [continue?] with it without regard of anything in the earth but the duty to my prince, and pray you think that there is nobody I desire to be more in that predicament with than with you, and ever have done, and ever will do, and whensoever you will make what trial you think good of anything I can, you shall try whether the increase of your fortune, which I pray for, or the decrease of it, which I do not fear, shall make me alter any point of my affection when I promise it.

For my two men, if I might receive that favor at your hands that I might have them sent over to me and withal that you advise me with reason to put them away, let myself have that credit to do, you shall favor me greatly. For the one, truly I will tell you I never meant to serve myself of him after his return to me for a particularity to myself, which I grew in a great misliking with him for, and in truth did not mean if he come to keep him long, and to look well enough to his water while he remaineth here. For Lilly I must tell your honor truly I have no cause that I do know to be offended with him, and truly I have sought into as much as a man could do, and he is not so wise as not to be found halting. For those things which you send me word of by Stallings, which I knew afore that he was examined upon, except that matter of my Lord of Arundel's, I could answer myself. For that of my Lord of Leicester, your honor did mistake me that I took him for a private person but in one kind, which was that I being a public person here for her Majesty could do no more than I did if it had been for my father, for to complain against anybody that had written against anybody but against the Queen I could not. And to go about to suppress it I could do no more, for as I could get books into my hand I burnt them all, to the number of thirty-two or three, till so great numbers of them came as I saw it was to no purpose. And for Lilly, if he perchance saw or read a book surely that were in reason no such criminal cause, but sure I had rather cause to think that my Lord of Leicester should be so incensed against him for the love the poor fellow bare to me than for any cause else.

Well, Sir, to avoid all causes, and that you shall see I will follow your counsel and advice in anything, I will if you think good send of purpose to my Lord of Leicester and write in the best manner I can to see if by craving it of him I can obtain his good will, which yet I know no cause of why I should leese it. And the letters and the bearer shall come by you first that you may see them, and if you will be so good to me as to send Lilly, I will send him over to him himself, that he may carry them to my Lord from me, and that my Lord may use him as he shall see cause or pardon him if he find none, and send him to me again with his pleasure. Surely, Sir, the man might stand me in some stead, and if you will favor me so much as to send him presently I shall take it a thing that I shall be beholding to you for. For Grimston hath very great business in England for a three weeks' going and coming, and I would fain have him to serve me here in his absence, and as soon as ever Grimston is returned I will presently send him back, first to you and so to my Lord of Leicester, or if you think not good for other causes, which I beseech you to look well into afore you condemn the poor man, he hath had a mind to travel a great while; I will give him wherewithal to travel for a year or such a thing into Italy, and after to place him the best I can. Mr. Stallings told me of some unkindness between my mother and you, which I am very sorry for; I will [. . .] both write and send my mind plainly to her. For the one cause which you conceived for my man's usage, truly upon my honesty I writ nor never sent any word to her nor to anybody else of it, and if she hath conceived anything of that it is of opinion that everybody else hath done that heard it. For that of my Lord of Arundel I will by him write my mind plainly and send to her by Stallings, and so would I do to my Lord of Arundel himself if I could tell how it would be taken. For surely, Sir, you should do me great wrong if you do not think that I myself desire to be as much beholding to you, and to have all my friends of the same mind, as any man in England, and I pray you, Sir, think so and let me by this poor suit I make to you for my men have cause to think so, and withal I pray you assure yourself that no poor gentleman in England loveth and honoreth his friends more everlastingly than I do.

5. POEMS

There are several extant poems concerning Leicester, most derived from *Leicester's Commonwealth*, but two will suffice by way of example. The "Epitaphium" survives in several similar versions,[9] but what seems to be the most authoritative form follows.

Epitaphium
Here lies the valiant soldier
  that never drew his sword.
Here lies the loyal courtier
  that never kept his word.
Here lies the noble lecher
  that used art to provoke.
Here lies the constant husband
  whose love was firm as smoke.
Here lies the politician
  and nut worm of the state,

> Here lies the Earl of Leicester
> that God and man did hate.[10]

The second example also illustrates some of the odd things that associated themselves with the Leicester legend. The puzzling, pious little effusion headed "Notable talk herein taught" is inscribed before a manuscript copy of *Leicester's Commonwealth* that is otherwise unremarkable (Folger Shakespeare Library, MS. G.b.11).

> Notable talk herein taught,
> In these words are many caught.
>
> Read you but not to speak again;
> Speak but not what thou readest here.
> News for to learn all men are fain,
> But wisely few that news can bear.
>
> The Ragged Staff that stay was to the state
> (As some men thought) is bent another way
> (As here is taught), so fickle is the stay
> Of those that use to bear the greatest sway.
>
> Let all take head how they aspire too high,
> For when they fall, of all, they lowest lie.
>
> The stately Bear that at the stake would stand
> 'Gainst all the mastiffs stout that would come forth
> Is muzzled here and ringed with our hand,
> Yea, vile reputed and of little worth.
>
> Great Robin, whom before all could not take,
> Is here by shepherd's curs made for to quake.
>
> Thus may we learn, there is no staff so strong
> But may be broken into shivers small,
> No beast so fierce the cruel beasts among
> But age or cunning gins may work his fall.
>
> Let no man trust in earth to find a place
> Which can preserve him from a foul disgrace.

Truths or untruths, whats'ere they be
Which here you read, yet not in vain.
Read over these and you shall see
That this doth prove the greatest gain,

To be content and not desire,
For all do fall that do aspire.

NOTES TO APPENDIX E

1. Hotson reads "worst."
2. "Fautor": partisan, supporter (*O.E.D.*). Walsingham appears to fear that someone at Court will persuade the Queen not to act to suppress the libel.
3. Burghley's *Execution of Justice in England*; the reply is Dr. Allen's *Defence of English Catholics*.
4. That is, his wife, Douglass Howard, Lady Sheffield.
5. Stafford's informants were correct: In the French translation Lady Sheffield's name, as well as everything else that might serve to identify her, has been carefully omitted from every place it occurs in the English original.
6. "Geason": rare, scarce (*O.E.D.*).
7. The calendarist misleadingly has "with some other tokens" (*C.S.P. Foreign, 1584–85*, p. 412).
8. Michael Moody was in Stafford's service, but was suspected by him of having been planted by Walsingham. Early in 1587, when Elizabeth would not proceed with the sentence of death already passed against the Queen of Scots, Walsingham came up with the "Stafford Plot," in which Des Trappes, secretary to the French ambassador Châteauneuf, and William Stafford (1554–1612), Sir Edward's brother, were to have employed Moody (then in Newgate prison for debt) to blow up Queen Elizabeth with gunpowder under her bed.
9. Other versions: Huntington Library MS. EL 6183 (signed "Wa. Ra."); Verstegan, *Declaration of the True Causes of the Great Troubles*, p. 54; Latham, *Poems of Sir Walter Ralegh*, p. 172. Raleigh's authorship is not now accepted.
10. British Library, Stowe MS. 156, fol. 204v. For discussion, see Peck, "Another Version of the Leicester Epitaphium."

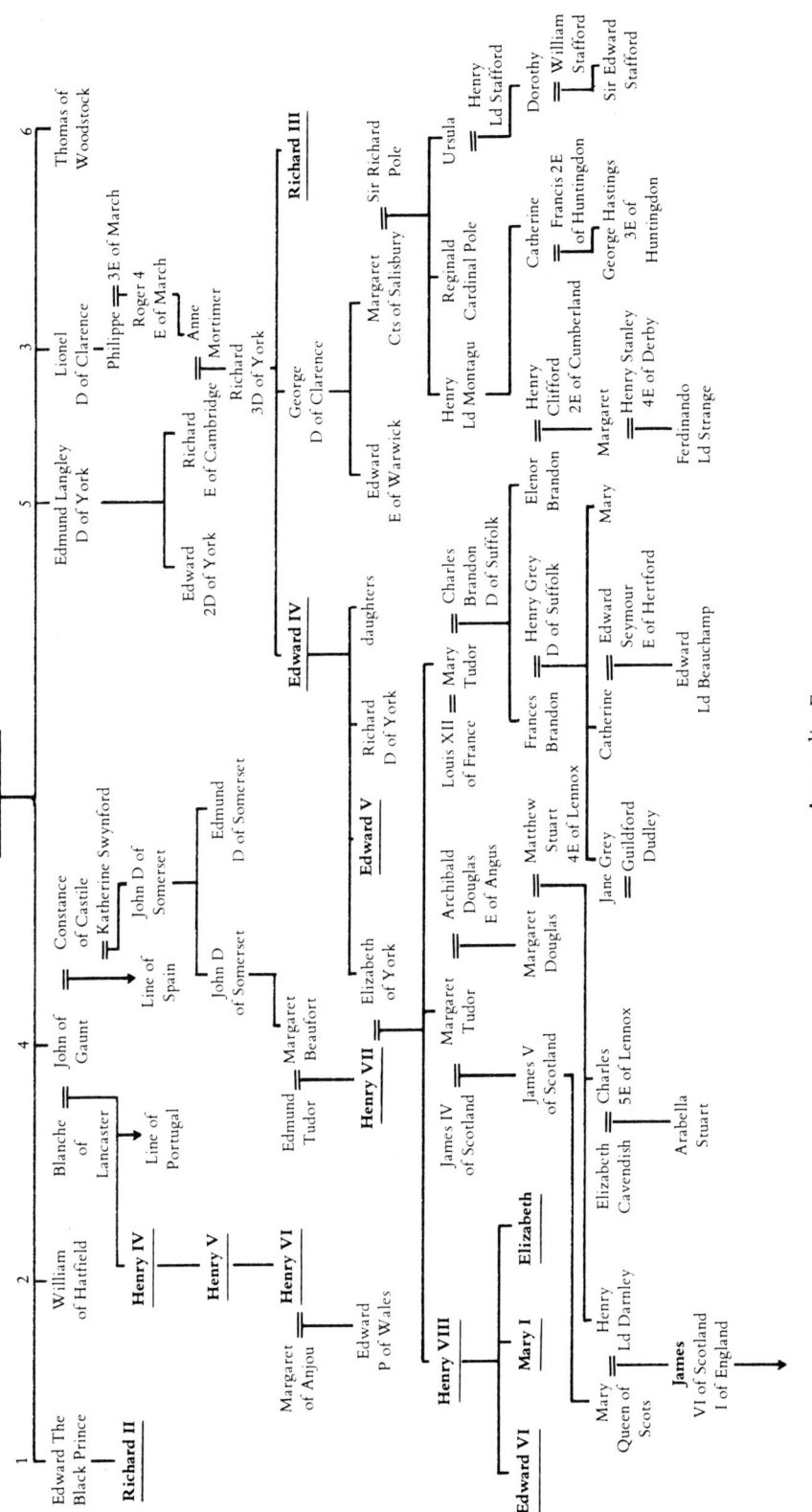

Appendix F
A. The Succession

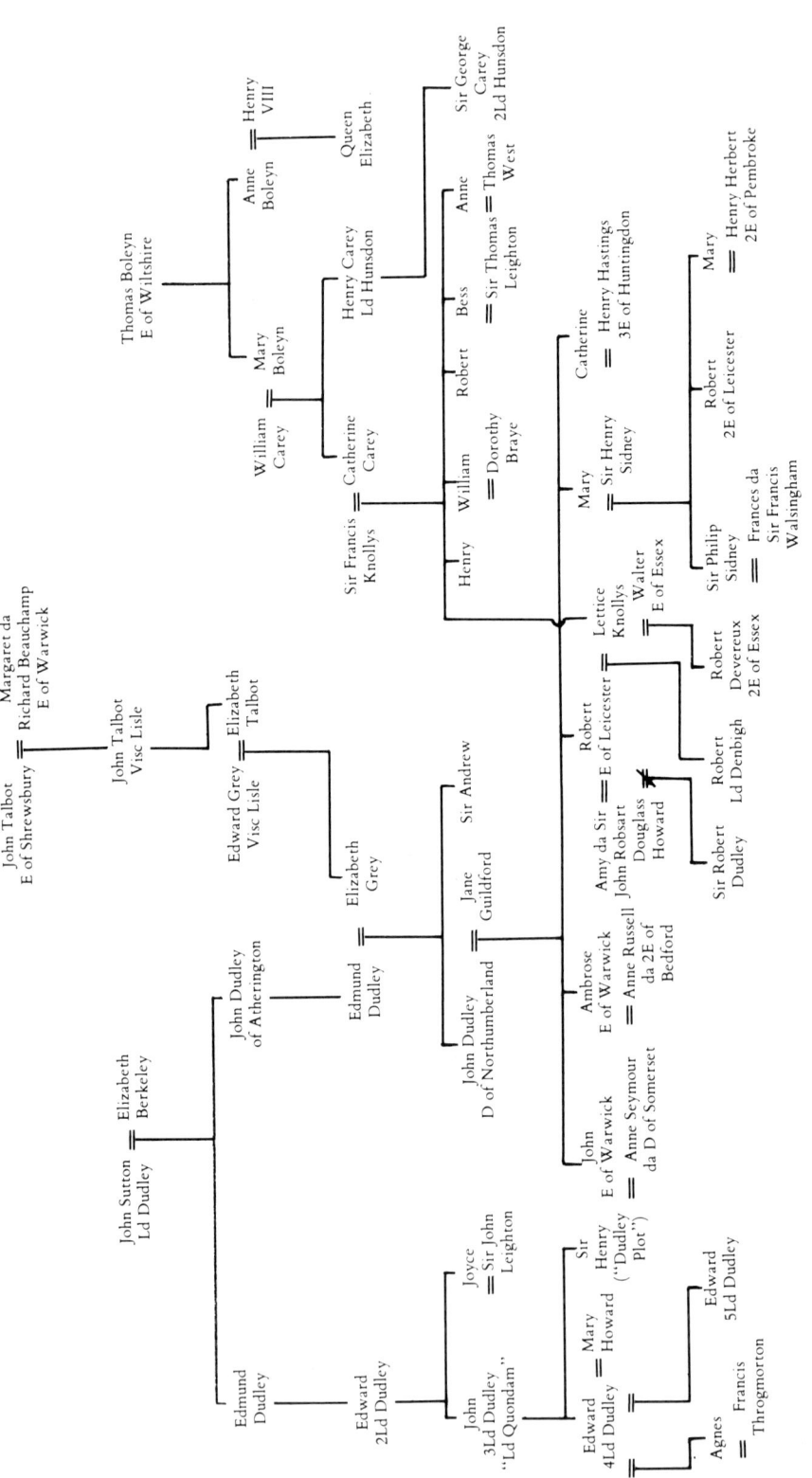

Appendix F
B. Major Dudley Connections

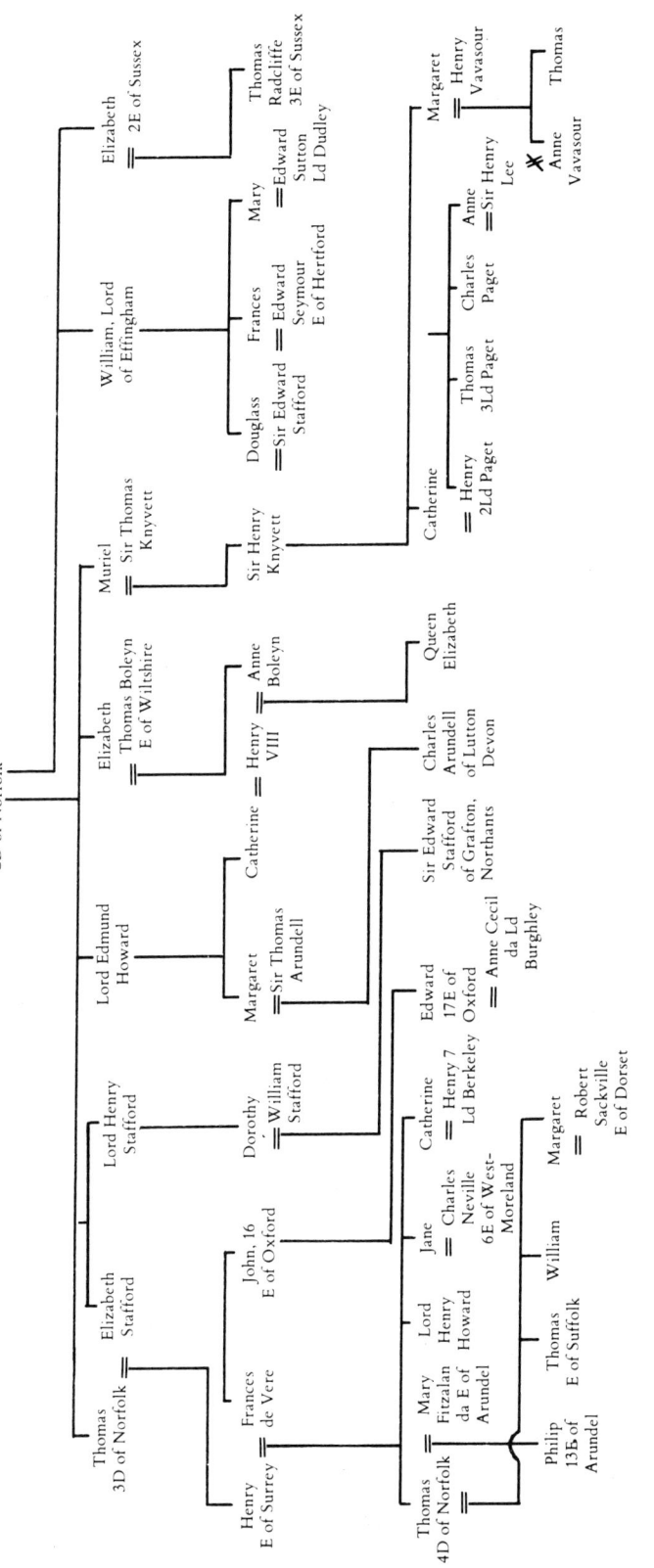

Appendix F
C. Major Howard Connections

Bibliography of Printed Works Cited

Adlard, George. *Amye Robsart and the Earl of Leycester.* London, 1870.
Aird, Ian. "The Death of Amy Robsart." *English Historical Review*, 71 (1956): 69–79.
Akrigg, G. P. V. *Shakespeare and the Earl of Southampton.* London: Hamish Hamilton, 1968.
Alberti, Leandro. *Descrittione di tutta Italia.* Bologna, 1550.
Allen, William. *An Admonition to the Nobility and People of England.* 1588. S.T.C. 368.
―――. *The Copy of a Letter Written by M. Doctor Allen.* 1587. S.T.C. 370.
―――. *A True, Sincere and Modest Defence of English Catholics.* 1584. S.T.C. 373. Edited by Robert M. Kingdon. Folger Documents Series. Ithaca: Cornell University Press, 1965.
Allison, A. F., and D. M. Rogers. *A Catalogue of Catholic Books in English Printed Abroad or Secretly in England, 1558–1640. Biographical Studies*, 3 (1956), nos. 3–4.
Arber, Edward, ed. *A Transcript of the Registers of the Company of Stationers of London, 1554–1640.* 5 vols. 1875–1877. Reprinted New York: Peter Smith, 1950.
Ashmole, Elias. *The History and Antiquities of Berkshire.* Vol. 1. London, 1719.
Atkinson, E. G. "The Cardinal of Châtillon in England, 1568–1571." *Proceedings of the Huguenot Society*, 3 (1892): 172–285.
Aubrey, John. *Aubrey's Brief Lives.* Edited by Oliver Lawson Dick. 3d ed. London: Secker & Warburg, 1958.
Axton, Marie. "The Influence of Edmund Plowden's Succession Treatise." *Huntington Library Quarterly*, 37 (1973/74): 209–26.
Baldwin, T. W. *On the Literary Genetics of Shakspere's Plays.* Urbana: University of Illinois Press, 1959.
Beer, Barrett L. *Northumberland: The Political Career of John Dudley.* Kent, Ohio: Kent State University Press, 1973.

BIBLIOGRAPHY OF PRINTED WORKS CITED   299

Bellamy, John. *The Tudor Law of Treason.* London: Routledge & Kegan Paul, 1979.
Bennett, Josephine Waters. "Oxford and *Endimion.*" *PMLA,* 57 (1942): 354–69.
Bindoff, S. T., J. Hurstfield, and C. H. Williams, eds. *Elizabethan Government and Society: Essays Presented to Sir John Neale.* London: Athlone Press, 1961.
Boas, Frederick S. *Christopher Marlowe: A Biographical and Critical Study.* Oxford: Clarendon Press, 1940.
Bossy, John. "The Character of Elizabethan Catholicism." *Past and Present,* 21 (1962): 39–59. Reprinted in T. Aston, ed. *Crisis in Europe, 1560–1660.* London: Routledge & Kegan Paul, 1965. Pp. 223–46.
―――. *The English Catholic Community, 1570–1850.* London: Darton, Longman & Todd, 1975.
―――. "English Catholics and the French Marriage, 1577–1581." *Recusant History,* 5 (1959): 2–16.
Bowers, Fredson T. "Kyd's Pedringano: Sources and Parallels." *Harvard Studies and Notes in Philology and Literature,* 13 (1931): 241–49.
Briegerus, Julius. *Flores Calvinistici decerpti ex vita Roberti Dudlei Comitis Lecestriae.* Naples [false]: Zangarum, 1585 [1586]. (British Library 1345.a.25 and 1017.a.22.)
Brodie, D. M. "Edmund Dudley, Minister of Henry VII." *Transactions of the Royal Historical Society,* 4th ser., 15 (1932): 133–61.
Brooke, C. F. Tucker, ed. *Shakespeare Apocrypha.* Oxford: Oxford University Press, 1908.
Brooks, Eric St. John. *Sir Christopher Hatton: Queen Elizabeth's Favourite.* London: Cape, 1946.
Broughton, Richard. *The English Protestants Plea and Petition.* 1621. S.T.C. 10415.
Bruce, John, ed. *Correspondence of Robert Dudley, Earl of Leycester, During His Government of the Low Countries in the Years 1585 and 1586.* Camden Society 27 (1844).
Burgoyne, F. J., ed. *Collotype Facsimile and Type Transcript of an Elizabethan Manuscript Preserved at Alnwick Castle, Northumberland.* [*Leicester's Commonwealth* MS.] London: Longmans, Green, 1904.
―――. ed. *The History of Queen Elizabeth, Amy Robsart, and the Earl of Leicester.* [*Leicester's Commonwealth.*] London: Longmans, Green, 1904.
Calendar of Patent Rolls, Elizabeth. [Cited by inclusive years.] London, 1934– .
Calendar of State Papers, Domestic Series, of the Reigns of Edward VI, Mary, Elizabeth. Edited by Robert Lemon and Mary A. E. Green. 12 vols. London, 1856–1872.
Calendar of State Papers, Foreign Series, of the Reign of Elizabeth. Edited by Joseph Stevenson. 23 vols. London, 1863–1950.

Calendar of State Papers Relating to Scotland and Mary, Queen of Scots, 1547–1603. Edited by Joseph Bain. 13 vols. London, 1898–1969.
Calendar of State Papers, Spanish, Elizabeth. Edited by Martin A. S. Hume. 4 vols. London, 1892–1899.
Calendar of State Papers, Venetian. Edited by Rawdon Brown, G. Cavendish Bentinck, Horatio F. Brown. 9 vols. London, 1864–1898.
Camden, William. *The Historie of the Most Renowned and Victorious Princess, Elizabeth.* Translated by Richard Norton. London, 1630.
———. *The History of the Most Renowned and Victorious Princess Elizabeth: Selected Chapters.* Edited by Wallace T. MacCaffrey. Chicago: University of Chicago Press, 1970.
Canny, Nicholas. *The Elizabethan Conquest of Ireland.* New York: Barnes & Noble, 1976.
Cecil, William. *The Execution of Justice in England.* 1583, S.T.C. 4902. 1584, S.T.C. 4903. Edited by Robert M. Kingdon. Folger Documents Series. Ithaca: Cornell University Press, 1965.
Chamberlin, Frederick. *Elizabeth and Leycester.* New York, 1939.
———. *The Private Character of Queen Elizabeth.* New York: Dodd, Mead, 1922.
Chambers, E. K. *Sir Henry Lee: An Elizabethan Portrait.* Oxford: Oxford University Press, 1936.
Cicero. *Letters.* Loeb Classical Library, 1928.
———. *De Officiis.* Loeb Classical Library, 1913.
———. *Philippics.* Loeb Classical Library, 1926.
Clancy, Thomas H. *Papist Pamphleteers: The Allen-Persons Party and the Political Thought of the Counter-Reformation in England, 1572–1615.* Chicago: Loyola University Press, 1964.
———. "A Political Pamphlet: The *Treatise of Treasons*, 1572." *Loyola University Studies in the Humanities*, 1962, pp. 15–30.
Clark, Peter, Alan G. R. Smith, and Nicholas Tyacke, eds. *The English Commonwealth, 1547–1640: Essays in Politics and Society Presented to Joel Hurstfield.* Leicester: Leicester University Press, 1979.
Clifford, Anne. *The Diary of Lady Anne Clifford.* Edited by Victoria Sackville-West. London: Heinemann, 1923.
Collier, John Payne, ed. *The Egerton Papers.* Camden Society 12 (1840).
Collins, Arthur, ed. *Letters and Memorials of State.* [Sidney Papers.] 2 vols. London, 1746.
Collinson, Patrick. "The Downfall of Archbishop Grindal and Its Place in Elizabethan Political and Ecclesiastical History." In Clark, *The English Commonwealth, 1547–1640*, pp. 39–57.
———. *The Elizabethan Puritan Movement.* Berkeley: University of California Press, 1967.
Commynes, Philippe de. *The Memoirs of Philippe de Commynes.* Translated by

Isabelle Cazeaux. 2 vols. Columbia: University of South Carolina Press, 1969.
Cooper, J. P. "Henry VII's Last Years Reconsidered." *Historical Journal*, 2 (1959): 103-29.
Copley, Anthony. *An Answer to a Letter of a Jesuited Gentleman.* 1601. *S.T.C.* 5735.
Corbett, Julian. *Drake and the Tudor Navy.* 2 vols. 1898. Rpt. London: Longmans, 1917.
Cotgrave, Randle. *A Dictionarie of the French and English Tongues.* 1611. Facsimile rpt. Columbia: University of South Carolina Press, 1950.
[Creswell, Joseph?] *An Advertisement Written to a Secretary of my L. Treasurer's of England.* 1592. *S.T.C.* 19885.
Cross, Claire. *The Puritan Earl: The Life of Henry Hastings, Third Earl of Huntingdon, 1536-1595.* London: Macmillan, 1966.
Darnton, Robert. *The Literary Underground of the Old Regime.* Cambridge: Harvard University Press, 1982.
Dasent, John R., ed. *Acts of the Privy Council of England.* [*A.P.C.*] 32 vols. London, 1890-1907.
"The Dead Man's Right." [By Nicholas Breton?] *The Phoenix Nest*, 1593. Reprinted in D. Wilson, *Sweet Robin*, pp. 339-41.
Dee, John. *The Private Diary of Dr. John Dee.* Edited by James Halliwell. Camden Society 19 (1842).
D'Ewes, Simonds. *Journals of All the Parliaments.* London, 1682.
Dictionary of National Biography. Edited by Leslie Stephen and Sidney Lee. 22 vols. London, 1885-1900, and supplements.
Diodorus Siculus. *Diodorus of Sicily.* Vol. 8. Loeb Classical Library, 1963.
Discours de la vie abominable, ruses, trahisons, meutres, impostures, empoisonnements, paillardises, atheismes, & autres tres iniques conversations, desquelles a usé & use journellement le my Lorde de Lecestre Machiaveliste. 1585. (British Library, 10806.a.10)
Drake, James, ed. *The Perfect Picture of a Favorite.* [*Leicester's Commonwealth.*] London, 1708, 1711, 1721.
———. ed. *Secret Memoirs of Robert Dudley.* [*Leicester's Commonwealth.*] London, 1706.
Dudley, Edmund. *The Tree of Commonwealth.* Edited by D. M. Brodie. Cambridge: Cambridge University Press, 1948.
Dugdale, William. *The Antiquities of Warwickshire.* London, 1656.
Edwards, Edward. *The Life and Letters of Sir Walter Ralegh.* 2 vols. London, 1868.
Edwards, Francis. *This Marvellous Chance.* London: Hart-Davis, 1968.
Ellis, Henry, ed. *Original Letters Illustrative of English History.* 3rd ser. 4 vols. London, 1846.

Elton, G. R. "Henry VII: Rapacity and Remorse." *Historical Journal*, 1 (1958): 21–39.
―――. "Henry VII: a Restatement." *Historical Journal*, 4 (1961): 1–29.
Falls, Cyril. *Elizabeth's Irish Wars*. London: Methuen, 1950.
Fitzherbert, Thomas. *A Defense of the Catholic Cause*. 1602. S.T.C. 11016.
―――. *A Treatise Concerning Policy and Religion*. 1606. S.T.C. 11017.
Foster, Frank Freeman. *The Politics of Stability: A Portrait of the Rulers in Elizabethan London*. London: Royal Historical Society, 1977.
Freeman, Arthur. *Thomas Kyd: Facts and Problems*. Oxford: Clarendon Press, 1967.
Gairdner, James. "The Death of Amy Robsart." *English Historical Review*, 1 (1886): 235–59.
―――. "The Death of Amy Robsart." *English Historical Review*, 13 (1898): 83–90.
Gentili, Alberico. *De legationibus libri tres*. 1585. Edited by G. J. Laing. New York: Oxford University Press, 1924.
Harbison, E. Harris. *Rival Ambassadors at the Court of Queen Mary*. Princeton: Princeton University Press, 1940.
Harington, John. *Nugae antiquae*. Edited by Thomas Park. 2 vols. London, 1804.
―――. *A Tract on the Succession to the Crown (A.D. 1602)*. Edited by Clements R. Markham. Roxburghe Club, 1880.
Harris, P. R. "William Fleetwood, Recorder of the City, and Catholicism in Elizabethan London." *Recusant History*, 7 (1963): 106–22.
Hawarde, John. *Les Reportes del cases in Camera Stellata*. Edited by W. P. Baildon. London, 1894.
Haynes, Samuel, ed. *A Collection of State Papers*. London, 1740.
Hazen, Allen T. "Literary Forgeries and the Library." *Columbia Library Columns*, 22 (1972): 6–13.
Hicks, Leo. *An Elizabethan Problem: Some Aspects of the Careers of Two Exile-Adventurers*. New York: Fordham University Press, 1964.
―――. "An Elizabethan Propagandist: The Career of Solomon Aldred." *The Month*, 1945, pp. 181–91.
―――. "The Growth of a Myth: Father Robert Persons, S.J., and Leicester's Commonwealth." *Studies: An Irish Quarterly*, 46 (1957): 91–105.
―――, ed. *Letters and Memorials of Robert Persons, S.J.: To 1588*. Catholic Record Society 39 (1942).
―――. "Sir Robert Cecil, Father Persons, and the Succession, 1600–1." *Archivum Historicum Societatis Jesu*, 24 (1955): 95–139.
Higginson, J. J. *Spenser's Shepherd's Calendar in Relation to Contemporary Affairs*. New York: Columbia University Press, 1912.
Historical Manuscripts Commission. Bath MSS.

BIBLIOGRAPHY OF PRINTED WORKS CITED 303

———. Hastings MSS.
———. Hereford MSS.
———. Penshurst MSS.
———. Rutland MSS.
———. Salisbury (Hatfield) MSS.
Holinshed, Raphael. *Chronicles of England, Scotland, and Ireland.* Edited by Henry Ellis. 6 vols. London, 1808.
Holles, Gervase. *Memorials of the Holles Family, 1493–1656.* Edited by A. C. Wood. Camden Society, 3rd ser., 55 (1937).
Holmes, Peter. "The Authorship of 'Leicester's Commonwealth.'" *Journal of Ecclesiastical History,* 33 (1982): 424–30.
Hotson, Leslie. "Who Wrote 'Leicester's Commonwealth'?" *The Listener,* 43 (1950): 481–83. Continued exchanges, pp. 567, 659, 745.
Howell, Roger. *Sir Philip Sidney, the Shepherd Knight.* London: Hutchinson, 1968.
Hughes, Paul L., and James F. Larkin, eds. *Tudor Royal Proclamations.* 3 vols. New Haven: Yale University Press, 1964–1969.
Hume, David. *The History of England from the Invasion of Julius Caesar to the Revolution of 1688.* 1754–1762. Rpt. London, 1829.
Hume, Martin A. S. *The Courtships of Queen Elizabeth.* London: Macmillan, 1898.
Hurstfield, Joel. "The Succession Struggle in Late Elizabethan England." In Bindoff, *Elizabethan Government and Society,* pp. 369–96. Reprinted in his *Freedom, Corruption and Government in Elizabethan England.* London: Cape, 1973. Pp. 104–34.
James, Thomas. *The Jesuits Downfall.* 1612. S.T.C. 14459.
Jebb, Samuel. *The Life of Robert Dudley, Earl of Leicester.* London, 1727.
Jenkins, Elizabeth. *Elizabeth and Leicester.* New York: Coward-McCann, 1962.
Jerome, Saint. *Selected Letters.* Loeb Classical Library, 1933.
Johnson, Samuel. *Johnson's Dictionary: A Modern Selection.* London: Gollancz, 1963.
Jordan, Wilbur K. *The Development of Religious Toleration in England.* Vol. 1 Cambridge: Harvard University Press, 1932.
———. *Edward VI: The Threshold of Power.* Cambridge: Harvard University Press, 1970.
———. *Edward VI: The Young King.* Cambridge: Harvard University Press, 1968.
Kantorowicz, Ernst. *The King's Two Bodies: A Study in Mediaeval Political Theology.* Princeton: Princeton University Press, 1957.
Kempe, A. J., ed. *The Loseley Manuscripts.* London, 1836.
Kendall, Alan. *Robert Dudley, Earl of Leicester.* London: Cassell, 1980.

Kendall, Paul Murray. *Richard the Third*. New York: Norton, 1956.
Kinney, Arthur, ed. *Elizabethan Backgrounds*. Hamden, Conn.: Archon Books, 1975.
Knappen, M. M. *Tudor Puritanism*. Chicago: University of Chicago Press, 1939.
Knox, T. F., ed. *Letters and Memorials of William Cardinal Allen*. London, 1882.
Labanoff, Alexandre, ed. *Letters of Mary Stuart*. Selected and Translated by William Turnbull. London, 1845.
Latham, Agnes, ed. *The Poems of Sir Walter Ralegh*. Cambridge: Harvard University Press, 1951.
Law, T. G., ed. *The Archpriest Controversy: Documents Relating to the Dissensions of the Roman Catholic Clergy, 1597-1602*. 2 vols. Camden Society, n.s., 56 (1896) and 58 (1898).
Lecler, Joseph. *Toleration and the Reformation*. Translated by T. L. Westow. 2 vols. New York: Association, 1960.
Lee, A. G. *The Son of Leicester*. London: Gollancz, 1964.
Leicester's Commonwealth Fully Epitomiz'd. London, 1641. Reprinted in *Harleian Miscellany*. Vol. 4. London, 1809.
Leslie, John, Bishop of Ross. *Defense of the Honour of the Right High, Mighty and Noble Princess Mary, Queen of Scotland*. 1569. S.T.C. 15505.
———. *A Treatise Touching the Right*. 1584. S.T.C. 15507.
Levine, Mortimer. *The Early Elizabethan Succession Question, 1558-1568*. Stanford: Stanford University Press, 1966.
———. "The Last Will and Testament of Henry VIII: A Reappraisal Appraised." *Historian*, 26 (1964): 471-85.
[Lewknor, Lewis] *A Discourse of the Usage of the English Fugitives by the Spaniard*. London, 1595. S.T.C. 15562.
Lodge, Edmund. *Illustrations of British History, Biography, and Manners*. 2nd ed. 3 vols. London, 1838.
Loomie, Albert J. *The Spanish Elizabethans: The English Exiles at the Court of Philip II*. New York: Fordham University Press, 1963.
MacCaffrey, Wallace T. "The Anjou Match and the Making of Elizabethan Foreign Policy." In Clark, *The English Commonwealth, 1547-1640*, pp. 59-75.
———. "Place and Patronage in Elizabethan Politics." In Bindoff, *Elizabethan Government and Society*, pp. 95-126.
———. *Queen Elizabeth and the Making of Policy, 1572-1588*. Princeton: Princeton University Press, 1981.
———. *The Shaping of the Elizabethan Regime*. Princeton: Princeton University Press, 1968.
Machiavelli, Niccolo. *The Prince*. Translated by Robert M. Adams. New York: Norton, 1977.

Maclean, John, ed. *The Berkeley Manuscripts.* 3 vols. Gloucester, 1883–85.
Malden, Henry E., ed. *The Devereux Papers, 1575–1601.* Camden Society, 3rd ser., 34 (1923).
Matthew of Westminster. *Flores historiarum.* London, 1853.
Mattingly, Garrett. "William Allen and Catholic Propaganda in England." In *Travaux d'Humanisme et Renaissance* (Geneva), 28 (1957): 325–39.
Mickle, William. "Cumnor Hall." In Thomas Evans, *Old Ballads, Historical and Narrative.* Vol. 1. London, 1784. Rpt. in Scott, *Kenilworth*, preface to the 1831 edition.
More, Thomas. *History of King Richard III.* In Richard Sylvester, ed., *The Complete Works.* Vol. 2. New Haven: Yale University Press, 1963.
Murdin, William, ed. *Collection of State Papers . . . Left by William Cecil.* London, 1759.
Naunton, Robert. *Fragmenta regalia.* 1641. London, 1834.
Neale, John E. *Elizabeth I and Her Parliaments, 1559–1581.* New York: St. Martin, 1958.
———. *Elizabeth I and Her Parliaments, 1584–1601.* New York: St. Martin, 1958.
———. "The Elizabethan Political Scene." *Essays in Elizabethan History.* London: Cape, 1958. Pp. 59–84.
———. "The Fame of Sir Edward Stafford." *English Historical Review*, 44 (1929): 203–19.
———. *Queen Elizabeth I.* 1934. Rpt. London: Cape, 1952.
Nichols, John. *The Progresses and Public Processions of Queen Elizabeth.* 3 vols. London, 1823.
Nicolas, Nicholas Harris, ed. *Memoirs of the Life and Times of Sir Christopher Hatton.* [*Hatton Memoirs.*] London, 1847.
Orwell, George, and Reginald Reynolds, eds. *British Pamphleteers.* Vol. I. London: Wingate, 1948.
Osborn, James M. *Young Philip Sidney, 1572–1577.* New Haven: Yale University Press, 1972.
Ovid. *Metamorphoses.* Translated by Arthur Golding, 1567. Edited by John Frederick Nims. New York: Macmillan, 1965.
Oxford Dictionary of English Proverbs. Edited by William George Smith. 2nd ed., rev. by Paul Harvey. Oxford: Clarendon Press, 1948.
Oxford English Dictionary: Compact Edition. 2 vols. New York: Oxford University Press, 1971.
Painter, William. *The Palace of Pleasure.* 1566. Edited by Joseph Jacobs. 3 vols. New York: Dover, 1966.
Parsons, Robert. *A Brief Discourse Containing Certain Reasons Why Catholics Refuse to Go to Church.* 1580. S.T.C. 19394.

306   LEICESTER'S COMMONWEALTH

———. *A Conference about the Next Succession to the Crown of England.* By "R. Doleman." 1595. *S.T.C.* 19398.
———. *A Discussion of the Answer of M. William Barlow.* 1612. *S.T.C.* 19409.
———. *An Epistle of the Persecution of Catholics in England.* 1582. *S.T.C.* 19406.
———. *The Judgment of a Catholic Englishman.* 1608. *S.T.C.* 19408.
———. *A Temperate Ward-word to the Turbulent and Seditious Watchword of Sir Francis Hastings.* 1599. *S.T.C.* 19415.
———. *Warnword to Sir Francis Hastings' Wast-word.* 1602. *S.T.C.* 19418.
Peck, D. C. "An Alleged Early Draft of 'Leicester's Commonwealth.'" *Notes and Queries,* n.s. 22 (1975): 295–96.
———. "Another Version of the Leicester Epitaphium." *Notes and Queries,* n.s. 23 (1976): 227–28.
———. "The Earl of Leicester and the Riot at Drayton Basset, 1578." *Notes and Queries,* n.s. 27 (1980): 131–35.
———. "Government Suppression of Elizabethan Catholic Books: The Case of *Leicester's Commonwealth.*" *Library Quarterly,* 47 (1977): 163–77.
———. ed. "'The Letter of Estate': An Elizabethan Libel." *Notes and Queries,* n.s. 28 (Feb. 1981): 21–35.
———. ed. "'News from Heaven and Hell': A Defamatory Narrative of the Earl of Leicester." *English Literary Renaissance,* 8 (1978): 141–58.
———. "Raleigh, Sidney, Oxford, and the Catholics, 1579." *Notes and Queries,* n.s. 25 (1978): 427–31.
Peck, Francis. *Desiderata Curiosa: or A Collection of Divers Scarce and Curious Pieces.* 2 vols. London, 1732–1735.
Petti, A. G., ed. *Letters and Despatches of Richard Verstegan.* Catholic Record Society 52 (1959).
Plutarch. *Plutarch's Lives.* Edited by Arthur Hugh Clough. 2 vols. London: Dent, 1910.
Pollard, A. F. *England under the Protector Somerset.* London: Paul, Trench, Trübner, 1900.
Pollard, A. W., and G. R. Redgrave, eds. *A Short-Title Catalogue of Books Printed in England, Scotland, & Ireland and of English Books Printed Abroad, 1475–1640.* [*S.T.C.*] London: Bibliographical Society, 1926.
Pollen, John Hungerford, ed. *Memoirs of Robert Persons, S.J.* Catholic Record Society 2 (1905), 4 (1907).
Pollen, John Hungerford, and William McMahon, eds. *The Ven. Philip Howard, Earl of Arundel.* English Martyrs, 2. Catholic Record Society 21 (1919).
Porter, H. C. *Reformation and Reaction in Tudor Cambridge.* Cambridge: Cambridge University Press, 1958.
Pritchard, Arnold. *Catholic Loyalism in Elizabethan England.* London: Scolar Press, 1979.

Prothero, G. W., ed. *Select Statutes and Other Constitutional Documents.* 4th ed. Oxford: Clarendon Press, 1913.
Pulman, Michael Barraclough. *The Elizabethan Privy Council in the Fifteen-Seventies.* Berkeley: University of California Press, 1971.
Read, Conyers. "The Fame of Sir Edward Stafford." *American Historical Review,* 20 (1915): 292–313.
——. "The Fame of Sir Edward Stafford." *American Historical Review,* 35 (1930): 560–66.
——. "A Letter from Robert, Earl of Leicester, to a Lady." *Huntington Library Bulletin,* 9 (1936): 15–26.
——. *Lord Burghley and Queen Elizabeth.* New York: Knopf, 1960.
——. *Mr. Secretary Cecil and Queen Elizabeth.* New York: Knopf, 1955.
——. *Mr. Secretary Walsingham and the Policy of Queen Elizabeth.* 3 vols. Oxford: Clarendon Press, 1925.
——. "Walsingham and Burghley in Queen Elizabeth's Privy Council." *English Historical Review,* 28 (1913): 34–58.
——. "William Cecil and Elizabethan Public Relations." In Bindoff, *Elizabethan Government and Society,* pp. 21–55.
Rogers, Thomas. *Leicester's Ghost.* Edited by Franklin B. Williams, Jr. Renaissance English Text Society 4. Chicago: Newberry Library and University of Chicago Press, 1972.
Rose, Elliott. *Cases of Conscience: Alternatives Open to Recusants and Puritans under Elizabeth I and James I.* Cambridge: Cambridge University Press, 1975.
Rosenberg, Eleanor. *Leicester, Patron of Letters.* New York: Columbia University Press, 1955.
Ross, Charles. *Richard III.* Berkeley: University of California Press, 1981.
Rowse, A. L. *Sir Walter Ralegh.* 1962. Reprinted Westport: Greenwood, 1975.
Salmon, J. H. M. *The French Religious Wars in English Political Thought.* Oxford: Oxford University Press, 1959.
Scarisbrick, J. J. *Henry VIII.* Berkeley: University of California Press, 1968.
Scott, Walter. *Kenilworth.* 1821. Reprinted with preface, 1831.
Sidney, Philip. *Miscellaneous Prose of Sir Philip Sidney.* Edited by Katherine Duncan-Jones and J. A. van Dorsten. Oxford: Clarendon Press, 1973.
——. *Prose Works of Sidney.* Edited by A. Feuillerat. 4 vols. 1912. Rpt. Cambridge: Cambridge University Press, 1962.
Smith, Alan G. R. *The Government of Elizabethan England.* London: Arnold, 1967.
——. *Servant of the Cecils: The Life of Sir Michael Hickes, 1543–1612.* London: Cape, 1977.
Smith, Lacey Baldwin. "The Last Will and Testament of Henry VIII: A Question of Perspective." *Journal of British Studies,* 2 (1962): 14–27.

Southern, A. C. *Elizabethan Recusant Prose, 1559–1582*. London: Sands, 1950.
Southwell, Robert. *An Humble Supplication to her Majestie*. 1600. *S.T.C.* 7586. Edited by R. C. Bald. Cambridge: Cambridge University Press, 1953.
Stone, Lawrence. *The Crisis of the Aristocracy, 1558–1641*. Oxford: Oxford University Press, 1965.
Stopes, Charlotte. *The Life of Henry, Third Earl of Southampton*. Cambridge: Cambridge University Press, 1922.
―――. *Shakespeare's Warwickshire Contemporaries*. Stratford-on-Avon: Shakespeare Head Press, 1897.
Stow, John. *The Chronicles of England*. 1580. *S.T.C.* 23333.
Strype, John. *Annals of the Reformation*. 4 vols. Oxford, 1824.
―――. *History of the Life and Acts of the Most Reverend Father in God, Edmund Grindal*. London, 1710.
Stubbs, John. *John Stubbs's Gaping Gulf*. Edited by Lloyd Berry. Folger Documents Series. Charlottesville: University Press of Virginia, 1968.
Suetonius. [*Works*.] 2 vols. Loeb Classical Library, 1928.
Tenison, E. M. *Elizabethan England*. 9 vols. Leamington, 1932–1951.
A Treatise of Treasons against Q. Elizabeth and the Crown of England. 1572. *S.T.C.* 7601.
Trimble, William R. *The Catholic Laity in Elizabethan England*. Cambridge: Harvard University Press, 1964.
Vergil, Polydore. *Anglica historia*. Camden Society 29 (1844), 36 (1846), 3rd ser. 74 (1950).
Verstegan, Richard. *An Advertisement Written to a Secretary of my L. Treasurers*. 1592. *S.T.C.* 19885.
―――. *A Declaration of the True Causes of the Great Troubles*. 1592. *S.T.C.* 10005.
Victoria History of the Counties of England. Compiled by William Page et al. London, 1900– .
Virgil. *Aeneidos, liber tertius*. Edited by R. D. Williams. Oxford: Clarendon Press, 1962.
Waldman, Milton. *Elizabeth and Leicester*. London: Collins, 1944.
Walpole, Richard, and Robert Parsons. *News from Spain and Holland*. 1593. *S.T.C.* 22994.
Warner, G. F., ed. *The Voyage of Robert Dudley*. Hakluyt Society, 2nd ser., 3 (1899).
Watson, William. *A Decacordon of Ten Quodlibetical Questions Concerning Religion and State*. 1602. *S.T.C.* 25123.
Wernham, R. B. *Before the Armada: The Growth of English Foreign Policy, 1485–1588*. London: Cape, 1966.
Williams, E. C. *Bess of Hardwick*. London: Longmans, 1959.
Williams, Franklin B., Jr. "Leicester's Ghost." *Harvard Studies and Notes in Philology and Literature*, 18 (1935): 271–85.

Williams, Neville. *Elizabeth I, Queen of England.* 1967. Rpt. London: Sphere, 1971.

———. *Thomas Howard, Fourth Duke of Norfolk.* New York: Dutton, 1964.

Williams, Penry. *The Council in the Marches of Wales under Elizabeth I.* Cardiff: University of Wales Press, 1958.

———. *The Tudor Regime.* Oxford: Clarendon Press, 1979.

Willson, David Harris. *King James VI and I.* 1956. Rpt. London: Cape, 1963.

Wilson, Charles. *Queen Elizabeth and the Revolt of the Netherlands.* Berkeley: University of California Press, 1970.

Wilson, Derek. *Sweet Robin: A Biography of Robert Dudley, Earl of Leicester, 1533–1588.* London: Hamish Hamilton, 1981.

Wilson, Thomas. *State of England A.D. 1600.* Edited by F. J. Fisher. Camden Society, 3rd ser., 52 (1936).

Wing, Donald, ed. *Short-Title Catalogue of Books Printed in England, Scotland, Ireland, Wales, and British America and of English Books Printed in Other Countries, 1641–1700.* 3 vols. New York: Index Society, 1948.

Wood, Anthony à. *Athenae Oxonienses.* Edited by Philip Bliss. 4 vols. Oxford, 1813–1820.

Yorke, Philip, Earl of Hardwicke, ed. *Miscellaneous State Papers from 1501 to 1726.* [Hardwicke State Papers.] 2 vols. London, 1778.

INDEX OF PROPER NAMES

Page numbers in italics refer to the texts of *Leicester's Commonwealth* and the 1585 Addition; those in Roman type refer to introductory or supplemental matter. Marginalia in the original are found with the notes but indexed to the places in the text where they occur.

Abingdon, Berkshire, 265
Acteon, *100*, *204*
Adamson, Patrick, Archbishop of St. Andrews, *171*, 218
Admonition to the Nobility and People of England (1588), 3
Agazzari, Alfonso, S.J., 286
Agincourt, Battle of (1415), *214*
Ahasuerus, King of Persia, *135*, *212*
Aird, Ian, 266
Aiax, *104*
Alberti, Leandro, *121–22*
Aldred, Solomon, *173*, 219
Alençon, Duke of. See Anjou, François, Duke of
Alexander the Great, *180*
Allen, Giles, 245
Allen, Thomas, Dr., *116*, *208*
Allen, William, Dr., 3, 5, 13, 33–35, 59, 228, 285
Amadis, of Gaul, *136*, *213*
Aman, Duke, See Haman
Anglesey, Isle of, Wales, *120*, *209*
Angus, Earl of. See Douglas, Archibald
Anjou, François, Duke of ("Monsieur"), 2, 5, 11, 15, 17–19, 22, 36, *69*, *75–79*, *168*, *197–99*, *201*, *230–33*, *238*, *244*, 245–47
Anne of York, *151*, *214*
Antipater, *180*
Antonio, Don, Prior of Crato, *214*
Antwerp, Netherlands, 55, *69*, *231*, *244–45*, *247*
Appletree, Thomas, *213*
Appleyard, John, *235–37*, 246, 267
Aquitaine, *161*
Arden, Edward, of Park Hall, *173*, 219, 273
Aristotle, *77*, *125*
Arran, Earl of. See Stuart, James
Arthur, Duke of Brittany, *160*, *213*, *216*
Arundel Castle, Sussex, 261
Arundel, Earl of. See Fitzalan, Henry; Howard, Philip
Arundell, Charles, ix, 6, 9, 13–31, 36, 54, 56–60, *202*, *204*, *206*, 217–19, 229, *243*, 246–47, 271–72, 285, 297

Arundell, Margaret Howard, 14, 297
Arundell, Thomas, Lord, of Wardour, 14, 219, 297
Ashby de la Zouch, Leicestershire (Huntingdon's house), *106*, *206*
Ashmole, Elias, 45
Askew, Anne, Lady, *128*, *211*
Assuerus, King. See Ahasuerus, King of Persia
Athenians, *148*, *183*
Atkins, Robert, 10, 54
Attalus, Duke, *187*
Augustine, Saint, 199
Augustus Caesar, *258*, *260*

Babington Plot (1586), 3, 211
Babington, Anthony, 59
Babington, Francis, Dr., *91*, 201
Babylon, *180*
Bacon, Nicholas, Sir, *99*, 203
Barnet, Battle of (1471), *145*, *212*, *214*
Basing, Hampshire, *172*
Bayley, Henry, Dr., *91*, 201
Bayley, Walter, Dr., *82–83*, *116*, 200, 208
Beaton, James, Archbishop of Glasgow, 27, 29, 60
Beauchamp, Henry, Earl of Warwick, 263
Beauchamp, Margaret. See Talbot, Margaret Beauchamp
Beauchamp, Richard, Earl of Warwick, 257, 263–64
Beaufort, Edmund, Duke of Somerset, *131*, *181*, *212*, 295
Beaufort, John, Duke of Somerset, *149*, *214*, 295
Beaufort, John, 2d Duke of Somerset, *149*, 295
Beaufort, Margaret, *149*, 295
Beaumaris, Anglesey, 209
Bedford, Earl of. See Russell, Francis
Belvoir Castle, Leicestershire, 269, 277
Berden, Nicholas. See Rogers, Thomas
Berkeley Castle, *210*
Berkeley, Catherine Howard, Lady, 297
Berkeley, Henry, 7th Lord Berkeley, *99*,

310

INDEX OF PROPER NAMES   311

123, 210, 264, 297
Berkeley, James, 264
Berkeley, James, 1st Lord Berkeley, 264
Berkeley, Thomas, 5th Lord Berkeley of first creation, 264
Bertha, Queen of Kent, *78*, 199
Berwick, Northumberland, *104*, 205
Beza, Theodore, *171*, 218
Blackfriars, Greenwich, *92*
Blanche of Lancaster, *149-50*, 214, 295
Bleke, Gabriel, of Gloucestershire, 207, 225
Blount, Thomas, Leicester's man, 246, 265
Bodin, Jean, 36
Bohemia ("Boemland"), *184*
Boleyn, Anne, Consort of Henry VIII, King of England, 12, 296-97
Boleyn, Elizabeth Howard, Countess of Wiltshire, 297
Boleyn, Mary. See Carey, Mary Boleyn
Boleyn, Thomas, Earl of Wiltshire, 296-97
Bolingbroke, Henry of. See Henry IV, King of England
Borgarucci, Guilio ("Dr. Julio"), *80, 82, 116, 123*, 269, 274-76
Bossy, John, 16, 20
Bosworth, Battle of (1485), *152*
Boulogne, France, *111*, 207
Bourne, Warden of the Company of Stationers, 224
Bowes, Jerome, Sir, 44, *97*, 203
Bramshot, Sussex, 260-61
Brandon, Charles, Duke of Suffolk, *152-53, 155*, 215, 295
Brandon, Eleanor. See Clifford, Eleanor Brandon
Brandon, Frances. See Grey, Frances Brandon
Braye, Dorothy, Lady Chandos, *82*, 200, 296
Bridget of York, *151*
Briegerus, Julius, 12, 55
Brinkley, Stephen, 7
Brittany, *160*
Bromley, Thomas, Sir, Lord Chancellor, 284
Broughton, Richard, 267
Browne, Anne, wife of Charles Brandon, 215
Browne, Anthony, Viscount Montagu, 19
Browne, Mary. See Wriothesley, Mary Browne
Bruges, Netherlands, *69*, 275
Brutus, Marcus, 44, *179-80*

Brydges, Edmund, Lord Chandos, 200
Buchanan, George, 217
Buckingham, Duke of. See Stafford, Henry
Bulkeley, Richard, Sir, 209
Burghley, Lord. See Cecil, William
Burgoyne, F. J., 224
Butler, Thomas, 10th Earl of Ormonde, 8, *92-93*, 202
Buttler, Bald, *81*, 199, 225
Bysse, Margaret, 268
Bysse, Robert, 268

Caesar, Julius, 144, *179-80*, 255, 258
Calais, France, *110, 151*, 207
Calvin, Jean, 12, 218
Calvinists, 67
Cambridge University, *65, 76-77, 115, 125, 146, 175, 191-92*, 208, 214, 247
Cambridge, Earl of. See Richard (Plantagenet)
Camden, William, 13, 45, 47, 51, 213, 267
Campion, Edmund, S.J., 32, 201, 219
Canterbury, Archbishop of. See Cranmer, Thomas; Grindal, Edmund; Parker, Matthew
Capet, Hugh, 260
Carey, Catherine. See Knollys, Catherine Carey
Carey, George, Sir (later 2d Lord Hunsdon), 59, *105*, 205, 296
Carey, Henry, Lord Hunsdon, *104*, 203, 205, 284, 296
Carey, Mary Boleyn, 296
Carey, William, 296
Carnarvonshire, Wales, *119*
Carthaginians, *148, 183*
Casimir, John, of the Palatinate, *67, 76*, 198
Castile, *150*
Câteau-Cambrésis, Treaty of (1559), 207
Catherine de Medici, Queen Mother of France, 17, 200, 288
Catherine, Duchess of Braganza, 214
Catilina, Lucius Sergius, 43, *185*, 220, *233*
Cavendish, Charles, Sir, *173*, 219, 248
Cavendish, Elizabeth. See Stuart, Elizabeth Cavendish
Cavendish, William, 248
Cecil, Anne. See De Vere, Anne Cecil
Cecil, John, priest, 26
Cecil, Robert (later Earl of Salisbury), 286
Cecil, William Lord Burghley, 1-5, 7, 9, 11, 14, 16-17, 21, 32-34, 43, 47, 51, 59, 62, 77,

312 INDEX OF PROPER NAMES

84-85, 103, 115, 176, 197-98, 200, 202-5, 207-8, 213, 215-17, *243,* 245, 247-48, 266, 276, 283-84, 286-87
Cecily of York, *151,* 214
Chandos, Lady. See Braye, Dorothy
Chandos, Lord. See Brydges, Edmund
Charles I, King of England, 270
Charles V, Holy Roman Emperor, *69,* 197, 214
Charles, Archduke of Austria, 62, *79,* 199
Charles, Duke of Burgundy, "the Bold", *144*
Châteauneuf, French ambassador, 294
Châtillon, Odet, Cardinal de, *79, 80, 83,* 200, 225
Cheapside, London, *167*
Cheke, Edward, 203
Cheke, John, 21
Chester, England, *175,* 210, 220
Christ, 34, *111,* 254
Christian Directory (1584 et seq.), 7
Christmas, Robert, *240,* 246-47
Cicero, Marcus Tullius, *185, 192,* 220-21, 255
Clancy, Thomas, S.J., 42, 224
Clarence, Duke of. See George; Lionel
Clark, a pirate, *92,* 202
Clerc (Clark), William, *166,* 217
Clerk, Augustine, Captain, 202
Clifford, Anne, Countess of Dorchester, Pembroke, and Montgomery, 5
Clifford, Eleanor Brandon, Countess of Cumberland, *152-53, 155, 162, 164-66*, 215, 295
Clifford, George, 3d Earl of Cumberland, *152,* 215
Clifford, Henry, 2d Earl of Cumberland, 215, 295
Clifford, Margaret. See Stanley, Margaret Clifford
Clinton, Edward, Earl of Lincoln, 16
Cockyn, Henry, 16, 219
Colepeper, Martin, Dr., *95, 116,* 203, 208
Coligny, Gaspard de, seigneur de Châtillon, 200
Collinson, Patrick, 19, 276
Cologne, Germany, 228, 287, 289
Commynes, Philippe, *144*
Compton, William, Lord, 56
Condé, Henri I de Bourbon, Prince of, *168*
Condé, Louis I de Bourbon, Prince of, 197
Conference about the Next Succession (1595), 40

Constance of Brittany, *160*
Constance of Castile, *150,* 214, 295
Constans, (legendary) King, 202
Constantinople, *67*
Conway, John, Sir, 210
Cordell, William, Sir, Master of the Rolls, 275
Cornwallis, William, 56
Courtenay, Edward, Earl of Devon, 215
Courtenay, Henry, Marquess of Exeter, 215
Courtenay, William, 214
Coventry, England, 203, 266
Cranmer, Thomas, Archbishop of Canterbury, 12
Creighton, William, S.J., 61, 263, 285
Croft, James, Sir, 77, 198
Croker, Gerald, Sir, 209-10
Crompton, Rowland, Essex's man, *82-83,* 200, 268
Culpepper, Doctor. See Colepeper, Martin
Cumberland, Earl of. See Clifford, George; Clifford, Henry
Cumnor, near Oxford, *81, 91,* 265

Dacres, Ann. See Howard, Ann Dacres
Dale, Valentine, Dr., *80,* 199, 275
Darcy, George, *236-37,* 246
Darnley, Lord. See Stuart, Henry
Darnton, Robert, 45
Davies, Hugh, 5, 10, 54
Davis (Davies), Mother, sorceress, *241-42*
Davison, William, 203
Davus (character in Roman comedy), *79,* 199
Dawson, John, printer, 224
De la Pole, William, Duke of Suffolk, 44, *188-89,* 220-21, 252
De La Warr, Lord, See West, Thomas
De Vere, Anne Cecil, Countess of Oxford, 16, *243,* 248, 271, 297
De Vere, Edward, 17th Earl of Oxford, 14, 16, 18-21, 56-57, 201, *243,* 247-48, 271-72, 297
De Vere, Frances. See Howard, Frances de Vere
De Vere, John, 16th Earl of Oxford, 297
De Vere, Robert, 1st Earl of Oxford, *188-89,* 220, 252
Dee, John, Dr., *116,* 208
Defence of English Catholics (1584), 5, 7, 12, 33, 54, 279, 285, 294
Defense of Leicester (1584-85), 8-9, 249-51

INDEX OF PROPER NAMES 313

Denbigh, Lord. See Dudley, Robert
Denbigh, Wales, 99, 117–18, 121
Derby, Countess of. See Stanley, Margaret Clifford
Derby, Earl of. See Stanley, Henry; Stanley, Thomas
Des Trappes, French ambassador's secretary, 294
Desmond, Earl of. See Fitzgerald, Gerald
Despenser, Hugh, Earl of Winchester, 188–89, 220
Despenser, Hugh, Sir, 188–89, 220
Deucalion, 260
Develing. See Dublin
Devereux, Robert, 2d Earl of Essex, 208, 296
Devereux, Walter, 1st Earl of Essex, 21, 76, 80, 82–84, 200, 204, 267–68, 277, 296
Devon, Earl of. See Courtenay, Edward
Diana (goddess), 100
Dieppe, France, 23
Digby, George, Sir, of Coleshill, 116, 208, 273
Discours de la vie abominable (1585), 10–12, 26, 30, 223, 228, 287–90
Dorset, Marquess of. See Grey, Henry, Duke of Suffolk
Douai, France, 197
Doughty, Thomas, 100, 204
Douglas, Archibald, 6th Earl of Angus, 152, 155, 215, 295
Douglas, Margaret. See Stuart, Margaret Douglas
Dover Strait, 221
Drake, Francis, Sir, 100, 204
Drake, James, Dr., 224
Draycot, Alice, 83–84, 268, 277
Draycot, Mary, 268
Drayton Basset, Staffordshire, 28, 117, 225, 272–74
Drury, Drew, Sir, 123, 210–11
Drury, William, Sir, 210, 212
Dublin, Ireland, 83, 200, 267–68
Dublin, Marquess of. See De Vere, Robert
Dudley Castle, Staffordshire, 86, 89, 259
Dudley Plot (1556), 205
Dudley, Agnes. See Throgmorton, Agnes Dudley
Dudley, Ambrose, Earl of Warwick, 17, 76, 95, 105, 117, 122–23, 197, 205, 208, 255, 269, 272, 275, 296
Dudley, Amy. See Robsart, Amy

Dudley, Anne Russell, Countess of Warwick, 76, 198, 296
Dudley, Arthur (putative son of Leicester), 53
Dudley, Catherine. See Hastings, Catherine Dudley
Dudley, Edmund, 75, 111, 113–14, 189–90, 193, 198, 207, 260–61, 263–64, 296
Dudley, Edward, Lord, See Sutton, Edward
Dudley, Elizabeth Grey, 257, 296
Dudley, Guildford, 152, 155, 198, 295
Dudley, Henry, Sir, 296
Dudley, Jane Grey. See Grey, Jane, Lady
Dudley, Jane Guildford, Duchess of Northumberland, 212, 296
Dudley, John, Duke of Northumberland, 14, 49, 56, 74–75, 77, 94–95, 98–99, 105, 111, 113–14, 123, 125, 131–33, 137, 146, 152, 154, 163, 165, 174–75, 181, 193–94, 198, 206–7, 209, 212, 214, 217, 256–58, 261, 263–64, 296
Dudley, John, Earl of Warwick, 296
Dudley, John, Lord. See Sutton, John
Dudley, John, of Atherington, 251, 264, 296
Dudley, John, of Stoke Newington, 269
Dudley, Mary. See Sidney, Mary Dudley
Dudley, Piers (error for John), 251, 260–61
Dudley, Robert, Earl of Leicester, ix–x, 1–32, 35–52, 54–55, 57–58, 60–62, 72–110, 112–37, 146, 154–55, 163, 167, 169, 171–77, 186–95, 197–212, 217–20, 227–28, 229–44, 245–55, 261–63, 265–76, 278, 282–93, 296
Dudley, Robert (Leicester's base son), 86, 207, 269–70, 296
Dudley, Robert, Lord Denbigh, 5, 55, 58, 81, 89, 131, 133, 199, 296
Dugdale, William, 45
Duncan-Jones, Katherine, 263
Dundee, Scotland, 282
Dutch rebels, 17, 244
Dyer, Edward, Sir, 81, 199
Dymock, Southampton's man, 248

Edgar Etheling, 160
Edgar, King of England, 201
Edmund "Crookback", Earl of Lancaster, 148–50
Edmund Langley, 1st Duke of York, 150–51, 214, 295
Edward, the Black Prince, 150, 159, 214, 295
Edward "the Confessor", King of England, 160, 202

Edward "the Outlaw", *160*
Edward (Plantagenet), Earl of Warwick, *144–46, 151, 178–79,* 295
Edward I, King of England, *148*
Edward II, King of England, *138, 188,* 220, 253
Edward III, King of England, *148–51, 157–59, 162, 165,* 214, 295
Edward IV, King of England, *104, 132, 135, 145–46, 149, 151–53, 157, 165, 169, 178–79,* 202, 212, 214, 256, 263, 295
Edward V, King of England, *134, 151,* 295
Edward VI, King of England, *71, 74, 94, 98–99, 111, 123, 125–26, 131, 137–38, 152, 163, 165, 193,* 198, 217, 295
Edward, 2d Duke of York, 214, 295
Edward, Prince of Wales (son of Henry VI), *134, 149,* 214, 295
Edwin (Edwy, Eadwig), King, *88,* 201
Elizabeth I, Queen of England, 1–2, 7–9, 14–24, 30, 33, 35, 37–39, 45–50, 52–54, 57–60, *71, 73–81, 83, 85–86, 88, 93, 95–98, 102–12,* 118–20, *124, 126–28, 130, 133–34, 136–42, 145–46, 150, 152–55, 163–64, 167–74, 176–94,* 198, 200, 202–4, 206–11, 213, 215, 218–19, *230–33, 237, 239, 243,* 244–45, 247–50, 252–53, 255, 261, 263, 265–67, 269–72, 274–77, 279–88, 290–91, 294–97
Elizabeth of York, Consort of Henry VII, *133, 145–46, 151–52,* 212, 295
Emerson, Ralph, Jesuit lay brother, 6, 54, 286
Englefield, Francis, Sir, 11–12, 61
English Mercurie, 56
Eric XIV, King of Sweden, *79–80,* 199, *237,* 246
Errington, George, 10
Esher, Surrey, 269
Essex, Countess of. See Knollys, Lettice
Essex, Earl of. See Devereux, Robert; Devereux, Walter
Esther (biblical figure), 212
Ethelbert, King of Kent, *78,* 198
Eu, France, 289
Execution of Justice in England (1583) 5, 32–33, 43, *66,* 197, 285, 287, 294
Exeter, Marquess of. See Courtenay, Henry

Fagan, Cicely, 268
Fagot, Henry, spy, 23

Fairfax (error for Fervaques), *238,* 247
Family of Love ("Familians"), *185,* 220
Farnese, Alexander, Duke of Parma, 214
Ferrers, Humphrey, Sir, of Tamworth, *122,* 209, 273–74
Fervaques, Anjou's man, *238,* 246–47
Finland, Duke of. See John, Duke of Finland
Fitzalan, Catherine, *155,* 215
Fitzalan, Henry, 12th Earl of Arundel, 16, 18, *111, 155, 167, 172, 174–75,* 207, 215, 218–19
Fitzalan, Mary. See Howard, Mary Fitzalan
Fitzalan, William, 11th Earl of Arundel, 215
Fitzgerald, Gerald, 15th Earl of Desmond, 202
Fitzherbert, Thomas, of Swinnerton, 7, 9, 24, 29, 31
Flanders, *67, 69, 149, 185–86, 230, 239,* 286
Fleetwood, William, Recorder of London, *105,* 206, 273
Fleix, Treaty of (1580), 220
Flinton, George, printer, 7, 9
Flores Calvinistici (1586), 3, 12, 51, 227
Flushing, Netherlands, *92,* 202, 244
Forster, Anthony, *81,* 265
Fortescue, John, Sir, of Salden, *104,* 205
Fowler, Thomas, *86,* 201
Fowler, William, 201
France, *67, 69, 78–79, 83–85, 92, 110, 142, 148, 159, 165, 168, 184*
Frederick III of the Palatinate, 198

Galen, *116*
Gates, John, Sir, *166,* 204, 217
Gates, one, 43, *100–2,* 204
Gaunt (Ghent), Netherlands, *69, 149,* 197
Gaveston, Piers, Earl of Cornwall, 44, *188–89,* 220, 252
Geneva, *171,* 218
Gentili, Alberico, 55, 263
Geoffrey, Count of Brittany, *160*
George, Duke of Clarence, *144–46, 151, 169, 178–79,* 295
Germany, *69, 72, 148, 168, 184*
Gerrard, William, Lord Chancellor of Ireland, 268
Ghibellines, *144*
Gifford, George, 56
Gifford, Gilbert, priest, 59–60, 210
Gifford, John, of Chillington, *123,* 210
Gifford, Thomas, 210

INDEX OF PROPER NAMES 315

Gifford, William, Dr., 210
Glasgow, Archbishop of. See Beaton, James
Gloucester, Duke of. See Humphrey; Richard III, King of England
Gorges, Arthur, 56
Gracious (Gracechurch) Street, London, 43, *64*, 197
Grecians, *67-69, 148, 187*
Greenwich Palace, *76*, 201, 284
Greville, Fulke, Lord Brooke, 210
Greville, Lodovick, *122*, 210
Grey, Arthur, Lord Grey of Wilton, *104*, 205
Grey, Catherine. See Seymour, Catherine Grey
Grey, Edward, 263, 296
Grey, Elizabeth. See Dudley, Elizabeth Grey
Grey, Frances Brandon, Duchess of Suffolk, *152, 155, 162, 164-66*, 215, 217, 295
Grey, Henry, Duke of Suffolk, *131-33, 137, 152, 155*, 212, 215, 217, 295
Grey, Jane, Lady, *152, 155*, 198, 214, 295
Grey, Mary, *152*, 295
Grimston, Stafford's man, 292
Grindal, Edmund, Archbishop of Canterbury, *81, 99, 123*, 274-76
Guaras, Antonio de, 267
Guelphs, *144*
Guernsey, Isle of, *105*, 206
Guildford, Jane. See Dudley, Jane Guildford
Guinea, *71*
Guise, Henri, Duc de, 23, 25, 59, 200, 220
Gunpowder Plot (1605), 3

Hackney, London, *86*, 201
Hakluyt, Richard, 6, 54
Hales, John, 217
Hall, Hugh, priest, *173*, 219
Haman (biblical figure), *135*, 212
Hampton Court, 7, 53, *106*, 279
Harcourt, Dorothy Robinson, 273
Harcourt, Walter, Sir, *122*, 273
Hardwick, Elizabeth, Countess of Shrewsbury, 58, *133, 152*, 211-12, 219, *243*, 248
Harington, John, Sir, 8, 13, 41, 216, 218
Harold II, King of England, *94*, 202
Harris, a pirate, *92*, 202
Hastings, Catherine Dudley, Countess of Huntingdon, *132*, 199, 296
Hastings, Catherine Pole, Countess of Huntingdon, *151, 177, 179*, 215, 220, 295
Hastings, Francis, 2d Earl of Huntingdon, 215, 295
Hastings, Henry, 3d Earl of Huntingdon, 3, 37-40, 61, *94-95, 103-6, 114, 126-27, 131-34, 138, 143-47, 150-51, 153, 163-64, 168, 177, 179, 193,* 204-6, 212, 214-15, 255, 295-96
Hastings, William, Lord, *134*, 212, 256, 263
Hatton, Christopher, Sir, 2, 17, 22, 43, 47, 49, 57-58, *139-40, 173, 175*, 208, 213, 219, 284
Hector, *104*
Heiward, Rowland, Sir, Lord Mayor of London, *105*, 206
Heliogabalus. See Varius Avitus Bassasius
Heneage, Thomas, Sir, *76*, 198, 246
Henri III, King of France, 46, *79*, 199-200, 247
Henri IV, King of France, *168*, 218
Henry II, King of England, *160*
Henry III, King of Castile, *150, 160*, 214
Henry III, King of England, *148-49*
Henry IV, King of England, *94, 132, 135, 147, 149-50, 157, 177*, 202, 212, 295
Henry V, King of England, *147, 149*, 258, 295
Henry VI, King of England, *99, 104, 131, 134-35, 138, 147, 149, 151, 158, 165, 181, 188*, 221, 253, 295
Henry VII, King of England, *74, 94, 113-14, 123, 126, 131, 142, 144-47, 149-54, 160, 179, 189-90*, 212, 214, 295
Henry VIII, King of England, *74, 94, 113, 126, 151-52, 154-56, 162-67, 169, 177, 179, 190*, 201, 217, 295-97
Herbert, Henry, 2d Earl of Pembroke, *104, 155, 167*, 202, 205, 215, *235*, 255, 296
Herbert, Mary Sidney, Countess of Pembroke, *104*, 205, 296
Herbert, William, 1st Earl of Pembroke, *130, 167*, 211, 218
Hercules, 262
Hereford, Bishop of. See Scory, John
Hertford, Earl of. See Seymour, Edward
Hibbott, John. See Huband, John, Sir
Hicks, Leo, S.J., 4, 31, 54, 56, 58
Holdenby (Hatton's house), 219
Holmes, Peter, 31, 56
Holyrood House, Edinburgh, 8, 282
Hook Norton, Oxfordshire, *122*, 209

316 INDEX OF PROPER NAMES

Hopton, Owen, Sir, Lieutenant of the Tower, *105*, 206
Horsey, Edward, Sir, *104, 112*, 205, 207, 246, 269
Hotson, Leslie, 27–28, 31, 54
Howard, Ann Dacres, Countess of Arundel, *243*, 247–48
Howard, Catherine, Consort of Henry VIII, 14, 297
Howard, Catherine. See Berkeley, Catherine Howard
Howard, Charles, Earl of Nottingham, 277, 284
Howard, Charles, Lord, 56
Howard, Douglass. See Sheffield, Douglass Howard, Lady
Howard, Edmund, Lord, 297
Howard, Elizabeth Stafford, Duchess of Norfolk, 297
Howard, Elizabeth. See Boleyn, Elizabeth Howard; Radcliffe, Elizabeth Howard
Howard, Frances de Vere, Countess of Surrey, 297
Howard, Frances. See Seymour, Frances Howard
Howard, Henry, Earl of Surrey (poet), 14, 297
Howard, Henry, Lord (later Earl of Northampton), 14, 16, 18–23, 26, 30–31, 56–58, 61, 198, 204, 210, 229, *243*, 248, 270–72, 297
Howard, Jane. See Neville, Jane Howard
Howard, Margaret. See Arundell, Margaret Howard
Howard, Mary Fitzalan, Duchess of Norfolk, 218, 297
Howard, Mary. See Sutton, Mary Howard
Howard, Muriel. See Knyvett, Muriel Howard
Howard, Philip, Earl of Arundel, 14, 18, 23, 26, 56, 218, 229, *243*, 247–48, 291–92, 297
Howard, Thomas, 2d Duke of Norfolk, 297
Howard, Thomas, 3d Duke of Norfolk, 214, 254, 263, 297
Howard, Thomas, 4th Duke of Norfolk, 1, 14–16, 21, 50, *167, 172–73*, 218, *243*, 246–48, 297
Howard, Thomas, Earl of Suffolk, 297
Howard, Thomas, Lord, 56
Howard, William, Lord Howard of Effingham, 279, 297

Huband, John, Sir, 77, 198
Hume, David, 45
Humphrey, Duke of Gloucester, *188*, 220
Hungary, *160, 184*
Hunnis, Robin, *83–84*, 267–68
Hunnis, William, *84*, 200
Hunsdon, Lord. See Carey, George; Carey, Henry
Huntingdon, Earl of. See Hastings, Henry

Indies, 258
Inner Temple, London, 204
Ireland, *100, 102, 104, 177, 186*, 205, 267–68
Isabella, Consort of Charles V, Holy Roman Emperor, 214
Isabella, Queen of Castile, 214
Israel, *148*
Italy, *82, 121, 144, 183*, 252

James IV, King of Scotland, *152*, 215, 295
James V, King of Scotland, 295
James VI, King of Scotland (James I of England), 4, 8, 12, 37–38, 41, 61, *154, 156, 161–62, 169–71, 178*, 212, 215–16, 218, 281–82, 295
James, Thomas, 3
Jebb, Samuel, 45
Jermine, Robert, Sir, *127*, 211
Jersey, Isle of, *105*, 205
Jerusalem, Palestine, *138, 160*
Joanna the Mad, 214
John of Gaunt, Duke of Lancaster, *147, 149–50, 152, 160*, 214, 295
John, Duke of Finland, 199, 246
John, King of England, *160*
John, King of Portugal, *150, 160*
Jones, Robert, secretary to N. Throgmorton, 200, 266
Judah, *148*
Judas Iscariot, *172, 232*
Julio, Doctor. See Borgarucci, Guilio

Kafka, Franz, 28
Katherine of York, *151*, 214
Katherine, Consort of Henry III of Castile, *150, 160*, 214
Kenilworth (Leicester's house), 12, 21, *76, 95, 99, 105–6, 117–19, 123*, 198, 202–3, 206, 209, 267
Killigrew, Henry, Sir, 202
Killigrew, William, *93*, 202, 211

INDEX OF PROPER NAMES 317

Killingworth. See Kenilworth
Kingsley, Charles, 26
Knell, T., Essex's chaplain, 268
Knollys, Anne. See West, Anne Knollys
Knollys, Catherine Carey, *105*, 205, 296
Knollys, Elizabeth. See Leighton, Elizabeth Knollys
Knollys, Francis, Sir, 17, *95, 105*, 206, 284, 296
Knollys, Lettice, Countess of Essex, of Leicester, 19, *76, 80, 82, 87, 89, 95, 105,* 116, *127-28, 136,* 199-200, 205, 208, 213, 219, *234,* 267, 269-70, 274, 296
Knollys, Robert, *128,* 211, 296
Knollys, William (later Earl of Banbury), 82, 200, 296
Knox, John, 12
Knyvett, Catherine. See Paget, Catherine Knyvett
Knyvett, Henry, Sir, 297
Knyvett, Margaret. See Vavasour, Margaret Knyvett
Knyvett, Muriel Howard, 297
Knyvett, Thomas, 272
Knyvett, Thomas, Sir, 297
Kyd, Thomas, playwright, 204

Lacedaemonians, *183*
Lafin, one, 247
Lais, of Corinth, courtesan, *88*
Lambeth Palace, London, 16
Lancaster, Duke of. See Henry IV, King of England; John of Gaunt
Lancaster, Earl of. See Edmund "Crookback"
Lancaster, House of, *104, 143-50, 152-53, 183*
Lane, Ralph, Sir, *106, 123,* 206
Lea, an Irishman, *83-84*
Leander, See Alberti, Leandro
Lee, Anne Paget, Lady, 58, 272, 297
Lee, Benedict, of Bigging, 200
Lee, Henry, Sir, Queen's Champion, *122,* 200, 209-10, 269, 272, 297
Lee, Richard, *122,* 209-10
Lee, Thomas, 200
Leicester's Commonwealth (1584), ix-x, 1-13, 16-22, 25-46, 50-52, 55-56, 60, 204, 210-11, 213-17, 221-29, 245-46, 249-50, 252-56, 260-63, 268-69, 271-72, 274, 276, 279, 281-87, 291-92

Leicester's Ghost, 13, 223, 227
Leicester, Countess of. See Knollys, Lettice
Leicester, Earl of. See Dudley, Robert; Sidney, Robert
Leighton, Elizabeth Knollys, *105,* 206, 296
Leighton, John, Sir, 296
Leighton, Thomas, Sir, 23, 43, 77, *105, 128,* 200, 205-6, 296
Lennox, Countess of. See Stuart, Margaret Douglas
Lennox, Duke of. See Stuart, Esmé
Lennox, Earl of. See Stuart, Charles; Stuart, Matthew
Leslie, John, Bishop of Ross, 7, 31, 40, 61, 214, 216-17, 221, 279
Lethington. See Maitland, William
Letter of Estate (ca.1585), 13, 46, 50, 204, 219, 226-27, 267, 269
Lever, Thomas, preacher, 266
Lieth, Scotland, siege of (1560), *104,* 205
Lilly, Stafford's man, 10, 30, 290-91
Lincoln, Earl of. See Clinton, Edward
Lionel, Duke of Clarence, *149-51, 160,* 295
Lleyn Peninsula, Wales, *120,* 209
Lloyd, Richard, Essex's man, *82-83,* 200
London, England, 6, 9-10, 27, 54, *65, 81, 83, 85, 103, 105, 112, 120, 132, 146, 171, 173, 175,* 202, 204, 206, 214, 219, *234,* 245, 262, 267, 272-73, 282-83
Lopez, Roderigo, Dr., *116,* 208
Lorraine, Cardinal of, 200
Loughton (F. Stonor's house), 203
Louis XI, King of France, *144*
Louis XII, King of France, *152,* 215, 295
Ludlow, Shropshire, 77, *120,* 198, 209
Lutherans, 67
Lyons, France, *173,* 219

Machiavelli, Niccolo, *132, 192,* 254
Maitland, William, of Lethington, 216
Mallet, *86*
Manuel Fortunatus, King of Portugal, 214
March, Earl of. See Mortimer, Edmund; Mortimer, Roger
Mardocheus. See Mordecai
Margaret of Anjou, Consort of Henry VI, King of England, *188-89,* 221, 295
Margaret, Countess of Salisbury, *151, 179,* 215, 295
Marius, Gaius, *144*
Marlowe, Christopher, 211

318 INDEX OF PROPER NAMES

Marsh Annotator, 53, 201, 211–12, 216, 218
Martelli, Hieronimo. See Samerie, Henri, S.J.
Martin Marprelate, 8, 42
Mary I, Queen of England, 71, 74–75, 123, 132–34, 137, 146, 152, 163–64, 166–68, 198, 206, 214, 217, 295
Mary Stuart, Queen of Scots, 4, 12–16, 21, 23, 26–27, 29, 31–32, 35–41, 59–61, 130, 142, 152, 154, 156, 161–62, 167–69, 171, 174, 178, 200, 206, 211–12, 215–21, 243, 248, 285, 294–95
Matius, Gaius, 255
Matthew of Westminster, 216
Mauvissière, Michel de Castelnau, Seigneur de la, 9, 17–20
Medici, See Catherine de Medici
Megarians, 148
Mendoza, Bernardino de, 9, 20–21, 23, 39, 57, 59, 61, 198, 202, 204, 212, 219, 228, 245
Merchant Adventurers Company, 207
Midas, 263
Milan, Italy, 29, 160, 219
Mildmay, Walter, Sir, Chancellor of the Exchequer, 206, 284
Moffett, Thomas, Captain, 239, 247
Montagu, Lord, See Pole, Henry
Montagu, Viscount. See Browne, Anthony
Montague, Edward, Sir, 166, 217
Montmorency, Anne de, Constable of France, 85, 200
Moody, Michael, Stafford's man, 290–91, 294
Mordecai, 135, 212
More, Thomas, Sir, 212, 256, 263
Morgan, Thomas, 6, 13, 24, 26–28, 31, 54, 58, 60, 245, 285
Mortimer, Anne, 150–51, 214, 295
Mortimer, Edmund, 3d Earl of March, 150, 214, 295
Mortimer, Philippe, 150, 295
Mortimer, Roger, 4th Earl of March, 177, 214, 295
Mowbray, Thomas, Duke of Norfolk, 188–89, 220

Naples, Kingdom of, 148
Nashe, Thomas, author, 42
Nau, Queen Mary's secretary, 27, 218
Naunton, Robert, Sir, 13, 45
Navarre, King of. See Henri IV, King of France

Neale, John Ernest, 25, 198
Nero, Emperor of Rome, 86, 121, 201, 209
Netherlands, 3, 12–13, 17, 29, 47, 197, 220, 244–46
Neville, Anne, Consort of Richard III, 133, 212
Neville, Charles, 6th Earl of Westmoreland, 29, 70, 197, 239, 247, 297
Neville, Henry, Sir, 43, 128, 211, 217
Neville, Jane Howard, Countess of Westmoreland, 297
Neville, Richard, Earl of Salisbury, 135, 212
Neville, Richard, Earl of Warwick, 94, 104, 132, 135, 202, 212, 257, 263
Newhaven (Le Havre), France, 69, 122, 197, 272, 275
News from Heaven and Hell (ca.1590), 13, 46, 50, 99
Nicholas, Edward, Sir, 224
Nicholson, William, Dr., 285
Niklas, Hendrik, sectarian, 220
Noel, Henry, 56
Norfolk, Duke of. See Howard, Thomas; Mowbray, Thomas
Norfolk, England, 173, 246
Normandy, 161
North Hall, Hertfordshire, 117, 208
North, Roger, 2d Lord, 18, 73, 95, 127, 197
Northumberland, Duke of. See Dudley, John
Northumberland, Earl of. See Percy, Henry
Norton, Richard, the "Old Rebel", 70, 197
Norton, Thomas, lawyer, 33, 54
Norwich Castle, Norfolk, 246
Nottingham, Earl of. See Howard, Charles

O'Neill, Shan, Irish rebel, 203–4
Octavius, See Augustus Caesar
Orange, Prince of. See William, Prince of Orange
Ormonde, Earl of. See Butler, Thomas
Osborne, Edward, Sir, Lord Mayor of London, 6, 285–86
Oxford University, 82, 91, 109, 115–17, 146, 191, 201, 208, 269
Oxford, Earl of. See De Vere, Edward; De Vere, John; De Vere, Robert
Oyselet, George L', printer, 7

Pace, John, jester, 254, 263
Paget, Anne. See Lee, Anne Paget

INDEX OF PROPER NAMES

Paget, Catherine Knyvett, Lady, 271, 297
Paget, Charles, 23–24, 26, 28, 58–60, 197, 248, 297
Paget, Henry, 2d Lord, 271, 297
Paget, Nazareth Newton, Lady, 24
Paget, Thomas, 3d Lord, 6, 13, 23–25, 27–29, 31, 56–59, 205, 212, 217, 271–73, 285, 297
Paget, William, 1st Lord, *166*, 217
Paget, William, 4th Lord, 59, 205
Painter, William, author, 201
Papists, *66–70, 72–73*, 77, *115–16, 130, 141, 169, 173, 181–82, 185*
Paramore, Richard, of London, 272–74
Paris, France, 5–7, 9, 19, 23–27, 29, 36, 59, *173*, 227, 266
Parker, Matthew, Archbishop of Canterbury, 9, *155*, 215
Parker, Warden of the Company of Stationers, 224
Parliament, 75, *97, 108, 134, 162, 164–66, 191*
Parma, Duke of. See Farnese, Alexander
Parry Plot (1585), 60
Parry, William, Dr., 2, 24, 54, 213
Parsons, Robert, S.J., 3–7, 13, 24, 26–29, 31, 56, 58, 60–61, 206, 219, 227, 248
Patagonia, 204
Paul's Cross, London, *146*, 214
Paulet, Amias, Sir, *105*, 205–6, 211, 219
Paulet, William, Marquess of Winchester, *167*, 218
Pausanias, assassin, *187*
Pembroke, Earl of. See Herbert, Henry; Herbert, William
Penteneis, the merchant, *83*, 200
Percy, Henry "Hotspur", *135*, 212
Percy, Henry, 1st Earl of Northumberland, *135*, 212
Percy, Henry, 8th Earl of Northumberland, 18–19, 21, 23, 26, 55–56, 58
Percy, Thomas, Earl of Worcester, *135*, 212
Perrot, John, Sir, 5, *104*, 205
Persecutione anglicana, De (1582), 2
Persons, Robert. See Parsons, Robert
Perth, Scotland, 282
Peter I, King of Castile, 214
Petworth, Sussex (Northumberland's house), 21, 23
Phalaris, Tyrant of Agrigentum, *117*, 208
Phelippes, Thomas, Walsingham's man, 59
Philip II, King of Spain, 59–60, *69, 110, 150, 185*, 197, 202, 207, 214, 228, *239*
Philip of Macedon, *187*

Philippe, Consort of John, King of Portugal, *150, 160*, 214
Plowden, Edmund, lawyer, 40, 217
Poland ("Polonia"), *184*
Pole, Catherine. See Hastings, Catherine Pole
Pole, Henry, Lord Montagu, *151, 179*, 215, 295
Pole, Reginald, Cardinal, *151*, 215, 295
Pole, Richard, Sir, *151*, 215, 295
Pole, Ursula, See Stafford, Ursula Pole
Poley, Robert, 10, *127*, 211
Politiques, 36
Pollen, John Hungerford, S.J., 31, 54
Polydore Vergil. See Vergil, Polydore
Pompey, "the Great", *144*
Pontefract Castle, Yorkshire, *134*, 212
Popham, John, Sir, Attorney General, *243*, 248
Portugal, *69, 146, 150, 159*, 197
Prisons: Bastille (Paris), 13, 27; Fleet, 246, 273; Marshalsea, 210; Newgate, 219, 247, 294; Poultry Street Counter, 6
Privy Council, 8, 16, 19–20, *99, 161, 164, 166–67, 170–71, 194*, 202, 205–6, 210, 212, 217, 224, *233, 239*, 245, 248, 267, 273, 280
Puritans, *67–69, 72–73, 104–5, 185, 232, 239–40*, 287

Quadra, Alvarez de, Bishop of Aquila, 266

Raby, House of, 259
Radcliffe, Elizabeth Howard, Countess of Sussex, 297
Radcliffe, Henry, 2d Earl of Sussex, 297
Radcliffe, Thomas, 3d Earl of Sussex, 14–15, 17–23, 29, 43, 51, 55, 77, *85, 92, 99, 102–3, 176*, 198, 202–5, 246, 270, 297
Raleigh, Walter, Sir, 22, 54, 56, *92*, 202, 271, 294
Randolph, Thomas, Diplomat, 215
Ratclif, Charles, 1
Read, Conyers, 31, 203, 269
Rheims, France, 10, *115*, 197, 210, 228, 285, 287, 289
Richard (Plantagenet), 3d Duke of York, *99, 131, 135, 150–51, 181*, 203, 212, 214, 295
Richard (Plantagenet), Earl of Cambridge, 214, 295
Richard I, King of England, *138, 160*, 213, 259

Richard II, King of England, *96*, *135*, *138*, *144*, *149–51*, *159*, *177*, *188*, 202, 212, 220, 253, 295
Richard III, King of England, 49, *94*, *131*, *133–34*, *146–47*, *151–52*, *165*, *169*, *178*, 202, 212, 214–15, 263, 295
Richmond, Earl of. See Henry VII, King of England; Tudor, Edmund
Ridley, Nicholas, Bishop of London, 214
Ridolfi Plot (1571), 15
Roberts, Peter R., x, 203
Robinson, Dorothy. See Harcourt, Dorothy Robinson
Robinson, John, 273–74
Robinson, Thomas, of Drayton Basset, *99*, *122*, 272–75
Robinson, William, of Drayton Basset, *122*, 272
Robsart, Amy, Lady Dudley, 31, 55, *81–82*, *86*, *90–92*, 200–1, *235*, 246, 265–67, 296
Roger of Wendover, 216
Rogers, Thomas (alias Nicholas Berden), 9–10
Rogers, Thomas, of Bryanstone, 13, 227
Romans, *94*, *144*, *148*, *179*, *183*, 259
Rome, Italy, 26, *115*, *173*, 197
Ross, Bishop of. See Leslie, John
Rouen, France, 5–7, 9, 31, 61, 286
Rousseau, Jean-Jacques, 45
Royal Exchange, London, *238*, 247
Russell, Anne. See Dudley, Anne Russell
Russell, Francis, 2d Earl of Bedford, 17, *104*, 198, 205, 284
Ruthven, Scotland, 282

Sackville, Robert, Earl of Dorset, 297
Sadler, Ralph, Sir, 219
St. Albans, Battle of (1455), 212
St. Andrews, Archbishop of. See Adamson, Patrick
St. Asaph, Bishop of, 287
St. Paul's, London, 214, *241*
Salamis, Isle of, *148*
Salic Law, *142*
Salisbury, Countess of. See Margaret, Countess of Salisbury
Salisbury, Earl of. See Neville, Richard
Salmon, J. H. M., 223
Salvariccia, Bartolome, 204
Salvatore, a stranger, *100*
Samerie, Henri, S.J., 60

Sander, Nicholas, Dr., 19, *70*, 197
Sands (Sandys), Edwin, Archbishop of York, *146*, 214
Sardanapalus, King of Assyria, *86*, 201
Savage, Mr., 209
Saxony, 67
Scarborough, Yorkshire, 10, 54
Scory, John, Bishop of Hereford, 10, *233–34*, 245
Scory, Sylvan, 10, *234–35*, 245–46
Scotland, *78*, *104*, *161–62*, *168*, *170–71*, *186*, 201, 215–16
Scotland, Line of *134*, *152–54*, *156–57*, *162–63*, *176–78*, 217
Scott, George, *97*, 203
Scott, Walter, Sir, 45
Seymour, Anne Stanhope, Duchess of Somerset, *137*, 213
Seymour, Catherine Grey, Countess of Hertford, 38–39, *152*, *155*, 215–16, 295
Seymour, Edward, Duke of Somerset, 14, *85*, *94*, *111*, *131*, *137*, *174*, *181*, 207, 212–13, 219
Seymour, Edward, Earl of Hertford, 38, *152*, *155*, 215, 295, 297
Seymour, Edward, Lord Beauchamp, 215, 295
Seymour, Frances Howard, Countess of Hertford, *176*, 220, 269, 297
Seymour, Thomas, 216
Seymour, Thomas, Lord, *137*, 213
Sha (Shaw), Ralph, Friar, *146*, 214
Sheares, William, printer, 224
Sheffield (Shrewsbury's house), 12
Sheffield, Douglass Howard, Lady, 10, 15, 24–25, 29–30, 52, 59–60, *81–82*, *86–90*, 199, 201, 207, 220, *237–38*, 246–47, 269–71, 277, 288–89, 294, 296–97
Sheffield, John, 2d Lord of Butterwick, *82*, 200, 269
Shelley, William, of Michelgrove, 8, 23–24
Shrewsbury, Countess of. See Hardwick, Elizabeth
Shrewsbury, Earl of. See Talbot, George; Talbot, John
Sicily, *148*
Sidney, Frances Walsingham, 296
Sidney, Henry, Sir, *104*, 202–3, 205, *233*, *235*, 245, 255, 268–69, 284, 296
Sidney, Mary Dudley, Lady, 199, 205, 256, 296

INDEX OF PROPER NAMES

Sidney, Mary. See Herbert, Mary Sidney
Sidney, Philip, Sir, 8–9, 18, 42, *81*, 199, 202, 205, 211, *231, 233*, 244, 249–51, 263–64, 296
Sidney, Robert, 2d Earl of Leicester, 199, 296
Simier, Jean de, diplomat, 17–19, *85, 92, 95*, 201–2, 204, 213, *238–39*, 246–47
Smerwick, Ireland, massacre (1579), 205
Smith, Thomas, Customer of the Port of London, 207, 246
Smith, Thomas, Sir, 17
Smithfield, London, *116*
Snowden Forest, Wales, *99, 117, 119*, 209
Somerset, Duchess of. See Seymour, Anne Stanhope
Somerset, Duke of. See Beaufort, Edmund; Beaufort, John; Seymour, Edward
Somerville Plot (1583), 59, 219
Somerville, John, 219
Southam, Warwickshire, *99*, 203
Southampton, Earl of. See Wriothesley, Henry; Wriothesley, Thomas
Southern, A. C., 54
Southouse, Christopher, Huntingdon's man, *132*, 212
Southwell, Francis, 16, 19–20, 56–57
Spain, *78, 148, 159, 186*
Spencer, See Despenser
Spenser, Edmund, poet, 270
Spoleto, Italy, *121*
Stafford Plot (1587), 294
Stafford, Dorothy, Lady, 18, 24, 292, 295, 297
Stafford, Edward, Sir, 5–6, 9–11, 13, 15, 17–18, 24–25, 29–31, 59–61, 197, 202, 215, 228–29, 246–47, 270, 285–92, 294–95, 297
Stafford, Elizabeth. See Howard, Elizabeth Stafford
Stafford, Henry, Duke of Buckingham, *131*, 212, 215
Stafford, Henry, Lord, 215, 273, 295, 297
Stafford, Robert, Sir (error for Edward), 229, *237*
Stafford, Ursula Pole, Lady, 215, 295
Stafford, William (Sir Edward's brother), 294
Stafford, William, of Grafton, 295, 297
Stallings, a courier, 290–92
Stanhope, Anne. See Seymour, Anne Stanhope

Stanley, Ferdinando, Lord Strange, 5th Earl of Derby, 38, 283, 295
Stanley, Henry, 4th Earl of Derby, 38, 60, *153*, 284, 295
Stanley, Margaret Clifford, Countess of Derby, 38, *153, 155*, 295
Stanley, Thomas, 1st Earl of Derby, *131*, 212
Stanley, William, Sir, 212
Star Chamber, 210, *233*, 269–70, 273
Stephen, King of England, *160*
Stephens, Richard, priest, 56–57
Sterling, Scotland, 282
Stinter, a courier, 6, 286
Stoke Newington, London, *86*, 269
Stokes, Adrian, *165*, 217
Stonor, Francis, *95*, 203
Story, John, Dr., 247
Stow, John, *113*
Strafford, Earl of. See Wentworth, Thomas
Strange, Lord. See Stanley, Ferdinando
Strype, John, 45, 276
Stuart, Arabella, 12, 38, 58, *131, 133–34, 152, 154–56*, 211–12, 215, 295
Stuart, Charles, 5th Earl of Lennox, 12, *152*, 211, 215, 295
Stuart, Elizabeth Cavendish, Countess of Lennox, *152*, 211, 215, 295
Stuart, Esmé, Duke of Lennox, 12
Stuart, Henry, Lord Darnley, 12, 38, *161*, 215, 295
Stuart, James, Earl of Arran, 282
Stuart, James. See James VI, King of Scotland
Stuart, Margaret Douglas, Countess of Lennox, 38, *86, 152*, 201, 212, 215, 295
Stuart, Mary. See Mary Stuart, Queen of Scots
Stuart, Matthew, 4th Earl of Lennox, *152*, 201, 215, 295
Stubbs, John, 54
Suetonius, *119*
Suffolk, Duke of. See Brandon, Charles; De la Pole, William; Grey, Henry
Suffolk, House of, *94, 126, 146, 153–56, 162–63, 167*
Sulla, Lucius Cornelius, *144*
Surrey, Earl of. See Howard, Henry; Howard, Philip
Sussex, Earl of. See Radcliffe, Henry; Radcliffe, Thomas
Sutton, Edward, 2d Lord Dudley, 296

INDEX OF PROPER NAMES

Sutton, Edward, 4th Lord Dudley of Dudley Castle, 201, 258, 260, 264, 273, 296–97
Sutton, John, 1st Lord Dudley, 258–61, 264, 296
Sutton, John 3d Lord Dudley, 296
Sutton, Mary Howard, Lady Dudley, 201, 296–97
Sutton, Richard, Sir, 259
Sweden, Duke of, King of. See Eric XIV
Swynford, Hugh, Sir, 214
Swynford, Katherine, *149*, 214, 295

Tadcaster, Battle of (1461), *145*, 214
Talbot, George, 6th Earl of Shrewsbury, 12, *133, 174, 178–79*, 212, 219–20, *243*, 248, 284
Talbot, Gilbert (later 7th Earl of Shrewsbury), *133*, 212, 219
Talbot, John, 1st Earl of Shrewsbury, 257, 263, 296
Talbot, John, Viscount Lisle, 257, 263, 296
Talbot, Margaret Beauchamp, Countess of Shrewsbury, 257, 263, 296
Tamworth, Staffordshire, 209, 273
Tarquins of Rome, *87*
Tartary, Great Cham of, *67, 117*
Tewkesbury, Battle of (1471), *145*, 214
Thames River, 213, *241*
Thames Street, London, 224
Thomas of Denbigh, Dr. Julio's man, 275
Thomas of Woodstock, *160*, 295
Throgmorton, Agnes Dudley, 296
Throgmorton, Francis, 12, 23–24, 29, 59, 200, 210, 296
Throgmorton, George, 210
Throgmorton, John, Sir, Justice of Chester, *99, 123*, 210, 219
Throgmorton, Nicholas, Sir, *84–85, 173*, 199–200, 205, 210, 266
Throgmorton, Thomas, 11, 24, 29, 31, 200, 210, 228, 245, 288
Tiber River, *121*
Tiberius, Roman Emperor, *108*
Tider (Teuder), Robin, *92*, 202
Tilney, Edmund, *81*, 199
Timon of Athens, *239*, 247
Tindall, Humfrey, Dean of Ely, 203
Tournay, Netherlands, *185*
Tower of London, 8, 14, 22–24, *105, 134, 151, 174*, 206, 216, 219, 246, 248, 271–72
Towton, Battle of (1461), 214

Treatise of Treasons (1573), 9, 213
Tree of Commonwealth, 113, 208
Tresham, Thomas, Sir, 29
Tresham, William, 6, 23–24, 29, 31, 56, 58, 285
Tudor, Edmund, Earl of Richmond, *150*, 295
Tudor, Margaret, Wife of James IV and Archibald Douglas, *152, 154, 161–62*, 212, 215, 295
Tudor, Mary, Wife of Louis XII of France, *152–53, 155, 162*, 215, 295
Tully. See Cicero, Marcus Tullius
Tutbury (Shrewsbury's house), 12, 59
Tyburn, London, *100*, 204

Ulster, Ireland, 267
Umbria, Italy, *121*
Umpton (Unton), Edward, 219
Umpton, Henry, Sir, diplomat, *173*, 219

Varius Avitus Bassanius ("Heliogabalus"), *86–87*, 201
Varney, Richard. See Verney, Richard, Sir
Vaux, George, yeoman of Leicester's bottles *238*, 246
Vavasour, Anne, 22, *61*, 271–72, 277, 297
Vavasour, Henry, of Copmanthorpe, 271, 297
Vavasour, Margaret Knyvett, 297
Vavasour, Thomas, 272, 297
Venetians, *148*
Vere, Robert. See De Vere, Robert
Vergil, Polydore, *96, 161, 188*, 199, 213–14, 220–21
Verney, Richard, Sir, *81, 90, 116*, 265
Verstegan, Richard, 60–61, 208
Vitellius, Roman Emperor, *121*
Vortigern, King, *94*, 202

Waad, William, 290
Wakefield, Battle of (1460), *151*, 212
Wales, 1, *81, 103–4, 119*, 205, 209
Wales, Prince of. See Edward
Walsingham, Frances. See Sidney, Frances Walsingham
Walsingham, Francis, Sir, 2–3, 6–7, 9–11, 14, 17, 19, 22–23, 25–31, 47, 57–60, 74–75, 198, 201–2, 219–20, 244–45, 248, 268, 276, 284, 286, 289–90, 294
Wanstead, Essex (Leicester's house), *95, 127*, 202–3

INDEX OF PROPER NAMES 323

Warde, Tristram, 273
Warner, Edward, Sir, Lieutenant of the Tower, 206
Warwick, Earl of. See Beauchamp; Dudley, Ambrose and John; Edward (Plantagenet); Neville, Richard
Warwick, England, *76*
Watson, William, priest, 5
Webster, John, playwright, 13, 199, 275
Welles, John, Viscount, 214
Wentworth, Thomas, Earl of Strafford, 223–24
West, Anne Knollys, Lady De La Warr, *128*, 211, 296
West, Thomas, Lord De La Warr, 211, 296
Westminster, London, 245, 258
Westmoreland, Earl of. See Neville, Charles
Weston, William, priest, 54
Whitney, George (error for Whitton), *122*
Whitton, George, Controller of Woodstock, 210
Wigges, William, 10
Wight, Isle of, *104*, 205
William I, King of England ("the Conqueror"), 202
William of Hatfield, *150–51*, 295
William, Prince of Orange, *230–31*, 244–45
Willoughby, Francis, Sir, 273
Wilson, Derek, x, 47, 57, 199, 223, 271

Wilson, Thomas, 13, 41, 217
Wilson, Thomas, Dr., 247
Wiltshire, Earl of. See Boleyn, Thomas
Winchester, Marquess of. See Paulet, William
Windsor Castle, 43, *128*, 211
Windsor, Frederick, Lord, 56, 219
Wood, Thomas, 47
Woodshaw, Edward 247
Woodstock, *122*, 210
Worcester, Earl of. See Percy, Thomas
Wray, Christopher, Sir, Chief Justice, *243*, 248
Wriothesley, Henry, 2d Earl of Southampton, 56, 229, *243*, 248
Wriothesley, Mary Browne, Countess of Southampton, *243*, 248
Wriothesley, Thomas, 1st Earl of Southampton, *111*, 207

Xerxes I, 212

Yale, Thomas, Dr., 275
York, Duke of. See Edmund Langley; Edward IV; Richard
York, England, *103*, 204–5
York, House, of *104, 143–52, 183*

Zangarum, John Baptist, printer, 55